SANDRA GUSTAFSON'S

GREAT SLEEPS PARIS

www.paris-paris.com

NINTH EDITION

D1026241

CHRONICLE BOOKS
SAN FRANCISCO

Printed in the United States of America.

NINTH EDITION
ISBN: 0-8118-2921-9
ISSN: 1074-505X

Cover design: Benjamin Shaykin
Book design: Words & Deeds
Typesetting: Jack Lanning
Series editor: Jeff Campbell
Author photograph: Marv Summers

Distributed in Canada by
Raincoast Books
9050 Shaughnessy Street
Vancouver, B. C. V6P 6E5

10 9 8 7 6 5 4 3 2 1

Chronicle Books LLC
85 Second Street
San Francisco, CA 94105

www.chroniclebooks.com
www.greateatsandsleeps.com

*For Great Sleepers in Paris: Barbie, Sunny,
Michael, Will, Mary, Sara, Sandy, and Marty . . .
merci beaucoup!*

Contents

To the Reader

You, who have ever been to Paris know;
And you who have not been to Paris—go.
> —*John Ruskin,*
> A Tour through France, *1835*

The crowds in the streets, the lights in the shops, the
elegance, variety, and beauty of their decorations,
the brilliant cafés with their vivacious groups at little
tables on the pavement soon convince me that this is
no dream: that I am in Paris . . .
> —*Charles Dickens*

La Belle France continues to beckon visitors to her shores. Indeed, it should not be surprising that Paris is one of the most popular travel destinations in the world, playing host to more than 22 million visitors yearly, or nearly ten times the city's population. The American passion for Paris has not ebbed despite wars, riots, occupations, and the rise and fall of hemlines and the dollar. Whether seen for the first time or the tenth, Paris never leaves you, and it becomes a never-ending love affair for most of us. Walk a block, turn a corner—in Paris there is always something interesting, something beautiful and new, something that has been there forever but that you never noticed until now. No matter what time of year you visit, it is impossible to keep from losing your heart to the city, with its grand boulevards, beautiful men and women, breathtaking monuments and museums, glorious food, famous art, and sweeping views—from place de la Concorde up the Champs-Élysées, from the steps of the Sacré Coeur over the entire city, and standing at Trocadéro looking across the fountains to the Eiffel Tower.

Then again, first priority for visitors to Paris is get a roof over their heads. Despite Paris's reputation for high prices, there are fifteen hundred hotels in all price ranges, so even travelers on very tight budgets can enjoy a pleasant stay in the city. However, the French have learned to make do with cramped quarters, sitting elbow-to-elbow in bistros, standing nose-to-nose on a crowded métro, or inching their way through narrow, traffic-clogged streets. This intimacy is part of the city's charm, and it translates even to the size of hotel rooms, which by American standards are very small.

The essence of any Parisian hotel is its individuality, and no two are alike. You can, of course, find here the most luxurious pleasure palaces in the world as well as those few people would even consider, and it is always possible to check into the Hilton or any other big-name chain hotel. But only in Paris can you sleep in a romantic hideaway in Montmartre and be served breakfast in bed while looking out the window and seeing all of Paris below, rent a sixteenth-century apartment with views of Notre Dame Cathedral and the Seine, or check into a suite in a renovated hotel a block from the Ritz, but light-years away in price.

It is certainly true that a trip to Paris will cost more today than it did a few years ago, but what doesn't? Europe—or Paris—on $20 or $30 a day no longer exists for any traveler. Most of those romantically thread-bare hotels of our youth are thankfully gone for good. More and more smaller hotels are being renovated—adding bathrooms, fluffy towels, fax machines, and buffet breakfasts served in sixteenth-century stone-walled *caves* (or cellars). This, of course, means higher prices. Yet there are still many ways to save money and maximize the buying strength of the dollar without feeling *nouveau pauvre* in the process, and *Great Sleeps Paris* will show you how.

Great Sleeps Paris is a highly selective guide to the hotels that I have discovered to be the best value in their category, be it a no-star with the shower and toilet down the hall or an antique-filled, three-star Left Bank hotel with a Jacuzzi in the marble bathroom. The purpose of this book is to offer fail-safe advice for first-time visitors, as well as for Paris veterans, on the best-priced accommodations for a range of tastes and needs, but all of which maintain a minimum standard of quality and cleanliness. The selections include hotels—from the center of Paris to the fringes—for lovers and honeymooners, nostalgia buffs, backpackers, and families. Other options include camping, renting an apartment, or living in a hostel, and for students, a wealth of inexpensive beds await. Each hotel listing has been included because I feel it has something special to offer. Some represent a particular style or era; others have been beautifully restored; and some are in nontourist neighborhoods where people like you and I live and work, send their children to school, get their cars repaired, eat lunch, shop, and go to the dentist. Some accommodations are basic, many are charming, and a few are starkly modern. Many are inexpensive, others moderately priced, and some fall into the Big Splurge category for those with more flexible budgets and demanding tastes. All have one vital feature in common: the potential for providing a memorable stay that will make you feel you have discovered your own part of Paris, one that you will savor and want to return to as often as possible.

It is important for readers to know that no hotel can purchase a listing or ask to be included in this book. I pay my own way and I do all the research and writing for the book myself; the buck stops right here. In reviewing the hotels, I pull no punches and call the shots as I see them . . . good, bad, and otherwise, including giving the specifics about the best and worst rooms, so that you will know exactly what to expect when you check into your room during your Parisian holiday.

What are the guidelines I use for selecting a hotel? The two primary concerns are value for money and cleanliness, followed by location, pleasant surroundings in the room, and management attitude and service. On my visits to the hotels, which are always unannounced, I wipe my fingers across the door tops, check closets, turn on the showers, look for mold, flush toilets, spot thin towels and waxed or sandy toilet paper, open and close windows, bounce on the beds, look under them for dust, and visit the dining room where breakfast is served. I have stumbled along dimly lit corridors, climbed endless flights of stairs, and been squeezed into minuscule cage elevators that seem to have been in operation since the fall of the Bastille all so that I can warn you about avoiding the same.

In addition to giving the value-conscious traveler the inside track to the best hotel prices in Paris, *Great Sleeps Paris* offers insider information on shopping. If you are like I am and believe the eighth deadly sin is paying full retail price for anything, then you will love the "Great Buys and Savvy Chic" shopping section (see page 285). There you will learn where to find everything from designer discount shops and big-name cosmetics to the latest models of shoes—all sold for less than their regular retail cost.

Longtime readers of the *Cheap Sleeps* series will notice one obvious change from the last edition: the title. I have done this to more accurately reflect the nature of these guides, which are my personal discoveries and hand-picked selections of what I consider the best-value places to sleep well in Paris in a range of price categories. But while the title has changed, the purpose of the series remains the same—to save you money without sacrificing quality, and to share with you Paris's great sleeps.

On my most recent trip for this ninth edition of this guide, I inspected every hotel and shop listed in the eighth edition, along with scores of others that did not make the final cut for one reason or another. In so doing, I walked 648 miles, wore out my walking shoes, and was asked for directions 57 times. And yet, no matter what the weather, how long the day, or the personalities and moods of the people I met along the way, it never seemed like work. I loved every minute of it. I hope that *Great Sleeps Paris* shows you how to cut corners with style, so that traveling on a budget will not make you give up the good life by lowering your standards, and that it gives you enough information on the hotels listed to help you select the one that will make your stay in Paris truly special and set the stage for many return visits. If I have been able to do this, I will have done my job well. I wish you *bonne chance* and *bon voyage.*

Tips for Great Sleeps in Paris

1. Unless you enjoy standing in long lines in French government tourist offices or rail stations, or wandering the streets looking for a hotel, never arrive in Paris without confirmed hotel reservations in writing.

2. Dealing directly with the hotel almost always insures the best rate. However, if a hotel has an Internet site or a toll-free 800-number you can call from the United States and Canada, do check the site and/or call to find out about special package deals for seniors, weekends, families, the off-season, and so on. Then call the hotel directly and see if you can better the price. Chances are good that you can.

3. Luxury does not necessarily have to be beyond your budget if you go when everyone else does not. The weather may not always cooperate in the off-season months, but there will be far fewer tourists and hotels will be cutting deals. The two weeks in mid-January and mid-February and the months of May, June, September, and October are the hardest times to find a hotel room in Paris. During the height of winter and summer, hotel rates are at their lowest.

4. You pay for the room, not for the number of people occupying it. Back rooms often face blank walls or dreary courtyards and are usually smaller, but they cost less and are quieter. Twin beds cost more than a double, and any room with a private shower only will be less than one with a bathtub. If you ask for a double room, you must specify if you want a double bed or twin beds.

5. Don't be surprised if your shower, either stall or over the bathtub, has no curtain. In smaller hotels, towels are usually changed every two or three days.

6. Many hotels do not allow outside guests to visit you in your room. This is an iron-clad rule in hostels, student digs, and almost every no-star and one-star hotel in Paris.

7. Inquire about the hotel's refund policy in case you send a deposit and then have to cancel at the last minute. Some smaller hotels have draconian ideas about refunds.

8. If you have booked an apartment and paid a chunk of money in advance, are flying charter, or have a nonrefundable and nonchangeable airline ticket, seriously consider purchasing trip insurance. If you have to change dates, interrupt travel, or cancel altogether, you will be grateful for it. The Automobile Club of America has a

list of carriers. Some are Access America, Inc., 800-284-8300; Carefree Travel Insurance, 800-323-3149; and Travel Guard International, 800-782-5151.

9. Always check out the room before you check in. Confirm the rate and discuss the cost of any extras (such as telephone calls, both local and long distance) ahead of time, not when paying the bill. All hotels must clearly post their rates by the reception desk, but they are not required to list "hidden" charges they may add on later.

10. Avoid eating breakfast at your hotel if you want to save money. Instead, join the Parisians standing at the bar at the corner café. Be sure to tell the hotel when reserving, and again at the beginning of the stay, that you will not be eating breakfast, and see that the cost is deducted per person, per day, from your hotel bill if it is included in the original room rate. Only a few hotels refuse to deduct breakfast, but you must ask; it is never done voluntarily.

11. Do major laundries at the local laundromat and take your cleaning to the neighborhood dry cleaner yourself. Laundry and dry cleaning sent from the hotel can blow a budget to shreds. If you do wash out a few things, be sure they do not drip over carpeting or fabric. And please, do not hang things in the windows!

12. Notify the hotel if you expect to arrive after 6 P.M. Even if you paid the room deposit, the hotel can technically resell your room to someone else if they do not know your arrival time.

13. Change money at a bank, never at a hotel.

14. For security's sake, avoid rooms on the *rez-de-chaussée*. In France, the ground floor (*rez-de-chaussée*) is what Americans call the first floor; the French first floor (*premier étage*) is our second floor.

15. Paris is a very noisy city both day and night, making it heaven for night owls and a nightmare for insomniacs. Traffic, sirens, motor scooters, and voices magnify on the narrow streets, echoing throughout the night. Street-cleaning crews and trash trucks start their rounds at zero-dark-hundred, which provide many a rude awakening for those still sleeping, or wishing they could. If noise is a problem, ask for a room away from the street, in the back of the hotel, or facing an inner courtyard. For added insurance, buy or bring earplugs (*boules de quiès*).

16. It is important to realize that a *hôtel* is not always a hotel. The word *hôtel* has more than one meaning in French. Of course it means a lodging place for travelers, but it also means a mansion or town house, like the Hôtel Lambert, or a large private home (a *hôtel particulier*). The city hall is the *Hôtel de Ville;* auctions are held at the *Hôtel des Ventes; Hôtel des Postes* refers to the general post office;

and the *Hôtel des Invalides,* once a home for disabled war veterans, is now the most famous military museum in the world and the final resting place for Napoléon Bonaparte. Finally, if you are in the hospital, you are in a *Hôtel-Dieu.*

17. Traveler: Know thyself. It has often been said that all a person needs for adventure is the desire to have one. Your trip to Paris (or to any other destination) should be an adventure filled with treasured memories that last a lifetime. In any adventure, there will always be surprises. If you aren't willing to risk some unexpected turns in your plans, but insist on absolute predictability, especially with your accommodations, then I recommend you do one of two things: reserve a room at the Hôtel Ritz (Tel: 01-43-16-30-30, Fax: 01-43-16-36-68/69), or invest your travel money elsewhere and stay home.

General Information

When to Go

If you don't travel when you can, your heirs probably will.
—*Anonymous*

How wonderful it would be to drop everything and fly to Paris whenever the spirit moved us! If such romantic impulses do not quite fit into your schedule or budget, then the high and low seasons must be taken into consideration. These times of year affect not only the availability of hotel rooms and the rates but also airline fares. High season in Paris is considered to be May, June, September, and October—as well as the fashion weeks in January and early July for haute couture, again in March and October for prêt-à-porter, and the spring and fall trade shows. It is very important for Paris visitors to note that when fashion shows fill the city to the bursting point, and whenever there is a big trade show, many hotels add on surcharges of at least 50 percent. Dates vary slightly from year to year, so the best bet is to check with the French Government Tourist Office in New York or Los Angeles for the latest information. This leaves mid-July, August, November, December (except for the week to ten days around Christmas and New Year's), and parts of January and February as the best times to go to Paris. The drawback in July and August is that you will be sharing your Parisian holiday with many other tourists and very few French. Despite government pleadings and tourist demands, August is still the traditional vacation month for most Parisians, and many restaurants and shops are closed for at least a week or two, if not the entire month. The good news is that hotels are always open—and many offer lower rates—and everything is easier to come by, including métro seats, café tables, and good-natured waiters.

Holidays and Events

Holidays (*les jours fériés*) are vital dates to bear in mind when planning any trip to Paris. Banks, post offices, and most retail stores are all closed, and museums that are open may run on different time schedules. In addition, banks may be closed a half day before each holiday as well as the day after in some instances. The traffic is horrendous, especially if the holiday falls on a Tuesday or Thursday, since many French will take off Monday or Friday to make it a long weekend. Restaurant holiday policies vary with the rise and fall of the economy. Always call ahead to make sure—even if they say they are open, they may change their mind and be closed. Skeleton or third-string crews man the hotel desks, and there is often a laid-back attitude during a holiday period, resulting in quick excuses for things not working. It can all add up to some very frustrating times for a traveler.

January 1	New Year's Day	*Jour de l'An*
Easter Sunday		*Pâques*
and Monday		*et Lundi de Pâques*
Ascension Day		*Ascension*
(40 days after Easter)		
May 1	Labor Day	*Fête du Travail*
May 8	VE Day	Armistice 1945
July 14	Bastille Day	*Quatorze Juillet/Fête Nationale*
August 15	Assumption Day	*Assomption*
November 1	All Saints' Day	*Toussaint*
November 11	Armistice Day	Armistice 1918
December 25	Christmas Day	*Noël*

For motorists, the time to avoid is the last weekend in August, when Parisians return from their vacations en masse via the autoroutes. This grand *rentrée* creates traffic snarls of world-class proportions.

Events in Paris

The two best sources for events in Paris are the weekly magazines *Pariscope: Une Semaine de Paris* and *l'Officiel des Spectacles*. They come out on Wednesday, cost 3 to 4F (0.46–0.61€) and are sold at every kiosk in the city. In these magazines you will find listings for the opera, theater, films, concerts, art exhibitions, special events, naughty nightlife, weekly TV programs, swimming pool hours, and interesting guided tours. Although the magazines are printed in French (with the exception of a small English-language section in *Pariscope* devoted to weekly highlights), a non-French speaker can quickly decipher the information given.

What to Bring

I think every wife has a right to insist upon seeing Paris
—*Sydney Smith, letter to Countess Grey, September 11, 1835*

Why buy good luggage? You only use it when you travel . . .
—*Casey Stengel*

If you follow only one piece of advice in *Great Sleeps Paris,* let it be this: Travel light. Porters are no longer roaming airports or train stations, and bellboys are almost relics of the past for most hotels in the budget category. Therefore, you are going to have to carry your own luggage, and believe me, after the first ten minutes, less is definitely best. My travel rule of thumb is: Take twice as much money as you think you will need and half as much clothing. Keep it simple, color coordinate your outfits, and remember, this is Paris, not Mars, so you can go out and buy something wonderful if you need to fill a gap in your travel wardrobe.

One of the favorite pastimes of Parisians and their expatriate friends is to sit in a café along a busy boulevard and pick out the tourists. You can spot them a mile away, in their summer tank tops and shorts, a bottle of water dangling from a hook on their belt—and in winter, bundled up in parkas as if the ski slopes were just around the corner. Of course, they all wear jogging shoes and the men have baseball caps . . . often turned backward.

Parisians are some of the most stylish people on earth. They are also some of the most conservative in their dress. Yes, you will see some off-the-wall outfits on bionic, buffed bodies, but you will never see short shorts on any well-groomed Parisian man or woman. Big-city clothes are the call of the day, no matter what the weather may be.

Naturally, you will leave your heavy wool coat and long johns at home when you visit Paris in August. But what kind of coat makes sense in May or June? Knowing the monthly average temperatures will help: January 45.5°F (7.5°C); February 44.8°F (7.1°C); March 50°F (10.2°C); April 60.3°F (15.7°C); May 61-62°F (16.6°C); June 75°F (23°C); July 77°F (25.1°C); August 78°F (25.6°C); September 69–70°F (20.9°C); October 61.7°F (16.5°C); November 53°F (11.7°C); December 46°F (7.8°C).

If you are going during the warm months, wear light cottons and comfortable shoes. Synthetics don't breathe and add to the heat discomfort. For winter visits, layering makes sense, and so does a lined raincoat, a set of silk long underwear, and a hat (since 70 percent of body heat goes out through your head). Jeans are universal and certainly acceptable for sight-seeing and casual dining. However, they are not considered in vogue at more expensive restaurants or if you are invited to someone's home. Men will feel comfortable wearing slacks and a nice shirt or turtleneck, along with a jacket if it is cool. Women will feel best in simple, well-tailored outfits. Gauzy, lime-green jumpsuits with sequined Eiffel Tower T-shirts, along with jogging shoes for every occasion, spell tourist and can lead to such problems as poor service or being a target of pickpockets.

When packing your bags, use every bit of space to its fullest: stuff your shoes, roll your sweaters and underwear, use plastic garment bags between layers to prevent wrinkling and pack so things will not slip and slide to one end. Pack your toiletries and cosmetics in a waterproof bag. You only need one experience with the mess caused by airline pressure blowing off the top of your shampoo or nail polish remover to know what I am talking about.

The following list of useful items is by no means exhaustive, but is one compiled over the years by a veteran traveler.

- A bar or bottle of bath soap and your own shampoo
- As many moist towelettes as you can fit in, and a bottle of antiseptic hand wash
- Sunscreen lotion and sunglasses

- French dictionary or phrasebook
- Portable radio with earphones
- Pedometer to keep track of the number of miles you walk, so you can impress your friends when you return
- First-aid kit
- Sewing kit, with a pair of decent scissors
- Travel tool kit with Swiss army knife, screwdriver, tape, stapler, packing tape, Scotch tape, string
- A few hangers you can toss out at the end of the trip. You would be surprised at the condition and sparse number of hotel hangers.
- Rubber doorstop as a security measure
- Rubber sink stop for drip-dry laundries; blow up hangers, clothesline with clothespins, or clothespins you can hang up; and a small container of spot remover to use on tough stains before you wash your clothes in your room sink or bathtub. (However, don't pack laundry soap; it's cheap and readily available wherever you go.)
- Adapter plug and a transformer for electrical appliances (see "Voltage," page 42).
- Suction hook for the back of the bathroom or bedroom door
- Suction-cup magnifying mirror
- Alarm clock
- Mosquito repellent
- Flashlight
- Something to read
- Umbrella
- Camera, and five more rolls of film than you think you will need
- Extra batteries

Disabled Travelers

Paris is improving for wheelchair-bound travelers. Many hotels in *Great Sleeps Paris* do have rooms that have been somewhat refitted for handicapped guests, but the facilities may consist only of a wide door, a grab-bar by the tub, or just the fact that the room is on the *rez-de-chaussée* (ground floor). For more information, there are several agencies you can contact. The French Tourist Office publishes *Tourisme Pour Toute le Monde* (60F, 9.15€); it is located at 127, avenue des Champs-Élysées, 75008; Tel: 01-49-52-53-55; Métro: Charles-de-Gaulle-Étoile. A toll-free number offers advice in French for disabled persons living or visiting Paris (08-00-03-37-48). The Comité National de Laision Pour la Réadaptation des Handicapés (CNRH) publishes in French or English *Paris Île-de-France Pour Tous* (80F, 12.20€); contact them at 236 bis, rue de Tolbiac, 75013; Tel: 01-53-80-66-63; Métro: Glacière. *Où Ferons-Nous Étape?* ("Where Shall We Stop Off?") (85F, 12.96€), which lists French hotels that have handicapped accessibility, is published by the Association des Paralysés de France, 22, rue du Père-Guérain, 75013; Tel: 01-44-16-83-83; Métro: Place d'Italie. The Association des Paralysés de France also has lists of hotels in France with facilities for the disabled; contact them at 17, boulevard August Blanqui, 75013; Tel: 01-40-78-69-00; Métro: Corvisart.

Not all the métros and buses are suitable for wheelchair use. For information in English and a list of the most accessible métro and RER stations, call RATP, place de la Madeleine, 75008; Tel: 08-36-68-41-14; Open: daily 6 A.M.–9 P.M. Theoretically, taxis are obliged to pick up passengers in wheelchairs, but don't count on it. It is better to reserve with one of the following companies who specialize in service for the handicapped. They both like a forty-eight-hour notice.

Aihrop, 01-41-29-01-29; Open: Mon–Fri 8 A.M.–noon, 1:30–6:30 P.M.

GiHp, 01-41-83-15-15; Open: Mon–Fri 7:30 A.M.–8 P.M.

Auxiliaire des Aveugles (01-43-06-39-68) has a bilingual staff that provides information on services in Paris for the visually impaired.

Neuf Orthopedio is a store selling wheelchairs, canes, and other accessories for the handicapped. They are at 9, rue Léopold Bellan, 75002; Tel: 01-42-33-83-46; Métro: Sentier; Open: Mon–Fri 9 A.M.–6 P.M.

Other information for disabled travelers can be obtained from the following organizations in the United States:

Directions Unlimited
720 N. Bedford Road
Bedford Hills, NY 10507
Tel: 800-533-5343
A tour operator specializing in custom tours for the disabled.

Society for the Advancement of Travel for the Handicapped, Inc.
347 Fifth Avenue
New York, NY 10016
Tel: 212-447-7284

Travel Information Service
Moss Rehabilitation Hospital
1200 West Tabor Road
Philadelphia, PA 19141
Tel: 215-456-9600
Telephone information and a referral service.

Twin Peaks Press
Box 129
Vancouver, WA 98666

This group publishes the *Directory of Travel Agencies for the Disabled,* which lists hundreds of agencies around the world.

Discounts

Hotels

When booking your hotel room, it always pays to ask if any discounts are being offered, even in the middle of high season—you might get lucky. It makes good sense to check hotel Internet sites or to call 800-numbers to see about special package deals or lower rates. Savvy travelers check with airlines or their travel agents for package deals that include airfare coupled with a hotel at a fraction of the cost if paid for separately. Often included are airport transfers and/or car rentals. In July and August, many hotels offer a published 10 percent discount, and for others, you have to ask. Some hotels will give an automatic 5 to 10 percent discount to *Great Sleeps Paris* readers, and I have noted these in the listings.

If you are willing to take a chance and really lock yourself into a ticket that cannot be changed without an act of Congress, investigate discount air ticketers who advertise on Sunday in most major metropolitan newspaper travel sections. The fares are low enough to enable some to upgrade on a hotel or stay longer. However, the restrictions are many, so be sure you understand the fine print and are able to live with it.

Museums

For avid museum-goers in Paris, there are now one-, three-, and five-day French passes that provide direct access to more than sixty museums, including the Louvre, Musée d'Orsay, Musée Picasso, Versailles, and other famous sights and monuments. Called the *Carte Musées*—or the Paris Museum Pass—it covers your admission for each museum and allows you go to the head of any line, or through a special entrance, without waiting. You can also revisit your favorites as many times as you want at no extra charge. In general, entry is free for children under eighteen in most museums, and on Sunday, entrance to museums is free to anyone, but the crowds can be frightening. If you have the museum pass, you will at least avoid standing in lines to get in, and that is worth something, especially when it is freezing cold, pouring rain, or scorching hot. The passes are on sale in the museums, major métro stations, and tourism offices in Paris, including the one at 127, Champs-Élysées. In Paris, the pass costs 80F (12.20€) for one day, 160F (24.39€) for three days, and 240F (36.59€) for five days. For further information, check the Website at www.intermusees.com.

The passes can also be purchased before leaving the United States through Challenges International, Inc., 10 East 21st Street, Suite 600,

New York, NY 10010; Tel: 212-529-9069; Fax: 212-529-4838; Internet: www.ticketsto.com; Open: Mon–Fri 8:30 A.M.–5:30 P.M.

If your travels will be taking you beyond Paris, consider purchasing the National Museum Pass, which is valid for one year and allows unlimited free entrance, without having to stand on line, to more than one hundred national monuments in France, sixteen of which are in and around Paris. The pass is on sale at participating monuments or at the Caisse Nationale des Monuments Historiques et des Sites. Price is 280F (42.69€). Tel: 01-44-61-21-50; Internet: www.monuments-france.fr.

Seniors

If you have reached your sixtieth birthday, in France you are a member of the *troisième age* (third age) and are eligible for a Carte Vermeil (CV). This card entitles you to a number of significant discounts, including reductions on air and rail travel as well as on the bus and métro in Paris. The French domestic airline, Air Inter, honors "third agers" by giving 25 to 50 percent reductions on regular nonexcursion ticket prices. On French trains, you can save between 25 and 50 percent of the cost of a first- or second-class compartment and 10 percent of an excursion ticket. These air and rail reductions are not available during all times of the year, and restrictions do apply. However, if you can cash in on the savings, they can be significant. Other benefits include reduced entrance rates for theaters, museums, and cinemas. Wherever you go in France, ask if there are special rates for seniors; the answer will often be yes.

The Carte Vermeil is valid for one year from June 1 to May 31 of the following year. The card cannot be purchased in the United States, but it is available at any major railway station in France. Do not expect clerks to speak English, but you won't need much French to communicate your wishes, as most of them are used to dealing with foreigners who are privy to this super deal. When you go to purchase your card, you will have to show your passport as proof of age. For more information, contact the French National Railroads, 610 Fifth Avenue, New York, NY 10012; Tel: 212-582-2816. However, be prepared for frustrating waits that could speed your aging process.

In addition, members of the AARP (American Association of Retired Persons) are entitled to discounts on air tickets, rooms in selected major chain hotels, and some train and car rentals. Always inquire when booking a reservation. Elderhostel, another organization for seniors, operates programs throughout Europe, and many are in France. Contact them at 75 Federal Street, Boston, MA 02110-1941; Tel: 617-426-7788.

Students and Teachers

The best discounts for students and teachers are available with the International Student Identity Card (ISIC) and the International Teacher Identity Card (ITIC). Both are available through Council Travel offices in the United States and Paris. For complete information on this excellent travel discount card, see "Student Accommodations" in "Other Options," page 280. Anyone age twenty-six or younger, whether a student or not, can buy the Carte 12/25, which allows a 50 percent reduction on TGV train travel.

Theater and Concerts

You can buy half-price tickets for selected concerts, theaters, ballets, and other shows on the day of the performance only at 15, place de la Madeleine, 8th; Métro: Madeleine; and at Esplanade de la Tour Montparnasse, 75014; Métro: Montparnasse. Hours for both are Tues–Sat 12:30–8 P.M., Sun 1–4 P.M.; closed Monday.

Transportation

If you will be in Paris only a short time and plan on seeing a lot, the Paris Visite ticket is worth considering. This go-as-you-please ticket is good for one, two, three, or five days, and it is valid for the bus, métro, RER, and the SNCF trains to Disneyland Paris, Versailles, Fontainebleau, and Roissy-Charles-de-Gaulle and Orly airports. However, the card's main benefit is that it also offers reductions on a few museums and tourist sites in Paris. It is available at main métro stations, any RER or SCNF station, and from the Paris Tourist Information Office. Children under twelve pay half price. Rates depend on how many zones you travel to.

	1–3 zones	1–5 zones	1–8 zones
1 day	55F (8.38€)	110F (16.77€)	155F (23.63€)
2 days	90F (13.72€)	175F (26.68€)	225F (34.30€)
3 days	120F (18.29€)	245F (37.35€)	280F (42.69€)
5 days	175F (26.68€)	300F (45.73€)	350F (53.36€)

For longer stays in the main part of Paris, a better transportation deal is the Carte Hebdomadaire. This ticket is good for an entire seven-day week, which always begins on Monday and expires on Sunday. It costs 95F (14.48€) and requires a passport-sized photo, which you can get taken in major métro stations. This gives unlimited travel only in zones 1 and 2 (where most visitors are going to be) on the bus and métro, period. It does not cover trips to Versailles or Disneyland, or offer any reduced admission rates for Paris sites. A one-day Mobilis pass ranges from 30F (4.57€) for zones 1–2 to 110F (16.77€) for zones 1–8, but does not include the airports.

Tours and Classes

This section covers several popular walking tours of Paris, along with two very special people who provide tours as well as other unique services: Rachel Kaplan and Paule Caillat. In addition to being multilingual, extremely talented, and very well qualified, these two women are passionate about what they do and possess an intimate, detailed knowledge of Paris, a city they have come to love and call their own through many years of living and working here. Indeed, any of the tours here are wonderful ways to enhance your trip and learn more about the fascinating City of Light.

French Links–Rachel Kaplan

Whatever your needs, interests, or requirements, Rachel Kaplan will be up to the challenge. She never stops developing and perfecting her personalized tours of Paris, or her day trips to the countryside, which immerse participants in the refinements of France while enlightening them about the culture and dispelling myths about the people. Far from being stuffy, dry, pedagogical lectures, Rachel presents French art, history, and life in an entertaining, educational way. A day spent with her reveals many hidden treasures, whether it be on one of her tours covering Paris Gardens, Literary Paris, Children's Paris, Jewish Paris, Discount/ Upscale Shopping (including tickets to fashion shows), Women's History of Paris, or Flea Market visits (which include price negotiations and shipping). Her day trips outside Paris include the Chateaux of the Loire, Great Cathedrals, and Beaches of Normandy—to name only a few. In addition to her tours, she is a recognized authority on Paris's little-known museums, and has written four books on the subject: the *Little Known Museums In and Around* series, which covers Paris, London, Berlin, and Rome. If you need help with your travel itinerary, transportation, finding a gym to work off those buttery croissants, planning for a handicapped person, or purchasing advance tickets, Rachel is the person to call.

Telephone/Fax: 01-44-64-76-26
Email: kaplan@club-internet.fr.
Internet: www.frenchlinks.com
Credit Cards: None, cash only
Prices: Depends on your agenda and specific needs

Promenades Gourmandes–Paule Caillat

Not only did I learn a lot about cooking, but I had the opportunity to meet a wonderful person!
—*George Brooks, Attorney-at-Law*

It doesn't matter who you are—everyone from gourmet chefs to fledging novices will learn something from the dynamic Parisian chef Paule Caillat, whose love of cooking and culinary heritage transform everything she touches. Paule, who was born and raised in Paris and college-educated in the States, gives private and group cooking lessons in Paris, but I can assure you they are a quantum leap from the ordinary, stilted classes I have often attended. Menus are selected according to the season, student preferences, and a careful eye for product availability once you have returned home. Cooking with Paule means hands-on from the get-go: shopping at the market right through enjoying what you have prepared and cleaning up afterward. On the trip to the outdoor market, you will learn how to recognize the best ingredients, discern the different types of bread and cheese, detect a French apricot from one imported from Israel and know which one to buy, select the perfect meats and fish, and avoid anything that is not absolutely fresh. Through her knowledge of food you will also be able to place the products you buy into their historical and geographical context in France. After lunch (if you have signed up for a full-day session) Paule will take you on a Promenade Gourmande (gourmet walking tour) to visit famous bakeries, kitchens of well-known restaurants, the bistros of rising young chefs, landmark kitchen equipment emporiums, saffron producers, and much more.

Cooking lessons are not the half of Paule and her enthusiasm about food. She also leads small groups on excursions to areas in France that are specifically known for their exceptional food products. The trips include train travel, all meals and accommodations, and visits to points of interest.

Paule is a delightful, dynamic, knowledgeable woman. If you love food and cooking, please treat yourself to one of her cooking lessons or trips. You won't regret it for a minute. As one very happy participant said, "This was the best day I have ever spent in Paris, and the highlight of my entire trip!" I agree, and so does everyone lucky enough to spend time with Paule.

Note: No classes or tours are held in August.

187, rue du Temple, 75003
Telephone: 01-48-04-56-84
Fax: 01-42-78-59-77
Email: paule.caillat@wanadoo.fr
Credit Cards: None, cash only
Prices: Half day: market visit, cooking class, and lunch, $200; two half days, $360; full day: market visit, class, lunch, gourmet walking tour, $290; two full days, $560

Paris Contact–Jill Daneels and Anne Hervé

Jill Daneels and Anne Hervé lead small, two-hour walking tours of Paris in English. If you are interested in bohemian Montmartre, going back to the eighteenth century to retrace Thomas Jefferson's Parisian footsteps, or discovering hidden treasures of the Marais, join one of her informative walking tours. Customized tours for individuals or groups can be arranged.

Telephone/Fax: 01-42-51-08-04 (Jill Daneels); 01-47-90-52-16 (Anne Hervé)
Email: pariscontact@wanadoo.fr
Credit Cards: None, cash only
Prices: 60F (9.15€) per person; 50F (7.62€) students, retirees, children under 15

Paris Walking Tours–Peter and Oriel Caine

If you are fluent in French, finding an interesting walking tour in Paris is easy. Just look in the weekly issue of *Pariscope* and you will find several possibilities every day of the week. For those whose French is limited, an English-language walking tour with British expatriates Oriel and Peter Caine is the solution. The Caines are licensed "blue badge" guides in France. They and a small group of assistants have put together a series of well-researched walking tours through parts of Paris the casual visitor is likely to miss. Their comments are both educational and entertaining, filled with little-known tidbits that humanize the particular area covered. The tours are given year-round, last approximately an hour and a half, and all you have to do is to show up at the appointed time and place wearing comfortable shoes and be ready to learn and enjoy. For a schedule, contact them at the numbers listed below.

10, rue Samson
St Denis, 93200
Telephone: 01-48-09-21-40
Fax: 01-42-43-75-51
Email: Peter@pariswalkingtours.com
Internet: www.pariswalkingtours.com
Credit Cards: None, cash only
Price: 60F (9.15€) per person, collected at the beginning of the walk

Walking the Spirit Tours–Julia Browne

Julia Browne, a Canadian who moved to Paris in 1994, discovered that Langston Hughes wrote poetry in a sixth-floor garret a few streets from where she was then living. This discovery inspired her to do more research on the history of African Americans in Paris and the long-standing historical and cultural connection they have had. She now shares her knowledge with visitors on her Walking the Spirit Tours. African American musicians, writers, artists, and intellectuals have had a multi-faceted presence in Paris, and the tour shows you where James Baldwin, Richard Wright, Josephine Baker, Countee Cullen, and many more lived, worked, ate, drank, and died. Visit the oldest African American soul food restaurant in Paris, as well as the Casino de Paris, where the 369th Harlem Infantry Regiment played the city's first jazz. If you are interested in the African American–Paris connection, or want to learn more about this fascinating aspect of Paris culture, here is the perfect opportunity. Tours must be reserved, and can be arranged for individuals or groups.

Telephone: 01-42-29-60-12
Email: brownejulia@minitel.net
Credit Cards: None, cash only
Prices: Adults 150F (22.87€); two tours 125F (19.06€) per person, per tour; children under 16 half price; group rates on request

Tourist Offices and American Embassy

The main office of the French Government Tourist Office is at 127, avenue des Champs-Élysées, 75008; Tel: 08-36-68-31-12, 01-49-52-53-56; Métro: Charles-de-Gaulle-Étoile. They are open in summer daily 9 A.M.–8 P.M., and in winter Mon–Sat 9 A.M.–8 P.M., Sun and holidays 11 A.M.–6 P.M. Branches offices are Eiffel Tower; Tel: 01-45-51-22-15; Open: in summer daily 11 A.M.–7 P.M.; and at Gare de Lyon, Mon–Sat 8 A.M.–8 P.M.

On the Internet, you can contact the French Government Tourist Office at www.paris-touristoffice.com. You can get bilingual information on Paris from www.paris.org.

For information on Paris and Île de France, contact Espace du Tourisme d'Île de France at Carrousel du Louvre, 99, rue de Rivoli, 1st; Métro: Palais Royal–Musée du Louvre; Tel: 08-03-03-19-98; Open: Mon, Wed–Sun 10 A.M.–7 P.M.

In the United States, the French Government Tourist offices are located at 444 Madison Avenue, New York, NY 10020; Tel: 212-838-7300; and 9454 Wilshire Blvd., Beverly Hills, CA 90212; Tel: 320-271-6665. They are open Mon–Fri 9:30 A.M.–4 P.M. Or send them an email at fgto@gte.net or surf their Website at www.francetourism.com.

In Paris, the American Consulate is at 2, rue St-Florentin, 75001; Tel: 01-43-12-22-22; 01-43-96-14-88; Métro: Concorde. The American Embassy is at 2, avenue Gabriel, 75008; Métro: Concorde; Tel: 01-42-96-12-02.

Money Matters

There are few certainties when you travel. One of them is that the moment you arrive in a foreign country, the American dollar will fall like a stone.

—Erma Bombeck

If you charge big items on your credit card, carry some traveler's checks, convert as you go, and use ATMs, you will do fine. Also, remember to carry a few of your own personal checks. If you suddenly run out of money, you can use them to get cash advances, provided the credit card you have allows this. Try to have a few francs on hand when you arrive. This gets you out of the airport faster and keeps you from having to wait in line to get enough money to get into Paris. True, you may pay more for this convenience, but if you change $200 or so before you leave home, you will never miss the few cents extra it may cost. If you cannot get francs locally, you can order them by telephone, and they will arrive by Federal Express within two days. Please contact Thomas Cook Currency Service, 630 Fifth Avenue, New York, NY 10101; Tel: 800-287-7362; Open: Mon–Fri 8:30 A.M.–9 P.M., EST.

Automatic Teller Machines—ATMs

Automatic Teller Machines are all over Paris. You can use your bank ATM card, American Express, or a Visa or MasterCard. There will be fees involved, but you will be getting a wholesale conversion rate that is better than you would get at a bank or currency exchange office. Naturally, you are limited to the amount you can withdraw by the type of account you have and your cash advance balance and limit. Please—and I cannot stress this enough—do not assume your ATM card or credit card pin numbers will automatically work in Paris. They might, but you may have to obtain a special pin (personal identification number) or enroll in a special program. Contact the card issuer for the steps you need to take, and allow plenty of time. Setting up an account can take several weeks but costs the cardholder nothing. For the Paris Cirrus locations and details you will need to use your card there, call 800-4-CIRRUS (424-7787); Internet: www.mastercard.com. For foreign Plus locations and information, call 800-THE-PLUS; Internet: www.visa.com. To enroll in the American Express foreign ATM program, call 800-CASH-NOW (227-4669). Check the following sites for worldwide ATM locations: Visa, www.visa.com/pd/atm, and MasterCard, www.mastercard.com/atm.

Credit Cards

For the most part, I recommend using a credit card whenever possible. The benefits are many. It is the safest way purchase things because it eliminates the need for carrying large sums of cash, which you must obtain by standing in line at a bank or at another money-changing facility. The credit card company gives the rate of exchange on the day the receipt from the expenditure is submitted, and this can work to your advantage if the dollar is rising. It also provides you with a written record of your purchases, and best of all, you often get delayed billing of up to four to six weeks after you have returned home. If you pay in cash, the money is spent immediately. With a credit card, the money stays in your bank account drawing interest until you need it to pay the final bill. Emergency personal check cashing and access to ATM machines are benefits of many cards, as is free travel insurance. Check with your issuing bank to determine the benefits you have . . . you may be pleasantly surprised. Be careful, however, because many credit card companies have slapped on a foreign use surcharge of 1 to 5 percent per transaction. The cards tied to airline miles are some of the worst offenders, making the frequent flyer mile build up not very attractive when you consider you are paying more to get it. Again, check with the issuing bank of the credit cards you plan to use on your trip, and allow enough time to make necessary changes to another card.

Keep a copy of all of your credit card numbers with you, and treat it with the same importance you do your passport. Lock it up in the hotel safe—don't keep it in your wallet or purse. Save your receipts to check against the statement when it arrives. Errors are frequent. American

Express card members have a host of back-up services, including their American Express Global Assist program, which can be reached twenty-four hours a day, seven days a week, at 800-554-2639, or collect from abroad at 715-343-7977. This is a service for any American Express cardholder who needs emergency medical, legal, or financial assistance while traveling. Operators at this number will accept collect calls and give information on currency rates, weather, visa and passport requirements, customs, and embassy and consular telephone numbers and addresses. They also will help with urgent message relays, lost luggage location, prescription assistance, emergency hotel check-in if you have lost your credit card, and provide translations. It is worth having an American Express card just to have this service.

Finally, remember, in Europe a MasterCard is Eurocard, and Visa is Carte Bleu. Every listing in *Great Sleeps Paris* tells you whether or not plastic money is accepted. Thankfully, most hotels accept at least one credit card.

If, heaven forbid, your cards are lost or stolen, call one of these twenty-four-hour hotlines in Paris, or call collect in the United States to report the loss as soon as possible.

In Paris:

American Express (cards) 01-47-77-72-00

American Express
 (traveler's checks)   08-00-90-86-00

Diners Club   01-49-06-17-50/08-00-22-20-73

MasterCard (Eurocard)   01-45-67-84-84

Visa (Carte Bleu)   08-36-69-08-80

From Paris, you can call the following U.S. numbers to report a theft or loss of your cards:

American Express   Toll-free: 800-233-5432
                    collect: 336-393-1111
                    www.americanexpress.com

Diners Club   Toll-free: 800-234-6377
                    collect: 702-797-5532
                    www.dinersclubus.com

MasterCard   Toll-free: 800-302-7309
                    collect: 314-542-7111
                    www.mastercard.com

Visa   Toll-free: 800-336-8472
                    collect: 410-581-9994
                    www.visa.com

Cash Advances

If you are stuck for cash, don't panic. You can use your American Express, Diners Club, MasterCard, or Visa to get cash, either by writing a personal check and presenting your card, or going to a bank that gives cash advances for whatever card you are carrying (see also "Wiring Money to Paris," page 28).

American Express: Cardholders can get fast money by writing personal checks. For more information on this lifesaving service, contact American Express Global Assist at 800-333-2639.

Diners Club: For any Diners Club cardholder, a cash advance of $500 a day, or $1,000 a week, is easy. Just present the card and a picture ID at any Eurochange bank and that's it.

MasterCard or *Visa:* Available through banks displaying these card signs.

Currency Exchange

The use of traveler's checks has been almost totally replaced by ATMs, making currency exchange much less important than it once was. However, for some, traveler's checks may be preferable because if they are lost or stolen, there is recourse and they will be replaced. Estimate your needs carefully when changing money. If you overbuy, you will lose twice, buying and then selling. Every time you exchange currency, someone is making a profit, and I assure you, it is not you. The worst exchange rates are at the airport. The second-worst rates are at hotels, restaurants, and shops. These places should be avoided at all costs when it comes to money changing. Your best currency exchange rate will always be at a bank. Banking hours are Monday through Friday, 9:30 A.M. to 5 P.M. Many banks close at noon the day before a public holiday, and all remain closed on holidays and the day after Christmas, Easter, and Pentecost.

You will get a better rate for traveler's checks than for cash, but the real cost lies in what you spent to get the traveler's checks in the first place and the commission cost to convert them. If your bank gives free American Express traveler's checks, by all means try to get them in French francs or euros. This eliminates your exchange problems, including reading one word further in this section about currency exchange. If you are unable to get your traveler's checks in francs or euros, you can cash American Express traveler's checks commission-free at the American Express office in Paris. The drawbacks here are that the exchange rates are not always the best, and the lines are slow and oh, so long. The office is at 11, rue Scribe, 75009; Tel: 01-47-77-79-50 (exchange office); Métro: Opéra (exit rue Scribe); Open: Mon–Sat 9 A.M.–4:30 P.M.

Another bank with a multitude of services is Citibank, which has regular banking services plus currency exchange, traveler's checks, and cash advance with Visa cards. They accept Cirrus and most other ATM cards. They also have English-speaking representatives. There are two locations at 30 and 125, avenue Champs-Élysées, 75008; Tel: 01-49-05-49-05; Open: Mon–Sat twenty-four hours.

If you need currency exchange at any time of the day or night, Chequepoint is open twenty-four hours daily; it's at 150, avenue des Champs-Élysées, 75008; Métro: Charles-de-Gaulle-Étoile; Tel: 01-49-53-02-51.

Commission-free Rates. Banque Libanaise has one of the best exchange rates in Paris. They are across the street from American Express at 7, rue Auber, 75009; Métro: Opéra, (exit rue Scribe); Tel: 01-47-42-33-89; Open: Mon–Fri 9 A.M.–5 P.M.

You can also get commission-free rates from Comptoir de Change Opéra at 9, rue Scribe, 75009; Métro: Opéra; Tel: 01-47-42-20-96; Open: Mon–Fri 9 A.M.–5:15 P.M., Sat 9:45 A.M.–4:15 P.M.

You can also exchange money at rail stations and at scores of authorized money-changing booths, which are thick around tourist areas, especially along rue de Rivoli, the Champs-Élysées, and the Centre Pompideau (Beaubourg). Sometimes they advertise "commission-free" exchanges, and usually the rates are lower than at a bank, or even at American Express, but often you have to change large amounts. Your best bet with these is to use them only when all else fails, and then shop around for the best deal.

Wiring Money to Paris

When your money is history in Paris before you are, and you have exhausted (or preferred not to use) any of the above discussed ways to increase your cash flow, there is one recourse left: Call home for money. The fastest way to refill your wallet is to have the money wired from someone in the States using a moneygram. The transfer is accomplished in minutes and the sender pays the fees, which are based on the amount sent. Here is what to do:

Contact the sender in the United States, who in turn will send the money to you in either of two ways: by going to an office located in his or her city or via a credit card given over the telephone. Note, if the money is sent by credit card, there is a $500 limit. To send the money in person, the sender must call 800-926-9400 (twenty-four hours a day, 365 days a year). This is an information line that will provide the sender with the location of the agents nearest his or her home and any other particulars for sending the money. To send money by credit card, call 800-325-6000, Mon–Fri 6 A.M.–4:30 P.M., MST. This enables the sender to send up to $500 and charge it to a MasterCard or Visa credit card. No matter which way the money is sent, the cash-strapped person in Paris will be notified of the transaction and given a ten-digit confirmation number and an address to go to an Paris to pick up the money (using a photo ID). The main Western Union office in Paris is at 4, rue du Cloître-Notre-Dame, 75005; Métro: Cité; Tel: 01-42-54-46-12; Open: daily

9 A.M.–5 P.M. As you face Notre Dame Cathedral, rue du Cloître-Notre-Dame is the first street on the left.

Tipping

How much is too much, and what is enough? Here are a few guide-lines for appropriate tipping in Paris.

By law, in France, a service charge of 15 percent is added to all hotel and restaurant bills. This service charge *is* the tip, so that when you receive your final bill at a restaurant, you don't need to tip anything more. While this eliminates the need for tips in general, there are certain times when an additional tip is appropriate.

Bars, cafés, restaurants	Leave a few extra francs in a bar or café, and up to 10 percent if the waiter in a restaurant has gone to extra lengths for you.
Hotels	Bellboys 6F (0.91€) per bag; chambermaids about 20F (3.05€) for a three-day stay; room service 10F (1.52€)
Hairdressers	10 to 15 percent; shampoo girls 10–15F (1.25–2.20€)
Taxi drivers	10 to 15 percent
Theater ushers	2–3F (0.30–0.46€) for seating two people

NOTE: Beware of the tipping scam. There is an increasingly common practice in restaurants of putting the entire amount of the bill, to which a 15 percent service has already been added, in the top box of the charge slip, leaving the boxes marked "tip" and "total" empty. Do not be intimidated. Draw a line from the top figure to the total at the bottom and then write in the total figure yourself. If you are leaving a tip on top of this total (and remember you do not have to), leave it in cash. Often tips left on credit cards are not properly distributed.

The bottom line on tipping in Paris is the same as in anywhere else in the world: It is a matter of personal choice. If you liked the service, reward it; if not, do not feel guilty about not leaving an additional sou.

The Euro

The euro became the official currency of the eleven-nation European Union, of which France is a part, on January 1, 2000, but euro notes and coins will not be made available until January 2002, when they will be used alongside the national currencies until July 2002. At that point, the euro will become the sole legal tender for the European Union. Until then, travelers can continue to use national currencies (such as francs for France and pesetas for Spain), although you will notice prices being displayed in both the national currency and the euro. During the transition, while businesses convert to euro pricing, consumers will be able to use euro traveler's checks in denominations of 50, 100, and 200 euros to pay for goods and services. However, these are not yet fully accepted everywhere.

All prices in this book are given in both French francs and the euro (using the current conversion rate). At press time, 1 euro equalled 6.56 French francs and about one U.S. dollar.

Health Matters

Check with your medical insurance carrier before leaving home to see what your coverage abroad will be. Most will cover you for a limited period. If medical care is needed, many medical facilities will require that you pay for your treatment in full at the time of service. Don't think that they will file claims for you, or participate in any medical plan you may belong to. It will generally be up to you to get your claim processed and be reimbursed. Be sure you get an itemized bill to submit to your insurance company. You may wish to take out additional medical insurance, and if so, contact your own insurance carrier, the American Automobile Association for their list of medical insurance carriers, or Wallach & Company, 107 West Federal Street, P.O. Box 480, Middleburg, VA 20118; Tel: 800-237-6615; Email: info@wallach.com; Internet: www.wallach.com; Open: Mon–Fri 8:30 A.M.–5:30 P.M. Another company I have used is Travel Guard. They are open for questions twenty-four hours a day, seven days a week; Tel: 800-826-1399; Fax: 800-955-8785; Internet: www.noelgroup.com.

It is not difficult to stay healthy in Paris. The main complaints seem to be hangovers and/or exhaustion from too much late-night partying, and the usual stomach upsets caused from too much rich food. The water is safe to drink, but I always advise buying bottled water if only because it tastes better. Water from public fountains and spouts is not safe. Of course, it is always prudent to pack an extra set of glasses, an adequate supply of whatever medications you are taking, and a copy of prescriptions, perhaps translated into French. If you need medical attention, contact one of the following.

The American Hospital	63, boulevard Victor Hugo, Neuilly; Tel: 01-46-41-25-25; Métro: Porte Maillot, then bus No. 82
The Franco-British Hospital	3, rue Barbès, 92300, Levallois-Peret (a suburb of Paris); Tel: 01-46-39-22-22; Métro: Anatole-France
Search for hospitalized persons	01-46-39-22-22; 8:45 A.M.–5:50 P.M.

AIDS Information Hotline	01-42-70-03-00; daily 9 A.M.–7 P.M.
Burns (24 hours)	Hôpital de St-Antoine, 184, rue du Fbg-St-Antoine, 75012; Tel: 01-49-28-26-09; Métro: Faidherve-Chaligny
Children	Hôpital Necker, 149, rue de Sèvres, 75015; Tel: 01-44-49-40-00; Métro: Duroc
Children's Burns	Hôpital Armand-Trousseau, 26, avenue du Dr. Arnold-Netter, 75012; Tel: 01-44-73-74-75; Métro: Bel Air
Homeopathic Doctor	Académie d'Homéopathie et des Médecines Douces, 2, rue d'Isly, 75008; Tel: 01-43-87-60-33; Métro: St-Lazare; Open: Mon–Fri 10 A.M.–6 P.M. Many pharmacies also sell homeopathic medicines.
SOS Cardiac	01-45-45-41-00, 01-47-07-50-50
SOS Dentist (8 A.M.-10 P.M.)	01-43-37-51-00
SOS Depression (24 hours)	01-45-22-44-44
SOS Doctor (24 hours)	01-43-37-77-77, 01-47-07-77-77
SOS Drug Crisis	01-45-81-11-20
SOS Eye	01-40-92-93-94
SOS Handicap (medical assistance for the handicapped)	01- 47-41-32-33
SOS Help (Bilingual crisis hotline, 3–11 P.M.)	01-47-23-80-80, 01-47-20-89-98
SOS Nurse (will make house calls)	01-43-57-01-26, 01-43-57-01-26
SOS Pediatric	01-42-93-19-99
Alcoholics Anonymous	01-46-34-59-65

Pharmacies are marked with a green neon cross. They are serious places where health care advice is given out and quality skin and hair care products are sold by knowledgeable personnel. The pharmacist can help with many minor medical complaints, in addition to dispensing a prescription if you need one. A system of on-duty pharmacies ensures that at least one pharmacy in each arrondissement is always open. A closed pharmacy will have a sign giving the address of the nearest open pharmacy.

24-hour pharmacy	Pharmacie Dhèry, 84, avenue des Champs-Élysées, 75008; Tel: 01-45-62-02-41; Métro: George V; open 24 hours a day, 365 days a year
American Pharmacy	Pharmacie Anglo-Américaine, 6, rue Castiglione, 75001; Tel: 01-42-60-72-96; Métro: Tuileries; Open: Mon–Sat 9 A.M.–7:30 P.M.
Pharmacie des Halles	10, boulevard de Sébastopol, 75004; Métro: Châtelet; Open: Mon–Sat 9 A.M.–midnight, Sun noon–midnight
Pharma Presto-Night Pharmacy	01-42-42-42-50. Open 24 hours daily, will deliver
To find nearest all-night pharmacy	01-45-62-02-41

Emergency Numbers

In an emergency, dial these numbers. They are are free from any pay phone and are staffed twenty-four hours a day.

Police	17
Fire	18
Ambulance	15 or 01-45-67-50-50
Poison	01-40-05-48-48

Safety and Security

In comparison to other cities, Paris is not a dangerous place. It is still important, however, to take the same sensible precautions you would in any major metropolitan city in the world. If you are robbed or attacked, report the incident immediately at the police station in the arrondissement where the incident happened. Call 01-53-71-53-71 for the *commissariat* nearest you. If you are going to file a claim with your own insurance company, you will need this police report. In general, keep the following advice in mind as you tour Paris:

1. Be aware of your surroundings and do not go down dark streets at night, especially alone.

2. Wear a money belt or a neck pouch *inside* your clothing and carry in it only what you need with you: passport, some money, and so on. Carry your purse with the strap around your neck and the clasp

against your body, away from the street side. Fanny packs are magnets for thieves . . . they can cut and grab one before you even know it's missing. If you do wear one, don't wear it on your fanny; wear it in front of you, string the strap through your belt loops, and keep only a small amount of money in it. Do not carry any valuables in your wallet, purse, or bag. These all belong in your money belt, neck pouch, or in the hotel safe. Thread a safety pin through the toggle on your backpack's zipper to pin it closed.

3. Try to blend in and keep a low profile: don't wear flashy jewelry, wild colors or prints, or speak in a booming voice.

4. Keep a close eye on your possessions, and do not leave packages or suitcases unattended on the métro or when making a phone call or hailing a taxi. Be careful of your camera.

5. Trust your instincts: If someone or a situation seems suspect, it probably is, so beat a hasty retreat. Beware of pickpockets, especially on the métro and in tourist areas. Watch out for the bands of gypsy children who will surround you and distract your attention by fluttering papers in your face, and then strip you of your valuables before you can think to say, "Stop thief!"

6. Thieves in métro stations lurk around the turnstiles and try to grab your bag as you go through, or they reach for it as the train door closes. Always avoid métro stations late at night.

7. If you are alone, don't say so to a wide audience. Also, make sure someone at home knows your itinerary, and arrange times to call to check in, just to let them know all is well.

8. Before leaving home, make two photocopies of every document that is crucial to the successful completion of your trip—such as your passport, airline tickets, hotel vouchers, and list of credit card numbers (or the number of your credit card registry). Leave one copy at home with someone you can always contact, and take the other copy with you. In the horrible event that your documents are lost or stolen, you have a record of your various numbers, and the process of replacing everything will be easier. Lock up important papers, airline tickets, traveler's checks, extra money, and so on in the hotel safe. Even if there is a charge for this, it is nothing when you consider the cost, inconvenience, and hassle of a theft.

9. The U.S. Department of State publishes a pamphlet called *A Safe Trip Abroad*. For a copy, write the Superintendent of Documents, U.S. Government Printing Office, Washington, DC 20402.

Hotel Security

Security in your hotel mostly pertains to theft. Note that hotel liability tends to be limited and often provides slim protection for the traveler. If an item is stolen from your room, you may have little recourse, unless you can prove negligence. Here are some points to consider:

1. Avoid rooms on the ground floor and those near fire escapes.

2. Do not leave any valuables exposed in your room, even when you are sleeping.

3. When you leave your room, close and lock the windows and do not leave (or hide) any valuables. Lock them up in the hotel safe. There isn't a hiding place a thief doesn't know about.

4. Valuables include more than money and jewelry. Consider camcorders, cameras, computers, personal and travel documents, tape recorders, and so on.

5. If you leave luggage at the hotel after you check out, be sure the storage area is secure, and do not leave any bag containing valuables.

6. If you are a victim of a theft, insist on filing a complete report with the local police immediately. The more documentation you have, the better your chances are for compensation from your own insurance company.

7. Most important: If you don't absolutely need it in Paris, don't take it with you.

Lost and Found

If you think you've lost something, contact the Bureau des Objects Trouvés, 36, rue des Morillons, 75015; Métro: Convention; Tel: 01-55-76-20-20; Open: Mon–Fri 8:30 A.M.–7 P.M. You must visit in person to fill in a form detailing the date, time, and place where item was lost. If you lost an object in a street opening, you can call 01-44-66-49-25 and a sewer worker will try to rescue that key or diamond earring that fell through the sewer grate.

Staying in Touch

Email and the Internet

The worldwide love affair with the Internet and email is rapidly becoming a part of everyday life in France. However, logging on in your hotel room is far from hassle-free, and it's very expensive by U.S. standards. To avoid paying an arm and a leg to surf the Internet or to send email, go to a cyber café. If you are going to be in Paris for more than a few days and know you will be doing alot of digital communicating, buy a subscription card that is good for from either a couple of hours to 250 hours. Then check with your provider to see that your email address will work over the Web and in Paris. If not, you can set up a free email account through Yahoo! Mail (www.mail.yahoo.com), Hotmail (www.hotmail.com), or Netscape (www.netscape.com). In Paris you will need your user name or ID number and your account password. For a list of central cyber cafés in Paris, see page 347.

Here are some numbers for a few Internet providers in France: AOL, 08-00-90-39-10 (www.aol.fr); CompuServe, 01-70-70-01-70 (www.compuserve.fr); and Wanadoo, 08-01-63-34-34 (www.wanadoo.fr).

Fax

To send a fax to Paris from the U. S., dial 011+33+the number. Remember to eliminate the 0 at the beginning of the ten-digit number; for instance, if the fax number is 01-47-12-34-56, dial 011-33-1-47-12-34-56. To fax the U.S. from Paris, dial 00+1+area code+number.

Regular Mail

How quaint! Other than sending postcards, I cannot imagine too many travelers in Paris spending much of their time letterwriting. For postcards, you can buy stamps at any tobacconist shop. This eliminates standing in line at the post office, and the price is exactly the same.

Every *quartier* has a post office; they are open Monday to Friday from 8 A.M. to 7 P.M., Saturday until noon. The main post office at 52, rue du Louvre (Métro: Louvre-Rivoli; Tel: 01-40-28-20-00) is open twenty-four hours daily for *Poste Restante,* telephones, telegrams, stamps, and faxes, and for sending boxes not exceeding two kilos. Larger boxes have to be sent during regular post office hours. They also sell boxes in various sizes that are very sturdy and cheap.

If you do not have an address in Paris, you can use *Poste Restante.* Mail addressed to you must have your name in block capitals, followed by the words *Poste Restanate,* then the post office address: 52, rue du Louvre, 75001, Paris. To get your mail, you must show your passport and pay a small fee for each letter you receive. You can also receive mail c/o American Express, 11, rue Scribe, 75009; Métro: Opéra; Tel: 01-47-14-50-00 (main office); Open: Mon–Fri 9 A.M.–6 P.M., Sat 9 A.M.–5 P.M.

If speed is a factor for sending parcels, then Federal Express is probably your answer. They have an office at 63, boulevard Haussmann, 75008; Métro: Havre-Caumartin; Tel: 08-00-12-38-00; Internet: www.fedex.com/fr; Open: Mon–Fri 9 A.M.–7:30 P.M., Sat 9 A.M.–5:30 P.M.

Telephone

French telephone numbers have ten digits. Paris numbers begin with 01, the rest of France is divided into four regional zones with prefixes 02, 03, 04, and 05. Free telephone numbers begin with 08; cell phone numbers begin with 06. If you are calling France from abroad, leave off the 0 at the beginning of the ten-digit number; dial 0+country code+area or city code+number. For instance, if you are in the United States, and the Paris number is 01-42-22-33-44, dial 011-33-1-42-22-33-44

Making a call from a public telephone is not as simple as dropping a coin into the pay telephone, dialing 0, and requesting connection. Most public phones in Paris now require a prepaid phone card (*télécarte*), which you buy in increments or units (*unités*). To make a call, pick up the phone, insert the card into a slot on the phone, wait for the dial tone, then start dialing the number. The amount of your call is automatically deducted from the remaining value. These cards offer several advantages: you do not need a pocketful of change; calling from a public phone eliminates the surcharges in hotels, cafés, and restaurants; and the card has no expiration date, so you can use what is left on your card on your next trip. Where to buy the *télécarte*? Post offices, *tabacs,* airports, and train and métro stations all sell them. Telephone books are in all post offices and hotels; the white pages list names of people and businesses, yellow pages list businesses and services by category.

Every time you pick up a phone in Paris it will cost you money, even if you are calling next door. If you are calling abroad, the rates can be downright frightening. Avoid going through your hotel switchboard when calling home. Even if you reverse the charges, use a telephone service such as AT&T, or use a calling card, you will be charged a surcharge, sometimes up to 100 percent of the call. Check with the hotel operator about your hotel's policy, as they all differ. To avoid the surcharge, go to a pay telephone booth, on the street or at a post office, and use your *télécarte* or calling card to reach whatever service you have: MCI, AT&T, and so on. This is simple, painless, and definitely the least expensive way to stay in touch.

For further savings, call when the rates are low. Within France and Europe, call Monday through Friday from 7 P.M. to 8 A.M., and from Saturday noon to 8 A.M. Monday. The cheap rates to the United States and Canada are Monday through Friday, 7 P.M. to 1 P.M., and all day Saturday and Sunday. Remember, when calling the United States, Paris is six hours ahead of Eastern Standard Time and nine hours ahead of Pacific Standard Time.

Some numbers you might need to make domestic or international calls:

To call Paris from the United States	011+33+number
To call the United States from Paris	00+1+area code+number
To reach an English-speaking operator	
AT&T	0800-99-00-11
MCI	0800-99-00-19
Sprint	0800-99-00-87
Directory information	12
Operator	10
International information	00-33-12+country code (1 for U.S.)
Traffic	01-48-94-33-33
Weather	
For France and abroad	08-36-70-12-34
Paris	08-36-68-02-75

Transportation

Public transportation in and around Paris is some of the best in Europe. Because it is so efficient, why would any foreign traveler willingly subject him- or herself to driving in this city? Parking is impossible, traffic is from hell, gasoline is expensive, and the one-way streets will drive you crazy. Did you know that of Paris's 988 miles of streets, 435 miles are one way?! Isn't this a vacation? Behind the wheel, Parisian drivers are kamikaze pilots taking no prisoners. They think nothing of driving and parking on the sidewalk, blocking traffic on narrow streets, cutting in and out with inches to spare, and flashing their lights to indicate displeasure (honking the horn is forbidden until the moment of impact). Then there is the *priorité à droite* to get used to: this gives the right of way to the car approaching from the right, regardless of the size of the street, the traffic on it, or the safety hazard of the moment. Adding to this frightening horror show are the devil-may-care, insane motorcyclists who drive, often at rapid speed, on the sidewalk when the traffic is too thick for them to squeeze through it. The best reason to drive a car in Paris is to get out of town and head for the provinces.

Instead, Paris is a city that invites walking. Exploring the narrow streets or strolling the grand boulevards is the best way to discover your own special Paris. Save yourself a great deal of aggravation by using the métro, the buses, the RER suburban railway, and your own feet to get around the city. However, even as a pedestrian, you must keep up your guard. In Paris, anyone behind the wheel of a car—or traveling by any kind of wheeled conveyance, be they rollerbladers, bicyclists, scooter riders, or motorcyclists—considers the pedestrian a monumental nuisance in the effort to get from A to B in the least amount of time possible. Even when the pedestrian has a green light . . . don't assume that drivers will concede the right of way. By law, drivers are only required to come to a full stop at a red light. When there is a crosswalk, whether or not it has a flashing amber light or a sign saying *priorité aux pietons* ("priority to pedestrians"), drivers will ignore this and step on the gas.

Getting to and from the Airports

Roissy–Charles de Gaulle Airport

For general information in English, twenty-four hours daily, call 01-48-62-22-80.

A taxi is the easiest and most comfortable way to get from Roissy to Paris, but it is expensive. The ride into central Paris takes about fifty minutes on a good day; during rush hour, add at least thirty minutes. Taxis will take no more than three people and charge a 6F (0.91€) surcharge for every piece of luggage. Fares range between 250 and 300F (38.11–45.73€) during the day and are higher from 8 P.M. to 7 A.M. A 15 percent tip is expected.

A more economical way is by the direct RER B train to Paris. There is direct access from Terminal 2. A free shuttle bus (look for the word *navette*) runs from Terminal 1 and takes passengers to the Roissy train station, where you board the Roissy Rail (RER B) into the city, with stops at Gare du Nord, Châtelet–Les Halles, St-Michel, Luxembourg, Port Royal, and Denfert–Rochereau. The train leaves every twenty-five minutes between 5 A.M. and 11 P.M. and costs under $10. The train trip takes around forty-five minutes, and the shuttle to the airport station about fifteen minutes. For more information, call SNCF at 01-53-90-20-20.

Air France buses (you do not have to be a passenger on one of their flights to use them) leave from both terminals every twenty minutes from 5:30 A.M. to 11 P.M.; they take about forty minutes to reach Paris and costs around 60F (9.15€). The buses stop at place de la Porte Maillot/Palais des Congrès, Arc de Triomphe/Charles de Gaulle Étoile at avenue Carnot, Gare Montparnasse at 113, boulevard Vaugirard, and Gare de Lyon. For information, call 01-41-56-89-00.

The RATP-run Roissybus runs every twenty-five minutes between the airport and rue Scribe, near place de l'Opéra and beside the American Express office; it takes about forty-five minutes and costs around 60F (9.15€), and that includes all of your luggage. Tickets are sold on the bus. Call the main RATP number, 08-36-68-41-14, for information in English.

There are also various shuttle services between both Roissy–Charles de Gaulle and Orly Airports, which take passengers door-to-door from the airport to their hotel. Advance reservations are necessary. Paris Shuttle works seven days a week; rates start around 85F (12.96€) per person (this rate requires a two-person minimum). Contact them as follows: Tel: 01-43-90-91-91; Fax: 01-43-90-91-10; Email: Parishuttle@aol.com; Internet: www.parishuttle.com. Another company is Airport Shuttle, which costs 125F (19.06€) for one person, with better rates for two or more. To contact them: Tel: 01-45-38-55-72; Fax: 01-43-21-35-67; Internet: www.airportshuttle.fr.

Orly Airport

For English-speaking information, daily 6 A.M.–11:30 P.M., call 01-49-75-15-15.

A taxi from Orly to Paris takes thirty to forty minutes and costs between 150 and 190F (22.88–28.97€), plus 6F (.091€) for each piece of luggage.

The easiest way to get into Paris is on the RER C line on the métro. The high-speed Orlyval shuttle train runs every five to eight minutes (Mon–Fri 6 A.M.–10 P.M., Sat–Sun 7 A.M.–11 P.M.) to RER B station Antony, costs 60F (9.15€), and takes thirty minutes.

There is the courtesy bus Orlyrail to RER station Pont de Rungis, where you get a train to Paris for 30F (4.57€). Trains run daily every fifteen to twenty minutes from 6:30 A.M. to 11:30 P.M. and take fifty minutes.

Air France buses leave both terminals every twelve minutes between 5:50 A.M. and 11 P.M. to the Air France air terminal at Les Invalides or

Montparnasse. The fare is around 40F (6.10€), and the trip takes between thirty and sixty minutes, depending on traffic. Another bus option is the Orlybus to and from the Denfert-Rochereau métro station, which leaves daily every ten minutes between 6 A.M. and 11:30 P.M. Cost is 30F (4.50€); tickets are bought on the bus. Call 01-41-56-89-00 for more information.

Le Bourget

For information on Le Bourget, call 01-48-62-12-12.

This is where Charles Lindbergh landed after his transatlantic flight. Now the airport is used mainly for charter flights within France. If you land here, take bus No. 350, which leaves every fifteen minutes from 6 A.M. to 11:45 P.M. and costs two métro tickets; it goes to Gare du Nord and Gare de l'Est, where you can get the métro to your Paris destination. You can also catch the No. 152 bus, which makes the same two stops and also goes to Porte de la Villette, if this is better. Hours of operation and costs are the same.

Métro and Regional Express Railway (RER)

The Paris métro system has fourteen lines, each identifiable by its number and destination. With 370 stations, it is one of the most efficient in the world. The RER (Regional Express Railway) has five lines in Paris—A, B, C, D, and E—and is joined to the city métro network and some of the SNCF trains (France's national train system). Using a combination of the métro and the RER can take you within walking distance of almost everything you would want to see and do in the city. Trains run from 5:30 A.M. until 12:30 A.M.

You can buy individual tickets, but a *carnet* of ten is much more practical and cheaper by 40 percent. Either of these can be purchased at métro stations, tourist offices, and *tabacs*. There is a special Paris Visite card that is not a particularly good deal unless you will be in Paris only a short time and want to see a lot. If you are staying in Paris more than a few days, buy the weekly Carte Hebdomadaire or the monthly Carte Orange Coupon Mensuel, both of which allow unlimited travel on the métro and buses. To buy either, go to any major métro station. You must have a passport-size photo (there are photo booths in some larger métro stations). Always hold on to your ticket. If you are caught without it, you will be fined. You may buy these two types of métro passes at the cashier window in almost any métro station, or from the RATP offices: place de la Madeleine, 75008; Tel: 01-40-06-71-45, in English 08-36-68-41-14; Métro: Madeleine; Open: May to September only, Mon–Fri 8:30 A.M.– noon, 1–4:30 P.M., Sat 8:30 A.M.–noon, 2–4:30 P.M. The other RATP office is at 53 bis, quai des Grands Augustins, 75006; Tel: 01-40-46-44-50; Métro: St-Michel; Open: year-round Mon–Sat, same hours. To help you decide which type of ticket or pass is best for you, see "Transportation" under "Discounts," page 20.

For the most detailed Paris maps showing all streets with métro stops, consult the *Plan de Paris par Arrondissement* (see page 51). Métros are generally safe. Just use common sense and do not leave a wallet in a back pocket or your purse unzipped. Late at night, the following stations should be avoided: Barbes-Rochechouart, Pigalle, Châtelet, Les Halles, Trocadéro, and Anvers.

Bus

Because the métro is so fast and efficient, visitors often overlook the buses in Paris. The routes of each bus line are generally posted at each stop. They are also listed in the back of the *Plan de Paris par Arrondissement* (see page 51), or you can pick up a free bus map, *Autobus Paris-Plan de Reseau,* at tourist offices and in some métro stations. If you have a métro ticket, or a weekly or monthly métro pass, these will all work on the bus; just show your pass to the driver. Warning: Do not punch your *weekly* ticket when you board the bus, just show it. Punching it will render it unusable. You can punch your *individual* ticket, which, if you don't already have one, you can purchase from the bus driver. Always hold on to your ticket until you get off the bus. If caught without it, you will be fined. All buses run Monday to Saturday from 6:30 A.M. to 8:30 P.M. Some continue until 12:30 A.M., and some run on Sunday. The Noctambus runs all night, but the routes are fewer. The pamphlet printed by the RATP–Paris Bus, Métro, RER Routes–lists several scenic bus routes and gives directions to major museums and monuments. For RATP information in English, call 08-36-68-41-14, or visit their Website at www.ratp.fr.

Important warning: Buy your métro or bus tickets and passes from cashiers inside métro stations, or from one of the RATP offices listed above. Do not, under any circumstances whatsoever, buy from independent shysters who work the train stations claiming to be authorized RATP employees, which they are not. They are cheats out to steal your money through their scam.

Taxi

The challenge of finding a taxi in Paris often rivals that of New York City on a busy Friday afternoon. Add rain to that and you are better off riding public transportation or walking. Hailing a cab on a corner is difficult. It is smarter to go to a taxi stand; they are located on most major thoroughfares and at all the railroad stations. Taxis are required by law to stop for you if the large white light on top is on (unless it is the driver's last half hour on duty or the passenger is less than fifty meters from a taxi stand). A glowing orange light means the taxi is not available. Taxi drivers will take you anywhere you want to go in Paris or to either airport, follow a route of your choosing, accept all handicapped passengers, and give you a receipt. They are not required to take animals (even though they may have their own dog riding with them in the front seat), take more than three persons, or accept an unreasonable amount of luggage. They might do any of these things, but there will be a supplemental charge. There is a minimum fee of 15F (2.29€), plus 6F (0.91€) for every piece of luggage. Normal taxi fares are based on area and time of day. Beneath the taxi light are three little lights—A, B, and C. One of these will light up according to what tariff applies. The tariff is also shown on the meter display inside the taxi. A 15 percent tip is customary. If you want an early-morning taxi to take you to the airport, book it the night before. If you need a taxi at a specific time and don't want to chance not finding one, call ahead. If you do call a taxi, the fare starts when the driver gets the call, not when you get in. Here is a list of some of the bigger taxi companies; all take credit cards (minimums vary), but only Taxi G7 takes reservations in English.

Alpha	01-45-85-85-85
Artaxi	01-42-03-50-50
Taxis Bleu	01-49-36-10-10
Taxi G7	01-47-39-47-39

Paris taxi drivers are quite honest and above-board, and they provide receipts upon request. Ask for *un reçu, s'il vous plat.* If you have problems, note the cab number and company name and write to the Bureau de la Réglementation publique de Paris, 36, rue des Morillons, 75732, Paris Cedex 15; Tel: 01-45-31-14-80.

You can hire a chauffeured limousine with a bilingual driver from Paris Major Limousines; Tel: 01-44-52-50-00; Fax: 01-44-52-50-05; Email: pml@Paris.limousines.fr.

Train

The SNCF is the acronym for the French national train system. There are six train stations in Paris: Gare de Lyon for trains going to the southeast of France, the Alps, Provence, and Italy; Gare d'Austerlitz for trains going to the southwest of France and Spain; Gare de l'Est for trains to Alsace and southern Germany; Gare St-Lazare for the northwest and Normandy; Gare du Nord for trains to Brussels, London via the Chunnel, and other destinations to the north; and Gare Montparnasse for trains to the west, Brittany, and Bordeaux. At each station is a métro stop with the same name.

You can buy tickets at the station, or call ahead to reserve your seat, but you must pick it up within forty-eight hours. If you are under twenty-six years old, you can save up to 50 percent on TGV fares with the Carte12/25. Without the card, you still get a 25 percent reduction. People over sixty also get good deals with a Carte Vermeil (see "Discounts," page 19). Before boarding the train you must remember to validate your ticket in an orange *composteur;* these are located at the beginning of the platforms, and when the conductor checks your ticket, he could fine you for not having done it. For information, go to 16, boulevard des Capucines, 75002; Métro: Opéra; or call 01-45-82-50-50 or 08-36-35-35-35; Open: daily 7 A.M.–7 P.M.

Time

France is one hour ahead of Greenwich Mean Time (GMT). Time is based on the twenty-four-hour clock. To check the time and set your clock, dial 36-99. Paris is six hours ahead of Eastern Standard Time and nine hours ahead of Pacific Standard Time. Daylight Savings Time is observed from April 1 to October 31.

Standards of Measure

France uses the metric system. Here are the conversions:

1 inch = 2.54 centimeters	1 centimeter = 0.4 inch
1 mile = 1.61 kilometers	1 kilometer = 0.62 miles
1 ounce = 28 grams	1 gram = 0.04 ounces
1 pound = 0.45 kilograms	1 kilogram = 2.2 pounds
1 quart = 0.95 liter	1 liter = 1.06 quarts
1 gallon = 3.8 liters	

How much is that in miles, feet, pounds, or degrees? Here is how to do the conversions:

Kilometers/miles: To change kilometers to miles, multiply the kilometers by .621. To change miles to kilometers, multiply the miles by 1.61.

Meters/feet: To change meters to feet, multiply the meters by 3.28. To change feet to meters, multiply the feet by .305.

Kilograms/pounds: To change kilograms to pounds, multiply the kilograms by 2.20. To change pounds to kilograms, multiply the pounds by .453.

Celsius/Fahrenheit: To change Celsius to Fahrenheit, double the Celsius figure and add 30. If the Celsius figure is below zero, double the sub-zero number and subtract it from 32.

Voltage

French electrical circuits are wired at 220 volts. You will need a transformer and an adapter plug for appliances you bring that operate on 110 volts. Things such as hair dryers and hair curling irons may have switches that convert the appliance from one voltage to another. This only eliminates the need for a transformer, not for the adapter plug. If you are planning on using a computer, be sure you have a surge protector and the adapter plug, otherwise you could end up damaging your machine. Don't worry if you find yourself without the proper adapters or transformers. Go to the basement of BHV department store (see "Shopping," page 311) and take the appliance with you. If they don't have what you need, chances are it doesn't exist.

How to Use
Great Sleeps Paris

Big Splurges

Hotels in the Big Splurge category are higher priced and are included because their amenities, ambiance, service, and overall appeal will suit those travelers with more flexible budgets and demanding tastes. Even though the prices are higher, they still offer the same good value for money as the lower priced accommodations in this guide, and they make ideal places to stay for special occasions. All Big Splurge hotels are marked with a dollar sign ($). The index includes a separate list of these special hotels.

Stars

Hotels throughout France are controlled by a government rating system that ranks them from no stars to four-star deluxe. Every hotel must display prominently the number of stars it has. In Paris, there are currently 19 hotels with no-star ratings and 179 one-star, 611 two-star, 563 three-star, and 121 four-star hotels.

Because the number of stars has to do with the size of the room, the distance from the bed to the light switch, and whether or not there is an elevator, and absolutely nothing to do with the level of cleanliness, attitude of management or personnel, location, or value for money, you cannot always judge the quality or even the price of a hotel by its stars. In older hotels, many of the rooms are not standardized, and they can range in size and price from a dark little cavelike cell on the back to a sumptuous suite facing a leafy garden.

However, the star ratings do act as a general guide. A no-star hotel is usually mighty basic, with few, if any, private bathrooms and rarely anyone behind the desk who speaks any English. Many of them, however, are spotlessly clean, well located, and excellent budget values. A one-star hotel has minimum facilities, but again, it may be well located and very clean. Two stars means a comfortable hotel with direct-dial phones in all rooms and an elevator in buildings of four or more stories. Three stars means a very comfortable hotel where all rooms have direct-dial phones, a majority have private plumbing, and there is an elevator. A four-star hotel is first class all the way, usually with a restaurant, and a four-star deluxe is a virtual palace, with every service you could dream of. This book covers no-star to three-star hotels, with the exception of a single four-star that was too good to leave out.

Reservations

People always ask me, "Do I need advance hotel reservations in Paris?" The answer is yes, positively! In order to be assured of a room, you must reserve as far in advance as possible. Paris experiences some of the worst hotel bottlenecks in Europe, and a confirmed reservation, even on the slowest day in the low season, will save you frantic hours spent searching for a room after your arrival. It will also save you money, since without advance reservations you will probably be forced to take something beyond your budget, perhaps in a part of the city you do not like. Do not reserve for more nights than you think you will need. If you decide to leave before you intended, or if you want to switch hotels, you may not get back any money you have paid ahead, or you could be charged on your credit card for the nights you do not stay.

The easiest way to reserve is to let your travel agent do all the work. However, it is not hard to do it yourself, and frankly, with the ease and speed of the telephone, faxes, and email, it is not only easy but better because you will be able to ask questions, inquire about exact rates, and arrange just what you want without going through a intermediary. In addition, the hotel may pass along to you their savings of the travel agent's commission. After reserving by one of these methods, you will be asked to guarantee your booking by fax with a major credit card, or in a few cases, a money order in French francs.

The one way *not* to reserve is by letter. Transatlantic mail can take more than two weeks each way—and if there is a strike, who knows how long mail will take to reach its destination? Now with the speed and ease of email, a letter makes no sense; in fact, in today's world, writing for reservations is about as *au courant* as the bustle. In other words, don't do it.

When reserving, the following points should be covered:

1. Dates of stay, time of arrival, and number of persons in the party.

2. Size and type of room (double or twin beds, extra beds, adjoining rooms, suite, and so on).

3. Facilities needed: private toilet, shower and/or bathtub, or hall facilities if acceptable.

4. Location of room: view, on the street, on the courtyard, or in the back of the hotel.

5. Rates. Determine what the nightly rate will be, including the per person City of Paris tourist tax, called the *taxe de séjour* (see "Rates: Paying the Bill," page 47, for details). Be sure to state whether or not you will be eating breakfast at the hotel (and remember you will save money if you do not).

6. Deposit required and form of payment.

7. Refund policy if you should have to cancel.

8. Request a faxed confirmation and take it with you to the registration desk.

Email and the Internet

The attraction and convenience of the Internet and email is beginning to sweep the French hotel industry in the magnitude it has in the States. Even some of the smallest hotels have realized that an email address and/or a Website can increase business significantly. Whenever applicable, each hotel's email and/or Internet address have been given. In many cases, hotels subscribe to a general service rather than have their own. Because the digital revolution is still growing in France, please be understanding and patient and expect some snafus.

Fax

All but the smallest budget hotels in Paris have joined the electronic age and have, at the very least, a fax machine. Faxing is the best way to secure a confirmed booking because it ensures that all parties get the details correct. Insist on a confirmation fax from the hotel, acknowledging your reservation and all pertinent details. To fax a hotel in Paris, dial 011 + 33, and then the fax number in Paris, remembering to drop the first zero. For instance, if the fax is 01-42-12-34-56, compose 011 + 33 + 1-42-12-34-56.

Telephone

Always call Paris during regular, local weekday business hours to avoid talking to a hotel night clerk who has no authority to negotiate prices. Before calling, write down all your requests and questions. The hotel will ask you to send a fax with your credit card number as a guarantee for your reservation. In this fax to the hotel, cite the details of the conversation, the name of the person with whom you spoke, and the date and time of the call. It is vital to ask the hotel to fax you a confirmation of your reservation in return, and then take it with you in case there are any problems at check-in. To dial direct to Paris from the United States, dial 011 + 33, and then the number of the hotel, dropping the first 0 of the ten-digit phone number. For instance, if the hotel phone number is 01-42-11-22-33, you dial 011 + 33 + 1-42-11-22-33.

Making Your Reservation in French

If the hotel in question has no English-speaking staff, or you just want to try your luck with French, here are a few simple phrases for making your reservation (see also the glossary, page 350).

Bonjour/Bonsoir Madame/Monsieur
Hello/Good evening Madam/Sir

Parlez-vous Anglais?
Do you speak English?

Je voudrais réserver ____ chambre(s) (tranquille) pour une/deux/trois personnes qui donne sur (le jardin/la rue/la cour) à deux lits (avec un grant lit/à un lit) avec salle de bains et WC (avec douche ou bain et WC/sans douche ou bain et WC) pour ____ nuit(s) à partir du ____ au ____.

I would like to reserve ____ (quiet) room(s) for one/two/three persons that is/are on (the garden/the street/the courtyard) with two beds (one big bed/one regular-size bed) with bath and toilet (with shower or bath and toilet/without shower or bath and toilet) for ____ night(s) beginning on ____ to ____.

Je voudrais prendre la (les) chambre(s) avec (sans) le petit déjeuner
I would like to have the room(s) include (without) breakfast.

Quel est le tarif?
What is the price?

Quel est votre tarif meilleur? Avez-vous des prix basse-saison?
What is your best price? Do you have a low-season price?

Voici mon numéro de carte de credit.
Here is my credit card number.

Mon numéro de fax/email est_____.
My fax/email number is_____.

Veuillez-vous confirmer ma reservation des que possible?
Would you please confirm this reservation as soon as possible?

Merci beaucoup, Monsieur/Madame.
Thank you very much, sir/madame.

If you are sending a confirming fax, you will want to add:

Vous trouvez ci-joint____ (mon carte de credit) à titre d'arrhes.
You will find attached ____ (my credit card number and expiration date) as a first-night deposit.

Auriez-vous le bonté de bien vouloir me confirmer cette réservation dès que possible? Je vous remercie de votre obligeance, et je vous prie de croire, Monsieur/Madame, à l'assurance de mes sentiments distingués.
Would you please be kind enough to confirm this reservation as soon as possible? Thank you for your assistance.
Yours sincerely,

Deposits

After making a reservation, most hotels will require at least a one-night deposit, even if you have been a guest there before. This is smart insurance for both sides. The easiest way to handle a deposit is with a credit card. If the hotel does not take credit cards, there are other options. You can sometimes send your own personal check, which the hotel will only cash if you are a no-show. They will return uncashed check to you upon arrival. The next best option is to send the hotel an international money order in U.S. dollars. This can be converted into French francs (or euros) by the hotel, and it saves you from having to secure a deposit in French francs (or euros) on this side of the Atlantic. While this option is more convenient for you, it is added work for the hotel, costs them money to exchange, and some, especially in the lower price ranges, simply refuse. If your hotel insists on a deposit in French francs, you will have to purchase them in the form of a money order through your bank.

Checking In/Checking Out

The lobby is usually one of the most attractive parts of a hotel, both because first impressions are important and because it is where the owner and manager spend their day. When you arrive at your hotel, ask to see your room. This is a normal and expected practice in all hotels in France. If you are dissatisfied, ask to see another room. After approving the room, reconfirm the rate and whether or not you will be eating breakfast at the hotel. This advance work prevents any unpleasant surprises at checkout time.

In most hotels, you pay for the room, not for the number of persons occupying it. Thus, if you are alone and occupy a triple, you will pay the triple price, unless negotiated otherwise. Watch out! Most rooms are set up for two, and the few singles tend to be tiny and located on a top floor without much view or along the back facing a blank wall. Most hotels have two kinds of double rooms: those with a double bed (*un grand lit*) and those with twin beds (*deux lits*). If you ask for a double, you will get a room with a double bed, so when reserving, be sure to be specific about exactly what type of bed arrangement suits you.

In Paris, the hotel day begins and ends at noon. If you overstay, you can be charged the price of an extra day. If you are arriving before noon after a long international flight, the room will probably not be ready if the hotel is fully booked. If you must have your room at 8 or 9 A.M., you will have to book (and pay) for it the night before. If you think you might arrive after 6 P.M., be sure to notify the hotel; otherwise your room can legally be given away, even if you have a deposit.

Rates: Paying the Bill

Just like French restaurant menus, hotel rates and the number of stars must be posted.

The city of Paris levies a visitors' tax on persons not liable for the resident tax (a tax raised on habitual residents of the City of Paris). This visitors' tax, called the *taxe de séjour,* applies to all forms of paying accommodations: hotels and tourist residences, furnished flats, holiday campsites, and RV parking. The tax is charged per person, per night. Some hotels charge it over and above the quoted rate, which is technically illegal, but no one seems to be looking; others include it in the total hotel rate. All *Great Sleeps Paris* listings state whether or not this tax is included or extra. However, policies on this tax change, so to avoid confusion, be sure to inquire at the time of booking whether or not the *taxe de séjour* is included or extra. The following categories apply:

Type of accommodation	Price per person, per day
4-star hotels and other equivalent establishments	7 francs, 1.07€
3-star hotels and other equivalent establishments	6 francs, 0.91€
2-star hotels and other equivalent establishments	5 francs, 0.76€
1-star hotels and other equivalent establishments	3 francs, 0.46€
No-star hotels and other equivalent establishments	1 franc, 0.15€
Camping and RV areas	1 franc, 0.15€

The proceeds of the *taxe de séjour* are allocated for the development and promotion of tourism in Paris.

The French government no longer tightly controls hotel prices, but they do give special authorization for hotels to increase prices by a certain percentage every year. Many hotels do this around April; others have held steady for two and three years at a time. It usually depends on the economy. Most hotels offer different rates at different times of the year, getting what they can when they can, based on the law of supply and demand. This is especially true during the fashion and trade shows, when hotels in premium Paris locations have been know to double prices—and have people fight to pay them.

All rates listed in *Great Sleeps Paris* are for full price and do not reflect any special deals. If a hotel does offer discounted rates at certain times of the year, that is noted. The rates tell whether or not breakfast is extra or included and, if included, whether or not the hotel will allow you to deduct it if not taken. While I have made every effort to be accurate on the rates, I cannot control changes or fluctuations of the dollar against the franc or the euro, so be prepared for the prices vary (unfortunately, usually upward). All listings state which credit cards are accepted. In most hotels, payment is required one night in advance. Some low-priced hotels, youth hostels, and student accommodations do not accept credit cards. It is cash up front in French francs or euros only. I have yet to see one of these hotels bend on this important point, so be prepared.

The following abbreviations are used to denote which credit cards a hotel will accept:

American Express	AE
Diners Club	DC
MasterCard	MC
Visa	V

Hotel exchange rates are terrible. If you plan to pay your bill in cash, convert your money at a bank before checkout time (see "Currency Exchange," page 27). Before leaving the hotel, go over your bill carefully, question anything you do not understand, and get a receipt marked paid.

Complaints

If you have a serious complaint about some aspect of your hotel stay (and this does not mean noise or mismatched colors in your room), complain directly to the manager, not to the desk clerk, who has no authority and will rarely pass on your comments to the boss for fear of losing his or her job. If the problem cannot be solved at this level, then put your concerns in writing and send them to the Direction du Tourisme, 2, rue Linois, 75015, Paris; Métro: Charles-Michels. I also encourage you to let me know about any major problems you encounter. While I cannot intercede on your behalf, it is important for me to know if a hotel is no longer measuring up so that I can take up the matter with the hotel on my next visit. Please see "Readers' Comments," page 363, for my address.

If you have a consumer complaint with a shop or store, write to Direction Départmentale de la Concurrence, de la Consommation, et la Répression des Fraudes, 8, rue Froissart, 75153, Paris, Tel: 01-40-27-16-00. This office is in the Ministry of Finance. Be sure to include an explanation, copies of your receipt, and any correspondence you have had with the seller.

Breakfast

Hotel breakfasts are almost always a bad buy. It is much cheaper, and twice as interesting, to join the locals at the corner café for a *café crème* and a croissant, or to stop by a neighborhood *pâtisserie* or *boulangerie* that has a few tables and chairs and indulge in freshly baked treats. Almost every Parisian hotel charges extra for their Continental breakfast, which consists of coffee, tea, hot chocolate, bread, croissants or other rolls, butter, and jam. Some throw in a glass of juice or a piece of cheese. Watch out for the "breakfast is offered" ruse. No, it isn't . . . you are paying for it in the room rate; it just has not been separately charged. In general, if a hotel charges breakfast separately, you can usually have it taken off your bill if, when you first check in, you tell them you will be declining breakfast during your stay and don't want to be charged for it; if the hotel has included breakfast in the room rate, it is virtually impossible to have it deducted. Hotels stand to make as much as a 200 percent profit on this meal, so they naturally encourage their guests to take it at the hotel. If you want anything extra, it will cost dearly and is usually not worth the extra expenditure. Many hotels are now offering a buffet downstairs for the same price as a Continental, which they will serve in your room. An all-you-can-eat buffet with cereals, yogurt, hard-boiled eggs, cheese, cold meat, and fruit added to the standard Continental fare can sometimes be worth the price, especially if you plan to skip lunch. But please! Do not treat the buffet as a free feed for the rest of the day by loading up a bag with the fixings for lunch and a predinner snack. This is extremely bad form, and hoteliers will be furious if they catch you doing it.

Unless otherwise noted, none of the hotels listed serve meals other than breakfast.

English Spoken

All the hotel listings in this book state whether or not English is spoken. If you do not speak any French and want to avoid the stress of trying to communicate without it, it is important to know whether someone at the hotel speaks English. If you can dust off a few French phrases, smile, and display good will, you will find that the hotel staff will prove to be friendly and go out of their way to help you. While it is fun to practice your high-school French, it is not fun to try to deal with a problem while struggling to speak it.

Smoking/Nonsmoking Rooms

Bon chance on this one! Statistics show that 50 percent of Parisian men are smokers and 30 percent of Parisian women light up. I think these figures are very low, considering that three tons of cigarette butts are cleaned off the streets of Paris every day! There is only one hotel group in Paris that devotes at least one entire floor of rooms to its nonsmoking guests. This is Libertel, three of which are listed in *Great Sleeps Paris*. Many other hotels will say they have nonsmoking rooms, but what they really mean is that the maid will open the window and spray air freshener on the day you arrive. If the hotel provides exclusive nonsmoking rooms, it is definitely noted under Facilities and Services category. Fortunately, many of the hotel breakfast dining rooms are nonsmoking. The index has a list of hotels that have rooms exclusively set aside for nonsmoking guests.

Facilities and Services

A brief summary at the end of each hotel listing states which facilities and services are offered by the hotel. The may include: air-conditioning, bar, direct-dial telephone, hair dryer, elevator, Internet connections, laundry service, minibar, parking, room service, television with international reception, pay-per-view television or videos, safe in office or in the room (and if there is a charge), and exclusive nonsmoking rooms. Of course, the better the hotel, the more offerings there will be.

Nearest Tourist Attractions

Each hotel listing tells you if the hotel is on the Right or Left Bank and gives you the nearest tourist attractions within a reasonable walking distance.

Transportation

The closest métro stops are given with each hotel listing. That is not to say that taking the bus might not be a better way for you to get where you want to go. It is beyond the scope of *Great Sleeps Paris* to give the bus routes, but there are free métro and bus maps available in métro stations and at your hotel. When in doubt, just ask at the hotel desk. You can bet the clerk rides either the métro or the bus to work. (See "Transportation," page 37, for complete information on public transportation in Paris.)

Maps

The maps in *Great Sleeps Paris* are meant to help locate all the hotels and shops; they are not meant to replace detailed street maps to guide you as you walk about the city. The free maps you will pick up at your hotel are worth what you paid for them: nothing. If you plan to be in Paris for more than a day, a necessary investment, and one that will last forever, is a copy of the *Plan de Paris par Arrondissement*. This Parisian "bible" offers a detailed map of each arrondissement, with a completely keyed street index, métro and bus routes, tourist sites, churches, and other valuable information. It is available at major newsstands and bookstores. All Parisians have a copy, and so should you. One of the easiest for visitors is the fold-out *Plan de Paris*, Editions Coutarel, with monuments shown and a complete street index.

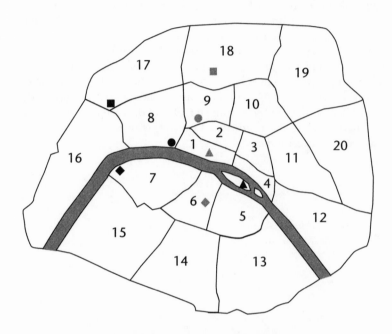

● Place de la Concorde   ● Opéra
■ Arc de Triomphe   ■ Sacré Cœur
▲ Notre Dame   ▲ Louvre
◆ Tour Eiffel   ◆ Jardin du Luxembourg

HOTEL LISTINGS BY ARRONDISSEMENT

Paris has more than nine million inhabitants occupying 432 square miles. Despite these numbers, it is a very compact city, bound by a ring road known as the *périphérique* and divided into twenty districts called *arrondissements*. Anything outside the *périphérique* is the *banlieu* and is considered the suburbs. In the late nineteenth century, Paris was reorganized and modernized by Baron Haussmann, the far-sighted planner who gave the city its wide boulevards, beautiful parks, and system of arrondissements that make up the city today. Each arrondissement has a character all its own, as well as its own mayor, city hall, police station, and central post office.

Knowing which arrondissement is which is the key to understanding Paris and quickly finding your way around. Starting with the first arrondissement, which is the district around the Louvre, the numbering of the districts goes clockwise in a rough spiral. From a visitor's standpoint, the arrondissements of greatest interest are the first through the eighth, although there are interesting things to see and do in all of them. For instance, Montmartre occupies most of the eighteenth, and to attend a performance at the Opéra Bastille, you will journey to the eleventh. The River Seine divides Paris into the Right Bank (*Rive Droite*) and the Left Bank (*Rive Gauche*). Right Bank arrondissements are one, two, three, four, eight, nine, ten, eleven, twelve, sixteen, seventeen, eighteen, nineteen, and twenty. Left Bank arrondissements are five, six, seven, thirteen, fourteen, and fifteen. For mailing purposes, the Paris zip code is 750 followed by a two-digit number indicating the arrondissement: 75001 is the first, 75002 is the second, and so on. For every address in *Great Sleeps Paris,* the postal zip code is given.

First Arrondissement

Paris began on Île de la Cité, and Parisians still regard it as the center not only of their city but of all France. Anchored in the middle of the Seine, Île de la Cité has some of the oldest and most treasured monuments of Paris. La Conciergerie is the Gothic prison where thousands, including Robespierre and Marie-Antoinette, were incarcerated during the French Revolution. Le Palais de Justice, a royal palace, became the seat of the judicial system after the French Revolution. Ste-Chapelle, located within the walls of Le Palais de Justice, has seven-hundred-year-old, breathtakingly beautiful red-and-blue stained-glass windows. The Tuileries Gardens and Louvre Museum form the cornerstone of this regal *quartier*. In the first you will find the rejuvenated Les Halles, with Forum des Halles housing two hundred or more boutiques along with movie theaters, fast-food joints, and the largest métro station in the world (which has the reputation of being unsafe after dark). Two famous churches are here: St-Germain-l'Auxerrois, the Gothic church parish of French kings, and St-Eustache, the largest Gothic Renaissance church in Paris. For many, place Dauphine, with its white brick buildings, is one of the most peaceful and harmonious in the city. The palaces surrounding the moneyed place Vendôme include the famed Cartier jewelry store, the Ministry of Justice, and the world-renowned Ritz Hôtel, where room prices are within the budget of any average emir or Texas oil mogul.

RIGHT BANK
Conciergerie, Île de la Cité, Pont Neuf, Place Dauphine, Les Halles, Louvre, Palais de Justice, Palais Royal, place Vendôme, Ste-Chapelle, St-Eustache

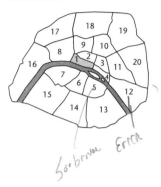

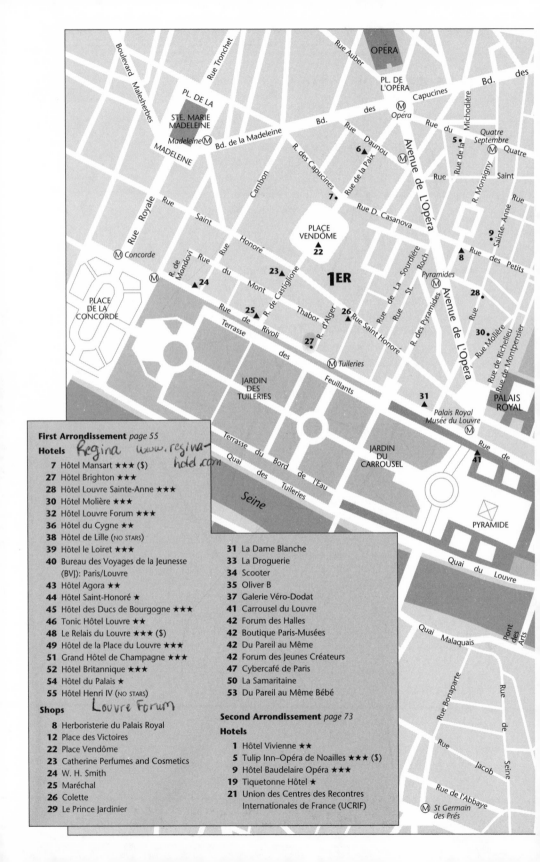

First Arrondissement *page 55*

Hotels Regina www.regina-hotel.com

- **7** Hôtel Mansart ★★★ ($)
- **27** Hôtel Brighton ★★★
- **28** Hôtel Louvre Sainte-Anne ★★★
- **30** Hôtel Molière ★★★
- **32** Hôtel Louvre Forum ★★★
- **36** Hôtel du Cygne ★★
- **38** Hôtel de Lille (NO STARS)
- **39** Hôtel le Loiret ★★★
- **40** Bureau des Voyages de la Jeunesse (BVJ): Paris/Louvre
- **43** Hôtel Agora ★★
- **44** Hôtel Saint-Honoré ★
- **45** Hôtel des Ducs de Bourgogne ★★★
- **46** Tonic Hôtel Louvre ★★
- **48** Le Relais du Louvre ★★★ ($)
- **49** Hôtel de la Place du Louvre ★★★
- **51** Grand Hôtel de Champagne ★★★
- **52** Hôtel Britannique ★★★
- **54** Hôtel du Palais ★
- **55** Hôtel Henri IV (NO STARS)

Shops Louvre Forum

- **8** Herboristerie du Palais Royal
- **12** Place des Victoires
- **22** Place Vendôme
- **23** Catherine Perfumes and Cosmetics
- **24** W. H. Smith
- **25** Maréchal
- **26** Colette
- **29** Le Prince Jardinier
- **31** La Dame Blanche
- **33** La Droguerie
- **34** Scooter
- **35** Oliver B
- **37** Galerie Véro-Dodat
- **41** Carrousel du Louvre
- **42** Forum des Halles
- **42** Boutique Paris-Musées
- **42** Du Pareil au Même
- **42** Forum des Jeunes Créateurs
- **47** Cybercafé de Paris
- **50** La Samaritaine
- **53** Du Pareil au Même Bébé

Second Arrondissement *page 73*

Hotels

- **1** Hôtel Vivienne ★★
- **5** Tulip Inn–Opéra de Noailles ★★★ ($)
- **9** Hôtel Baudelaire Opéra ★★★
- **19** Tiquetonne Hôtel ★
- **21** Union des Centres des Recontres Internationales de France (UCRIF)

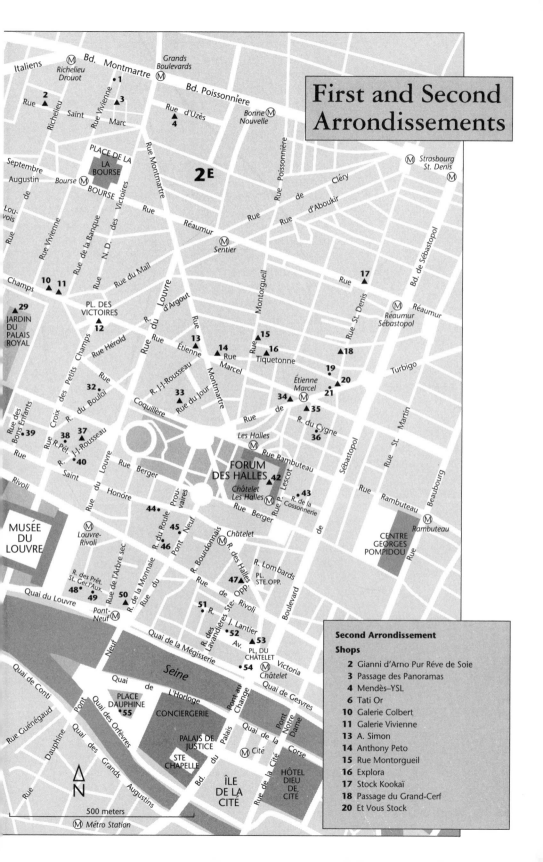

First and Second Arrondissements

Italiens
Bd. Montmartre Ⓜ
Richelieu Drouot Ⓜ
● 1
Grands Boulevards Ⓜ
Bd. Poissonnière

Rue
2 ▲
Richelieu
Saint
Marc
Rue Vivienne
▲ 3
Rue d'Uzès
4 ▲
Bonne Nouvelle Ⓜ

Septembre
Augustin
Bourse Ⓜ
de
Lou-vois
Rue

PLACE DE LA BOURSE
LA BOURSE
Rue Montmartre
2E

Rue
Rue N.-D.
des Victoires
Rue de la Banque
Rue Vivienne

BOURSE

Réaumur
Rue
Rue d'Aboukir
Rue de
Cléry

Strasbourg St. Denis Ⓜ
Ⓜ

Champs
10 ▲ 11 ▲

29 ▲
JARDIN DU PALAIS ROYAL

Rue du Mail
Ⓜ Sentier

PL. DES VICTOIRES
12 ▲
Rue Hérold
Rue Étienne
13 ▲
14 ▲
Rue Marcel

15 ▲
16 ▲
Rue Tiquetonne
Montorgueil
Rue St. Denis

17 ▲
Rue

Réaumur Sébastopol Ⓜ
Réaumur
Bd. de Sébastopol

▲ 18

Rue du Bouloi
32 ●

33 ▲
Coquillière
Rue du Jour
Rue Montmartre
R. J.-J.-Rousseau

Étienne Marcel
19 ●
▲ 20
21 ●

34 ▲ Ⓜ
▲ 35
R. du Cygne
36

Turbigo

Rue des Bons Enfants
39 ●
38 ▲ 37 ▲
R. Pél. R. J.-J.-Rousseau
40 ●
Croix des Petits Champs
Rue du Louvre

Rue
de
Les Halles Ⓜ
Rue Rambuteau

Rue
Saint
Honoré
Rue Berger

FORUM DES HALLES
42 ▲
Châtelet Les Halles Ⓜ
Rue P. Lescot
43 ●
R. de la Cossonnerie
Rue Berger

Rue St. Martin
Sébastopol
Rambuteau Ⓜ

CENTRE GEORGES POMPIDOU
Beaubourg
Rue Rambuteau

MUSÉE DU LOUVRE

Louvre-Rivoli Ⓜ
44 ●
Prou-vaires
R. du Roule
45 ●
46 ●
Pont-Neuf

R. de l'Arbre sec
R. de la Monnaie
Rue du
Rue des Bourdonnais
Châtelet
R. des Halles
47 ▲
PL. STE.OPP.

R. Lombards
PL. STE.OPP.

Boulevard de

Rivoli
Rue
48 ● 49 ● 50 ●
R. des Prêt.
St. Ger.l'Aux.
Quai du Louvre
Pont-Neuf Ⓜ

R. des Lavandières Ste.-Op.
51 ●
R. J. Lantier
52 ●
Av.
▲ 53
PL. DU CHÂTELET
54 ●
Victoria
Châtelet Ⓜ
Cité Ⓜ

Quai de la Mégisserie
Quai de Gesvres

Quai de Conti
Seine
Quai
de
L'Horloge
PLACE DAUPHINE
55 ●
CONCIERGERIE

Rue Guénégaud
Pont Neuf
Quai des Orfèvres
Dauphine
Quai des Grands

PALAIS DE JUSTICE
STE CHAPELLE
Bd.
Augustins

Pont au Change
Palais
du
Quai de la Cité
Cité Ⓜ
Corse
Pont Notre Dame
Quai de la Cité

ÎLE DE LA CITÉ
Rue de la Cité

HÔTEL DIEU DE CITÉ

△ N

500 meters
Ⓜ Métro Station

HOTELS IN THE FIRST ARRONDISSEMENT

($) indicates a Big Splurge

GRAND HÔTEL DE CHAMPAGNE ★★★ (51)
17, rue Jean-Lantier, at 13, rue des Orfèvres, 75001
Métro: Châtelet (exit rue de Rivoli, *nos impairs*, or Bertin Poirée)

TELEPHONE
01-42-36-60-00; toll-free from U.S., 1-800-44-UTELL

FAX
01-45-08-43-33

CREDIT CARDS
AE, DC, MC, V

RATES
Single 750F (114.34€), double 880F (134.16€), suites 1,430F (218.00€); *taxe de séjour* 6F (0.91€) per person, per day

BREAKFAST
60F (9.15€) per person, buffet downstairs or Continental in room

ENGLISH SPOKEN
Yes

43 rooms, all with shower or bath and toilet

Hidden on a small corner near the River Seine and the Châtelet métro stop, the family-owned Grand Hôtel de Champagne appeals to travelers looking for an A+ location for exploring the Louvre, the islands, St-Michel, and St-Germain-des-Prés.

If you look carefully in the sitting area off the reception, you will see the date 1562 carved on one of the original wooden pillars. This tells you when the building was built, but it doesn't tell you that it is the oldest structure on rue Jean-Lantier, and that before its present charmed transformation, it served as a residence for members of the tailor and shoemaker guilds, an inn during the Empire period, and until 1854, a Christian girls' school.

Different themes are carried out in each of the forty-three rooms and suites, with interiors running the gamut from masculine modern to frankly feminine. Generally speaking, they tend to be small by American standards. Many have hand-painted murals done by artists over the years (perhaps in lieu of a final payment?). Room 304 has a fanciful scene of Venice on the bathroom wall, and No. 302, one of my favorites, shows a pretty girl peeking through a cloud-filled sky. No. 105, a twin-bedded room, is done in a red-and-white English print. The nice corner bath makes up in part for the lack of sitting and luggage space. The viewless No. 308 reminds me of a chapel, with its stone walls, high beamed ceilings, and extra-quiet location. No. 301, in bright turquoise, with black and white accents, has a divided sitting area and a fantasy bathroom with double sinks. Rooms 502 and 504 have terraces. The unusual two-room suites are large. If you like sunken bathtubs, platform beds, conversation pits, and lots of open space splashed with color, these will undoubtedly please you.

Management is justifiably proud of its buffet breakfast served downstairs. Designed to appeal to lumberjack appetites, it includes fresh fruit, juices, a variety of breads and rolls, several selections of meat and cheese, pâté, eggs, and cereals. After this meal, you won't need to eat until dinnertime.

FACILITIES AND SERVICES: Direct-dial phone, elevator to fifth floor (stairs to three rooms on sixth floor), hair dryer, laundry service, minibar in suites, TV with international reception, safe in office (no charge)

NEAREST TOURIST ATTRACTIONS (RIGHT BANK): Forum des Halles, Centre Georges Pompideau (Beaubourg), Louvre, Île St-Louis, St-Michel, St-Germain-des-Prés

HÔTEL AGORA ★★ (43)
7, rue de la Cossonnerie, off rue Pierre Lescot, 75001
Métro: Châtelet–Les Halles
29 rooms, all with shower or bath and toilet

The decor at the Hôtel Agora is an eclectic pastiche of flea market nostalgia that gives new meaning to the phrases frou-frou and hand-me-downs. The rooms are not large, and neither are the bathrooms, but if you want something different in an active, animated section of Paris, read on.

TELEPHONE
01-42-33-46-02
FAX
01-42-33-80-99
CREDIT CARDS
AE, MC, V

RATES
)0–595F (60.98–
double 540–730F
(82.32–1 1 1.29€), triple 830F
(126.53€); *taxe de séjour* 5F
(0.76€) per person, per day

BREAKFAST
Continental 45F (6.86€)
per person

ENGLISH SPOKEN
Yes

The location, in the midst of a Les Halles block of touristy shops, is hardly inspiring. A short flight of stairs leads to a rather formally outfitted reception room with living plants draped all over the windows. A mirrored breakfast room has two covered tables and a sitting area to one side with several antique pieces and a photo of an Italian film star, who stayed here in leaner times.

The rooms are whimsically individual, mixing the old with the new in a way that comes together. No. 31, a twin, features an armchair covered in a leopard print, a fireplace, and a gold-framed headboard with hand-painted flowers. In No. 64 you will have a rooftop view of St-Eustache Church, sleep in a double bed, and use a small bathroom with a mini—corner shower and wash basin. No. 66, on the top floor, is a sweet single with a four-color slat park chair and a white bedspread with appliquéd floral hearts. Room 61 is the biggest and will hold three, but I think it is better for two. The room is dominated by a nineteenth-century painting of a woman and a mixture of similar-era art scattered on the walls. A Tunisian wood sculpture looms over the twin beds. The warm mustard-colored No. 51 is one of my favorites. Besides its tiny terrace, I like the entryway with its large oval mirror, the marble fireplace, and the gold scrolled piece of wood that forms a backdrop for the bed.

FACILITIES AND SERVICES: Direct-dial phone, elevator from first floor, TV with international reception, room safe (no charge)

NEAREST TOURIST ATTRACTIONS (RIGHT BANK): Heart of Les Halles, Centre Georges Pompidou (Beaubourg), Île de la Cité, Île St-Louis, Louvre

HÔTEL BRIGHTON ★★★ (27)
218, rue de Rivoli, 75001
Métro: Tuileries

60 rooms, all with shower or bath and toilet

TELEPHONE
01-47-03-61-61

FAX
01-42-60-41-78

EMAIL
hotel.brighton@wanadoo.com

CREDIT CARDS
AE, DC, MC, V

RATES
Single or double 680–950F
(103.67–144.83€), suite
1,400F (213.43€); extra bed
150F (22.87€)); *taxe de séjour*
included

The Hôtel Brighton dates from the end of the ninteenth century, and takes its name from the friend-ship that developed between Great Britain and France during the reign of Queen Victoria. The location is fabulous, overlooking the Tuileries Gardens and many of the most beautiful Parisian monuments. It is also only a short walk from the Louvre, place Vendôme, wonderful shopping, the Opéra, and the Seine.

The hotel is currently undergoing a complete redeco-ration, and when it is completed, it will be even more impressive that it is now. Until everything is finished,

I recommend requesting a redone room. Some on the back are ready. No. 401 is a large, quiet twin on the back with a rooftop view. The traditionally decorated room includes a desk, luggage space, and a bathroom large enough to hold a table and small stool in addition to the regular bathroom fixtures. Another choice on the back is No. 403, with a double brass bed and a leather armchair. The long, narrow marble bathroom is light and has a shower over the tub. These rooms are nice if you are willing to sacrifice a view and accept a certain minimum amount of noise. Frankly, when staying here I want a room with a view, so I can't wait for No. 418—and the twenty rooms similar to it—to be completed. These rooms have views that are nothing short of spectacular, encompassing almost all of Paris from the Arc de Triomphe and La Defense to the Eiffel Tower, Invalides, Notre Dame, and more. Yes, there is some noise, but double windows and air-conditioning buffer most of it. Also under the same ownership are the Hôtels Mansart, Place du Louvre, and Parc Saint-Séverin (see pages 68, 62, and 116).

NEAREST TOURIST ATTRACTIONS: Air-conditioning in new rooms, direct-dial phone, elevator, hair dryer, laundry service, minibar, TV with international reception, room safe (no charge)

NEAREST TOURIST ATTRACTIONS (RIGHT BANK): Tuileries Gardens, Louvre, place de la Concorde, Madeleine, place Vendôme, shopping, Opéra, Seine

HÔTEL BRITANNIQUE ★★★ (52)
20, avenue Victoria, 75001
Métro: Châtelet

40 rooms, all with shower or bath and toilet

The history of this hotel goes way back. In 1870–71, it was run by a Quaker mission to aid war victims. During World War I, it was where war casualties recuperated. Today it is a gracefully restored, sound choice between Châtelet and Hôtel de Ville. In the refashioning of the hotel several years ago, the owners wisely kept many original parts. The winding stairway with polished banister and the carved reception counter are two examples of how the old can blend beautifully with the new. Granite hallways lined with red print carpet lead guests to their rooms, which are behind eggplant-purple doors. Best choices are on the top three floors, just high enough to escape the brunt of the street noise and to avoid blank-wall views on the back. The rooms, though

BREAKFAST
45F (6.86€) per person, buffet or Continental in room

ENGLISH SPOKEN
Yes

TELEPHONE
01-42-33-74-59

FAX
01-42-33-82-65

EMAIL
mailbox@hotel-britannique.fr

INTERNET
www.hotel-britannique.fr

CREDIT CARDS
AE, DC, MC, V

RATES
Single 760F (115.86€), double 920–1,050F (140.25–160.07€); extra bed 135F (20.58€); lower rates depend on season and availability; *taxe de séjour* 6F (0.91€) per person, per day

BREAKFAST
65F (9.91€) per person, buffet
or Continental in room
ENGLISH SPOKEN
Yes

small, are professionally decorated in soft colors with tone-on-tone wallpaper, faux marble accents, and coordinated print fabrics.

Classical music soothes early morning diners in the pretty breakfast room. A buffet is laid out here, or you can have a Continental breakfast sent to your room for the same price. The sunken, mirrored lounge, with eye-level windows on the street, is accented with some lovely old heirlooms. Be sure to notice the bird cage, the early record player, and the intricately detailed model of an old sailing vessel.

FACILITIES AND SERVICES: Bar, direct-dial phone, hair dryer, elevator, minibar, TV with international reception, room safe (no charge), computer modems (two rooms)

NEAREST TOURIST ATTRACTIONS (RIGHT BANK): Louvre, Tuileries, Centre Georges Pompidou (Beaubourg), Forum des Halles, Île de la Cité, Île St-Louis, St-Michel

HÔTEL DE LA PLACE DU LOUVRE ★★★ (49)
21, rue des Prêtres St-Germain l'Auxerrois, 75001
Métro: Pont-Neuf, Louvre–Rivoli
20 rooms, all with shower or bath and toilet

TELEPHONE
01-42-33-78-68
FAX
01-42-33-09-95
EMAIL
hotel.place.louvre@wanadoo.fr
CREDIT CARDS
DC, MC, V
RATES
Single 540–740F (83.32–112.81€), double 740–880F (112.81–134.16€), triple 940F (143.30€); *taxe de séjour* included
BREAKFAST
Continental 55F (8.38€) per person
ENGLISH SPOKEN
Yes

The name of the hotel gives you a hint. From the front door the Louvre is only a five-minute stroll, the quais along the Seine a block away, and all the Left Bank has to offer is just a few minutes across the Pont Neuf to St-Michel. The hotel is imaginatively done from start to finish. Portions of the original stone walls are artistically exposed to the dramatically modern entry. Murals on curving walls lead to a tented sitting area with a purple chamois wall covering highlighted by black and tangerine leather and chrome furniture. A multicolored curtain hangs above the front window, which faces the St-Germain l'Auxerrois Church across the street.

All of the rooms are named for famous artists whose work hangs in the Louvre. The brilliant pink, third-floor Picasso suite has a view of the church, marble-topped bedside tables, a corner desk, mirrored wardrobes, and a wonderful upstairs bathroom with a skylight. If you check into the green-and-white Kandinsky double, you will have good luggage space and a salmon-colored tile bath with gray monogrammed towels and plenty of shelf space. The Robert Delauny room on the second floor has a good view of the church and the side of the Louvre. Breakfast is served in the original fourteenth-century stone-walled *cave* in the basement. When making reservations, try to avoid the weekends when the front desk is drastically understaffed, forcing the hardworking receptionist to do everything at a frustratingly frantic pace . . . from answering the constantly ringing telephone to checking in guests and trying to call for taxis.

NOTE: This hotel is run by the same management and owners as the Hôtels Parc Saint-Séverin, Mansart, and Brighton (see pages 116, 68, and 60).

FACILITIES AND SERVICES: Bar, direct-dial phone, room fans, hair dryer, elevator, minibar, radio, TV with international reception, room safe (no charge)

NEAREST TOURIST ATTRACTIONS (RIGHT BANK): Louvre, Centre Georges Pompidou (Beaubourg), Seine, St-Michel, Île de la Cité, Île St-Louis

HÔTEL DE LILLE (NO STARS, 38)
8, rue du Pelican, 75001
Métro: Palais Royal–Musée du Louvre
14 rooms, 6 with shower, none with bath and toilet

No private toilets, no closets (only hooks), no English spoken, no breakfast served, and no elevator in a five-floor hotel housed in a thirteenth-century building. Who needs this? Seekers of a very cheap sleep near the Louvre do, and believe me, they stay here in droves. If you do decide to stay here, don't expect thick towels, a particularly helpful staff, minibars (but there is a drink machine between the second and third floors), TVs, or other services or amenities. This is a cheap thrill all right, but it is also a safe and clean one that you can count on if all you need is a place to hang your hat and rest your weary head after a long day in Paris.

FACILITIES AND SERVICES: None

NEAREST TOURIST ATTRACTIONS (RIGHT BANK): Louvre, Palais-Royal, Les Halles, Tuileries, shopping on rue St-Honoré, Seine, Île de la Cité, Île St-Louis

TELEPHONE
01-42-33-33-42
FAX
None
CREDIT CARDS
None, cash only
RATES
Single 220F (33.54€), double 250–300F (38.11–45.73€); coin-operated shower 30F (4.57€); *taxe de séjour* included
BREAKFAST
None served
ENGLISH SPOKEN
None

HÔTEL DES DUCS DE BOURGOGNE ★★★ (45)
19, rue du Pont Neuf
Métro: Pont-Neuf, Châtelet
50 rooms, all with shower or bath and toilet

When you walk in the door, you can't miss the English hat rack with its collection of vintage hats. The owner originally had it in the lobby as a place for guests to hang their coats, but it was too fragile for this purpose. Rather than dispose of it, he went to the flea market and bought a collection of fanciful *chapeaux*.

TELEPHONE
01-42-33-95-64
FAX
01-40-39-01-25
EMAIL
hotelduc@MicroNet.fr
INTERNET
www.france-hotel-guide.com
CREDIT CARDS
AE, DC, MC, V

RATES
Single 800F (121.96€), double
915F (139.49€); children under
12 free; *taxe de séjour* included

BREAKFAST
Buffet 60F (9.15€) per person

ENGLISH SPOKEN
Yes

Now the hat rack, with the hats, has become the symbol of the hotel, and no one would *think* of hanging a coat on it. Another intersting feature along the wall leading to the downstairs breakfast room is the rogues' photo gallery of French and American astronauts, which is a tribute to the many clients who come here to attend meetings at the Centre Nationale Spatial Français (at the end of the street).

Besides the hat rack and the photos, there are many appealing things about the hotel. First, the A+ location puts guests in the heart of Paris. Next, children under twelve are free, and discounts are often available on the Internet. The rather plain, air-conditioned rooms are very clean, bathrooms have good mirror and sink space, but unfortunately, no shower curtains . . . which is the norm, not the exception, in Paris hotels. Finally, the staff, headed by Natalie Dupont, the assistant manager, is always ready to help.

FACILITIES AND SERVICES: Air-conditioning, direct-dial phone, elevator, hair dryer, laundry service, public parking across the street, TV with international reception, office safe (no charge)

NEAREST TOURIST ATTRACTIONS (RIGHT BANK): Louvre, Les Halles, Centre Georges Pompidou (Beaubourg), Seine, Île St-Louis, Île de la Cité, Notre Dame

HÔTEL DU CYGNE ★★ (36)
3, rue du Cygne, 75001
Métro: Étienne-Marcel, Les Halles
20 rooms, 18 with shower or bath and toilet

TELEPHONE
01-42-60-14-16

FAX
01-42-21-37-02

CREDIT CARDS
AE, DC, MC, V

RATES
Single 385–455F (58.69–
69.63€), double 510F (77.75€);
taxe de séjour included

BREAKFAST
Continental 40F (6.10€) per
person

ENGLISH SPOKEN
Yes

Two-star hotels in this corner of Les Halles are very scarce, so I was happy to find the Hôtel du Cygne, located in a seventeenth-century building on a short, pedestrianized street leading off the busy boulevard de Sebastopol. The owners have taken this old hotel and made it livable and appealing on almost every count. The pretty tiled entryway leads to a homey sitting room with padded wicker chairs and a partial glass ceiling. While the hallways could use a facelift, the rooms are good for the price. In fact, some three-star hotel rooms can't begin to compare with the twenty here, almost all of which have a desk and chair, luggage rack, bedside tables with good lights, and decent towels in adequate bathrooms. The twin-bedded nests have bathtubs; the single- and double-bedded rooms come with showers. Room 560, with a bright Provençal theme, is the biggest. The divided room has the beds on a platform mezzanine and a sitting area with a sofa bed, table, and chairs below. If you are willing to walk up one flight of stairs (from the third to the fourth floor), you can enjoy the quiet, quaint, and romantic No. 41, which is under the eaves, with mansard windows on the slanting roof; it has a shower and a marble desk. Single travelers should book Room 11, which faces out and has a wicker armchair, but avoid Room 38, which has no closet or drawer space and needs paint.

FACILITIES AND SERVICES: Direct-dial phone, elevator to all but top floor, hair dryer in most bathrooms, TV with international reeption, room safe (no charge)

NEAREST TOURIST ATTRACTIONS (RIGHT BANK): Centre Georges Pompidou (Beaubourg), Les Halles

HÔTEL DU PALAIS ★ (54)
2, quai de la Mégisserie, 75001
Métro: Châtelet (exit place du Châtelet)
19 rooms, 14 with shower or bath and toilet

While the location is dynamite and the views from most rooms spectacular, the hotel in general is a true fixer-upper. No elevator services any of the floors; dim-watt bulbs sway from high-pitched ceilings; exposed pipes wrap themselves around the rooms; and the double beds roll to the middle. In addition, if you open the windows or forget your industrial-strength earplugs, it can be hopelessly noisy twenty-four hours a day. However, for the budgeteer who can sleep through anything, the Hôtel du Palais has prices that are hard to ignore. Unless drastic renovations have taken place, I would absolutely refuse No. 18, a top-floor, beat-up cell with no heat. However, for a bargain sleep in Paris that won't disappoint—as long as you don't mind the attic school of decorating or a *laissez-faire* approach to cleaning—try to land one of the fourteen view rooms, all of which have private bathrooms and million-dollar vistas across the Seine to Nôtre Dame and the Left Bank. When booking a reservation, owner Monsieur Benoît asks that guests phone first to check availablity, and then confirm with a fax.

FACILITIES AND SERVICES: Direct-dial phone, TV in rooms with private facilities, no elevator

NEAREST TOURIST ATTRACTIONS (RIGHT BANK): Louvre, Centre Georges Pompideau (Beaubourg), Forum des Halles, Île de la Cité, Île St-Louis, St-Michel

TELEPHONE
01-42-36-98-25

FAX
01-42-21-41-67

CREDIT CARDS
MC, V

RATES
Single 183–353F (27.90–53.81€), double 236–386F (35.98–58.85€), triple 429F (65.40€); extra bed 75F (11.43€); free hall showers; 10 percent reduction Jan 15–Feb 28; *taxe de séjour* 3F (0.46€) per person, per day

BREAKFAST
Continental 35F (5.34€) per person

ENGLISH SPOKEN
Yes

HÔTEL HENRI IV (NO STARS, 55)
25, place Dauphine, 75001
Métro: Pont-Neuf, St-Michel, Cité

TELEPHONE
01-45-54-44-53

FAX
None

CREDIT CARDS
None, cash only

RATES
Single 150–190F (22.87–
28.97€), double 185–270F
(28.20–41.16€); extra bed 35F
(5.34€); shower 18F (2.74€);
taxe de séjour 2F (0.30€) per
person, per day

BREAKFAST
Included (hot beverage, bread
and butter)

ENGLISH SPOKEN
Yes

21 rooms, 4 with shower, none bath and toilet

Four hundred years ago, King Henri IV's printing presses occupied this narrow townhouse on Île de la Cité's pretty place Dauphine. Today, it is a twenty-one-room hotel that has been touted in every budget guide to Paris, becoming a mecca for the seriously thrifty and anyone else eager for a romantically threadbare hotel adventure in Paris. Despite improvements, such as hall linoleum, new wallpaper in a few rooms, and showers installed in four rooms, all guests must continue to be philosophical about both the accommodations and the plumbing. The rooms, which passed their prime decades ago, could be a shock to some: the furniture looks like leftovers from a garage sale; the lighting is dim; the mattresses are spongy; most of the wallpaper has seen better days; and the exposed peeling pipes gurgle and sputter all day—and all night—long. Only a bidet and basin come with each room, and the communal shower and toilets are reached via a steep, winding staircase in a dark and freezing-cold airshaft. On the other hand, it is so cheap, so perfectly located, so quiet, and the owners— M. and Mme. Balitrand and their son, François, who now runs it—are so friendly that thousands of young-at-heart guests continue to flock here from around the world and reserve many months in advance.

FACILITIES AND SERVICES: None. Office open for reservations 8 A.M.–7 P.M.

NEAREST TOURIST ATTRACTIONS (ON ÎLE DE LA CITÉ): Île St-Louis, St-Michel, St-Germain-des-Prés, Latin Quarter, Left Bank, Louvre, Musée d'Orsay, place Dauphine

HÔTEL LE LOIRET ★★★ (39)
5, rue des Bons Enfants, 75001
Métro: Palais Royal–Musée du Louvre

TELEPHONE
01-42-61-47-31

FAX
01-42-61-36-85

EMAIL
reservation@hotelleloiret.com

INTERNET
www.hotelleloiret.com

CREDIT CARDS
MC, V

31 rooms, all with shower or bath and toilet

The rooms at the three-star Hôtel le Loiret are up to one-third *less* than those just around the corner in a nationally known two-star chain hotel. And they are better than many other three stars in the same neighborhood. Alain and Madeleine Diguet have owned the hotel for twenty years. Even though their rooms and bathtubs are small, the good location and friendly tabs keep guests returning regularly. Each of the compact rooms have been customized with built-ins to take advantage of every inch of space. In addition to access to modems, a minibar, a room safe, and international TV reception, each guest is given a private fax and telephone number with voice mail. You also have the option of ordering a meal sent in by a catering service. The fax, phone number, and computer connection can be allocated when reserving or upon check-in.

FACILITIES AND SERVICES: Direct-dial phone with private number, elevator to 4th floor, hair dryer, laundry service, modems, parking 100F (15.24€) per day, radio, room safe (no charge), room service by outside caterer

NEAREST TOURIST ATTRACTIONS (RIGHT BANK): Louvre, Tuileries Gardens, Les Halles, Palais Royal, shopping

RATES
Single 490–530F (74.70–80.80€), double 570–630F (86.90–96.04€), triple 670–730F (102.14–111.29€); *taxe de séjour* included

BREAKFAST
Continental 45F (6.86€) per person

ENGLISH SPOKEN
Yes

HÔTEL LOUVRE FORUM ★★★ (32)
25, rue du Bouloi, 75001
Métro: Palais Royal–Musée du Louvre
27 rooms, all with shower or bath and toilet

The Hôtel Louvre Forum is a small, family-owned hotel well located for Louvre visitors and rue St-Honoré shoppers. The simple, cookie-cutter rooms have color-coordinated spreads and curtains, nice bathrooms, built-ins that include a work space, and open closets with a few shelves. Best rooms are those with bathtubs facing the street. Those along the back are cramped and viewless. Breakfast is served in a stone *cave* lined with farm implements, wooden shoes, and baskets. An ox yoke serves as an overhead light.

FACILITIES AND SERVICES: Direct-dial phone, elevator, hair dryer, TV with international reception, office safe (no charge)

NEAREST TOURIST ATTRACTIONS (RIGHT BANK): Louvre, Tuileries Gardens, Les Halles, Palais Royal

TELEPHONE
01-42-36-54-19

FAX
01-42-33-66-31

CREDIT CARDS
AE, DC, MC, V

RATES
Single 450F (68.60€), double 515–570F (78.51–86.90€); *taxe de séjour* included

BREAKFAST
Continental 45F (6.86€) per person

ENGLISH SPOKEN
Yes

HÔTEL LOUVRE SAINTE-ANNE ★★★ (28)
32, rue Ste-Anne, 75001
Métro: Palais Royal–Musée du Louvre, Pyramides
20 rooms, all with bath or shower and toilet

The hotel was completely renovated in 1997. The owners, M. and Mme. Bernie, said the work took one year to complete to their stringent specifications. Believe me, they did a great job. Each air-conditioned room is color coordinated in soft peach with blue or green accents, and the marble bathrooms have towel warmers and stretch tubs. All rooms can be recommended, but if it is a view of Sacre Coeur you are after or a balcony, these rooms are on the fifth floor. In the

TELEPHONE
01-40-20-02-35

FAX
01-40-15-91-13

EMAIL
ste-anne@worldnet.fr

INTERNET
www.worldnet.fr/ste-anne

CREDIT CARDS
AE, DC, MC, V

RATES
Single 700F (106.11€), double
790–900F (120.43–137.20€);
taxe de séjour included

BREAKFAST
Buffet 60F (9.15€) per person

ENGLISH SPOKEN
Yes

morning, a buffet breakfast is served in a stone room brightened by a bouquet of sunflowers complementing the yellow-and-blue tablecloths.

FACILITIES AND SERVICES: Air-conditioning, direct-dial phone, elevator, one handicapped-accessible room, hair dryer, laundry service, minibar, TV with international reception, room safe (no charge)

NEAREST TOURIST ATTRACTIONS (RIGHT BANK): Opéra, Louvre, Tuileries Gardens, Palais Royal, shopping

HÔTEL MANSART ★★★ ($, 7)
5, rue des Capucines, at place Vendôme, 75001
Métro: Opéra, Madeleine
57 rooms, all with shower or bath and toilet

TELEPHONE
01-42-61-50-28

FAX
01-49-27-97-44

EMAIL
hotelmansart@wanadoo.fr

CREDIT CARDS
AE, DC, MC, V

RATES
1–2 persons 930F (141.78€),
superior 1,020F (155.50€),
deluxe 1,350–1,650F (205.81–
251.54€); extra bed 110F
(16.77€); lower rates depending
on season and availability; *taxe
de séjour* 6F (0.91€) per person,
per day

BREAKFAST
60F (9.15€) per person, buffet
or Continental in room

ENGLISH SPOKEN
Yes

To be close to the Ritz, except in price—because your budget does not allow spending upwards of $700 per night for a double (breakfast extra)—consider staying at Hôtel Mansart, named after the architect of Louis XIV, who designed the place Vendôme, Versailles, and the dome on Les Invalides. The hotel used to be the Hôtel Calais, a rambling wreck totally devoid of style, with labyrinth halls, creaking floors, and turn-of-the-century plumbing. Not anymore! What a stunning transformation the owners have achieved.

By not making any structural changes other than adding spectacular new bathrooms, the owners kept the spirit of the building intact. You will still find long hallways, high ceilings, marble fireplaces, stained-glass windows, well-loved period furnishings, and in some cases, slightly sloping floors. No two rooms are alike, but all reflect the same high level of style and good taste. Some favorites include No. 603, a top-floor choice done in blue and gray with a mirrored armoire, marble bedside tables, and a tiled bathroom with double sinks. No. 400 is a large, twin-bedded room with good work space, plenty of light, and a bathroom large enough to accommodate a long tub and a marble-top table. No. 505, a sunny, rear twin room, has a separate stall shower in addition to a stretch-out bathtub that is perfect for luxurious bubble baths. Rooms 506, 507, and 508 have their own terraces. No. 502, facing the street, is enormous, with a fireplace, built-in armoire, large round table with chairs, and a writing desk. A showcase room is No. 204, overlooking place Vendôme. This room is done in royal blue with gold carpeting, and its high ceilings, collectable furniture, and lovely oil painting over the marble dresser are reminiscent of hotels on the Grand Tour of Europe that our grandmothers stayed in decades ago.

The stark simplicity of the lobby is created by an interesting mixture of geometric wall designs based on the gardens at Versailles. Antique chairs and love seats and tiny glowing ceiling lights complete the room by mixing a touch of contemporary with the past in an elegant way. A Continental breakfast is served in a formal room with arched stained-glass windows and suede-cloth-covered chairs placed around tables covered with damask cloths. Everything works together throughout this impressive hotel and adds up to a smart address in a fine location. Three other hotels are under the same ownership: Hôtel Parc Saint-Séverin, Hôtel de la Place du Louvre, and Hôtel Brighton (see pages 116, 62, and 60).

FACILITIES AND SERVICES: Air-conditioning in some rooms, bar, direct-dial phone, hair dryer, elevator to fifth floor only, minibar, TV with international reception, room safe (no charge), computer modems in most rooms

NEAREST TOURIST ATTRACTIONS (RIGHT BANK): Place Vendôme, place de la Concorde, Opéra, Madeleine, Louvre, shopping on rue St-Honoré

HÔTEL MOLIÈRE ★★★ (30)
21, rue Molière, 75001
Métro: Palais Royal–Musée du Louvre, Pyramides
32 rooms, all with shower or bath and toilet

The Molière has benefited from a recent redecoration and is once again a recommended midcity choice. The faux-finished, pillared lobby has azure blue velvet armchairs and an Art Nouveau beaded lamp on the reception desk. Toward the back is another sitting area with a red sofa and an assortment of magazines and daily newspapers, and just beyond is the breakfast room with glass-topped tables and metal chairs, overlooking a small interior garden.

The rooms, which are above average in size and layout, are tastefully done in a rather formal French style. The amount of living space is exceptional; the views, even along the back, are pleasant; and the location puts guests within walking distance of many of the tourist "musts" of Paris. If you are looking for space, book No. 56, a three-room suite with two bedrooms and a sitting room done in soft mauve. The sitting room offers a comfortable sofa, two armchairs, and a desk. The double

TELEPHONE
01-42-96-22-01

FAX
01-42-60-48-68

EMAIL
molière@worldnet.fr

INTERNET
www.123france.com

CREDIT CARDS
AE, DC, MC, V

RATES
Single 750F (114.34€), double 850F (129.58€), triple 980F (149.40€), apartment 1,500F (228.67€); extra bed 100F (15.24€); lower rates in off-season on request; *taxe de séjour* included

BREAKFAST
Buffet 70F (10.67€) per person

ENGLISH SPOKEN
Yes

bedroom has a wonderful brass bed with matching dressing table, marble bedside tables, a walk-in closet with wide shelves and double hanging space, and a tango-sized bathroom. Finally, there is a small single bedroom that would be perfect for a child. Less grand, but no less comfortable, is No. 41, a double with a new bathroom that has a magnifying mirror, large tub, and sink space. The bedroom, with a brass bed a mirrored armoire, has good living space. Room 42, also with a new bathroom, is another good choice if you want twin beds. No. 43 is a pleasant single with a large working desk and a stall shower.

FACILITIES AND SERVICES: Air-conditioning in all rooms except the suites, bar, direct-dial phone, elevator to all but top floor, hair dryer, laundry service, minibar, television with international reception, room safe (no charge)

NEAREST TOURIST ATTRACTIONS (RIGHT BANK): Louvre, Tuileries Gardens, Palais Royal, shopping, Opéra

HÔTEL SAINT-HONORÉ ★ (44)
85, rue St-Honoré, 75001
Métro: Louvre–Rivoli
29 rooms, all with shower or bath and toilet

TELEPHONE
01-42-36-20-38

FAX
01-42-21-44-08

INTERNET
www.123france.com

CREDIT CARDS
AE, MC, V

RATES
Single 290F (44.21€), double 410–450F (62.50–68.60€), triple 510F (77.75€); look for deals on Internet site; *taxe de séjour* included

BREAKFAST
Continental 29F (4.42€) per person

ENGLISH SPOKEN
Yes

The Hôtel Saint-Honoré is owned by Mr. Brice, whose grandfather opened it in 1975. For a one-star within walking distance to the Louvre, Palais Royal, Les Halles, and across the Pont Neuf to the Left Bank, it will be hard to top this budget choice. You can work off those extra pastries by climbing up the stairs (five floors' worth) to the plain rooms, all with the same built-in bed backing, gray closet, table, and one or two chairs. All but a few singles have televisions, and the older style bathrooms have showers with curtains. Rooms facing the street are preferable to the stuffy ones along the inside, expecially No. 320, a triple that is too narrow for negotiation. A Continental breakfast is served next to the lobby or on a small patio in the summer.

FACILITIES AND SERVICES: Direct-dial phone, no elevator (five floors), some hair dryers, French TV in twenty rooms, office safe (no charge)

NEAREST TOURIST ATTRACTIONS (RIGHT BANK): Louvre, Palais Royal, Les Halles, Pont Neuf

LE RELAIS DU LOUVRE ★★★ ($, 48)
19, rue des Prêtres St-Germain l'Auxerrois, 75001
Métro: Louvre–Rivoli, Pont-Neuf
20 rooms, all with shower or bath and toilet

Just down the street from the Hôtel de la Place du Louvre (see page 62) is Le Relais du Louvre, another top three-star pick hard by the Musée du Louvre. The small lobby, draped in dark red watermarked linen, offers comfortable seating. A massive fresh floral spray sitting atop an antique bureau adds color. The rooms live up to the elegant promise of the lobby. All are attractively furnished with designer fabrics and have good closet space and marble bathrooms with fluffy towels. No. 35, a standard twin-bedded room, offers an armchair covered in a quilted pink hydrangea pattern and a writing desk overlooking the church across the street. Appealing prints of Victorian ladies hang on the walls. If you need a little more space, consider No. 52, a suite with a direct view of the gargoyles on the St-Germain l'Auxerrois Church, or request Rooms 24 and 25, which connect and can be closed off together to form a nice family suite. Even larger is the apartment occupying the entire sixth floor. Aside from a beautiful, fully equipped kitchen complete with dishwasher, microwave, refrigerator, and separate freezer, the apartment has two television sets, a tape player, a comfortable living area with two sofas, and a wall of windows that let in light all day long. The singles are small and on the back, but the interior view is not depressing. An added bonus of this hotel is the friendly, English-speaking staff, composed of Brigitte and Marie.

FACILITIES AND SERVICES: Direct-dial phone, hair dryer, elevator, laundry service, minibar, TV with international reception, room safe (no charge)

NEAREST TOURIST ATTRACTIONS (RIGHT BANK): Louvre, Centre Georges Pompidou (Beaubourg), Seine, St-Michel, Île de la Cité, Île St-Louis

TELEPHONE
01-40-41-96-42

FAX
01-40-41-96-44

EMAIL
au-relais-de-louvre@dial.oleane.com

INTERNET
www.hotelguide.com

CREDIT CARDS
AE, DC, MC, V

RATES
Single 650–800F (99.09–121.96€), double 800–1,000F (121.96–152.45€), suite 1,300–1,500F (198.18–228.67€), apartment 2,400F (365.88€); extra bed 150F (22.87€); *taxe de séjour* 6F (0.91€) per person, per day

BREAKFAST
Continental (in room only) 60F (9.15€) per person

ENGLISH SPOKEN
Yes

TONIC HÔTEL LOUVRE ★★ (46)
12–14, rue du Roule, 75001
Métro: Louvre–Rivoli, Châtelet
34 rooms, all with shower or bath and toilet

Physical fitness buffs who stay at this central budget address can keep themselves in top shape. If you are a morning jogger or walker, it is only a hop, skip, and a jump to join fellow exercisers in the Tuileries or along the banks of the Seine. The hotel is also located well

TELEPHONE
01-42-33-00-71

FAX
01-40-26-06-86

EMAIL
tonic.louvre@wanadoo.fr

INTERNET
www.tonichotel.com

CREDIT CARDS
AE, DC, MC, V

RATES
Single 700–760F (106.71–
115.89€), double 800–860F
(121.96–131.11€), triple 860F
(131.11€); extra bed 100F
(15.24€); *taxe de séjour* 5F
(0.76€) per person, per day

BREAKFAST
45F (6.86€) per person, buffet
or Continental in room

ENGLISH SPOKEN
Yes

from a sight-seeing standpoint, and there are many good restaurants within easy walking distance (see *Great Eats Paris*).

The hotel consists of two parts: the main building and the new annex next door. In the main part, the simple, pastel rooms include luggage racks, mirrored wardrobes, and double-paned windows to keep out street noise. The bathrooms have either a built-in steam bath, a Jacuzzi in the bathtub, or a pulsating shower massage to ease away the aches and pains of daily tourist safaris through Paris. No. 101, a double, is better than No. 302 because it has more space, a Jacuzzi tub, and is nicely coordinated in rich reds and golden yellows.

In the annex, Rooms 106, 306, and 406 are winners. The dark wood furniture in each goes well with the exposed stone walls, beams, and double floor-to-ceiling windows. The booby prize is shared between Room 207, a dark space on the back facing a wall, and No. 505, a two-level arrangement with steep steps leading upstairs to a pitched roofed room with no view and no air circulation.

FACILITIES AND SERVICES: Bar, direct-dial phone, elevator to fourth floor in main building, no elevator in annex, hair dryer, minibar, TV with international reception, shower massage or steam bath in most rooms, Jacuzzis in some, safe in office (no charge)

NEAREST TOURIST ATTRACTIONS (RIGHT BANK): Louvre, Tuileries, Seine, Palais-Royal, Île de la Cité, Île St-Louis, St-Michel

Second Arrondissement

The second arrondissement is known as the area of finance (around the stock exchange, or Bourse), the press, and the rag trade (around place du Caire). It makes up for its small size with the beautiful Victorian shopping *passages* and the boutiques around place des Victoires. The second is within walking distance to the Marais, Centre Georges Pompidou (or Beaubourg), the Palais Royal, and the Louvre Museum. The southern half around rue Montorgueil has some of the best food markets in Paris. The seedy northern half around rue d'Aboukir should definitely be avoided, and so should rue St-Denis, home of Paris hookers and other assorted netherworld characters.

RIGHT
BankBourse, Cognacq-Jay Museum, *passages,* place des Victoires, rue Montorgueil shopping street

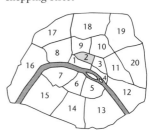

HOTELS IN THE SECOND ARRONDISSEMENT
(see map page 56)

OTHER OPTIONS
Student Accommodations

($) indicates a Big Splurge

HÔTEL BAUDELAIRE OPÉRA ★★★ (9)
61, rue Ste-Anne, 75002
Metro: 4-Septembre, Pyramides
29 rooms, all with shower or bath and toilet

TELEPHONE
01-42-97-50-62

FAX
01-42-86-85-85

EMAIL
hotel@cybercable.fr

INTERNET
www.paris-hotel.net

CREDIT CARDS
AE, DC, MC, V

RATES
Single 560–590F (85.37–89.94€), double 705–770F (107.48–117.39€), duplex for 2–3 people 810–1,000F (123.48–152.45€); *taxe de séjour* 6F (0.91€) per person, per day

BREAKFAST
Continental 45F (6.86€) per person

ENGLISH SPOKEN
Yes

The area has an interesting history. When Cardinal Richelieu bought the Palais Royal, he developed the area around it, including the rue Ste-Anne. The Hôtel Baudelaire Opéra began as a shop, then became a *hôtel particulier* (private townhome). It is named after the writer who lived here in 1854 and wrote letters to his mother pleading, "do not refuse me both your money and your company at the same time." The hotel now welcomes your visit, and asks a fair price for it. It is owned by a friendly couple who bought it a few years ago and have spent considerable time and money on improvements, which on the whole have been very successful. However, despite attractive color-coordinated fabrics and new beds and carpets, the tightly fitted rooms will never be anything but small. Yet they are a three-star value if you are traveling light and plan to spend little time in your hotel room.

FACILITIES AND SERVICES: Direct-dial phone, elevator, hair dryer, TV with international reception, room safe (no charge), some trouser presses

NEAREST TOURIST ATTRACTIONS (RIGHT BANK): Opéra, Palais Royal, place des Victoires, shopping

HÔTEL VIVIENNE ★★ (1)
40, rue Vivienne, 75002
Métro: Richelieu-Drouot, Grands Boulevards
44 rooms, 30 with toilet, all with shower or bath

TELEPHONE
01-42-33-13-26

FAX
01-40-41-98-19

EMAIL
paris@hotel-vivienne.com

CREDIT CARDS
MC, V

RATES
Single 300–500F (45.73–76.22€), double 400–540F (60.98–82.32€); extra bed is 30 percent of room rate; children under 10 are free; *taxe de séjour* 5F (0.76€) per person, per day

BREAKFAST
Continental 40F (6.10€) per person

ENGLISH SPOKEN
Yes

The picture on the reception desk was taken at the hotel in 1917. The little girl in the photo was born in this hotel, which her parents owned along with a restaurant next door. The present owner, Claudine Haycraft, bought the hotel from the family twenty-five years ago. Since then, she has slowly redone it, making it a popular budget destination in this part of Paris. The rooms are kept spotlessly clean by a team of career maids. Room decor falls into the typical two-star category: mix-and-match furniture, some chenille here and there, and industrial-strength carpeting. Ten have balconies. New beds throughout and remodeled bathrooms in most rooms have improved things immeasurably. Best rooms in the house? I think No. 14, which faces the street and is large enough to feel at home in for more than overnight; No. 6, a double on the street with two windows opening onto a balcony; and No. 3, in bright orange, yellow, blue, and aqua, also with a balcony, new tiled bathroom, and sleeping space for four.

FACILITIES AND SERVICES: Direct-dial phone, elevator to fifth floor, hair dryer, some modems, TV with international reception, safe in office (no charge)

NEAREST TOURIST ATTRACTIONS (RIGHT BANK): Bourse, Opéra

TIQUETONNE HÔTEL ★ (19)
6, rue Tiquetonne, 75002
Métro: Étienne-Marcel

46 rooms, 30 with shower and toilet, no bathtubs

Anyone looking for an old-fashioned, budget-minded family hotel that offers basic, clean rooms in central Paris will hit pay dirt here. The old-fashioned hotel has been run for a half century by Mme. Sirvain, her niece Marie-Jo, and the hotel dog, Ganish, a strapping German shepherd who surveys the scene from a command post in the lobby.

All the doubles have showers, but only some singles do, and with limited success. For example, in No. 34, you enter the pink-papered room through the bathroom, red curtains hang at the windows, and furniture consists of a bed and a hard chair. There is nothing wrong with No. 20, provided you can live in a room with an orange chenille bedspread, red curtains, and floral wallpaper in peach, pink, and green. Furnishings include a small table with a laminated top displaying sailing ships and two hard chairs. The bathroom has a shelf over the sink and a curtain shielding the enclosed tile shower. No. 30, an inside double, demonstrates an attempt to color coordinate the aqua blue chenille spread with the blue trim on the curtains.

Rock-bottom prices insure popularity, so book early, but don't plan on a room in August or during the week between Christmas and New Year's, when the family shuts the hotel and goes on their own vacation.

FACILITIES AND SERVICES: Elevator

NEAREST TOURIST ATTRACTIONS (RIGHT BANK): Centre Georges Pompidou (Beaubourg), Forum les Halles, rue Montorgueil shopping street

TELEPHONE
01-42-36-94-58

FAX
01-42-36-02-94

CREDIT CARDS
MC, V

RATES
Single 153–225F (23.32–34.30€), double 260F (39.64€) (double beds only); shower 30F (4.57€); *taxe de séjour* included

BREAKFAST
Continental 28F (4.27€) per person (no croissants)

ENGLISH SPOKEN
Yes

TULIP INN–OPÉRA DE NOAILLES ★★★ ($, 5)
9, rue de la Michodière, 75002
Métro: Opéra, 4-Septembre
61 rooms, all with shower or bath and toilet

TELEPHONE
01-47-42-92-90; toll-free in the U.S., 800-344-1212 (Golden Tulip Hotels)

FAX
01-49-24-92-71

EMAIL
Tulip.Inn.denoailles@wanadoo.fr

INTERNET
www.hoteldenoailles.com

CREDIT CARDS
AE, DC, MC, V

RATES
Single 700–1,050F (106.71–160.07€), double 780–1,100F (118.91–167.69€), suites 1,560–2,000F (237.82–304.90€); ask about promotional rates; *taxe de séjour* included

BREAKFAST
Buffet 60F (9.15€) per person

ENGLISH SPOKEN
Yes

If you are allergic to gilt and cherubs, you will appreciate this sleek hotel, which owner Martine Falck has turned into a smart, Art Deco–inspired site with different bold color schemes of gray, black, midnight blue, and yellow distinguishing each floor. The street entrance leads into a wide-spaced reception room with designer chairs and tables overlooking a new bar and an atrium garden to one side.

All sixty-one rooms and suites can be recommended, from the four on the first floor that open onto their own garden and the smart suites to the smallest room, No. 507, done in gray and black with green accents. Room 601 is a step up in size and has a terrace, built-in desk, and comfortable reading chair. Room 510, in red and black, is a double with a modern twist on 1920s decor, especially in the bathroom, which has the latest in fixtures, including a great-looking, free-standing sink. Consider one of the masculine suites if you are in Paris for business. Each has a separate sitting room with a sofa, TV, large working desk, and halogen lighting. There is a second remote-controlled TV in the bedroom, and in one suite, you can walk onto a wood-planked terrace equipped with a table and chairs for al fresco dining . . . or working. A free sauna and workout gym are added bonuses for many. The attractive weekend and off-season rates make this a contender if this is your area of choice in Paris.

FACILITIES AND SERVICES: Air-conditioning, bar, conference room, direct-dial phone, elevator, gym and sauna, hair dryer, TV with international reception, safe in office (no charge), laundry service, room service

NEAREST TOURIST ATTRACTIONS (RIGHT BANK): Opéra, shopping at Galeries Lafayette and Au Printemps, Louvre

Third Arrondissement

RIGHT BANK
Carnavalet Museum (City of Paris Museum), French National Archives, Marais, Picasso Museum (Hôtel Salé), Musée des Arts et Métiers

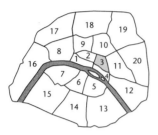

This area includes the northern parts of the revitalized Marais, a thirteenth-century swampland, which later became the residential suburb of the French nobility. It later fell from favor, and until it was rescued by Minister of Culture André Malraux in the 1960s, it was the worst slum in Paris. Today the magnificent seventeenth-century *hôtel particuliers* (private mansions) have been turned into museums, the most famous of which is the Picasso Museum in the Hôtel Salé. The Musée des Arts et Métiers, occupying the medieval abbey of St-Martin-des-Champs, has a fascinating collection of industrial and scientific objects displayed on the abbey's altars, apses, and choir stalls.

HOTELS IN THE THIRD ARRONDISSEMENT

Third and Fourth Arrondissements

Rue de Cléry

Strasbourg Ⓜ St. Denis

Boulevard

Rue

Rue St. Martin

Sébastopol

1 • R. Sal. de Caus

R. Montgolfier

Réaumur Ⓜ Sébastopol

Arts et Métiers Ⓜ

R. Montgolfier

Rue

Rue de Louvre

Rue

Rue Réaumur

Rue Montmartre

Étienne

Étienne Marcel Ⓜ

de

Turbigo

Rue

St. Martin

Rue

des Gravilliers

Marcel

Rue

Rambuteau

Rue

Les Halles Ⓜ

Rue

Rue du Grenier-St. Lazare

5 ▲

6 •

3E

Rue Berger

FORUM DES HALLES

Châtelet Les Halles

Châtelet Les Halles Ⓜ

Sébastopol

Beaubourg

Imp. Berthaud

Rambuteau Ⓜ

Rue

Temple

R. de

Châtelet Ⓜ

Pont Neuf

Rue

de

de

R. des Halles

R. des

Boulevard

Lombards

Rambuteau

7 •

CENTRE GEORGES POMPIDOU

du

Rambuteau

Archives

8 ▲

R. des Blancs

Manteaux

Rue du

12 ▲

Martin

13 •

14 ▲

R. N. Flam.

R. de la

de Renard

R. Ste. Croix de la Bret.

18 •

21 •

R. des

Veille

Rue

Rivoli

Avenue

St.

15 ▲

16 •

Rue

Verrerie

R. Bourg-Tibourg

22 ▲

19 ▲

20 ▲

Quai de la Mégisserie

Voie

G. Pompidou

TOUR ST. JACQUES

PL. DU CHÂTELET

Châtelet Ⓜ

17 ▲

Hôtel de Ville Ⓜ

24 ▲ • 25

23 ▲

Rue de Roi

R. des Écouffes

Seine

Quai

de

l'Horloge

PLACE DAUPHINE

CONCIERGERIE

P. au Change

Quai

de Gesvres

Pont Notre Dame

Victoria

HÔTEL DE VILLE

4E

Rue

de

Rue

R. des

Miror

PALAIS DE JUSTICE

STE CHAPELLE

Bd. du Palais

ÎLE DE LA CITÉ

Cité Ⓜ

HÔTEL DIEU DE CITÉ

Rue de la Corse

P. d' Arcole

Quai de l'Hôtel de Ville

Fr.

R. Pt. L. Philippe

38 ▲

Seine

Rue de la Cité

46 •

Rue d'Arcole

Quai

aux

Fleurs

P. L. Philippe

Voie

Pont Marie

Q. d'Anjou

St. Michel Ⓜ

Quai St. Michel

Saint Michel

Q. de

Montebello

NOTRE DAME

Pont St. Louis

Q. de Bourbon

ÎLE ST. LOUIS

Georges

Pont Marie

Saint Jacques

47 •

Rue

48 • ▲ 50

49 ▲

Q. de Béthune

Bd.

Cluny La Sorbonne Ⓜ

Rue

St. Germain

△ N

500 meters

Ⓜ Métro Station

R. des Deux Ponts

St. Louis en l'île

ST. LOUIS

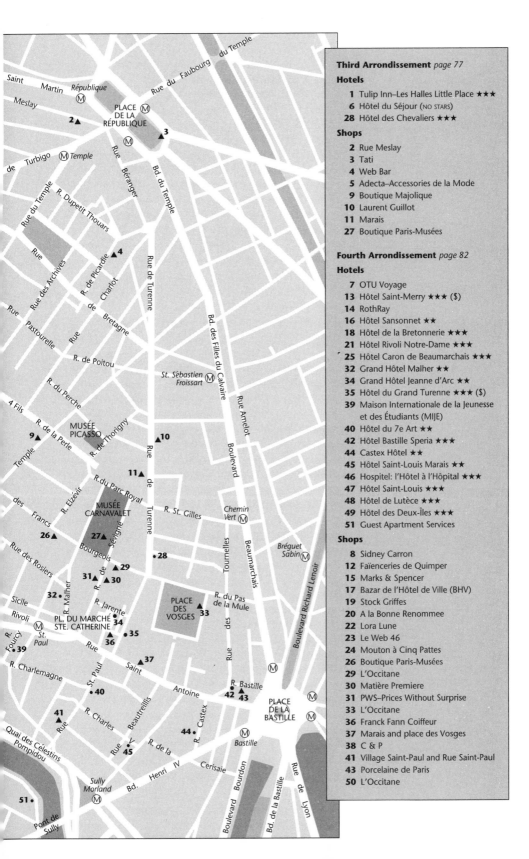

HÔTEL DES CHEVALIERS ★★★ (28)
30, rue de Turenne, 75003
Métro: Chemin-Vert

24 rooms, all with shower or bath and toilet

TELEPHONE
01-42-72-73-47
FAX
01-42-72-54-10
CREDIT CARDS
AE, MC, V
RATES
1–2 persons 760–850F
(115.86–129.58€); *taxe de séjour*
included
BREAKFAST
Continental 50F (7.62€), buffet
80F (12.20€), per person
ENGLISH SPOKEN
Yes

The location near the Picasso Museum and on the edge of the vibrant Marais puts the Hôtel des Chevaliers on the list of desirable, good-value sleeps in Paris. A yellow fabric–lined sitting room has a small bar, where you can read an assortment of international newspapers. The smartly done rooms are not large, but they are sound-proofed by double-paned windows and brightened by attractive fabrics and fresh flowers. I think those on the third and fourth floors are preferred. Those on the fifth floor require climbing one flight of stairs, and the rooms, while still appealing for many, are even tighter, given the configuration of the sloping roof lines. The five facing the inner courtyard, and No. 16, a dark twin with no sky view, are the least pleasant. The only other draw-back I found was the location of the room safes—on the floor in either the closet or the bathroom, forcing one into a prone position to gain access.

Sixteenth-century exposed supports line the stairway leading to the downstairs breakfast room, fashioned from an old *cave* (cellar), with the original water well still in one corner. Nicely upholstered chairs are placed around well-lit tables, where breakfast is served on individual trays. Management, headed by owner Mme. Truffaut, is very outgoing and friendly, and repeat guests are many.

FACILITIES AND SERVICES: Bar, direct-dial phone, elevator to fourth floor, hair dryer, minibar, TV with international reception, room safe (no charge)

NEAREST TOURIST ATTRACTIONS (RIGHT BANK): Marais, place des Vosges, Musée Picasso, Bastille Opéra

HÔTEL DU SÉJOUR (NO STARS, 6)
36, rue du Grenier-St-Lazare, 75003
Métro: Rambuteau, Étienne-Marcel

21 rooms, 11 with shower and toilet, no bathtubs

TELEPHONE AND FAX
01-48-87-40-36
CREDIT CARDS
None, cash only
RATES
Single 190–330F (28.97–
50.31€), double 290–330F
(44.21–50.31); shower 20F
(3.81€); *taxe de séjour* included
BREAKFAST
Not served
ENGLISH SPOKEN
Limited

If the bottom line is saving money, then visitors who do not mind a theatrically run-down, five-story walk-up will definitely be interested in this clean budget launching pad for their Paris sojourn. The building has been a hotel for three hundred years and is, and probably always will be, a quantum leap from modern. You enter from the street and walk up steps with a black rubber strip anchoring the laminated woodlike covering. Owners Jean and Maria have been here for over five years, and have been making improvements on a cautious basis, starting with new mattresses, hall toilets, and some paint. They probably won't replumb to add another shower: the lone one will have to do. Singles can snooze in No. 20, a top floor perch with a sink. Duos can go for Nos. 12 or 13; neither has a shower or toilet, and No.12 has a bare floor. No. 10 with a shower and sink is a sunny double facing out with a pink chenille draped bed. If there are two of you, and you each plan on bathing, definitely go for a room like No. 15, which has its own shower, toilet, and sink. Though showerless rooms are cheaper at first glance, once you add in the extra cost for the shared hall showers you will end up spending more.

FACILITIES AND SERVICES: Office safe (no charge)

NEAREST TOURIST ATTRACTIONS: Centre Georges Pompidou (Beaubourg), Musée Picasso, Les Halles

TULIP INN–LES HALLES LITTLE PLACE ★★★ (1)
4, rue Salomon de Caus, 75003
Métro: Réaumur-Sébastopol, Strasbourg-St-Denis
57 rooms, all with shower or bath and toilet

The hotel, overlooking the green Arts et Métiers Square, has an impressive facade with carved stones, scrolled balconies, and marble columns that is reminiscent of the roaring twenties. Inside, fabric-covered walls and drapes frame the entrance to the restaurant, where guests admire its lovely original stained-glass windows and floral patterned ceiling. The comfortable sitting room is furnished with back-to-back sofas and barrel armchairs, and to one side, a mosaic tiled bar overlooks a well-tended garden. The fifty-seven rooms have built-ins that allow for more space, and they are decorated in pleasing blends of orange, warm mustard, and green. The rooms have all the three-star perks, including modems and bathrooms with toiletries and a lighted magnifying mirror. The hotel restaurant serves lunch from Monday to Friday, and dinner Monday to Thursday.

FACILITIES AND SERVICES: Air-conditioning, bar, direct-dial phone, elevator, hair dryer, laundry service, minibar, modems, restaurant open for lunch and dinner during the week, TV with international reception, office safe (no charge)

NEAREST TOURIST ATTRACTIONS (RIGHT BANK): Centre Georges Pompidou (Beaubourg), Les Halles

TELEPHONE
01-42-72-08-15; toll-free in U.S., 800-344-1212 (Golden Tulip Hotels)

FAX
01-42-72-45-81

EMAIL
LittlePlaceHotel@compuserve.com

INTERNET
www.hotelbook.com/goldentulip

CREDIT CARDS
AE, MC, V

RATES
Single 790F (120.43€), double 890F (135.68€), triple 1,000F (152.45€); *taxe de séjour* included

BREAKFAST
Buffet 65F (9.91€) per person

ENGLISH SPOKEN
Yes

Fourth Arrondissement

RIGHT BANK
Centre Georges Pompidou (Beaubourg), Hôtel-de-Ville (City Hall), Île St-Louis, Jewish Quarter, Notre Dame Cathedral, place des Vosges, Maison de Victor Hugo, continuation of the Marais

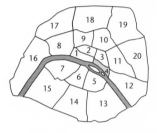

The fourth arrondissement stretches from the Marais through the ancient Jewish quarter on the rue des Rosiers to the Île St-Louis in the middle of the Seine. It is an area perfectly suited to exploring on foot, lending itself to discovery at almost every turn. Its immense charm comes from a wonderful mixture of past and present. Notre Dame Cathedral, the geographical and spiritual heart of France, sits majestically on the tip of Île de la Cité. Place des Vosges, with its historic pink-brick townhouses set above wide arcade walkways, is the oldest square in Paris and one of the most beautiful. Victor Hugo resided here at Number 6. Île St-Louis is one of the most desirable, and admittedly expensive, places to reside in Paris. The island is a capsule of all that is Parisian, with interesting shops, art galleries, boutiques, Baroque mansions, lines for the famous Berthillon ice cream, and lovely views along the romantic quais. Not to be missed is the architecturally controversial modern art museum, the Centre Georges Pompidou (also known as the Beaubourg), which logs more visitors each year than the Eiffel Tower.

HOTELS IN THE FOURTH ARRONDISSEMENT
(see map page 78)

OTHER OPTIONS

($) indicates a Big Splurge

CASTEX HÔTEL ★★ (44)
5, rue Castex, 75004
Métro: Bastille

29 rooms, 21 with shower or bath and toilet, 8 with shower and no toilet

The friendly Bouchand family who had been at the helm of the Castex since 1929 has sold. Virtually nothing has changed at the hotel, certainly not the prices, and unfortunately not much in the generic rooms, which have open closets, no drawers, and no televisions. Five rooms open onto what management calls "a patio." I think these claustrophobic spaces lack security, and the so-called patio is actually the storage area for the hotel's trash cans. The best rooms for budgeters are those with a shower but no toilet. The hall toilets are clean, and only two rooms share one on each floor. The location is tops for the place des Vosges, the islands, and the nightlife around the Bastille . . . giving you all the more reason to spend less, using your room only as a Paris pit stop.

FACILITIES AND SERVICES: Direct-dial phone, no elevator, hair dryer available, safe in office (no charge)

NEAREST TOURIST ATTRACTIONS (RIGHT BANK): Bastille Opéra, Marais, place des Vosges, Île de la Cité, Île St-Louis

TELEPHONE
01-42-72-31-52

FAX
01-42-72-57-91

EMAIL
info@castexhotel.com

INTERNET
www.castexhotel.com

CREDIT CARDS
AE, DC, MC, V

RATES
Single 240–320F (36.59–48.78€), double 320–360F (48.78–54.88€), triple 410–460F (62.50–70.13€), quad 530F (80.80€); *taxe de séjour* included

BREAKFAST
Continental 35F (5.34€) per person

ENGLISH SPOKEN
Yes

GRAND HÔTEL JEANNE D'ARC ★★ (34)
3, rue de Jarente, 75004
Métro: St-Paul, Bastille

36 rooms, all with shower or bath and toilet

The Grand Hôtel Jeanne d'Arc sits on a quiet street leading into the Marais. Discovered long ago by astute, wallet-conscious travelers, the hotel offers spotless rooms with a minimum of snags and tears. Sometimes it is hard to account for different types of decorating tastes, and I

TELEPHONE
01-48-87-62-11

FAX
01-48-87-37-31

CREDIT CARDS
AE, DC, MC, V

RATES
Single 340–430F (51.83–
65.55€), double 345–520F
(52.59–79.27€), triple 570F
(86.90€), quad 640F (97.57€);
taxe de séjour included

BREAKFAST
Continental 40F (6.10€) per
person

ENGLISH SPOKEN
Yes

will admit to being baffled about a few of the choices in the public areas of this hotel. My prize for the most bizarre mirror on the Continent goes to the one done by a local artist that hangs near the reception and defies rational description. The strange taste in art carries to the bright primary-colored fish painted on the first- and second-floor stairways. Fortunately, the rooms do not keep pace with the unusual decoration elsewhere, and they are actually quite acceptable.

Rooms 11 or 12 are good bets if there are two of you, and if there are four, No. 15 is a good choice. If you are alone, avoid No. 31, with dorm-style furniture and an old pink tiled shower. Instead, request No. 51, a small top-floor room with a desk, open closet, sunny view, and a compact bathroom with a stall shower. If bathroom floor space is needed, ask for No. 63, with two double beds, a huge blue bathroom, and a rooftop view. Repeat customers comprise the bulk of the clientele, so book early if this one appeals to you.

FACILITIES AND SERVICES: Direct-dial phone, elevator, TV with international reception, safe in office (no charge)

NEAREST TOURIST ATTRACTIONS (RIGHT BANK): Picasso Museum, Marais, place des Vosges, Bastille Opéra, rue des Rosiers (Jewish Quarter)

GRAND HÔTEL MALHER ★★ (32)
5, rue Malher, 75004
Métro: St-Paul

31 rooms, all with shower or bath and toilet

TELEPHONE
01-42-72-60-92

FAX
01-42-72-25-37

EMAIL
ghmalher@yahoo.fr

CREDIT CARDS
AE, DC, MC, V

RATES
Single 600–650F (91.47–
99.09€), double 700–750F
(106.71–114.34€), junior suite
900–1,000F (137.20–152.45€);
taxe de séjour included

BREAKFAST
Continental 50F (7.62€) per
person

ENGLISH SPOKEN
Yes

The Grand Hôtel Malher is a winning two-star with many three-star features. The lobby is dominated by a lovely gold mirror and blue velvet chairs attractively arranged against a backdrop of centuries-old stone walls. Fresh flowers and bowls of potpourri soften the setting. Breakfast is served in a seventeenth-century vaulted wine cellar. Coordinated bedrooms with tiled bathrooms are welcoming retreats. Nos. 32 and 62 are standard doubles on the back with space and good light in the bathroom. Other nice choices are on the sunny top floors in rooms with balconies. Room 55, a light lavender twin with a little balcony, faces front. No. 64, a suite, is ideal for a couple with one child. It has a double and a twin bed, an extra-large sink area in the gray tiled bathroom, and oil paintings on the walls. Pamela and Didier Fossiez are your gracious hosts, and your stay with them should be delightful.

FACILITIES AND SERVICES: Conference room, direct-dial phone, elevator, hair dryer, minibar, TV with international reception, safe in office (no charge)

NEAREST TOURIST ATTRACTIONS (RIGHT BANK): Marais, place des Vosges, Bastille Opéra, Picasso and Carnavalet Museums, rue des Rosiers (Jewish Quarter), Île de la Cité, Île St-Louis, St-Germain-des-Prés

HOSPITEL: L'HÔTEL À L'HÔPITAL ★★★ (46)
1, place du Parvis Notre-Dame de Paris, 75004
Métro: Cité

14 rooms, all with shower or bath and toilet

Wanted: A quiet, air-conditioned hotel room on the doorstep of Notre Dame Cathedral, only seconds away from all the fun and frolic going on around place St-Michel and the Left Bank. Impossible? *Mais non!* Not if you check into Hospitel: l'Hôtel a l'Hôpital, located within the walls of Paris's oldest and most prominent hospital: L'Hôtel Dieu de Paris. Originally opened to serve relatives of patients, the fourteen rooms are now open to anyone. Frankly, I had my doubts when I first heard about it. I could just imagine the depressing rooms with linoleum floors and institutional furnishings, all smelling like Lysol. How wrong I was. Actually, the hotel has a great deal going for it. In addition to the dynamite location, its contemporary rooms, done with Art Deco overtones and in vibrant primary colors, are blissfully quiet and air-conditioned. The tiled baths are above average; it is, of course, absolutely spotless; and above all, the low prices are amazing for this expensive, touristy sector of Paris. Room service for hot meals is available daily between 11 A.M. and 9 P.M. The only downside is that the hotel is situated on the sixth floor under a mansard roof. There are no real windows, only skylights—but they are ample and let in plenty of light and sunshine, and from No. 10, you can see the tower of Notre Dame. The closet and drawer spaces are not geared to long stays, and you might see a few hospital patients in bathrobes en route to your elevator. If you can live with this, it is a real value.

NOTE: To locate the hotel within the hospital, enter directly through the door just beside the main door. The entrance is marked. The hotel is located on the sixth floor of Building 2 (look for Galerie B-2, *6ème étage*).

TELEPHONE
01-44-32-01-00

FAX
01-44-32-01-16

EMAIL
hospitel@aol.com

CREDIT CARDS
AE, DC, MC, V

RATES
Single 480F (73.18€), double 550F (83.83€); *taxe de séjour* included

BREAKFAST
Continental 40F (6.10€) per person

ENGLISH SPOKEN
Yes

FACILITIES AND SERVICES: Air-conditioning, direct-dial phone, elevator, two handicapped-accessible rooms, TV, room service, office safe (no charge)

NEAREST TOURIST ATTRACTIONS (RIGHT BANK): Notre-Dame, Île de la Cité, Île St-Louis, St-Michel, St-Germain-des-Prés

HÔTEL BASTILLE SPERIA ★★★ (42)
1, rue de la Bastille, 75004
Métro: Bastille (exit boulevard Beaumarchais)
42 rooms, all with shower or bath and toilet

TELEPHONE
01-42-72-04-01
FAX
01-42-72-56-38
EMAIL
speria@micronet.fr
INTERNET
www.123france.com
CREDIT CARDS
AE, DC, MC, V
RATES
Single 560–600F (85.37–91.47€), double 600–750F (91.47–114.34€); extra bed 110F (16.77€); lower rates in off-season and through Internet; *taxe de séjour* included
BREAKFAST
Continental 50F (7.62€), buffet 70F (10.67€), per person
ENGLISH SPOKEN
Yes

With the opening of the new Bastille Opéra, along with many galleries, new wave boutiques, trendy restaurants, and hot night spots throughout the *quartier,* the Bastille is one of the most popular places in Paris today. Visitors longing to be in the center of all this action can stay at the Bastille Speria, which is next to the famed brasserie Bofinger (see *Great Eats Paris*) and only a few yards from the place de la Bastille. The interior of the hotel was renovated in the late 1980s and continues to be well maintained. The rooms have uncluttered lines, black contemporary furnishings, and brightly colored carpets. The modern breakfast area and lounge have the same trim lines and feature a small garden and large aquarium with colorful fish. Management is coolly efficient.

FACILITIES AND SERVICES: Air-conditioning, direct-dial phone, elevator, hair dryer, magnifying mirrors, minibar, TV with international reception, room safe (15F, 2.29€, per day), trouser press

NEAREST TOURIST ATTRACTIONS (RIGHT BANK): Bastille Opéra, Marais, place des Vosges, Picasso Museum, typical outdoor market on boulevard Richard Lenoir (Thur and Sun 8 A.M.–noon)

HÔTEL CARON DE BEAUMARCHAIS ★★★ (25)
12, rue Vieille-du-Temple, 75004
Métro: Hôtel-de-Ville, St-Paul
19 rooms, all with shower or bath and toilet

TELEPHONE
01-42-72-34-12
FAX
01-42-72-34-63
CREDIT CARDS
AE, DC, MC, V
RATES
1–2 persons 730–810F (111.29–123.48€); extra bed 100F (15.24€); *taxe de séjour* included

Named after the boisterous author of the *Marriage of Figaro,* the Caron de Beaumarchais is close to interesting shopping in the Marais, the Jewish Quarter, and the Bastille Opéra. The beautifully restored hotel opened for business in June 1993, and is run by father and son owners Étienne and Alain Bigeard. Between them they have all the credentials necessary to run a fine, small hotel. Service and attention to guests' needs is a dwindling commodity in today's hotel market, but not here. Every time I have been in the hotel, guests could not say enough about the care and consideration extended to them during their stay, and this is backed up by the many glowing letters I have received from contented readers who have stayed here.

The downstairs lobby features a Louis XVI fireplace, copies of eighteenth-century murals, an antique game table laid out with authentic old playing cards, and an atrium garden off to one side. A brunch with freshly squeezed orange juice, assorted pastries, fresh fruit, and yogurt is served in a comfortable room that lends itself to lingering while thumbing through the collection of guidebooks left here for everyone's use. If guests prefer, a Continental breakfast will be brought on a tray to their rooms.

The nineteen bedrooms are small, but effective design and elegant eighteenth-century decor overcome this. No detail has been overlooked in providing a coordinated look. The Gustavian III–style furniture was made specially for the hotel. Original pages from the *Marriage of Figaro* are framed and hang in each room. Handpainted and signed ceramic tiles highlight the bathrooms, where even the color of the soap in the soap dish has been taken into consideration. All rooms are air-conditioned and soundproofed, and six have balconies with tables and chairs. In operating the hotel, the family strives to re-create a typically French atmosphere where guests feel at home and want to return. They achieve their goal with great success.

FACILITIES AND SERVICES: Air-conditioned and sound-proofed rooms, bathrobes, direct-dial phone, hair dryer, elevator, minibar, TV with international reception, safe in office (no charge)

NEAREST TOURIST ATTRACTIONS (RIGHT BANK): Place des Vosges, Marais, Jewish Quarter, Centre Georges Pompidou (Beaubourg), Île St-Louis, Île de la Cité, Picasso Museum, Bastille Opéra

BREAKFAST
Continental in room 55F (8.38€), brunch 80F (12.20€), per person
ENGLISH SPOKEN
Yes

HÔTEL DE LA BRETONNERIE ★★★ (18)
22, rue Ste-Croix-de-la-Bretonnerie, 75004
Métro: Hôtel-de-Ville
30 rooms, all with shower or bath and toilet

A stay in this captivating hotel will make you feel like an inhabitant of old-world Paris. Set in a restored seventeenth-century townhouse in the heart of the picturesque Marais, it is just minutes from the Beaubourg,

TELEPHONE
01-48-87-77-63
FAX
01-42-77-26-78
INTERNET
www.labretonnerie.com

CREDIT CARDS
MC, V

RATES
1–2 persons 660–850F
(100.62–129.58€), suites
1,100F (167.69€); *taxe de séjour*
6F (0.91€) per person, per day

BREAKFAST
Continental 60F (9.15€) per
person

ENGLISH SPOKEN
Yes

place des Vosges, the Picasso Museum, the banks of the Seine, and Notre Dame. High praise goes to longtime owners M. and Mme. Sagot and their daughter, Valérie, now the managing director, for providing a warm welcome to their many returning guests, who rightfully consider this to be one of the best small hotels in Paris.

Quality and taste are evident from the minute you enter the comfortable cross-beamed lobby and sitting room, with a large tapestry on one wall and tapestry-covered armchairs. The rooms are individually decorated and all are recommended. For a special treat, reserve No. 25 with modern British colonial wicker and a four-poster metal bed. Bathroom touches include fabric wall coverings, a deep tub, and an inset sink with plenty of space for all the cosmetics one could possibly need. A special favorite is No. 28, a two-room suite with a double bathroom to die for . . . just wait until you sink into the massive oval tub. No. 35 is wonderful. Magnificently done in pale yellow and green with enviable antiques, it consists of a bedroom, a separate sitting room, and one of the most beautiful three-star marble baths in Paris. For something smaller, but just as appealing, try Room 14 or 37, both with a four-poster canopy bed. Breakfast is served in the arched, stone-walled *cave* (cellar), with colorful dried floral arrangements complementing the rich French red decor.

NOTE: The hotel is closed in August.

FACILITIES AND SERVICES: Direct-dial phone, elevator, hair dryer, laundry service, minibar, TV with international reception, room safe (no charge)

NEAREST TOURIST ATTRACTIONS (RIGHT BANK): Place des Vosges, Bastille Opéra, Beaubourg, Marais, Picasso Museum, Seine, Île de la Cité, Île St-Louis, rue des Rosiers (Jewish Quarter)

HÔTEL DE LUTÈCE ★★★ (48)
65, rue St-Louis-en-l'Île, 75004
Métro: Pont-Marie

23 rooms, all with shower or bath and toilet

TELEPHONE
01-43-26-23-52

FAX
01-43-29-60-25

EMAIL
hotel.lutece@free.fr

INTERNET
www.france-hotel-guide.com/
h75004lutece.htm

CREDIT CARDS
AE, V

Île St-Louis is a small island, a mere six blocks long and two blocks wide, in the middle of the Seine. Every day and night, and especially on the weekends, crowds of tourists and Parisians surge down the main street, browsing through the boutiques and art galleries or stopping for an ice cream at the famed Berthillon. Lovers of this unique part of Paris check into either the Lutèce or the Deux-Îles (see below), both owned by husband-and-wife team Roland and Elisabeth Buffat. Stepping inside the Hôtel de Lutèce from the island's main street, you are welcomed by bouquets of fresh flowers and a large stone fireplace surrounded by soft couches and armchairs. The rooms at the Lutèce are not large by any standards, but they are nicely decorated and have the requisite exposed beams, provincial prints, and pretty rooftop views (that is, if you are lucky enough to secure a top-floor room, particularly Nos. 51, 52, 53, or 62). Because the hotel exudes charm from top to bottom, it is booked months ahead, so you should reserve as far in advance as possible.

FACILITIES AND SERVICES: Air-conditioning, direct-dial phone, elevator, hair dryer, TV with international reception, safe in room (no charge)

NEAREST TOURIST ATTRACTIONS (ISLAND IN THE SEINE): Île St-Louis, Île de la Cité, St-Germain-des-Prés, Latin Quarter, St-Michel, Bastille, place des Vosges, Picasso Museum, Marais

RATES
Single 780F (118.91€), double 910F (138.73€), triple 1,030F (157.02€); *taxe de séjour* 6F (0.91€) per person, per day

BREAKFAST
Continental 60F (9.15€) per person

ENGLISH SPOKEN
Yes

HÔTEL DES DEUX-ÎLES ★★★ (49)
59, rue St-Louis-en-l'Île, 75004
Métro: Pont-Marie

17 rooms, all with shower or bath and toilet

To capture the enchantment of Paris, stay on Île St-Louis. But be forewarned—you may never want to leave!

Many people like being on the island because they are only steps away from Notre Dame Cathedral, Ste-Chapelle, and the Conciergerie; within walking distance to the Marais; and close to all the excitement and nightlife around the Bastille Opéra. Only a few feel isolated and frustrated by its narrow streets, weekend crowds, and lack of easy parking. Personally, I love it, but I am biased because this is where I lived the first year I spent in Paris.

The Hôtel des Deux-Îles is a beautiful seventeenth-century mansion owned by decorator Roland Buffat and his wife, Elisabeth (they also run Hôtel de Lutèce, above). This hotel displays their touches at every turn, from the lobby with its atrium garden to the Louis XIV tiled bathrooms. The snug hotel breakfast area downstairs has a big fireplace and several secluded nooks with soft overstuffed sofas, making it a perfect place to start your Paris day. The rooms, where the very essence of Paris can be viewed from the top-floor windows, are very small, but they are well done with provincial prints, fabric wall coverings, bamboo furniture, and tiled baths.

TELEPHONE
01-43-26-13-35

FAX
01-43-29-60-25

EMAIL
hotel.2iles@free.fr

INTERNET
www.france-hotel-guide.com/
h750042iles.htm

CREDIT CARDS
AE, V

RATES
Single 810F (123.48€), double 930F (141.78€); *taxe de séjour* 6F (0.91€) per person, per day

BREAKFAST
Continental 65F (9.91€) per person

ENGLISH SPOKEN
Yes

FACILITIES AND SERVICES: Air-conditioning, direct-dial phone, elevator, hair dryer, TV with international reception, room safe (no charge)

NEAREST TOURIST ATTRACTIONS (ISLAND IN THE SEINE): Île St-Louis, Île de la Cité, Latin Quarter, St-Michel, St-Germain-des-Prés, Marais, Picasso Museum, place des Vosges, Bastille Opéra

HÔTEL DU GRAND TURENNE ★★★ ($, 35)
6, rue de Turenne, 75004
Métro: St-Paul, Bastille
41 rooms, all with shower or bath and toilet

TELEPHONE
01-42-78-43-25, toll-free in U. S., 800-MERCURE

FAX
01-42-74-10-72

INTERNET
www.mercure.com; www.libertel-hotels.com; www.accor.com

CREDIT CARDS
AE, DC, MC, V

RATES
Single 875F (133.39€), double 940–995F (143.30–151.69€), suite 820–1,200F (125.01–182.94€); extra bed 200F (30.49€); lower rates depending on season and availability; *taxe de séjour* included

BREAKFAST
Buffet 80F (12.20€) per person

ENGLISH SPOKEN
Yes

The Libertel hotel group, which is now part of Mercure, has many smart lodgings in various price categories scattered throughout Paris. All are beautifully done from top to bottom with coordinated colors and furnishings. Hôtel du Grand Turenne offers forty-one charming rooms done in blues, greens, or soft reds. The first and second floors are devoted entirely to nonsmokers. There are several categories of rooms, and despite their slight increase in price, I recommend the Superior rooms because they offer more space, especially for a double. There is one exception, however, and that is No. 603, a top-floor Superior double. The big bathroom with windows and a tub is nicely appointed, but the slanted wall makes it awkward for a tall person. Junior suites are popular with some, but I don't think they offer enough value to justify the higher price tags. Full room service is available from the morning until 2 P.M., and again from 6 to 11 P.M. This is a lifesaver if you have children or are just arriving with a case of jet lag and need something to eat at an off hour. The hotel location, only a five-minute walk from place des Vosges, offers visitors a convenient base for exploring one of the most interesting *quartiers* in Paris. From here it is a pleasant stroll to the Picasso Museum, Île de la Cité, Île St-Louis, the Bastille Opéra, and all the wild and woolly nighttime fun in the eleventh arrondissement. In addition, many restaurants listed in *Great Eats Paris* are close by.

NOTE: The first and second floors are entirely nonsmoking.

FACILITIES AND SERVICES: Direct-dial phone, elevator, hair dryer, laundry service, minibar, room service, TV with international reception, safe in office (no charge)

NEAREST TOURIST ATTRACTIONS (RIGHT BANK): Place des Vosges, Picasso Museum, Bastille Opéra, Île St-Louis, Île de la Cité

HÔTEL DU 7E ART ★★ (40)
20, rue St-Paul, 75004
Métro: St-Paul, Bastille

22 rooms, all with shower or bath and toilet

The theme of the hotel is "yesterday's and today's movies." If you are a movie buff, especially if you love old films, you *must* at least drop by to admire the hotel's fabulous collection of film posters. For instance, the sitting room displays an irreverant takeoff on the Last Supper with Marilyn Monroe as the central figure and twelve male film stars, ranging from Laurel and Hardy to Elvis and Frankenstein, sitting and gesturing along the laden table.

The rooms are not posh, nor are they large, but they do have character . . . and at least one or two framed film posters. No. 27, a back double with a miniature bathroom squeezed into a closet, sports *A L'Est d'Eden* with James Dean, *Les Trafiquants de la Nuite* (*The Long Haul*) starring Victor Mature and Diana Dors, and *Ne Me Quitter Jamais* (*Never Let Me Go*) with Clark Gable and Gene Tierney. Room 21, with beige grass-cloth walls and brown paisley quilted spreads on twins, can fit three, but I think it's better for two. Posters here include *The Swan* with Grace Kelly and *Niagara* with Marylin Monroe, Joseph Cotten, and Jean Peters. From a nostalgic standpoint, my favorite in this room is *Scandle en Floride* (*Scandal in Florida*) featuring Ronald Reagan and Shirley Temple. If you can't live without your own bit of film memorabilia or collectable kitsch, check out the small boutique, and the front window display . . . almost everything is for sale

FACILITIES AND SERVICES: Bar, direct-dial phone, no elevator, hair dryer available, laundry room for guests, TV with international reception, room safe (no charge)

NEAREST TOURIST ATTRACTIONS (RIGHT BANK): Marais, place des Vosges, Bastille, the islands, Notre Dame, Latin Quarter, antiques and boutiques along rue St-Paul

TELEPHONE
01-44-54-85-00

FAX
01-42-77-69-10

CREDIT CARDS
AE, DC, MC, V

RATES
1–2 persons 440–700F (67.08–106.71€); extra bed 100F (15.24€); *taxe de séjour* 5F (0.76€) per person, per day

BREAKFAST
Continental 50F (7.62€) per person

ENGLISH SPOKEN
Yes

HÔTEL RIVOLI NOTRE-DAME ★★★ (21)
19, rue du Bourg-Tibourg, 75004
Métro: Hôtel-de-Ville

TELEPHONE
01-42-78-47-39
FAX
01-40-29-07-00
INTERNET
www.hotelrivolinotredame.com
CREDIT CARDS
AE, DC, MC, V
RATES
Single 580–740F (88.42–112.81€), double 740–760F (112.81–115.86€), triple 760F (115.86€); extra bed 50F (7.62€); *taxe de séjour* 6F (0.91€) per person, per day
BREAKFAST
Continental 50F (7.62€) per person
ENGLISH SPOKEN
Yes

31 rooms, all with shower, bath, and toilet

The Rivoli Notre-Dame has a rich quality about it, especially in the ground-floor sitting area, which incorporates a heavy tapestry–covered high-back settee, dark cocoa armchairs, and thick hemp carpeting. An enviable framed collection of prints of early French fashions and tradespeople lines one wall. Tucked around the corner by the atrium garden is an attractive fringed chaise lounge and floor lamp. The elevator hides behind a brass-studded suede-covered door. The rooms are small, but very well done, especially No. 34, done in white with brass lamps framing the bed and a soft blue-and-yellow wall covering hanging behind it. The pink tiled bathroom includes a tub and a few toiletries. No. 21 is a single on the back facing a wall. It is a quiet, corner choice, with a small table, extra chair, and a tub in the bathroom. Breakfast is served on round tables in a small stone cellar downstairs.

FACILITIES AND SERVICES: Direct-dial phone, elevator, hair dryer, laundry service, TV with international reception, room safe (no charge)

NEAREST TOURIST ATTRACTIONS (RIGHT BANK): Marais, Île St-Louis, Île de la Cité, Notre Dame, place des Vosges, Jewish Quarter

HÔTEL SAINT-LOUIS ★★★ (47)
75, rue St-Louis-en-l'Île, 75004
Métro: Pont-Marie

TELEPHONE
01-46-34-04-80
FAX
01-46-34-02-13
INTERNET
www.hotelsaintlouis.com
CREDIT CARDS
MC, V
RATES
Single 700F (106.71€), double 800–900F (121.96–137.20€); *taxe de séjour* 6F (0.91€) per person, per day
BREAKFAST
Continental 55F (8.38€) per person
ENGLISH SPOKEN
Yes

21 rooms, all with shower or bath and toilet

Real estate prices for even the tiniest studio on Île St-Louis are mind-boggling, so you can imagine there are no hotel bargains here. This former swamp was transformed into an elegant residential area in the seventeenth century, and it is still the favorite of artists, actresses, heiresses, and members of the Rothschild family. The tree-lined quays, magnificent townhouses, and narrow main street make it so intimate and romantic that it is one of the most enchanting and picturesque places to stay in Paris. The Hôtel Saint-Louis boasts those quintessentially charming Parisian hotel status symbols: exposed wood beams, arched stone basement breakfast room, tapestry-rich fabrics, a few well-positioned antiques, and big bouquets of fresh flowers.

The rooms are small, even by Paris standards, but if you get one with a balcony, this helps. No. 52, hidden under the eves, is the tiniest room, but its two balconies, including one off the bathroom with a peek at the Seine, make it a very popular choice. No. 41, either a twin- or king-bedded room, has two windows overlooking its balcony. In No. 42 the balcony is on the corner. The bathroom is narrow, but it does have good light and some shelf space.

FACILITIES AND SERVICES: Direct-dial phone, elevator, hair dryer, laundry service, TV with international reception, room safe (no charge)

NEAREST TOURIST ATTRACTIONS (ISLAND IN THE SEINE): Île St-Louis, Île de la Cité, Notre Dame, Latin Quarter, St-Germain-des-Prés, place des Vosges, Marais, Bastille

HÔTEL SAINT-LOUIS MARAIS ★★ (45)
1, rue Charles V, 75004
Métro: Bastille, St-Paul
16 rooms, all with shower or bath and toilet

Andrée and Guy Record, who also own Hôtel Saint-Louis (see above), have recently redone their second hotel located near the place des Vosges and the Bastille. Their efforts show they have kept the spirit and style of the centuries-old building intact, especially the antique-furnished lobby. The highly polished stone floor, accented by Oriental rugs, guides you to a staircase (there is no elevator in the five-floor hotel) that leads to the sixteen rooms, where rich red and blue fabrics hang on the walls and on brass rails behind the beds. No. 4 is one of my favorites because it has twin beds, a bit more room, and a nice writing desk and chair. Room 16 is just as nice, especially the new bathroom with a tub. If you are here alone, ask for No. 1, with exposed beams and a mirrored bath with a shower.

FACILITIES AND SERVICES: Direct-dial phones, no elevator (five floors), hair dryer, TV with international reception, room safe (no charge)

NEAREST TOURIST ATTRACTIONS (RIGHT BANK): Place des Vosges, Bastille, Marais, Île de la Cité, Île St-Louis, Notre Dame

TELEPHONE
01-48-87-87-04

FAX
01-48-87-33-26

INTERNET
www.saintlouismarais.com

CREDIT CARDS
MC, V

RATES
Single 485–585F (73.94–89.18€), double 685–785F (104.43–119.67€); *taxe de séjour* 5F (0.76€) per person, per day

BREAKFAST
Continental 50F (7.62€) per person

ENGLISH SPOKEN
Yes

HÔTEL SAINT-MERRY ★★★ ($, 13)
78, rue de la Verrerie, 75004
Métro: Châtelet, Hôtel-de-Ville

TELEPHONE
01-42-78-14-15

FAX
01-40-29-06-82

INTERNET
www.ibrguide.com

CREDIT CARDS
AE, MC, V

RATES
1–2 persons 500–1,200F
(76.22–182.94€), 3 persons
1,400F (213.43€); suite for
1–2 persons 1,800F (274.41€),
3 persons 2,000F (304.90€),
4 persons 2,200F (335.39€);
taxe de séjour included

BREAKFAST
Continental 65F (9.91€) per
person

ENGLISH SPOKEN
Yes

11 rooms, 9 with shower or bath and toilet; 1 suite with shower, bath, and toilet

The former presbytery of the seventeenth-century Gothic church of St-Merry is now the most unusual hotel in Paris, and it qualifies as its own tourist attraction! It is the labor of love of owner M. Crabbe, who for more than forty years has been working to create a true Gothic masterpiece. His immense pride in his achievement is well deserved, and the results are spectacular.

The entrance to the hotel is through a short hallway with exposed beams and stone steps leading up to the lobby and reception area. Each room in the hotel is different (and priced separately) and showcases a wonderful collection of authentic Gothic church and castle memorabilia mixed with custom-made pieces. All the back rooms share a common wall with the church, and wherever possible this stone wall has been kept visible. Room 9 contains a carved stone flying buttress, which flows from the floor to the ceiling over the bed. Others have rough red tiles from the Chateau de l'Angeres in the Loire Valley, hand-carved mahogany pews, converted confessionals serving as headboards, and impressive eight-lamp chandeliers. All of the windows in the hotel are stained glass, and the balcony rails still bear the St-Merry Church crest. Since each room is unique, room rates vary accordingly, depending on the plumbing and the level of Gothic detailing.

For years M. Crabbe has been working on Room 20, the Gothic Suite, and it is finally completed. It isn't just a hotel suite, it is an experience! The approach is through an entry hall and up seventeen steps into a huge, pitched-roof room with cross beams, a baronial dining table seating six, skylights, a ten-foot clock, a fireplace, a wall of carved wooden shelves, and a large sofa bed where you can view the big-screen television. The bedroom is equally as dramatic, with a view of the Church of St-Merry. Even the bathroom is fabulous, with an ornately carved door depicting the three wise men, Mary, Joseph, and baby Jesus.

Finally, don't miss visiting the St-Merry Church adjoining the hotel. It has a beautiful choir and the oldest church bell in Paris, cast in 1331.

NOTE: The hotel is located on a pedestrian walkway, making it accessible by car or taxi only to the determined.

FACILITIES AND SERVICES: Direct-dial phone, no elevator, TV in suite; office safe, no charge

NEAREST TOURIST ATTRACTIONS (RIGHT BANK): Centre Georges Pompidou (Beaubourg), Marais, Seine, Île de la Cité, Île St-Louis, St-Germain-des-Prés

HÔTEL SANSONNET ★★ (16)
48, rue de la Verrerie, 75004
Métro: Hôtel-de-Ville
26 rooms, 22 with shower or bath and toilet

The family-owned Sansonnet offers far better two-star values than most of its competitors in the neighborhood. The hotel is clean, reasonably modern, and has been managed for more than twenty-five years by M. and Mme. Neau. A colorful aquarium sits at the lobby entrance, which is up an easy flight of stairs from the street. Several of the singles without facilities are minuscule, but if you have only a small suitcase and plan to use your room only for sleep, these are buys. The doubles are good-sized, with uniform color schemes and blended fabrics. The closets have shelves and most of the showers have doors. Finally, the address couldn't be better located for exploring the area around the Beaubourg and the Forum des Halles. For sightseeing and shopping farther afield, it is a ten-minute walk to the islands, St-Michel, the big department stores on rue de Rivoli, and a number of recommended restaurants in Paris (see *Great Eats Paris*).

FACILITIES AND SERVICES: Direct-dial phone, hair dryer in rooms with full facilities, no elevator, TV with international reception, safe in office (no charge)

NEAREST TOURIST ATTRACTIONS (RIGHT BANK): Centre Georges Pompidou (Beaubourg), Forum des Halles, BHV and La Samaritaine department stores, Île de la Cité, Île St-Louis

TELEPHONE
01-48-87-96-14

FAX
01-48-87-30-46

CREDIT CARDS
MC, V

RATES
Single 270–410F (41.16–62.50€), double 370–460F (56.41–70.13€); shower 20F (3.05€); *taxe de séjour* included

BREAKFAST
Continental 35F (5.34€) per person

ENGLISH SPOKEN
Yes

Fifth Arrondissement

LEFT BANK

Cluny Museum, Jardin des Plantes, Latin Quarter, rue Mouffetard, Panthéon, Sorbonne, place de la Contrescarpe

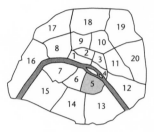

The fifth is known as the Latin Quarter for the students who came during the Middle Ages to study at the Sorbonne, which was founded in 1253 and remains a center of student life to this day, though not much Latin is spoken here anymore. The arrondissement stretches from the colorful street *marché* on rue Mouffetard to the dome of the Panthéon and through the botanical wonders of the Jardin des Plantes (opened by Louis XIV's doctor for the king's health). This ancient, interesting, and exhilarating part of Paris is crisscrossed with networks of narrow, curved streets lined on both sides with bookshops, restaurants, and cafés that surge with action twenty-four hours a day. It is youthful, cosmopolitan, bohemian, and fun. Even though St-Michel has lost its penniless chic, it is still the soul of the Latin Quarter. Crowds of all ages and types gather daily around the St-Michel fountain to flirt, eat, drink, argue, and watch the sidewalk entertainment. The area around place de la Contrescarpe is where Hemingway lived when he was a starving writer new to Paris. You can see two of his addresses: 39, rue Descartes, a studio; and 74, rue de Cardinal-Lemoine, where he lived with his wife, Hadley.

HOTELS IN THE FIFTH ARRONDISSEMENT

OTHER OPTIONS

Hostels

Student Accommodations

($) indicates a Big Splurge

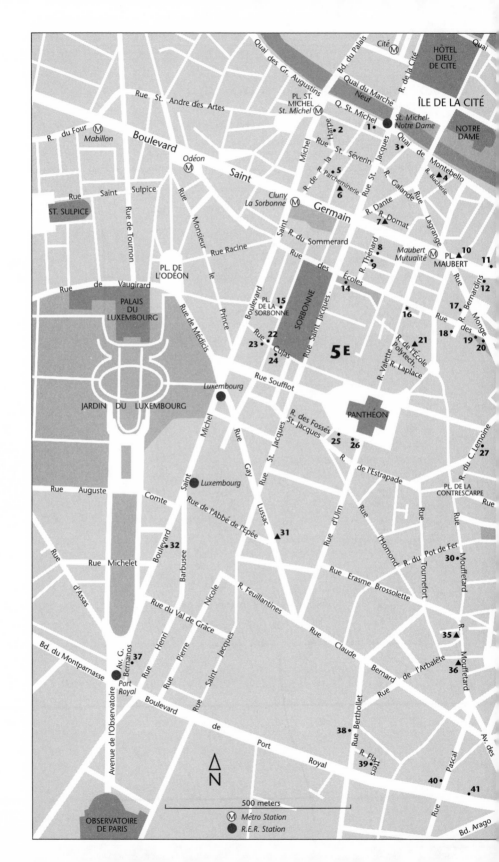

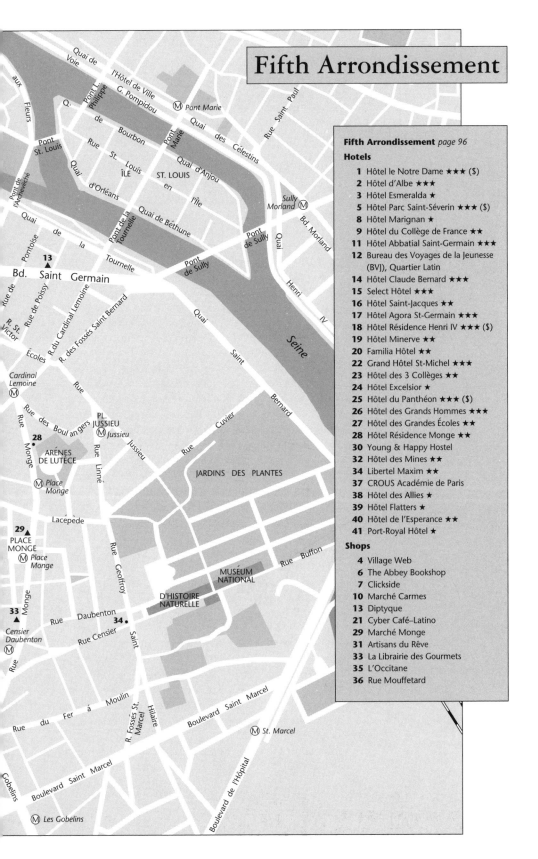

Fifth Arrondissement

FAMILIA HÔTEL ★★ (20)
11, rue des Écoles, 75005
Métro: Cardinal-Lemoine, Maubert-Mutualité

30 rooms, all with shower or bath and toilet

TELEPHONE
01-43-54-55-27

FAX
01-43-29-61-77

CREDIT CARDS
MC, V

RATES
Single 395–595F (60.22–90.71€), double 460–595F (70.13–90.71€), triple 650–700F (99.09–106.77€), quad 780F (118.91€); *taxe de séjour* 5F (0.76€) per person, per day

BREAKFAST
Continental 35F (5.34€) per person

ENGLISH SPOKEN
Yes

Many hotels on rue des Écoles are run by foreign managers for absentee owners in the Middle East. As a result, service, cleanliness, and upkeep are often drastically reduced because no one at the hotel has any stake in it or really cares. You will find none of this at the Familia Hôtel. M. and Mme. Gaucheron, who have owned the hotel for a decade, have turned the operating duties over to their son, Eric, whose hands-on management and high enthusiasm keep him on top of things every minute. Speaking rapid-fire French, Spanish, or English, he never stops doing whatever is necessary to insure that all guests are looked after properly. His wife, Sylvie, helps in the afternoon, or whenever she is not looking after their toddler, Charles, who is the apple of his grandfather's eye and adored by all the staff at the hotel.

The family is constantly on the lookout for ways to improve the hotel. The most recent was chipping away years of plaster and paint from the walls to expose the original stone from 1850, which now serves as a perfect backdrop for Eric's collection of original tapestries. Many rooms also have exposed walls; others have frescoes of famous Parisian landmarks. Room 62 has the Canal St-Martin painted over the twin beds; No. 43 has the famed Pont Neuf in sepia tones. I like No. 52, with the Pont Alexandre III and the Eiffel Tower gracing one wall and its little outdoor terrace with a view of Notre Dame. The same artist has painted a mural of old Paris along the front entry.

The bedrooms are on a rotating schedule for maintenance and improvements. Some rooms will have new mattresses one year, others a new bathroom, while still others will have new furniture. All have double-glazed windows. The size does not change, and they are still a tight fit for some, since they have limited space for bulky luggage or shopping purchases. But guests can always count on clean, snag- and tear-free accommodations. If you want a bird's-eye view of Notre Dame Cathedral, ask for a front room on the fifth or sixth floor. For a room with a balcony, you want something on the second or fifth floors, facing the street. Staying at the Familia puts guests only a few minutes from St-Germain-des-Prés, the islands, and all the famous cafés in the

Latin Quarter. Métro connections are good, and so is the bus transportation.

NOTE: If the Familia is booked, don't worry. The family now owns the Hôtel Minerve next door (see page 115), which they completely renovated into a very smart two-star.

FACILITIES AND SERVICES: Direct-dial phone, hair dryer, elevator, minibar, TV with international reception, safe in office (no charge)

NEAREST TOURIST ATTRACTIONS (LEFT BANK): Latin Quarter, St-Germain-des-Prés, Île de la Cité, Île St-Louis

GRAND HÔTEL ST-MICHEL ★★★ (22)
19, rue Cujas, 75005
Métro: Luxembourg
45 rooms, all with shower or bath and toilet

The Grand Hôtel St-Michel is an upscale pick between the boulevard St-Michel and the Panthéon. Before its recent transformation, it was a grim two-star that few could consider. Now, it is impossible not to be impressed with its elegant new look, which starts in the formal lobby and sitting rooms and continues along the tone-on-tone soft yellow hallways. Rooms are large enough to actually live in and are equipped with laptop friendly wiring, individual air-conditioning controls, and nice bathrooms. Those on the top floors have Panthéon views: in No. 503, a suite, you can see the dome from both balconies, including one off the bathroom. No. 604 has a view from both windows and one of the best bathrooms in the house.

FACILITIES AND SERVICES: Air-conditioning, bar, conference room; direct-dial phones, elevator, hair dryer, laundry service, modems, discounted public parking, TV with international reception, room safe (no charge)

NEAREST TOURIST ATTRACTIONS (LEFT BANK): Panthéon, Sorbonne, St-Michel

TELEPHONE
01-46-33-33-02
FAX
01-40-46-96-33
EMAIL
grand.hotel.st.michel@wanado.fr
INTERNET
www.grand-hotelst-michel.com
CREDIT CARDS
AE, DC, MC, V
RATES
Single 700F (106.71€), double 900F (137.20€), suite 1,300F (198.18€); *taxe de séjour* 6F (0.91€) per person, per day
BREAKFAST
Buffet 65F (9.91€) per person
ENGLISH SPOKEN
Yes

HÔTEL ABBATIAL SAINT-GERMAIN ★★★ (11)
46, boulevard St-Germain, 75005
Métro: Maubert-Mutualité
43 rooms, all with shower or bath and toilet

The Abbatial Saint-Germain offers comfort, convenience, and location. True, the rooms are generally small by American standards, but they are the norm in this popular sector of Paris, and they are carefully cleaned by a team of maids headed by Maria, who has spent a quarter century working here. The spirit of the

TELEPHONE
01-46-34-02-12
FAX
01-43-25-47-73
EMAIL
Abbitial@hotellerie.net
INTERNET
www.abbatial.com
CREDIT CARDS
AE, DC, MC, V

RATES
Single 600–720F (91.47–
109.76€), double 760–880F
(115.86–134.16€), triple
1,030F (157.02€); free baby
cot; *taxe de séjour* 6F (0.91€)
per person, per day

BREAKFAST
Buffet 50F (7.62€) per person

ENGLISH SPOKEN
Yes

nineteenth-century building is evident from the original cross beams along the halls, tapestry-covered furniture, and white antiqued furniture. The plaster plaques of nymphs and cherubs that grace almost every room seem a little over the top, but to each his own. The fifth- and sixth-floor rooms have balconies with views of Notre Dame and the Panthéon, and the sunny streetside rooms are soundproofed with double-glazed windows. Also under the same ownership is the Hôtel Agora St-Germain (see below).

FACILITIES AND SERVICES: Air-conditioning, direct-dial phone, elevator, hair dryer, laundry service, minibar, public parking across the street, TV with international reception, room safe (no charge)

NEAREST TOURIST ATTRACTIONS (LEFT BANK): St-Michel, Île de le Cité, Île St-Louis, Cluny Museum, St-Germain-des-Prés

HÔTEL AGORA ST-GERMAIN ★★★ (17)
42, rue des Bernardins, 75005
Métro: Maubert-Mutualité
39 rooms, all with shower or bath and toilet

TELEPHONE
01-46-34-13-00

FAX
01-46-34-75-05

EMAIL
agorastg@hotellerie.net

INTERNET
www.france-hotel-guide.com

CREDIT CARDS
AE, DC, MC, V

RATES
Single 610–650F (92.99–
99.09€), double 760–860F
(115.86–131.11€), triple 980F
(149.40); *taxe de séjour* 6F
(0.91€) per person, per day

BREAKFAST
Continental 50F (7.62€) per
person

ENGLISH SPOKEN
Yes

The Agora St-Germain continues to represent a success story for both owners and guests. It reopened in 1987 after undergoing a face-lift of remarkable proportions and has been popular ever since. Recently, an interior garden was added, giving the sitting area and lobby more dimension. The small, customized rooms with pretty silk wall coverings, ample space, and marble tiled bathrooms are beautifully maintained. A Continental breakfast is served in a stone-walled dining room with baskets of fresh flowers and linen napkins on each table. The friendly owners, Pascale and Michèle Sahuc, and their staff see to the wishes of every guest. Firmly recommended by all who have stayed here, this haven for weary travelers is less than five minutes away from good restaurants (see *Great Eats Paris*) and close to all the charm and excitement of this part of the Left Bank. Also under same ownership is the Abbatial St-Germain on boulevard St-Germain (see above).

NOTE: At the corner of rue des Bernardins and boulevard St-Germain is the church St-Nicholas du Chardonnet, the only church in Paris with all services conducted in Latin.

FACILITIES AND SERVICES: Air-conditioning, direct-dial phone, elevator, hair dryer, minibar, TV with international reception, room safe (no charge)

NEAREST TOURIST ATTRACTIONS (LEFT BANK): Latin Quarter, St-Michel, St-Germain-des-Prés, Île de la Cité, Île St-Louis

HÔTEL CLAUDE BERNARD ★★★ (14)
43, rue des Écoles, 75005
Métro: Maubert-Mutualité, Cluny–La Sorbonne
35 rooms, all with shower or bath and toilet

The Claude Bernard continues to be a Latin Quarter favorite, thanks to its friendly atmosphere and key location as a base for exploring St-Michel, St-Germain-des-Prés, and the islands in the Seine. Things have picked up considerably thanks to Paul Benjichou, a young, new owner with fresh ideas.The refurbished lobby incorporates a four-hundred-year-old Dutch inlaid cabinet, but the bar is new and so is the large wooden reception desk. A long, black leather sectional along the front window of the hotel provides a good place to rest a few minutes and watch the parade of people rushing by. Upstairs, the rooms combine English country pine furniture with French provincial fabrics, but color coordination has improved and so have most of the bathrooms. During the remodeling, the intricately carved moldings and doors were kept, along with the double French windows overlooking the street. The tremendous triple rooms are good for families, but these rooms face the noisy street, so heavy-duty earplugs would be a must for light sleepers. In fact, all the rooms facing the street should be considered off-limits for all but comatose sleepers.

FACILITIES AND SERVICES: Air-conditioning (100F, 15.20€, per day), fans are free, direct-dial phone, elevator, hair dryer, minibar, restaurant and tearoom, free sauna, TV with international reception, safe in office (10F, 1.52€, per day), sauna (50F, 7.62€, per person, free for readers of *Great Eats Paris*)

NEAREST TOURIST ATTRACTIONS (LEFT BANK): St-Michel, St-Germain-des-Prés, Île de la Cité, Île St-Louis, Latin Quarter

TELEPHONE
01-43-26-32-52
FAX
01-43-26-80-56
CREDIT CARDS
AE, DC, MC, V
RATES
Single 500–630F (76.22–96.04€), double 630–730F (96.04–111.29€); suite 1–2 persons 930F (141.78€), 3 persons 1,130F (172.27€), 4 persons 1,250F (190.56€); *taxe de séjour* included
BREAKFAST
55F (8.38€) per person, Continental in room or buffet downstairs
ENGLISH SPOKEN
Yes

HÔTEL D'ALBE ★★★ (2)
1, rue de la Harpe, 75005
Métro: St-Michel
45 rooms, all with shower or bath and toilet

This is the perfect site for Latin Quarter night owls and other urbanites who consider 11 P.M. the shank of the evening and the crack of dawn bedtime. Rue de la Harpe is just off place St-Michel, the twenty-four-hour,

TELEPHONE
01-46-34-09-70
FAX
01-40-46-85-70
EMAIL
albehotel@wanadoo.fr

INTERNET
www.hotelalbe.fr
CREDIT CARDS
AE, DC, MC, V
RATES
Single 645–670F (99.33–
102.14€), double 725–750F
(725–114.34€), triple 890F
(135.68€), quad
950F(144.38€); *taxe de séjour*
included
BREAKFAST
Buffet 60F (9.15€) per person
ENGLISH SPOKEN
Yes

nonstop, pulsating hub of this *quartier*. The street itself is lined with restaurants and cafés geared to tourists out for a good time. So, I must warn you, while this hotel has a good location and is the best on the street, it is going to be very noisy unless you use earplugs, sleep with the double-glazed windows tightly shut, and opt for the air-conditioning in a room on the top two floors. Good closet space and new bathrooms complement well-maintained rooms with quilted bedspreads, salmon-colored walls, and green carpets. Best choices are the corner rooms with three windows, but remember that they will be noisy. If there are four of you, look elsewhere; the quad here is too small. The bright modern breakfast room faces the street and plays relaxing classical music while you enjoy a morning croissant and *café au lait*.

FACILITIES AND SERVICES: Air-conditioning, bar, direct-dial phone, hair dryer, elevator to fifth floor (walk to sixth), laundry service, minibar, TV with international reception, room safe (no charge), room service for cold food

NEAREST TOURIST ATTRACTIONS (LEFT BANK): Notre Dame, Île de la Cité, Île St-Louis, St-Michel, Latin Quarter

HÔTEL DE L'ESPERANCE ★★ (40)
15, rue Pascal, 75005
Métro: Censier-Daubenton, Gobelins
38 rooms, all with shower or bath and toilet

TELEPHONE
01-47-07-10-99
FAX
01-43-37-56-19
CREDIT CARDS
AE, DC, MC, V
RATES
1–2 persons 410–510F (62.50–
77.75€), triple 610F (92.99€);
extra bed 75F (11.43€); *taxe de
séjour* included
BREAKFAST
Continental 40F (6.10) per
person
ENGLISH SPOKEN
Yes

Baubles, bangles, and beads—and then some— describes the over-the-top frilly decor and effervescent owner, Mme. Ellen Aymard, awaiting you at this hotel. Fortunately, you are not sleeping in her downstairs lobby, which is loaded with bowers of oversized fake flowers, Yugoslavian colored crystal, a doll collection, and an extensive array of hand-crocheted pillow covers, doilies, and lamp throws. Add to this a gurgling fountain and reproduction eighteenth-century furniture and some might need blinders to get to their rooms, which are all quite nice and tame by comparison. The color scheme revolves around coordinated yellow and soft rose florals. Bathrooms are all nice, and most have heated towel racks. At night you will always find a mint on your pillow. Room 11 is a double with a private garden and a large bathroom suitable for the handicapped. If you want quiet, book No. 21, a double on the back with its own balcony. The location is an interesting one, close to rue Mouffetard and within easy access to most Left Bank and Latin Quarter points of interest.

FACILITIES AND SERVICES: Bar, direct-dial phone, elevator, hair dryer, minibar, TV with international reception, safe in office (no charge)

NEAREST TOURIST ATTRACTIONS (LEFT BANK): Rue Mouffetard, Jardin des Plantes

HÔTEL DES ALLIES ★ (38)
20, rue Berthollet, 75005
Métro: Censier-Daubenton

43 rooms, 15 with shower or bath and toilet

Three generations of contented clientele continue to reserve rooms in this serviceable, frugal pick at the bottom of the fifth arrondissement. The location is not central by any means, but it is within walking distance to all the action and color around rue Mouffetard. Aside from a glass elevator, it is obvious that money has not been spent on fancy decorating touches, but all the rooms are clean, with few rips, tears, or dents in sight. The best part is that the rooms come with price tags no serious bargain hunter can ignore. The plain-Jane Room 22 is a steal, with a huge bathroom, twin beds, and nice wallpaper. It is, however, next to the hall shower. No. 2 is also across from a hall shower, and like most of the other rooms, is hose-down simple in every respect. It does have its own bathroom with orange sorbet–colored fixtures and a window. If you are single, avoid No. 51. Even though it has a view of the dome of l'Eglise du Val de Grace on the grounds of a nearby military hospital, the bed is too soft and lumpy. A better solo nest is sunny No. 52, recently redone with tiny flowered wallpaper and a new stall shower in the bathroom. No. 5, on the street, has space to spare, a double bed, new wallpaper, and a bathroom with a stall shower. Unfortunately, the windstorm in 1999, which damaged so many trees and buildings in and around Paris, caused damage to the hotel's sixth floor. Six rooms on this floor will be redone, and I imagine they will be well worth considering.

FACILITIES AND SERVICES: No TV, safe in office (no charge), desk open from 7 A.M. to 10:30 P.M., but keys given to guests

NEAREST TOURIST ATTRACTIONS (LEFT BANK): Rue Mouffetard

TELEPHONE
01-43-31-47-52

FAX
01-45-35-13-92

CREDIT CARDS
MC, V

RATES
Single 180–320F (27.44–48.78€), double 235–320F (35.83–48.78€), triple 325–420F (49.55–60.03€); public shower 15F (2.29€), towel 4F (0.61€) extra; *taxe de séjour* included

BREAKFAST
Continental 35F (5.34€) per person

ENGLISH SPOKEN
Yes

HÔTEL DES GRANDES ÉCOLES ★★ (27)
75, rue du Cardinal-Lemoine, 75005
Métro: Cardinal-Lemoine, Place Monge
51 rooms, all with shower or bath and toilet

TELEPHONE
01-43-26-79-23
FAX
01-43-25-28-15
INTERNET
www.hotel-grandes-ecoles.com
CREDIT CARDS
MC, V
RATES
Single 580–720F (88.42–
109.76€), double 580–760F
(88.42–115.86€), triple 710–
860F (108.24–131.11€); extra
bed 100F (15.24€); *taxe de séjour*
included
BREAKFAST
Continental 45F (6.86€) per
person
ENGLISH SPOKEN
Yes

Once found, this hotel address is one that its loyal followers whisper only to a select few. Nestled in a beautiful garden and hidden from the world behind towering wooden doors opening off the street, it is definitely one of the most romantic havens of peace and quiet in Paris. The grandmotherly owner, Leonore LeFloch, and her receptionist, Marie, treat their guests like family members. As you can imagine, reservations for this very special hotel are essential months in advance.

Two facing houses make up the hotel. In both, the rooms are decorated with a feminine touch, sparing no ruffle or pretty flowered fabric from the Laura Ashley school of decorating. Almost all of the rooms in both buildings look out onto the large tree-shaded garden with trellised roses, singing birds, spring daffodils, and summer wildflowers. Tables and chairs are placed here, making it a lovely spot for reading and sipping a cool drink. When you look out of your window between April and October, you will imagine you are in a French country village, not in the middle of Paris.

The hotel is an uphill climb from the métro, but once there you are close to place de la Contrescarpe, which played such an important part in Hemingway's Paris. You can also walk to rue Mouffetard, famous for its colorful, daily street *marché,* some good places to eat (see *Great Eats Paris*), and inexpensive clothing stores geared to cute young things.

FACILITIES AND SERVICES: Direct-dial phone, elevator, hair dryer, office safe (no charge), no TV

NEAREST TOURIST ATTRACTIONS (LEFT BANK): Rue Mouffetard, place de la Contrescarpe, Panthéon, Latin Quarter

HÔTEL DES GRANDS HOMMES ★★★ (26)
17, place du Panthéon, 75005
Métro: Luxembourg
32 rooms, all with shower or bath and toilet

TELEPHONE
01-46-34-19-60
FAX
01-43-26-67-32
CREDIT CARDS
AE, DC, MC, V

The Hôtel des Grands Hommes is a popular three-star choice, thanks to the personal management of the owner, Corinne Brethous-Moncelli. The hotel faces the Panthéon—the final resting place of many of France's great and near-great, including Napoléon. Rooms with a view are the same price as those without. In addition to its knockout location, it has historical significance: it was where André Breton invented automatic writing in 1919. When reserving, request one of the front rooms with a balcony, where you can have breakfast and gaze onto the Panthéon across the street and see Sacré Coeur gleaming in the distance. Honeymooners will want to stay in No. 22, with a canopied brass bed and two view balconies, or in No. 32, with a white metal-and-brass bed and a lovely marble bathroom filled with pink towels. Another good choice is No. 60, a two-room suite with a balcony facing the place du Panthéon. The bedroom has pitched beams, twin brass beds, and pink Venetian wall lights. There is also a sitting room with a sofa bed and a bathroom with a tub and hand-held shower. The gracious formal lobby is decorated in peach colors with faux marble finishes and outfitted with plenty of soft seating, a small corner bar, and an atrium garden filled with blooming plants.

NOTE: Also under the same ownership is the Hôtel du Panthéon next door (see page 109) and the Hôtel Résidence Henri IV on rue des Bernardins (see page 117).

FACILITIES AND SERVICES: Air-conditioning, bar, direct-dial phone, elevator, hair dryer, minibar, TV with international reception, safe in office (no charge)

NEAREST TOURIST ATTRACTIONS (LEFT BANK): Panthéon, Sorbonne, St-Michel, Jardin du Luxembourg

RATES
Single 850F (129.58€), double 900F (137.20€), sixth-floor suite 1,000F (152.45€), ground-floor suite 1,200F (182.94€); extra bed 100F (15.24€); *taxe de séjour* included

BREAKFAST
Buffet 50F (7.62€) per person

ENGLISH SPOKEN
Yes

HÔTEL DES MINES ★★ (32)
125, boulevard St-Michel, 75005
Métro: Port Royal
51 rooms, all with shower or bath and toilet

Charge reasonable prices for sensible, well-kept rooms and you also will enjoy the longevity of this great-value hotel in Paris. Owner Laurent Cuypers attributes the decorating to his mother, who personally made the curtains and bedspreads in all the rooms. Even though the hotel is on the far end of boulevard St-Michel, it is serviced by eight bus lines that will take you to Montmartre, Notre Dame, Ste-Chapelle, and almost everything in between.

Boulevard St-Michel is a major thoroughfare through this part of Paris. If peace and quiet is high on your list of requirements, I recommend a courtside room on a higher floor. If you don't mind some noise or can sleep

TELEPHONE
01-43-54-32-78

FAX
01-46-33-72-52

CREDIT CARDS
AE, DC, MC, V

RATES
Single 380–540F (57.93–82.32€), double 470–540F (71.65–82.32€), triple 630F (96.04€), quad 740F (112.81€); *taxe de séjour* included

BREAKFAST
Continental 40F (6.10€) per person

ENGLISH SPOKEN
Yes

with earplugs, No. 502 is a beamed twin-bedded room with dark blue carpeting and white stuccoed walls. There is luggage space, an open closet, a blue tiled bath, and a balcony. Even though it faces the street, it has double-paned windows to help diffuse the noise. Salmon is the color of choice in No. 305, which has a new bathroom and an interior view. American guests who value space should book Room 509, which is large enough to sleep four. The only room I would avoid is No. 508, a hot and stuffy room with a tiny bathroom and opaque glass-block windows.

FACILITIES AND SERVICES: Bar, direct-dial phone, elevator to 5th floor, hair dryer, TV, office safe (10F, 1.52€, per day)

NEAREST TOURIST ATTRACTIONS (LEFT BANK): Jardin du Luxembourg, St-Michel, Panthéon, St-Germain-des-Prés

HÔTEL DES 3 COLLÈGES ★★ (23)
16, rue Cujas, 75005
Métro: Luxembourg

44 rooms, all with shower or bath and toilet

TELEPHONE
01-43-54-67-30

FAX
01-46-34-02-99

CREDIT CARDS
AE, DC, MC, V

RATES
Single 420–645F (64.03–98.33€), double 525–735F (80.04–112.05€), triple 840F (128.06€); extra bed 100F (15.24€); *taxe de séjour* included

BREAKFAST
Continental 50F (7.62€) per person

ENGLISH SPOKEN
Yes

The hotel takes its name from the three colleges on the Montagne-St-Geneviève: La Sorbonne, founded in the thirteenth century; the fifteenth-century Collège St-Barbe, the oldest private school in France; and the prestigious Collège de France. If you want a modern room with a reasonable price tag in a good Left Bank neighborhood between the Sorbonne and the Panthéon, this is the place to go. The operative word here is simple. The small, off-white lobby has a California look, with modern chairs, large green plants, and bleached wooden floors. The pocket-size rooms have all the necessities: luggage racks, desks and chairs, full-length mirrors, wall-mounted television sets, and fitted bathrooms. No. 62 with a Sorbonne view, No. 63 with sloping roof, and No. 64 are best from a size standpoint, and No. 46 is a nice selection for the single traveler. The glass-roofed lounge off the lobby showcases a large, central tree that's surrounded by rattan chairs. A Continental breakfast is served in the tearoom on the street. Management, headed by Mme. Wyplosz and her staff, is pleasant and helpful in giving directions, making reservations, and confirming flights.

FACILITIES AND SERVICES: Direct-dial phone, elevator, hair dryer, laundry service, TV with international reception, safe in office (no charge), tearoom with a section for nonsmokers (open Mon–Fri 11 A.M.–7:30 P.M.)

HÔTEL DU COLLÈGE DE FRANCE ★★ (9)
7, rue Thénard, at rue Latran, 75005
Métro: Maubert-Mutualité, Cluny–La Sorbonne
29 rooms, all with shower or bath and toilet

Well placed in the heart of the Latin Quarter and across the street from the Collège de France, this is an outstanding value for a two-star hotel. The immaculate rooms are plainly yet uniformly done. The best ones are on the top floors; they have wooden beams and paneling, glimpses of Notre Dame Cathedral, and in summer are equipped with portable fans. No. 62 is the largest and most requested, probably due to the two floor-to-ceiling windows opening onto a small balcony, where you can see the Collège de France. The bathrooms are modern enough, with hair dryers, large towels, and space for more than just a toothbrush. The lobby and breakfast room have been redone with a rust red fabric covering the sectional seating. There's a nice collection of healthy green plants, and a statue of Joan of Arc guards the entryway. The popularity of this little hotel is reflected in its guest register, which is almost filled months ahead, so plan accordingly.

FACILITIES AND SERVICES: Direct-dial phone, fans, elevator to fifth floor, hair dryer, radio, TV with international reception, safe in office (no charge)

NEAREST TOURIST ATTRACTIONS (LEFT BANK): Latin Quarter, St-Michel, St-Germain-des-Prés, Sorbonne, Panthéon, Luxembourg Gardens, Île de la Cité, Île St-Louis

TELEPHONE
01-43-26-78-36

FAX
01-46-34-58-29

EMAIL
hotel.du.college.de.france@wanadoo.fr

INTERNET
www.france-hotel-guide.com/h75005college.htm

CREDIT CARDS
AE, MC, V

RATES
Single 525F (80.04€), double 580–610F (88.42–92.99€); extra bed 100F (15.24€), free for children under 14; *taxe de séjour* 5F (0.76€) per person, per day

BREAKFAST
Continental 40F (6.10€) per person

ENGLISH SPOKEN
Yes

HÔTEL DU PANTHÉON ★★★ ($, 25)
19, place du Panthéon, 75005
Métro: Luxembourg
34 rooms, all with shower or bath and toilet

The Hôtel du Panthéon, an elegantly converted townhouse, faces the imposing place du Panthéon in the fifth arrondissement. The métro is about five blocks away, but if you love this part of Paris, you know that almost everything is within walking distance. From the ground up, the hotel benefits from the impeccable taste and preservationist sensibilities of the gracious owner, Corinne Brethous-Moncelli, who also owns Hôtel des Grands Hommes next door (see page 106) and the Hôtel

TELEPHONE
01-43-54-32-95

FAX
01-43-26-64-65

EMAIL
henri4@hotellerie.net

INTERNET
www.france-hotel-guide.com/h75005pantheon.htm

CREDIT CARDS
AE, DC, MC, V

RATES
Single 800F (121.96€), double
1,000F (152.45€), triple
1,200F (182.94€); extra bed
100F (15.24€); *taxe de séjour*
included

BREAKFAST
Continental 50F (7.62€) per
person

ENGLISH SPOKEN
Yes

Résidence Henri IV on rue des Bernardins (see page 117).

The entry leads to the attractive lounge, with a corner coffee bar and a small atrium garden to one side. The Continental breakfast is served under the stone arches in the house's original cellar, or in the privacy of your own room. Guests will feel at home immediately in any one of the thirty-four rooms, decorated with antique furniture, textile-covered walls, and floor-length curtains hanging from fourteen-foot ceilings. The front rooms facing the Panthéon are naturally in demand, especially the five on the fifth floor with balconies. However, if you need absolute silence and calm, the viewless back rooms will guarantee this.

FACILITIES AND SERVICES: Air-conditioning, conference room, direct-dial phone, elevator, hair dryer, magnifying mirrors, minibar, porter, TV with international reception, safe in office (no charge)

NEAREST TOURIST ATTRACTIONS (LEFT BANK): Panthéon, Sorbonne, Latin Quarter, St-Germain-des-Prés, Luxembourg Gardens

HÔTEL ESMERALDA ★ (3)
4, rue St-Julien-le-Pauvre, 75005
Métro: St-Michel

TELEPHONE
01-43-54-19-20

FAX
01-40-51-00-68

CREDIT CARDS
None, cash only

RATES
Very small single 190F
(28.97€), 1–2 persons 365–
540F (55.64–82.32€), triple
600F (91.47€), quad 665F
(101.38€); *taxe de séjour*
included

BREAKFAST
Continental 45F (6.86€) per
person

ENGLISH SPOKEN
Yes

19 rooms, 16 with shower or bath and toilet; 4 apartments, all with shower or bath and toilet

Warning: This hotel is not for perfectionists!

The Esmeralda is an unconventional hideaway directly across the Seine from Notre Dame Cathedral. It has been owned for years by Madame Bruel, a sculptress and writer who lived in England and studied at Oxford. She and her former husband owned the first Bateaux Mouches that now take tourists up and down the Seine. After a bitter divorce, she bought the Esmeralda because she could see her beloved Seine from many of the windows. She told me most of the thirty-one rooms at the time were occupied by "permanent residents," all of whom shared one bathroom! She has made some improvements since then . . . notice I said *some*. It is a hotel people either love or absolutely hate. Maybe it does not have the most modern accommodations in town, but it does have one of the best Left Bank locations and some of the most interesting guests. The lack of embellishments, which might disappoint some, is the lure that brings others back again and again. This is a hotel with character for people with character.

No two rooms are alike, and they definitely are light years away from modern. Just like the unique owner, they flout convention and are eccentric to the core. Some are the size of a walk-in closet; others have chandeliers, marble fireplaces, and picture-perfect postcard views of Notre Dame Cathedral over the gardens of St-Julien-le-Pauvre, Paris's oldest church. All the rooms are reached by passing through a stone-walled lobby and climbing up a circular flight of ancient stairs. Some of the floors slant, a few areas need more than just a paint brush, and others have only a nodding acquaintance with the house-keeper. It is also noisy. But its many cult followers do not care because just being at the Esmeralda spells Paris for them. Be sure to bring earplugs and reserve way in advance.

NOTE: Insiders here for longer stays know to ask for one of the four apartments next door. These are, how-ever, not for everyone. Reached via a dark, winding, wooden staircase right out of a Victor Hugo novel, the apartments offer Paris without apologies. Yes, they are very old and dusty, and not everything works all the time. But for some, this faded charm with a definite past has a great appeal, especially when sitting by one of the large windows and looking across the Seine to Notre Dame bathed in moonlight.

FACILITIES AND SERVICES: Direct-dial phone, no elevator or TV, safe in office (no charge)

NEAREST TOURIST ATTRACTIONS (LEFT BANK): Notre Dame, Île de la Cité, Île St-Louis, St-Michel, St-Germain-des-Prés, Latin Quarter

HÔTEL EXCELSIOR ★ (24)
20, rue Cujas, 75005
Métro: Luxembourg

66 rooms, all with shower or bath and toilet

Acceptable one-star hotels are becoming an endangered species in this part of Paris. Either they have been totally renovated into three- or four-star addresses, or are so run-down and filthy that, for me, considering them is absolutely out of the question. Enter the Excelsior . . . still a one-star and still acceptable as long as you can live without air-conditioning or a direct-dial telephone in your room, don't need an elevator for the first two floors, and don't mind open closets, hard chairs, and some wear and tear around the edges. The rooms are clean, and the location is excellent. If you don't like noise, you will

TELEPHONE
01-46-34-79-50

FAX
01-43-54-87-10

EMAIL
htexcel5@club-Internet.fr

INTERNET
www.123france.com

CREDIT CARDS
AE, MC, V

RATES
Single 400F (60.98€), double 430–460F (65.55–70.13€), triple 540F (82.32€); lower rates in off-season on Internet; *taxe de séjour* included

BREAKFAST
Continental 35F (5.34€) per
person

ENGLISH SPOKEN
Yes

have to put up with some blank wall views in the second building. No. 204, a double, is one of these, but it does have newer carpeting, matching drapes and spreads, and a better closet, though the bathroom has a half tub. No. 34 is a safe twin bet. It faces front and has a bathroom with a shower over the tub. Forget No. 33—the toilet, sink, and shower are in an open area with no door!

FACILITIES AND SERVICES: Elevator from the second floor, hair dryer available, TV with international reception, office safe (no charge)

NEAREST TOURIST ATTRACTIONS (LEFT BANK): Panthéon, St-Michel

HÔTEL FLATTERS ★ (39)
3, rue Flatters, 75005
Métro: Gobelins, Port Royal

TELEPHONE AND FAX
01-43-31-74-21

CREDIT CARDS
None, cash only

RATES
Single 210–290F (32.01–
44.21€), double 260–340F
(39.64–51.83), triple 380F
(57.93€); *taxe de séjour* included

BREAKFAST
Continental 25F (3.81€) per
person (bread, no croissants)

ENGLISH SPOKEN
Yes

22 rooms, 18 with shower and toilet, 2 with shower and sink, 2 with toilet and sink (no public showers)

If you want to splurge on dinner or a new outfit rather than on a night's sleep, this one-star in the bottom of the fifth may be just the hotel you need. At one time, Madame Curie lived in the building; now it is owned by M. Lafond, who is slowly improving it.

Nineteen of the rooms have been redone, and all rooms on the first floor have private facilities. The location is quiet for Paris, and back room vistas are okay. Some rooms have carpeting; others bare wood floors and marble fireplaces. No. 2 has hardwood floors, but the black marble fireplace, peach walls, and newly tiled bathroom with a stall shower and good light (but no shelf space) compensate. Room 4, a twin on the back, has a view of a tree (which is lovely in the spring and summer) and a stall shower. If you are in No. 14, a twin on the top floor, you will have your own toilet, but no shower . . . and no possibility of taking one because the hotel does not have a public shower. Breakfast is served in a cozy room with three marble bistro tables and an Art Deco buffet. Management is friendly, and housekeeping, headed by the spirited Maria, is good. Everyone here knows the value of a smile and a kind word.

FACILITIES AND SERVICES: No elevator, TV (15F, 2.29€, per day)

NEAREST TOURIST ATTRACTIONS (LEFT BANK): Rue Mouffetard, Jardin des Plantes

HÔTEL LE NOTRE DAME ★★★ ($, 1)
1, quai St-Michel, 75005
Métro: St-Michel

26 rooms, all with shower or bath and toilet

The Hôtel le Notre Dame is welcomed back to the pages of *Great Sleeps Paris* after being eliminated in the last edition due to poor maintenance and indifferent management. Now, completely refashioned with verve by a new owner, the hotel offers twenty-six beautiful rooms, all with the latest bathrooms and the latest bold color schemes. Reserve one of the eighteen view rooms and you will look out across the *bouquinistes* (second-hand booksellers) lining the quays along the Seine and to the great western facade of the famed cathedral. Unless the windows are tightly shut and you are using earplugs, you will go to sleep and wake with the sounds of Paris, but for many of us, the majestic view will be worth it.

Entrance to the hotel is through a mirrored ground-floor hall and up a short flight of steps. The beautiful sitting room and breakfast area off the reception area have picture windows facing the cathedral and river. Warm dark woods show off the gold tartan-covered walls and form a backdrop for the comfortable seating that invites you to linger for hours and watch *toute* Paris surge by.

The rooms display an attractive mix of antiques and reproductions. If space is a prime concern, opt for No. 61, two-story duplex. When you walk in, voila! The river and Notre Dame are in full view. Upstairs there is a glass partition and a rooftop window with more views. I love the contemporary bathroom in No. 52 and the three windows in the room that allow you to lie in bed and gaze at the cathedral. In No. 53, you can still see the church, but not from bed. The new marble bathroom has a heated towel rack and good light. You definitely do not want to stay in Room 55, which faces a back air shaft and noisy fan.

FACILITIES AND SERVICES: Air-conditioning, bar, direct-dial phone, elevator from first floor (one flight of stairs to reception), hair dryer, minibar, modems, TV with international reception, room safe (no charge)

NEAREST TOURIST ATTRACTIONS (LEFT BANK): Notre Dame, Seine, Île de la Cité, Île St-Louis, Ste-Chapelle, St-Michel and Latin Quarter, St-Germain-des-Prés, Louvre, Musée d'Orsay

TELEPHONE
01-43-54-20-43

FAX
01-43-26-61-75

CREDIT CARDS
AE, DC, MC, V

RATES
1–2 persons 880–1,100F (134.16–167.69€), suite 1,500F (228.67€); *taxe de séjour* 6F (0.91€) per person, per day

BREAKFAST
Continental 45F (6.86€) per person

ENGLISH SPOKEN
Yes

HÔTEL MARIGNAN ★ (8)
13, rue de Sommerard, 75005
Métro: Maubert-Mutualité, Cluny–La Sorbonne
30 rooms, 6 with shower or bath and toilet

TELEPHONE
01-43-54-63-81
FAX
None
CREDIT CARDS
MC, V (800F, 121.96€, minimum)
RATES
Single 260F (39.64€), double 360–520F (54.88–79.27€), triple 490–620F (74.70–94.52€), quad 590–750F (89.94–114.34€); extra bed 70F (10.67€); showers free; *taxe de séjour* included
BREAKFAST
Included, cannot be deducted
ENGLISH SPOKEN
Yes, and German

The Marignan lives up to the three Cs of all lower priced accommodations: it is clean, convenient, and cheap, especially in November and December, when rooms for two, three, or four people are 15 percent less than the published prices. The hotel is usually jammed year-round with a frugal crowd of students, backpackers, and professors. A spirit of camaraderie prevails in this busy spot, making it impossible to feel lonely for long. The lineoleum-lined rooms are above average for a one-star. Mattresses are good, a few have private facilities, but don't look for views from the back singles or much in the way of reading lights.

To his credit, long-term owner Paul Keniger has provided guests with a wealth of information on Paris, including a large detailed map of the *quartier* showing the métro stops, banks, pharmacies, money-changing offices, bakeries, and tourist sites. The management also clearly states the rules of the hotel, and guests are expected to abide by them or move out. They are listed in plain sight at the check-in desk, so no one can claim "I didn't know" not to put my suitcase on the bed or to slam doors; to eat or leave empty bottles or cans in the room; to take a shower before 7 A.M. or after 10:45 P.M.; to turn off the light when leaving; and to ever go barefoot in public areas or on the stairs. Between March and September, reservations are taken for a minimum of two nights. All reservations are payable in advance by U.S. dollar check, *not* by credit card. Full refunds are granted if cancellation is more than seven days before arrival; otherwise, they charge the price of the room for one night. Last but not least in the rule department is the management's parsimonious breakfast philosophy. I quote Mr. Keniger: "If we give more, it encourages people to stay and eat, and then we won't have room to feed other guests." Since the breakfast, which is generous by one-star standards—it includes cheese, fruit salad, and orange juice along with bread and jam, but no croissant—is included in the rate and cannot be deducted, guests are stuck with an attitude that must reflect hard times for the owner.

FACILITIES AND SERVICES: Basement laundry and ironing area (no room laundry allowed); dining area where guests can eat food they bring in, boil water for a cup of tea, and use the refrigerator, microwave, and dishes; direct-dial phones; no elevator or TV; hair dryer in some rooms; safe in office (no charge); computer modems planned

NEAREST TOURIST ATTRACTIONS (LEFT BANK): Cluny Museum, Latin Quarter, St-Michel, St-Germain-des-Prés, Île de la Cité, Île St-Louis

HÔTEL MINERVE ★★ (19)
13, rue des Écoles, 75005
Métro: Cardinal Lemoine, Maubert-Mutualité
54 rooms, all with shower or bath and toilet

Eric Gaucheron had two important life-changing events in 1999: his wife, Sylvie, bore him a son, and he bought the fifty-four-room Hôtel Minerve, next door to the Familia Hôtel, which he and his family have owned for many years (see page 100). Despite the fact that the Minerve occupies an 1850 noble building, before Eric renovated it completely, the hotel was, in a word, terrible. No more! Thank goodness energy, imagination, and enthusiasm are three attributes Eric has in spades. He was right when he said to me, "Everyday I am working to do new things." It is true . . . he never stops! Twenty-four workmen toiled relentlessly for months to meet his exacting standards, and a phoenix has risen from the ashes of the old hotel.

Everything is new: the mattresses, the attractive antique-style furnishings, the coordinated fabrics, and of course, the marble tiled bathrooms with monogrammed towels. In addition to all the usual comforts. such as international television reception and triple-glazed windows to buffer the noise, all rooms have modems, four have cathedral ceilings, two have interior patios, ten have balconies, and many have hand-painted frescoes of French monuments. It is hard to pick a favorite, but I do like No. 607. The wall behind the bed was an old chimney, and from the balcony you have a view of Notre Dame and a twelfth-century abbey. No. 507 has two windows looking onto a balcony and a large bathroom with a tub. If you need absolute quiet, No. 608, with red-and-white *toile de Jouy* fabric (an eighteenth-century French scenic pattern), is on the back and can sleep three. Either of the two inside patio rooms (Nos. 102 and 103) are also quiet.

A mural montage of Paris greets guests as they enter the hotel. Original, old tapestries hang on the exposed stone walls in the lobby and in the downstairs breakfast room. The appealing lobby has burnt orange and gold

TELEPHONE
01-43-26-26-04,
01-43-26-81-89

FAX
01-44-07-01-96

CREDIT CARDS
MC, V

RATES
Single 395–650F (60.22–99.09€), double 460–680F (70.13–103.67€), triple 690F (105.19€); *taxe de séjour* included

BREAKFAST
Continental 40F (6.10€) per person

ENGLISH SPOKEN
Yes, and Spanish

armchairs and settees arranged in groups for twos and threes. Toward the back is a glass-enclosed atrium with a fountain, and an antique bookcase holding an antique book collection. It all adds up to an impressive new two-star hotel with many three-star attributes. Bravo Eric!

FACILITIES AND SERVICES: Direct-dial phone, elevator, hair dryer in most rooms; minibar, modems, TV with international reception, safe in office (no charge)

NEAREST TOURIST ATTRACTIONS (LEFT BANK): Latin Quarter, Île de la Cité, Île St-Louis, St-Germain-des-Prés

HÔTEL PARC SAINT-SÉVERIN ★★★ ($, 5)
22, rue de la Parcheminerie, 75005
Métro: St-Michel, Cluny–La Sorbonne
27 rooms, all with shower or bath and toilet

TELEPHONE
01-43-54-32-17

FAX
01-43-54-70-71

EMAIL
hotel.parc.severin@wanadoo.fr

INTERNET
hotel-espirit-de-france.com

CREDIT CARDS
AE, DC, MC, V

RATES
Single 560–1,070F (85.37–163.12€), double 655–1,070F (99.85–163.12€), suite 1,070–1,570F (163.12–239.34€); extra bed 120F (18.29€); children under 12 free; *taxe de séjour* included

BREAKFAST
60F (9.15€) per person, Continental in room or buffet downstairs

ENGLISH SPOKEN
Yes

Dyed-in-the-wool aficionados of life around St-Michel, who also like elegantly understated surroundings, will love this hotel. The owners are to be applauded for creating an alluring, modern establishment that is serene, serious, and pleasing to the eye. For someone very, very special, reserve No. 70, the private penthouse suite with its own elevator entrance. The wraparound terrace provides unequaled views of Notre Dame, St-Séverin Church (one of the most popular in Paris for weddings), the Panthéon, Collège de France, Tour Montparnasse, and in the distance, the Eiffel Tower and the Sacré Coeur on Montmartre. The interior of this dream suite glows with a blend of antiques and contemporary furnishings. The other rooms in the hotel display the same standards of excellence, and many have impressive views. The management and staff are exceptional in their attention and service for all of their guests. For those who want up-to-the-minute convenience and luxury in the heart of old Paris, the Parc Saint-Séverin is a favorite choice of many discriminating *Great Sleeps Paris* readers.

NOTE: For other hotels under the same ownership, see Hôtel de la Place du Louvre (page 62), Hôtel Mansart (page 68), and Hôtel Brighton (page 60).

FACILITIES AND SERVICES: Air-conditioning in most rooms, direct-dial phone, elevator, hair dryer, laundry service, minibar, TV with international reception, room safe (no charge)

NEAREST TOURIST ATTRACTIONS (LEFT BANK): St-Michel, Latin Quarter, Cluny Museum, St-Germain-des-Prés, Île de la Cité, Île St-Louis

HÔTEL RÉSIDENCE HENRI IV ★★★ ($, 18)
50, rue des Bernardins, next to Square Paul Langevin, 75005
Métro: Maubert-Mutualité, Cardinal Lemoine
14 rooms, all with shower or bath and toilet and fully fitted kitchenette

Eighteen years ago, when I began writing my Paris hotel guide, this hotel had another name and an image of faded respectability. Several years ago it was taken over by Corinne Brethous-Moncelli, who owns Hôtel des Grands Hommes (see page 106) and Hôtel du Panthéon (see page 109). Whatever Mme. Moncelli touches is transformed with style and distinction, and this property is no exception. Quietly situated opposite the leafy square Paul-Langevin, at the end of rue des Bernardins, the hotel offers fourteen spacious rooms, each with the added plus of fully fitted kitchenettes, as well as all the hotel services and facilities a guest could want. I think the best buys are the beautiful two-room suites because they offer separate sitting areas, marble fireplaces, and just enough extra space to make a long stay very comfortable. No. 22 has a magnificent gold-framed mirror over its fireplace. Hand-painted moldings and the original ceiling are carried through to the bedroom, which has a large armoire and a corner fireplace to add to its charm. Nos. 42 and 52 are large enough to accommodate a family. No. 10 on the ground floor has no fireplace and is my least favorite. The hotel is peaceful and calm, yet it is minutes away from almost everything on a visitor's A-list of things to see and do in the Latin Quarter and St-Germain-des-Prés.

FACILITIES AND SERVICES: Two air-conditioned rooms, direct-dial phone, elevator, hair dryer, TV with international reception, safe in room (no charge)

NEAREST TOURIST ATTRACTIONS (LEFT BANK): Latin Quarter, St-Michel, St-Germain-des-Prés, Île de la Cité, Île St-Louis, Cluny Museum

TELEPHONE
01-44-41-31-81
FAX
01-46-33-93-22
CREDIT CARDS
AE, DC, MC, V
RATES
1–2 persons 950–1,400F (144.83–213.43€); *taxe de séjour* 6F (0.91€) per person, per day
BREAKFAST
Continental 50F (7.62€) per person
ENGLISH SPOKEN
Yes

HÔTEL RÉSIDENCE MONGE ★★ (28)
55, rue Monge, 75005
Métro: Place Monge, Cardinal Lemoine
36 rooms, all with bath or shower and toilet

It isn't posh by any means, just a modest, family hotel run by a delightful owner, Mme. Chatillon. The exceptionally clean, well-priced rooms are done in rose, blue, peach, pale green, or yellow. No. 31 is one of the best in the house. This quiet room is done in hues of

TELEPHONE
01-43-26-87-90
FAX
01-43-54-47-25
EMAIL
hotel-monge@gofornet.com
INTERNET
www.hotelmonge.com

CREDIT CARDS
MC, V

RATES
Single 390–460F (59.46–
70.13€), double 400–560F
(60.98–85.37€); extra bed 100F
(15.24€); *taxe de séjour* 5F
(0.76€) per person, per day

BREAKFAST
Continental 40F (6.10€)
per person

ENGLISH SPOKEN
Yes

salmon and blue with two windows overlooking a play-ground and a bathroom with both a tub and shower. Three can live comfortably in No. 22, which has the bonus of a balcony. You can expect some noise in Rooms 1 and 15 because they face the street. Imitation flowers and plants abound, especially in the breakfast room, which is overflowing with many bright varieties sitting in floral trimmed pots.

FACILITIES AND SERVICES: Air-conditioning, direct-dial phone, elevator, hair dryer, minibar, TV with international reception, office safe (no charge)

NEAREST TOURIST ATTRACTIONS (LEFT BANK): Rue Mouffe-tard, Jardin des Plantes

HÔTEL SAINT-JACQUES ★★ (16)
35, rue des Écoles, 75005
Métro: Maubert-Mutualite, Cluny–La Sorbonne
35 rooms, 31 with shower or bath and toilet

TELEPHONE
01-44-07-45-45

FAX
01-43-25-65-50

CREDIT CARDS
AE, DC, MC, V

RATES
Single 275–495F (41.92–
75.46€), double 470–630F
(71.65–96.04€), triple 710F
(108.24€); free hall showers;
taxe de séjour included

BREAKFAST
Continental 40F (6.10€) per
person

ENGLISH SPOKEN
Yes

From the doorstep you can easily walk to Notre Dame, the Panthéon, the Louvre, the islands, and all the interesting streets that make up this part of the Latin Quarter. The thirty-five reasonably priced rooms are a mixture of modern comforts that flow easily with sculptured moldings and views of Notre Dame and the Panthéon. Everyone likes the tissue-lined No. 5, with two windows draped in fabrics that match the bed. The bathroom has a large tub and a shower guard. In No. 28, guests who don't mind climbing a few stairs are rewarded with a balcony and a new bathroom. Breakfast is served in a bright, streetside room with a wall mural of the Seine and Notre Dame.

FACILITIES AND SERVICES: Direct-dial phone, elevator to five floors (walk to sixth), hair dryer, magnifying mirrors in largest rooms, TV with international reception, office safe (no charge)

NEAREST TOURIST ATTRACTIONS (LEFT BANK): Latin Quarter, Panthéon, Sorbonne, the islands, rue Mouffetard

LIBERTEL MAXIM ★★ (34)
28, rue Censier, 75005
Métro: Censier-Daubenton
36 rooms, all with shower or bath and toilet

TELEPHONE
01-43-31-16-15; toll-free in
U.S., 800-MERCURE

FAX
01-43-31-93-87

INTERNET
www.mercure.com;
www.accor.com;
www.libertel-hotels.com

Most hotels that are part of a big chain leave me cold. The one distinct exception to this is Libertel, which operates under the umbrella of the Mercure Hotels. All the Libertels offer peaceful enclaves of comfort, high quality, and professional services. I applaud top management's bold (for Paris) decision to allocate at least two floors in each hotel exclusively for nonsmoking guests. The Maxim has three. The well-coordinated rooms are done in three different *toile de Jouy* fabrics in pink, gray, and blue. Bathrooms are tightly fitted with a tub and/or shower and modern free-standing marble sinks on a wrought-iron base. A filling buffet breakfast is served in a sky-lit room with fruit prints on the walls and red-and-green chairs. Walkers will enjoy strolling through the nearby Jardin des Plants, and shoppers won't want to miss rue Mouffetard, one of the most colorful and photographed markets and shopping streets on the Left Bank.

NOTE: Three floors are reserved for nonsmokers.

FACILITIES AND SERVICES: Direct-dial phone, elevator, fans, hair dryer available, laundry service, TV with international reception, office safe (no charge), handicapped-accessible room

NEAREST TOURIST ATTRACTIONS (LEFT BANK): Jardin des Plants, rue Mouffetard, Latin Quarter

CREDIT CARDS
AE, DC, MC, V

RATES
Single 605F (92.23€), double 670F (102.14€); *taxe de séjour* included

BREAKFAST
Continental 50F (7.62€) per person

ENGLISH SPOKEN
Yes

PORT-ROYAL HÔTEL ★ (41)
8, boulevard de Port-Royal, 75005
Métro: Gobelins, Censier-Daubenton
48 rooms, 20 with shower or bath and toilet

If you are looking for maximum value without sacrificing quality in either surroundings or service, you will find the Port-Royal Hôtel is impossible to beat. In fact, it is so far ahead of most other one-star hotels in Paris (and many two- and three-star hotels for that matter) that there simply is no contest. I will admit that I had my doubts at first, as I trudged on and on down the long boulevard de Port-Royal in a driving rainstorm looking for the hotel. Once inside, however, I found it nothing short of amazing. It is obvious that Claudine and Thierry Giraud are paying close attention to every detail and carrying on the traditions set by their father, who owned the hotel for over seventy years. On top of being an absolute steal for the money, it is spotless and, thanks to Claudine, exceptionally well decorated. The usual one-star dime-store taste—dusty plastic floral arrangements, mismatched colors, and exhausted, sagging furniture—is nowhere in sight. Instead, everything is in perfect order, from the red carpeted stairs and hallways with security and fire doors to the well-coordinated rooms, many with new wallpaper and carpeting, attractive fabrics, and ceiling fans. Those on the front have double-paned windows

TELEPHONE
01-43-31-70-06 (reservations accepted by phone 7 A.M.–7 P.M. only)

FAX
01-43-31-33-67

CREDIT CARDS
None, cash only

RATES
Single 216–425F (32.93–64.79€), double 275–425F (41.92–64.79€), deluxe 500F (76.22€); shower 15F (2.29€); *taxe de séjour* included

BREAKFAST
Continental 35F (5.34€) per person

ENGLISH SPOKEN
Yes

to let you sleep peacefully. Many have beautiful new bathrooms—especially No. 2, a double on the back. Even the showers have doors, a rare find in Paris and almost a curiosity in one-star hotels. Those selecting the smallest rooms need not feel deprived. These rooms have many of the nice touches of their more expensive neighbors, including a piece of candy on the pillow at night.

The facade has been repainted, enhancing the Art Deco glass gracefully curving over the front door. The inviting streetside sitting room, with its comfortable chairs and beautiful live green and flowering plants, belies the hotel's budget category. So does the breakfast room, overlooking a neatly manicured interior garden. Real flowers on the tables, caned chairs with upholstered seats, and an interesting collection of the family's antique woodworking tools displayed on the walls add to the appeal.

The hotel is easily accessible to St-Michel, the Musée d'Orsay, the Louvre, and the Champs-Élysées by bus. It connects to Orly by direct bus from the métro stop. Close by is a huge shopping complex with 150 boutiques and a branch of Au Printemps department store. Also near are cinemas—including the Grand Ecran, the largest screen in Europe—a selection of restaurants and cafés (see *Great Eats Paris*), and public parking. All in all, it adds up to one of the best hotels for the money in Paris.

FACILITIES AND SERVICES: Direct-dial phone, elevator, hair dryer and iron available, free street parking (Mon–Fri 7 P.M.–9 A.M. and all day Sat, Sun, holidays, and in Aug), TV in sitting room, safe in office (no charge)

NEAREST TOURIST ATTRACTIONS (LEFT BANK): Gobelins Museum (tapestries), rue Mouffetard, Jardin des Plantes

SELECT HÔTEL ★★★ (15)
1, place de la Sorbonne, 75005
Métro: Cluny–La Sorbonne, Luxembourg
68 rooms, all with shower or bath and toilet

TELEPHONE
01-46-34-14-80
FAX
01-46-34-51-79
EMAIL
Select.Hotel@wanadoo.fr
INTERNET
www.selecthotel.fr
CREDIT CARDS
AE, DC, MC, V

In 1937 Eric Sevareid paid 50¢ a night at the Select. Things have changed . . . considerably.

Dramatically renovated in late 1987, the hotel now has one of the most spectacular interior garden courts in Paris, complete with blooming tropical plants and a fountain. The lobby and reception area are studies in ultramodern design, with chrome and black leather furniture highlighted by posters of Paris. This sleek approach is carried into the intimate bar, breakfast room, and seating alcoves tucked around the skylit garden. Hallways showcase the work of Hyppolite Romain, who was commissioned specially to do all of the paintings you see.

Most of the rooms have as much appeal as the public areas, especially those overlooking the garden court or those ending in a 7 or 9, which overlook the place de la Sorbonne in front. Those on the backside and in the annex have all the perks but are dark, viewless, and done in some hideous wallpapers and colors. No. 41, a duplex, is also one to avoid due to the treacherous spiral staircase leading to the cavelike downstairs bedroom. Two of the nicest are Nos. 33 and 53, which display the original stone wall of the hotel and centuries-old oak beams. Two large floor-to-ceiling windows open onto the *place* below. Comfortable armchairs, good reading lights, a large working desk, hidden storage space, and a split bathroom make these favorites for longer stays. No. 65 is a good-looking double with a wraparound desk, two leather chairs, and a nice bath with good mirrors and space. An ideal Latin Quarter location, some lower off-season rates, three-star creature comforts, and the friendly reception staff (headed for more than twenty years by Jeanine) make the Select Hôtel a front-runner in the *quartier*. Unfortunately, it no longer costs only 50¢ a night.

FACILITIES AND SERVICES: Air-conditioning, bar with light snacks, direct-dial phone, elevator, hair dryer, modems, radio, TV with international reception, safe in office (no charge)

NEAREST TOURIST ATTRACTIONS (LEFT BANK): Latin Quarter, Sorbonne, St-Germain-des-Prés, Île de la Cité, Île St-Louis

RATES
1–2 persons 670–830F (102.14–126.53€), triple 950F (144.83€), duplex 1,250F (190.56€); extra bed 30 percent of room rate; children under 10 free during off-season; honeymooners receive complimentary champagne and breakfast during off-season; *taxe de séjour* 6F (0.91€) per person, per day

BREAKFAST
Continental 40F (6.10€) per person

ENGLISH SPOKEN
Yes

Sixth Arrondissement

LEFT BANK
École des Beaux-Arts, Luxembourg Gardens, Odéon National Theater, Académie Française, St-Germain-des-Prés Church, St-Sulpice Church

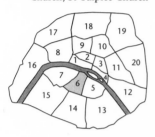

Literary and artistic Paris is the heart of the sixth, which is a continuation of the Latin Quarter and one of the most stimulating parts of the city. Intellectual, elegant, and very appealing, it has tiny side streets, old buildings, antique shops, a thriving café life, and more atmosphere block for block than anyone could ever soak up. The square by the St-Germain Church, the oldest Roman abbey church in Paris, is the main focus of the district. Les Deux Magots and Café de Flore, the two most celebrated cafés in Paris, were the hangouts of Hemingway, Sartre, Simone de Beauvoir, and James Joyce. Today they are jammed with Parisians and tourists alike engaged in some of the best people-watching in the universe.

HOTELS IN THE SIXTH ARRONDISSEMENT

OTHER OPTIONS

Residence Hotels

Student Accommodations

($) indicates a Big Splurge

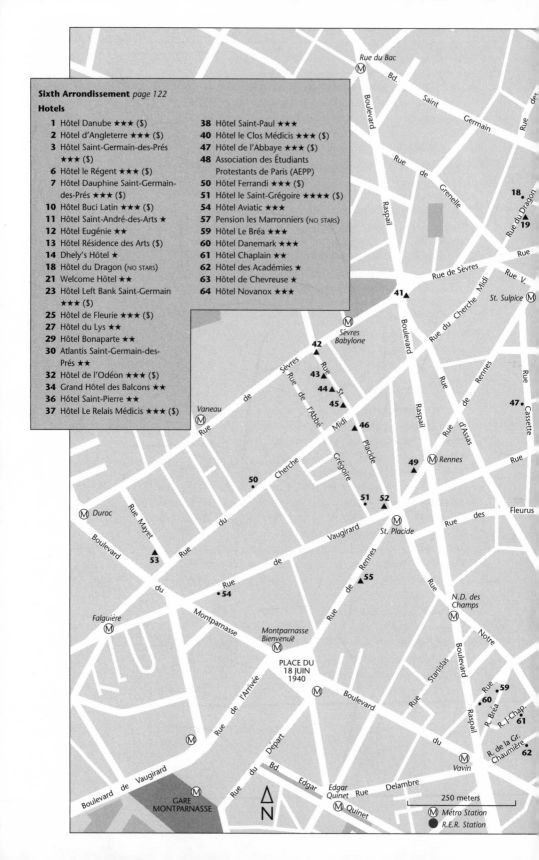

Rue du Bac
Bd.
Boulevard
Saint
Germain
Rue de
Rue
Grenelle
Raspail
Rue du Dragon
18
19
Rue
Rue de Sèvres
Rue V.
St. Sulpice
Rue du Cherche Midi
41
Sèvres
Babylone
42
Boulevard
Rennes
Rue
Sèvres
Rue de l'Abbé
43
44
St.
45
Rue de
Rue
Cassette
47
Vaneau
Rue
Midi
46
Placide
Grégoire
Rue d'Assas
Cherche
49
Rennes
Rue
Duroc
Rue Mayet
50
du
51 52
Vaugirard
St. Placide
Rue des
Fleurus
53
Boulevard
de
Rue
Rennes
55
N.D. des Champs
Falguière
54
Rue
Montparnasse
Montparnasse
Bienvenüe
Notre
Rue
Stanislas
Boulevard
PLACE DU
18 JUIN
1940
Boulevard
Rue
Rue
59
60
R. Bréa
R. J.-Chap.
61
Rue de l'Arrivée
du
Raspail
du
R. de la Gr.
Chaumière
62
Vavin
Rue
Départ
Bd.
Edgar
Edgar Quinet
Rue
Delambre
250 meters
Boulevard de Vaugirard
Rue du
Quinet
N
GARE
MONTPARNASSE
Ⓜ Métro Station
⬤ R.E.R. Station

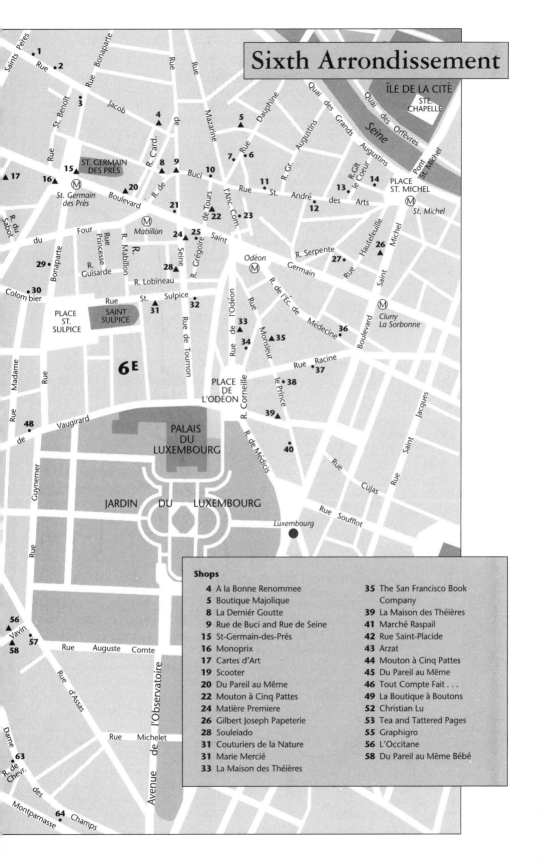

Sixth Arrondissement

ÎLE DE LA CITÉ

STE. CHAPELLE

PLACE ST. MICHEL

St. Michel

ST. GERMAIN DES PRÉS

St. Germain des Prés

PLACE ST. SULPICE

SAINT SULPICE

Odéon

Mabillon

Cluny La Sorbonne

6E

PLACE DE L'ODÉON

PALAIS DU LUXEMBOURG

JARDIN DU LUXEMBOURG

Luxembourg

Shops

4 A la Bonne Renommee
5 Boutique Majolique
8 La Derniér Goutte
9 Rue de Buci and Rue de Seine
15 St-Germain-des-Prés
16 Monoprix
17 Cartes d'Art
19 Scooter
20 Du Pareil au Même
22 Mouton à Cinq Pattes
24 Matière Premiere
26 Gilbert Joseph Papeterie
28 Souleiado
31 Couturiers de la Nature
31 Marie Mercié
33 La Maison des Théières

35 The San Francisco Book Company
39 La Maison des Théières
41 Marché Raspail
42 Rue Saint-Placide
43 Arzat
44 Mouton à Cinq Pattes
45 Du Pareil au Même
46 Tout Compte Fait . . .
49 La Boutique à Boutons
52 Christian Lu
53 Tea and Tattered Pages
55 Graphigro
56 L'Occitane
58 Du Pareil au Même Bébé

ATLANTIS SAINT-GERMAIN-DES-PRÉS ★★ (30)
4, rue Vieux Colombier, 75006
Métro: St-Sulpice, Mabillon

TELEPHONE
01-45-48-31-81
FAX
01-45-48-35-16
EMAIL
paris@hotelatlantis.com
INTERNET
www.hotelatlantis.com
CREDIT CARDS
AE, MC, V
RATES
1–2 persons 590–920F (89.94–140.25€); *taxe de séjour* included
BREAKFAST
Continental 45F (6.86€) per person
ENGLISH SPOKEN
Yes

27 rooms, all with shower or bath and toilet

Saving money with style is what you will be doing if you reserve at the Atlantis Saint-Germain-des-Prés, a two-star choice that outstrips many three-stars in comfort, service, and overall appeal . . . not to mention price. The hotel, located opposite St-Sulpice church, is in the thick of things in this corner of the St-Germain-des-Prés *quartier*. Within an easy five- to ten-minute walk you can be sipping a café at either Les Deux Magots or Café de Flore on the boulevard St-Germain; shopping at Bon Marché department store, browsing along the narrow streets lined with boutiques, or jogging off that last pastry in the Jardin du Luxembourg. The clean and efficient air-conditioned rooms are maintained by a staff of chambermen who take their job seriously. Furnishings are an interesting fusion of Art Deco and traditional French with brass beds, comfortable armchairs, good wardrobe space, and nicely coordinated fabrics. The tiled bathrooms are modern and functional. The downstairs sitting room adds another pleasant dimension to the hotel, as does the sky-lit breakfast room with a grandfather clock in one corner. The desk staff is exceptional.

FACILITIES AND SERVICES: Air-conditioning, direct-dial phone, hair dryer, elevator, some minibars (but not stocked), TV with international reception, room safe (no charge)

NEAREST TOURIST ATTRACTIONS (LEFT BANK): Jardin du Luxembourg, St-Germain-des-Prés, shopping, Île de la Cité, Île St-Louis

DHELY'S HÔTEL ★ (14)
22, rue de l'Hirondelle, 75006
Métro: St-Michel

TELEPHONE
01-43-26-58-25
FAX
01-43-26-51-06
CREDIT CARDS
AE, DC, MC, V
RATES
Single 210–230F (32.01–35.06€), double 310–400F (47.26–60.98€), triple 410–500F (62.50–76.22€); extra bed 100F (15.24€); shower 25F (3.81€); *taxe de séjour* 5F (0.76€) per person, per day

21 rooms, none with toilet or bathtub, 7 with shower

For the quintessential budget hotel, steps from the Seine and place St-Michel, Dhely's is the place. Many cut-rate choices in this Left Bank neighborhood are severely lacking in housekeeping, but not this one. Everything is shipshape, from the hall toilets and ground-floor showers to the rooms, most of which have pretty floral wallpaper and window boxes with real flowers. The larger rooms have carpeting; the smaller ones have linoleum floors. Of course, the higher you climb, the lower the price and the better the view. While the hotel is basic, it does have some redeeming architectural details, such as the original sixteenth-century tiled entryway and classified historical stairway, open beams, and exposed stone walls. In its most infamous moment, it was the home of Anne de Pisseleu, the favorite mistress of François Premier, king of France from 1515 to 1547. For the last twenty-one years, the hotel has been owned by Mme. Kenniche.

FACILITIES AND SERVICES: Direct-dial phone, TV with international reception, office safe (no charge), no elevator

NEAREST TOURIST ATTRACTIONS (LEFT BANK): St-Michel, Île de la Cité, Île St-Louis, St-Germain-des-Prés

BREAKFAST
Continental 35F (5.34€) per person

ENGLISH SPOKEN
Yes

GRAND HÔTEL DES BALCONS ★★ (34)
3, rue Casimir-Delavigne, 75006
Métro: Odéon

50 rooms, all with shower or bath and toilet

The Grand Hôtel des Balcons is one of the most dignified, inexpensive hotel choices in this part of the Left Bank, and it's a perennial favorite with older, cost-conscious budgeteers who have found that it is a much better value than the other three-star hotels on the same block.

The impressive lobby is a masterpiece of Art Nouveau design, with glorious stained-glass windows and masterfully turned wood. There are always beautiful fresh-flower displays, arranged by the manager's wife, who is a recognized ikebana expert. On the reception desk is a tin of biscuits, which you are invited to enjoy along with afternoon tea. Uniformed maids are relentless in keeping everything dust free. To management's credit, rooms have been redecorated with nice wallpaper and new bedspreads. Each has a desk where you can plug in your computer, at least one chair, and good reading lights. Many have double windows. Vintage baths tend to be small, but are spotless The location is tops, close to loads of budget restaurants (see *Great Eats Paris*), and near place de l'Odéon, boulevard St-Michel, St-Germain-des-Prés, and one of the city's most popular parks, the Jardin du Luxembourg.

FACILITIES AND SERVICES: Direct-dial phone, elevator, hair dryer, radio, TV with international reception, office safe (no charge)

NEAREST TOURIST ATTRACTIONS (LEFT BANK): St-Michel, St-Germain-des-Prés, Luxembourg Gardens, Île de la Cité, Île St-Louis

TELEPHONE
01-46-34-78-50

FAX
01-46-34-06-27

EMAIL
lesa@balcons.com

INTERNET
www.balcons.com

CREDIT CARDS
AE, DC, MC, V

RATES
Single 445-485F (67.84–73.94€), double 525–620F (80.04–94.52€), triple or quad 970F (147.88€); *taxe de séjour* 5F (0.76€) per person, per day

BREAKFAST
55F (8.38€) per person, Continental in room or buffet in dining room

ENGLISH SPOKEN
Yes

HÔTEL AVIATIC ★★★ (54)
105, rue de Vaugirard, 75006
Métro: Falguière, St-Placide, Montparnasse
43 rooms, all with shower or bath and toilet

TELEPHONE
01-53-63-25-50; toll-free in the U.S., UTELL 800-448-8355

FAX
01-53-63-25-55

EMAIL
welcome@aviatic.fr

INTERNET
www.aviatic.fr

CREDIT CARDS
AE, DC, MC, V

RATES
1–2 persons: *classique* 780–939F (118.91–143.15€), superior 950–1,100F (144.83–167.69€), suites 1,600–1,900F (243.92–289.65€); lower rates in Jan, Feb, July, Aug, Nov, and Dec; *taxe de séjour* included

BREAKFAST
65F (9.91€) per person, Continental in room or buffet downstairs

ENGLISH SPOKEN
Yes

The hotel is named after the aviators who came here to have drinks around the turn of the century. Today the Art Deco glass and the black wrought-iron awning over the door—flanked by matching lamps—set the welcoming stage for this businesslike hotel. The lobby has faux marble columns and small groupings of velvet chairs and antique marble chests topped with bouquets of fresh flowers. To one side is the breakfast room, papered with vintage Parisian art posters.

A wide, winding stairway with overhead skylights leads guests up to forest green carpeted hallways and the forty-three rooms in two buildings. There is more than just a touch of class in these well-thought-out chambers, which all have built-in luggage racks, good space to spread out and work, armchair seating, and ample closets. The rooms in the front building are bright and airy, with pretty views of the surrounding Montparnasse neighborhood. Those in the back are sunny, but they don't have much of a view. A change of ownership led to redecoration and needed improvements in most of the rooms, which now carry higher price tags. However, they have low-season discounts and deals throughout the year, so it's possible to avoid the sometimes Big Splurge rates.

FACILITIES AND SERVICES: Air-conditioning, bar, direct-dial phone, elevator, hair dryer, laundry service, minibar, modems in some rooms, parking (120F, 18.29€, per day), terry robes, TV with international reception, room safe (no charge)

NEAREST TOURIST ATTRACTIONS (LEFT BANK): Montparnasse, Jardin de Luxembourg

HÔTEL BONAPARTE ★★ (29)
61, rue Bonaparte, 75006
Métro: St-Sulpice, Mabillon
29 rooms, all with shower or bath and toilet

TELEPHONE
01-43-26-97-37, 01-43-26-54-10

FAX
01-46-33-57-67

CREDIT CARDS
AE, MC, V

The Hôtel Bonaparte is a thrifty two-star a whisper away from some of the best this Left Bank *quartier* has to offer. Not only are you in shopping heaven, but you'll be close to scores of restaurants and famous cafés (see *Great Eats Paris*), the Luxembourg Gardens, and the lovely St-Sulpice Church. Transportation to other parts of Paris is a snap either by bus or métro.

Most of the rooms have been refreshed, and for the price, they are well supplied with individually controlled air-conditioning, hair dryer, minibar, television, and room safe. An added plus is that the owner, Mme. Dumas, and her manager, Eric Lemaire, both speak English well. If it is twin beds you want, ask for the L-shaped No. 27, which has good cross-ventilation, a tiny front balcony, and a black marble fireplace; or ask for No. 16, with a large marble bath and white wicker furniture. No. 28, which has enough living and walking space, has been redone in pale yellow. It has a fireplace, large oval table with two chairs, a tiled bath with a window, and a balcony. A cozy single is the stone-walled No. 29, tucked under the mansard roof.

FACILITIES AND SERVICES: Air-conditioning, direct-dial phone, elevator, hair dryer, minibar, TV, room safe (no charge)

NEAREST TOURIST ATTRACTIONS (LEFT BANK): Seine, St-Germain-des-Prés, shopping, Île de la Cité, Île St-Louis

RATES
Single 510–620F (77.75–94.52€), double 650–840F (99.09–128.06€), triple 860F (131.11€); *taxe de séjour* included

BREAKFAST
Continental included, cannot be deducted

ENGLISH SPOKEN
Yes

HÔTEL BUCI LATIN ★★★ ($, 10)
34, rue de Buci, 75006
Métro: St-Germain-des-Prés, Odéon

27 rooms, all with shower or bath and toilet

Down the street from the picturesque Buci street *marché* is the Hôtel Buci Latin. To say the hotel is different is the understatement of the year. Owners Ronald MacLeod and Laurence Raymond have mixed an aggressively imaginative interior with an old period French building, and the results are nothing short of spectacular. The entrance announces immediately that this is a hotel where creativity and pure whimsy have been raised to new levels. A wooden-planked walkway leads guests to the reception desk, where three clocks display local time. To one side, zebra-patterned armchairs and comfortable sofas suggest lingering over a drink from the honor bar. Photos of all twenty-seven guest-room doors, which were crafted and hand painted by nine local artists, hang in the lobby. You'll have to see them, as they defy description. And if you take the elevator, you will miss the graffiti-covered stairway, authentically done by a knowledgeable New York artist.

The rooms are simple yet extremely well planned. Orange walls offset crisp white duvet covers on beds with built-in headboards hiding closets. Long, blond wall desks with halogen lights and a fabric-draped chair

TELEPHONE
01-43-29-07-20

FAX
01-43-29-67-44

EMAIL
hotel@bucilatin.com

INTERNET
www.bucilatin.com

CREDIT CARDS
AE, DC, MC, V

RATES
1–2 persons 1,200–1,400F (182.94–213.43€), duplex 1,850F (282.03€), junior suite 1,950F (297.28€); *taxe de séjour* 6F (0.91€) per person, per day

BREAKFAST
Included, cannot be deducted

ENGLISH SPOKEN
Yes

complement open-slat wooden armoires. What rooms are best? I can recommend them all, but No. 162, a top-floor junior suite with an electric bed, circular Jacuzzi bath, and a balcony with two chaise lounges, wins by a nose. A close second is No. 140, a duplex with a huge upstairs bathroom that has skylight views of St-Germain Church; an old-fashioned, claw-foot bathtub (and a modern stall shower for diehards); a beautiful antique sink; and an adobe tiled floor with an Indian rug under a marvelous wicker *coiffeuse* (dressing table). No. 123 has double windows facing out and, in the bathroom, black marble lining the white sink with chrome fittings. Clothes hang in two clever closets: one that looks like the gates to a fortress, and the other hidden behind the bed.

The downstairs breakfast room is no less unusual, with modern chairs covered in pink, green, orange, and turquoise leather. A steamer trunk that doubles as a buffet holds daily newspapers, a mirror made from beer caps set in cement, a collection of ceramic whiskey bottles, and a little roadster round out the experience.

FACILITIES AND SERVICES: Air-conditioning, bar, direct-dial phone, elevator, hair dryer, laundry service, minibar, room service, TV with international reception, office safe (no charge)

NEAREST TOURIST ATTRACTIONS (LEFT BANK): St-Michel, St-Germain-des-Prés, Île de la Cité, Île St-Louis

HÔTEL CHAPLAIN ★★ (61)
11 bis, rue Jules-Chaplain, 75006
Métro: Vavin, Notre-Dame-des-Champs
25 rooms, all with shower or bath and toilet

The lobby mural of Monet's lily pond at Giverny and a breakfast area opening onto a plant-filled patio make for a pleasing beginning at this attractive Montparnasse hotel. On the ground floor, five rooms open onto this little courtyard. Throughout the hotel, the coordinated rooms in yellow and green with blue accents display simple good taste, and they possess good desk space, chairs, room for luggage, and nice bathrooms. Within a five-minute walk of the hotel are scores of restaurants in all price categories (see *Great Eats Paris*), a dozen movie theaters, and the Luxembourg Gardens. For farther sightseeing jaunts, it's easy to catch a bus or the métro and be almost anywhere in Paris in fifteen minutes.

FACILITIES AND SERVICES: Direct-dial phone, elevator in front building, hair dryer, laundry service; TV with international reception, room safe (10F, 1.52€, per day)

TELEPHONE
01-43-26-47-64

FAX
01-40-51-79-75

EMAIL
chaplain-rg@wanadoo.fr

CREDIT CARDS
AE, DC, MC, V

RATES
Single 445F (67.84€), double 485F (73.94€), triple 680F (103.67€), quad 725F (110.53€); *taxe de séjour* included

BREAKFAST
Continental 45F (6.86€) per person

ENGLISH SPOKEN
Yes

NEAREST TOURIST ATTRACTIONS (LEFT BANK): Montparnasse, Luxembourg Gardens

HÔTEL DANEMARK ★★★ (60)
21, rue Vavin, 75006
Métro: Vavin, Notre-Dame-des-Champs
15 rooms, all with shower or bath and toilet

For the Nurit family, nothing seems to be too much
trouble when it comes to pleasing their guests. They
have a special fondness for Americans, many of whom
have been repeat guests for years, even before the hotel
was what it is today. The Nurits are proud of their
fifteen-room hotel in Montparnasse, and they should be.
It is an imaginative lesson in how to take an old student-
style hotel and turn it into an eye-catching spot on the
cutting edge of hotel chic.

Cool blues and grays dominate the downstairs color
scheme, with artist-inspired furnishings that look like
exhibits from New York's Museum of Modern Art. The
walls are dotted with a collection of dramatic posters of
Parisian landmarks and famous race cars, along with a
collection of bold paintings done by an architect friend
of the family. The rooms, done in soft yellows, green,
lavender, or cocoa brown, are constantly being upgraded.
While compact, they contain everything necessary for a
comfortable stay. All rooms have their own Italian
marble bathroom with heated towel racks, good makeup lighting, and in a few, a Jacuzzi. The rooms from the
third floor up have no interior views. Those on the front
face a pretty, white-brick apartment building with terrace gardens, and those on the top floor are under sloping, beamed ceilings with skylights.

FACILITIES AND SERVICES: Direct-dial phone, hair dryer,
elevator, some Jacuzzis, minibar, TV with international
reception, office safe (no charge)

NEAREST TOURIST ATTRACTIONS (LEFT BANK): Montparnasse

TELEPHONE
01-43-26-93-78

FAX
01-46-34-66-06

CREDIT CARDS
AE, DC, MC, V

RATES
1–2 people 690–890F (105.19–
135.68€); *taxe de séjour* 6F
(0.91€) per person, per day

BREAKFAST
Continental 60F (9.15€) per
person

ENGLISH SPOKEN
Yes

HÔTEL D'ANGLETERRE ★★★ ($, 2)
44, rue Jacob, 75006
Métro: St-Germain-des-Prés
27 rooms, all with shower or bath and toilet

Benjamin Franklin refused to enter this building to
sign the Treaty of Paris because at the time it was the
British Embassy and considered British soil. Ernest
Hemingway had no qualms when he occupied Room 14,
describing it to his friends as "good and cheap." Today

TELEPHONE
01-42-60-34-72

FAX
01-42-60-16-93

EMAIL
anglotel@wanadoo.fr

CREDIT CARDS
AE, DC, MC, V

RATES
1–2 persons: standard 785F
(119.67€), deluxe 1,050–
1,315F (160.07–200.47€),
2-person suite 1,680F
(256.11€), extra person 275F
(41.92€); *taxe de séjour*
6F (0.91€) per person, per day
BREAKFAST
Continental 65F (9.91€) per
person
ENGLISH SPOKEN
Yes

the Angleterre is no longer "cheap," but it is a declared national monument and a well-known classic hotel with a long list of guests clamoring to get in.

I can recommend all of the traditional rooms and suites; each one is different, but all are appointed with a high ceiling, exposed beams, large bed, exceptional closet space, and fabulous double-sink bathrooms. Room 5 on the back has a Venetian chandelier, a wicker armchair, and a great bathroom with an antique marble sink. In Room 38, a ground-floor favorite that opens onto a terrace, there is a Parisian beamed ceiling, a sitting room, and a stone wall in back of a curved wooden bed. The large closet with shelves allows for spreading out and settling in. No. 47 is in the part of the building without an elevator, but to me that doesn't matter. I could move right into this large antique-filled room, which overlooks the interior patio. This plant-filled, lovely spot is the perfect place to spend an hour or two in the afternoon, after a morning of browsing through all the interesting shops in the neighborhood. Breakfast is served in a sunny dining room with well-spaced tables and good lighting for reading the morning papers. The lobby is beginning to show its age, especially the worn, brown corduroy-covered sofas and chairs, which are out of place in this wonderful setting.

The rates are on the high side, but the hotel is included for those seeking a distinguished location in one of the most popular tourist *quartiers* in Paris. When reserving, be sure to specify either a standard or a deluxe room—or a suite (only two of which are serviced by an elevator)—and get written confirmation. While the accommodations are all lovely, the standard rooms probably will be too small for two people with bulky luggage.

FACILITIES AND SERVICES: Bar, direct-dial phone, elevator to most floors, hair dryer, two rooms with Jacuzzi, laundry service, TV with international reception, room safe (no charge)

NEAREST TOURIST ATTRACTIONS (LEFT BANK): Superb shopping and browsing, St-Germain-des-Prés, St-Michel, Île de la Cité, Île St-Louis

HÔTEL DANUBE ★★★ ($, 1)
58, rue Jacob, 75006
Métro: St-Germain-des-Prés
40 rooms, all with shower or bath and toilet

The building has an interesting history. The American Treaty of Independence from Britain was signed here on September 3, 1783. David Hartley represented the King of England and Benjamin Franklin, John Jay, and John Adams were the American representatives. During World War II, from September 1939 to June 1940, it was the home of General Sikorsky, head of the Polish government in exile. Today it is the Hôtel Danube, a St-Germain charmer with forty rooms offering good value for the price for those with more flexible budgets. The hotel is very well managed, and the desk staff are the friendliest and most accommodating in the neighborhood. It is also one of the few hotels that offers complimentary Internet access for guests to send and receive email.

A red floral wallpapered entry has a multicolored tile floor. To one side is an inviting sitting room with a fireplace flanked by two wing-back chairs. Just beyond an interior courtyard is a breakfast room with a collection of blue-and-white Oriental porcelain on display.

The large bedrooms are individually decorated with a mixture of styles that range from colonial Chinese and Indian to mid-Victorian. Double windows in Room 15 open onto the street. Seating is provided by two cane chairs positioned around a glass-topped table. Other appointments include a marble-topped chest of drawers, lighted closet, and gray monogrammed towels in the bathroom. No. 10 is the same size, and it has a beautiful double brass bed, but the bathroom has an older style of tile. For what Room 40 on the courtyard may lack in view, it more than makes up for in space. No. 41, a two-room apartment in pink and blue, is another large choice. It has an antique double bed in one room and two regular doubles in the second. The new marble tile bathroom has a tub with a hand-held shower over it and sink space for toiletries. No. 54 is a new room that's too elfin in size for two, but it probably would suit one person with light luggage. There are five rooms similar to No. 6, which has a table flanked by two armchairs, a marble-topped dresser, lighted closets, an older style bath, and a good working desk.

FACILITIES AND SERVICES: Direct-dial phones, elevator to most rooms, hair dryers in most or available, laundry

TELEPHONE
01-42-60-94-07 (reservations),
01-42-60-34-70

FAX
01-42-60-81-18

EMAIL
hoteldanube@wanadoo.fr

INTERNET
www.hoteldanube.fr

CREDIT CARDS
AE, MC, V

RATES
1–2 persons 680–1,080F
(103.67–164.64€), apartment
(2–4 persons) 1,400F
(213.43€), extra bed 200F
(30.49€); *taxe de séjour* 6F
(0.91€) per person, per day

BREAKFAST
Continental 60F (9.50€) per
person

ENGLISH SPOKEN
Yes

service, TV with international reception, office safe (no charge), complimentary Internet access to send and receive email

NEAREST TOURIST ATTRACTIONS (LEFT BANK): Excellent shopping, St-Germain-des-Prés, St-Michel, Île de la Cité, Île St-Louis, Seine

HÔTEL DAUPHINE SAINT-GERMAIN-DES-PRÉS ★★★ ($, 7)
36, rue Dauphine, 75006
Métro: Odéon

30 rooms, all with shower or bath and toilet

TELEPHONE
01-43-26-74-34, toll-free from the U.S., 800-44-UTELL

FAX
01-43-26-49-09

EMAIL
dauphine@cybercable.fr

INTERNET
www.dauphinestgermain.com

CREDIT CARDS
AE, DC, MC, V

RATES
1–2 persons 980F (149.40€); suite: 1–2 persons 1,215F (185.23€), 3–4 persons 1,410F (214.95€); lower rates in off-season; *taxe de séjour* included

BREAKFAST
Buffet 75F (11.43€) per person

ENGLISH SPOKEN
Yes

In the early days, the first and second floors of Parisian townhomes were for the nobility, the higher floors for the servants. This explains the larger rooms and higher ceilings you will encounter in this sixteenth-century building. Unfortunately, the rooms on the back (except on the top floor) and those ending in the number 4 face an uninspiring back view. However, they are quiet and certainly have the same three-star decorating standards and benefits found in the rest of the hotel. Otherwise, there is plenty to choose from, including Nos. 55, 56, 65, and 66, which are exclusively reserved for nonsmoking guests, and No. 52, decorated in a rose salmon Provençal print, with a recessed double bed and view of the neighboring rooftops. No. 61 is a blue-and-white sloped-roof suite that can accommodate up to four. The mansard windows let in plenty of light and have a view of Notre Dame Cathedral and the dome of the Panthéon.

A special feature of your morning routine here is the large breakfast buffet, which includes pastries and croissants baked in the hotel kitchen, fresh fruit, and cereals, as well as such extras as yogurt, ham, sausage, pâté, cheese, and mushrooms.

NOTE: There are several rooms reserved for nonsmokers.

FACILITIES AND SERVICES: Air-conditioning, bar, direct-dial phone with fax and Internet connections in each room, elevator, hair dryer, laundry service, minibar, radio, TV with international reception, room safe (no charge)

NEAREST TOURIST ATTRACTIONS (LEFT BANK): St-Michel, St-Germain-des-Prés, Île de la Cité, Île St-Louis, Seine, shopping

HÔTEL DE CHEVREUSE ★ (63)
3, rue de Chevreuse, 75006
Métro: Vavin
23 rooms, 15 with shower or bath and toilet

Nothing resembles a one-star at the Chevreuse but the prices. A hotel of some sort has been here for fifty years, but it took a new owner with some imagination to turn it into an eye-catching spot where no one need feel they are scrimping in order to stay within budget. It is all well done, from the minute you walk into the reception and lobby, which shows off the owner's penchant for collecting. The room is divided by a bookcase holding a vintage radio, flower vases, and a photo of the hotel as it was. Nearby is a 1930s clock, a trombone made into a floor lamp, and an old hat and umbrella rack next to a church pew. The sofa and chairs are covered in contemporary combinations of blue, white, and yellow. A small breakfast room with four tables and light metal and wood chairs is to one side.

Rooms are simple compositions with open closets, metal chairs, and built-ins. Since in-room showers resemble phone booths, and the shared hall showers are clean, acceptable, and free, you are actually better off and money ahead booking a showerless room. You will be able to improve your French comprehension by watching the French-only television channels, and if you are on the fifth floor, you can keep fit because there is no elevator in the building.

FACILITIES AND SERVICES: Direct-dial phone, TV, office safe (no charge), no elevator (five floors)

NEAREST TOURIST ATTRACTIONS (LEFT BANK): Montparnasse, Jardin du Luxembourg

TELEPHONE
01-43-20-93-16
FAX
01-43-21-43-72
CREDIT CARDS
MC, V
RATES
Single 255F–425F (38.87–64.79€), double 315–555F (48.02–84.61€); *taxe de séjour* 3F (0.46€) per person, per day
BREAKFAST
Continental 40F (6.10€) per person
ENGLISH SPOKEN
Yes

HÔTEL DE FLEURIE ★★★ ($, 25)
32–34, rue Grégoire-de-Tours, 75006
Métro: Mabillon, Odéon
29 rooms, all with shower or bath and toilet

If you enjoy the colorful, round-the-clock atmosphere of St-Germain-des-Prés, then the dynamic Hôtel de Fleurie is for you. This exceptional hotel is owned and managed by the Marolleau family, who for two generations owned Brasserie Balzar (see *Great Eats Paris*). When they sold the brasserie, they bought this down-and-out hotel, and with a year of hard work, they completely transformed it into a delightful three-star.

The facade of the hotel has been restored to its former glory and is embellished with statues that are lighted at

TELEPHONE
Information 01-53-73-70-00; reservations 01-53-73-70-10
FAX
01-53-73-70-20
EMAIL
bonjour@hotel-de-fleurie.tm.fr
INTERNET
www.hotel-de-fleurie.tm.fr
CREDIT CARDS
AE, DC, MC, V

RATES
Single 800–1,000F (121.96–
152.45€), double 900–1,200F
(137.50–182.94€), deluxe room
1,400–1,600F (213.43–
243.92€); family rooms (4
persons) 1,700–1,800F
(259.16–274.41€), extra bed
(only in deluxe rooms) 150F
(22.87€); children under 12
free; *taxe de séjour* included

BREAKFAST
55F (8.38€) per person,
Continental in room or buffet
downstairs; half price for
children under 12

ENGLISH SPOKEN
Yes

night. The lobby and sitting rooms are models of gracious comfort and charm. A spiral staircase leads from the reception desk down to a stone-walled *cave,* where a full buffet is served at tables covered with Provençal prints. Continental breakfasts, which include fresh orange juice, pound cake, and cheese in addition to the usual croissants and fresh bread, are served only in the rooms.

Almost all of the rooms have modern marble bathrooms and a good layout. All are air-conditioned—a welcome relief during the dog days of summer in Paris—and all come equipped with a minibar, remote-controlled television with CNN reception, international hookups for computers, and in the deluxe rooms, terry robes and slippers. Room 60, on the top floor with no elevator access, overlooks a beautiful mosaic-tiled building across the street. Other deluxe choices include Nos. 11, 14, 24, and 34. Nos. 14 and 24 have new bathrooms and *toile de Jouy* wallcovering in red and white. Room 54, a standard double, has a writing table, white cane headboard, lighted mirrored closet in the entry, and heated towel racks in the bathroom. No. 50, with a double bed, has a small window with a view and a pink marble bathroom; it would be nice for a single visitor. For reservations of more than seven nights, the hotel offers a three-day museum pass that enables visitors to bypass the lines at almost every museum and monument in Paris and at Versailles.

FACILITIES AND SERVICES: Air-conditioning, bar, direct-dial phone, international computer hookup in each room, elevator to all but top floor, hair dryer, laundry service, minibar, robes and skuffs in deluxe rooms, TV with international reception, room safe (no charge)

NEAREST TOURIST ATTRACTIONS (LEFT BANK): St-Michel, St-Germain-des-Prés, Île de la Cité, Île St-Louis

HÔTEL DE L'ABBAYE ★★★ ($, 47)
10, rue Cassette, 75006
Métro: St-Sulpice
46 rooms, all with shower or bath and toilet

TELEPHONE
01-45-44-38-11

FAX
01-45-48-07-86

EMAIL
Hotel.abbaye@wanadoo.fr.

INTERNET
www.Hotel-Abbaye.com

CREDIT CARDS
AE, MC, V

In the sixteenth and seventeenth centuries, the Abbaye Saint-Germain was a Catholic convent. Today it is a very special hotel for those who love its quiet location near St-Sulpice, its discreet staff, and its commendable service. The entrance is off the street through fifteen-foot-high green doors that open onto a cobblestone courtyard, where the nuns once gathered before going to chapel for daily prayers. The central reception room is handsomely furnished with magnificent antiques and comfortable sofas centered around a marble fireplace. Behind this is an exquisite salon with intimate seating, a wood-burning fireplace, a profusion of flowers, and a nice bar with big wicker armchairs. The addition of a glassed-in winter and summer garden where breakfast can be served has enhanced the hotel's charm and desirability even more.

Returnees vie for the top-floor terrace suites, with their arched ceilings, fireplaces and rooftop views, or the two ground-floor rooms with private gardens. I like No. 302, a two-level suite with a downstairs sitting room done in rose print wallpaper; it has a tufted leather armchair, comfortable sofa, big writing desk, and large lighted closet. Upstairs, the twin bedroom opens onto its own terrace. No. 303 is another two-level Oriental suite with a wonderful terrace and huge marble bath with plenty of shelf space. Other favorites are No. 11B, a standard twin on the back with brass beds and two windows overlooking ivy-covered walls, No. 4, a twin with its own patio; and No. 32, a nicely appointed, light room with a view over the trees and a sunken bathtub that is just right for one.

Because l'Abbaye is such a unique and outstanding choice, it is higher in price, and it is included for those with flexible budgets who are looking for a romantic Parisian address.

FACILITIES AND SERVICES: Air-conditioning in all rooms and suites, bar, direct-dial phone, elevator, hair dryer, modems, porter, TV with international reception, room service for light snacks, room safe (no charge)

NEAREST TOURIST ATTRACTIONS (LEFT BANK): Latin Quarter, Luxembourg Gardens, St-Germain-des-Prés, St-Sulpice, good shopping

HÔTEL DE L'ODÉON ★★★ ($, 32)
13, rue St-Sulpice, 75006
Métro: Odéon

29 rooms, all with shower or bath and toilet

Hôtel de l'Odéon has become a popular Paris destination for travelers who want luxury and impeccable service in a distinguished hotel that is still small enough to maintain a personal touch. The interior is in the style of a seventeenth-century inn, beautifully blending antique charm and atmosphere with all the modern conveniences

RATES
Single 1,000–1130F (152.45–172.27€), double 1160–1220F (176.84–185.99€), *grande* 1,680–1,750F (256.11–266.79€), suite 2300F (350.63€); *taxe de séjour* included

BREAKFAST
Continental included, cannot be deducted

ENGLISH SPOKEN
Yes

TELEPHONE
01-43-25-70-11

FAX
01-43-29-97-34

EMAIL
hotel.de.lodeon@wanadoo.fr

INTERNET
www.hoteldelodeon.com

CREDIT CARDS
AE, DC, MC, V

RATES
Single 780–900F (118.91–137.20€), double 900–1,300F (137.20–198.18€), triple 1,400–1,500F (213.43–228.67€), family room 1,500F (228.67€); *taxe de séjour* included

BREAKFAST
Continental 65F (9.91€) per person

ENGLISH SPOKEN
Yes

one expects in a top three-star hotel. In the charm department, the Odéon has it all: high beamed ceilings, stunning furniture, massive tapestries, intricately scrolled brass-and-metal beds with hand-crocheted coverlets, skylights, blooming flower boxes under the windows, lovely oil and watercolor paintings hanging throughout, and a manicured atrium garden sitting to one side of the sky-lit breakfast area. On the convenience side, the baths are large and the bedside lighting is good. Double-paned windows keep street noise to a minimum, air-conditioning allows warm-weather comfort, and the closets are large enough for more than the contents of an overnight bag.

FACILITIES AND SERVICES: Air-conditioning, direct-dial phone, elevator (but not in back building), hair dryer, TV with international reception, room safe (no charge)

NEAREST TOURIST ATTRACTIONS (LEFT BANK): St-Michel, St-Germain-des-Prés, Latin Quarter, St-Sulpice, Île de la Cité, Île St-Louis, Luxembourg Gardens

HÔTEL DES ACADÉMIES ★ (62)
15, rue de la Grande Chaumière, 75006
Métro: Vavin

TELEPHONE
01-43-26-66-44

FAX
01-43-26-03-72

CREDIT CARDS
MC, V

RATES
Single 235–380F (35.83–57.93€), double 320–380F (48.78–57.93€); shower 40F (6.10€); dogs free, no cats; *taxe de séjour* included

BREAKFAST
Continental (only bread and jam) 40F (6.10€) per person, in room only

ENGLISH SPOKEN
None

21 rooms, 17 with shower or bath and toilet

When planning your trip to Paris, you may begin to wonder where all the nonmillionaires sleep. Many of them have been sleeping at Hôtel des Académies for years because they do not have to dig too deeply into their pockets to pay the final bill. The owner, Mme. Charles, who was born in the hotel more than eighty years ago and still lives there, runs it with a firm hand, not standing for a *soupçon* of hanky-panky. Assisting her with the welcoming formalities is her dog, Diavolo, which she describes as "sort of a griffin." She is a devoted dog lover and welcomes guests who arrive with their own well-behaved canines.

Her plain, little, upstairs Montparnasse location delivers small but spotless rooms at unheard-of rates to a band of devoted regulars, who keep in touch by sending her postcards and souvenirs that she once proudly displayed in her tiny reception room. On my last visit I noticed that the postcard collection had been replaced by a new telephone system, but most of the knickknacks are still there, along with a cage of songbirds. There are no extras here, and the rooms mix 1950s chrome and plastic with varying color and pattern schemes. But with these breathtakingly low prices, especially for those who are willing to hike a few floors up to save even more money, who cares? Certainly not the generations of families who return year after year making it their home base in Paris.

FACILITIES AND SERVICES: Direct-dial phones, office safe (no charge)

NEAREST TOURIST ATTRACTIONS (LEFT BANK): Montparnasse, Luxembourg Gardens

HÔTEL DU DRAGON (NO STARS, 18)
36, rue du Dragon, 75006
Métro: St-Sulpice, St-Germain-des-Prés, Sèvres-Babylone

28 rooms, 24 with shower and toilet, 4 with shower only

Despite its no-star status and typical industrial carpeting, plastic plants, and calendar art, the Hôtel du Dragon is one of the last outposts for decent budget anchorage in the heart of the Left Bank. Sprinkled throughout the public rooms and in some of the guest rooms in this genuine family-owned cheapie are furnishings that belonged to the owner's grandparents when they started the hotel almost a century ago. The spotless rooms are bedecked in flowered or striped wallpaper and coordinating fabrics that look more up to date than some three-star hotels I could name. Of course, there is no elevator, and if you want air-conditioning, open the window. However, you do get orange juice with your morning baguette and jam (served in your room only), a television in your room, and a warm welcome from the Rabier-Roy family, who have owned the hotel since the 1920s.

The bottom line for prudent sleepers in Paris: You get a great sleep for your money, and today, that is not always easy to find.

FACILITIES AND SERVICES: Direct-dial phone, hair dryer, TV with international reception, office safe (no charge), no elevator (four floors in one part, three in another)

NEAREST TOURIST ATTRACTIONS (LEFT BANK): St-Michel, St-Germain-des-Prés, wonderful shopping and browsing

TELEPHONE
01-45-48-51-05

FAX
01-42-22-51-62

EMAIL
Hotel.Du.Dragon@wanadoo.fr

CREDIT CARDS
AE, MC, V

RATES
Single 295–420F (44.97–64.03€), double 480–540F (73.18–82.32€), triple 650F (99.09€); extra bed 30 percent of room rate; *taxe de séjour* included

BREAKFAST
Continental 40F (6.10€) per person

ENGLISH SPOKEN
Yes

HÔTEL DU LYS ★★ (27)
23, rue Serpente, 75006
Métro: St-Michel, Odéon

TELEPHONE
01-43-26-97-57
FAX
01-44-07-34-90
CREDIT CARDS
MC, V
RATES
Single 520F (79.27€), double
550F (83.85€), triple 690F
(105.19€); *taxe de séjour*
included
BREAKFAST
Continental included, cannot be
deducted
ENGLISH SPOKEN
Generally, yes

22 rooms, all with shower or bath and toilet

For those searching out cost-effective accommodations in Paris, the Hôtel du Lys has more French charm and romantic appeal than many three-star hotels in the area charging almost twice as much. Some readers have written to me complaining about the dark back rooms (which no one can remedy), the need for housekeeping to get busy with Lysol in the bathrooms, and the out-of-date no-credit-card policy. On my latest inspection of the hotel, I found that the owner, Marie-Hélène Decharne, who took over several years ago when her father retired after running the hotel for fifty years, had made some welcome improvements. Most rooms have been redecorated, housekeeping is back on its toes, and MasterCard and Visa are accepted. The location is dynamite, the prices are still in line, and if you hit the right room, your stay should be very nice.

The rooms are done in a cozy French style with beams, a stone wall here and there, and matching bedspreads and curtains. If you are reserving by telephone, please bear in mind that Mme. Decharne is usually at the hotel only on weekday mornings from 9 A.M. to noon. Otherwise, you will probably be dealing with a desk clerk with limited English and authority. When reserving, I would request No. 11, one of the better twin-bedded rooms with a high beamed ceiling and stone wall. Two windows opening onto flowerboxes let in plenty of light, and the room has two chairs, a large armoire, and a blue tiled bath with a nice tub. No. 16, in blue and white, has a new tiled bath with an enclosed shower. I would not request No. 14 because of its strange WC perched on a platform; No. 10, whose only window is in the bathroom; or No. 9, which has a new bathroom but is rather dark, and the TV is pitched from the ceiling above the closet.

FACILITIES AND SERVICES: Direct-dial phone, hair dryer, no elevator (four floors), TV with international reception, office safe (no charge)

NEAREST TOURIST ATTRACTIONS (LEFT BANK): St-Michel, St-Germain-des-Prés, Île de la Cité, Île St-Louis, Latin Quarter

HÔTEL EUGÉNIE ★★ (12)
31, rue St-André-des-Arts, 75006
Métro: St-Michel, Odéon

30 rooms, all with shower or bath and toilet

Situated on one of the busiest pedestrian streets in the very core of old Paris, the Eugénie offers good value for your hotel expenditure, while giving you pulsating, round-the-clock atmosphere in the bargain. The upbeat rooms in blues, greens, and soft maroon have air-conditioning, double-paned windows, and remote-controlled TVs, and they are big enough to turn around in. They are, however, short on luggage, closet, and seating space. The baths have the extras that tend to make a difference: hair dryers, enclosed stall showers or bathtubs with shower shields, and absorbent towels. As you can see, there will be few surprises, but it is a good choice in a popular location within easy walking distance to excellent shopping, sight-seeing, and dining (see *Great Eats Paris*).

FACILITIES AND SERVICES: Air-conditioning, direct-dial phone, elevator, hair dryer, minibar, TV with international reception, safe in room (20F, 3.05€, per day)

NEAREST TOURIST ATTRACTIONS (LEFT BANK): St-Michel, St-Germain-des-Prés, Île de la Cité, Île St-Louis, shopping

TELEPHONE
01-43-26-29-03

FAX
01-43-29-75-60

INTERNET
www.123france.com

CREDIT CARDS
AE, DC, MC, V

RATES
Single 580F (88.42€), double 680–770F (103.67–117.39€), triple 790F (120.43€); *taxe de séjour* 5F (0.76€) per person, per day

BREAKFAST
Continental 45F (6.86€) per person

ENGLISH SPOKEN
Yes

HÔTEL FERRANDI ★★★ ($, 50)
92, rue du Cherche-Midi, 75006
Métro: Vaneau, Falguière

42 rooms, all with shower or bath and toilet

Thoroughly dignified in every way, the hotel is unusually successful in combining the best in old-world style with modern comforts and expectations. The attractive owner, Mme. La Fond, and her exceptional staff are on top of the details that make a difference in a guest's stay. The downstairs sitting area is defined by an ornate marble fireplace and a crystal chandelier. Loads of comfortable chairs, fresh flowers, attractive art, and daily newspapers in French and English create a pleasing place to relax. Stained-glass windows add color to the front hall. The interior hallways, lined with ocher fabric to keep noise to a minimum, are gracefully joined by a winding staircase painted in a faux marble finish.

The rooms, all of which face the front, are furnished with period antiques and are color coordinated in soft shades of blues, browns, and pinks. Most have extra closet and luggage space and are just the ticket for those

TELEPHONE
01-42-22-97-40

FAX
01-45-44-89-97

EMAIL
hotel.ferrandi@wanadoo.fr

INTERNET
www.123france.com

CREDIT CARDS
AE, DC, MC, V

RATES
1–2 persons 640–1,000F (97.57–152.45€), deluxe room 1,300F (198.18€), suite 1,540F (234.77€); *taxe de séjour* 6F (0.91€) per person, per day

BREAKFAST
Continental 65F (9.91€) per person

ENGLISH SPOKEN
Yes

of us who do not travel lightly. For longer stays, I like Room 50, a ground-floor, two-room apartment with a roomy pink marble bathroom, or No. 43, with a four-poster bed, ornamental ceiling, plenty of drawer and closet space, good light, and inviting armchairs. Other favorites are No. 23, with a blue-and-white half-canopy bed, marble fireplace, and massive armoire; and No. 46, a twin or king in blue with a pink marble bathroom. No. 27, with a brass bed, double closet, and single chair, is the least expensive room; it's perfect for one. Some of the bathrooms, especially in the smaller rooms, tend to be cramped, but most are equipped with heated towel racks. Motorists will appreciate the hotel garage, and shoppers will love all the discount shopping stores within easy reach.

FACILITIES AND SERVICES: Air-conditioning, bar, direct-dial phone, elevator to four floors, hair dryer, laundry service, some minibars, modems, private parking (125F, 19.06€, per day, must reserve ahead), TV with international reception, office safe (no charge)

NEAREST TOURIST ATTRACTIONS (LEFT BANK): Montparnasse, Luxembourg Gardens, Bon Marché department store, good discount shopping (close)

HÔTEL LE BRÉA ★★★ (59)
14, rue Bréa, 75006
Métro: Vavin, Notre-Dame-des-Champs
23 rooms, all with shower or bath and toilet

TELEPHONE	01-43-25-44-41
FAX	01-44-07-19-25
CREDIT CARDS	AE, DC, MC, V
RATES	Single 750F (114.34€), double 820F (125.01€), triple 950F (144.83€), extra bed 100F (15.24€); *taxe de séjour* 6F (0.91€) per person, per day
BREAKFAST	Buffet 60F (9.15€) per person
ENGLISH SPOKEN	Yes

The floral theme of this attractive Montparnasse hotel starts the minute you enter the streetside orange-and-yellow sitting room, which has a framed art collage of rose petals and a big bouquet of silk red poppies in the window. Further charm is added by a marble-framed black metal fireplace and a terra cotta tiled bar facing a winter garden. The small, compact rooms have all been redone in yellow and blue and reflect good taste and three-star comforts. Two rooms (Nos. 7 and 8) open onto the garden. Number 7 is a small yellow double with a stall shower; No. 8, a king, has slightly more space, but for some the twelve steps down a narrow spiral stairway to reach the bathroom would not be appealing. Room 11, a twin on the courtyard, has a large bathroom with good lighting; No. 14, a double on the street, has the advantage of a bathtub and more luggage space.

FACILITIES AND SERVICES: Air-conditioning, bar, direct-dial phone, elevator in front building, hair dryer, laundry service, TV with international reception, room safe (no charge)

NEAREST TOURIST ATTRACTIONS (LEFT BANK): Montparnasse, Jardin du Luxembourg

HÔTEL LE CLOS MÉDICIS ★★★ ($, 40)
56, rue Monsieur-le-Prince, 75006
Métro: Odéon, Luxembourg
38 rooms, all with shower or bath and toilet

In 1773, this was a residence built for the Médicis family. Two centuries later it is a hotel displaying dignified good taste from top to bottom. The masculine-style rooms are named after famous French vintage wines. Each one has a large animal print on the wall, is handsomely furnished with sleek mahogany built-ins, and trimmed in navy, red, and brown. All the beds have duvet covers, the computer-friendly work spaces are excellent, and the tiled bathrooms are ample. Another nice feature is the hotel garden and the bar that faces it. The stone-walled sitting area has a pair of blue armchairs facing a double-sided glass fireplace and a sofa and more armchairs under the window. The hospitable staff is never too busy or rushed to handle the needs and requests of the guests.

FACILITIES AND SERVICES: Air-conditioning, bar, direct-dial phone, hair dryer, elevator, laundry service, modems, terry robes in most rooms, TV with international reception, office or room safe (no charge)

NEAREST TOURIST ATTRACTIONS (LEFT BANK): Jardin du Luxembourg, St-Germain-des-Prés; St-Michel, Musée de Cluny, Panthéon

TELEPHONE
01-43-29-10-80

FAX
01-43-54-26-90

EMAIL
clos_medicis@compuserve.com

INTERNET
www.closmedicis.com

CREDIT CARDS
AE, DC, MC, V

RATES
Single 800F (121.96€), double 900–1,000F (137.20–152.45€), deluxe 1,100F (167.69€), triple 1,250F (190.56€), duplex 1,250F (190.56€); *taxe de séjour* included

BREAKFAST
Buffet 65F (9.91€) per person

ENGLISH SPOKEN
Yes

HÔTEL LEFT BANK SAINT-GERMAIN ★★★ ($, 23) ✗
9, rue de l'Ancienne Comédie, 75006
Métro: Odéon
31 rooms, all with shower or bath and toilet

It is hard to imagine a small hotel in Paris more appealing than this one, which is, quite frankly, just the sort of hotel that will make anyone fall in love with Paris forever.

Located in the ever-popular St-Germain *quartier* and convenient to everything, it is run by Claude Teil and his family, who also operate the Hôtel Lido in the eighth arrondissement (see page 183). It is therefore no surprise to find the Hôtel Left Bank Saint-Germain just as beautiful, from the entrance where guests all admire an adorable antique baby carriage filled with authentically

TELEPHONE
01-43-54-01-70; toll-free in the U.S. and Canada, 800-528-1234 (Best Western)

FAX
01-43-26-17-14

EMAIL
LB@paris-hotels-charm.com

INTERNET
www.paris-hotels-charm.com

CREDIT CARDS
AE, DC, MC, V

RATES
Single 1,120F (170.74€),
double 1,400F (213.43€), triple
1,550F (236.30€), quad 1,700F
(259.16€); suite 1,860F
(283.56€); extra bed 100F
(15.24€); *taxe de séjour* 6F
(0.91€) per person, per day
BREAKFAST
Continental or buffet included,
cannot be deducted
ENGLISH SPOKEN
Yes

dressed vintage dolls to the large top-floor suite with dormer window views onto Notre Dame, Centre Georges Pompidou (Beaubourg), and Ste-Chapelle. To add to the overall allure, there are fresh flowers everywhere, museum-quality Aubusson tapestries, polished antiques mixed with special handmade furnishings from Perigord, excellent eighteenth-century reproductions, open oak beams, stone walls, and a very helpful, English-speaking staff.

The standard-size rooms are done in rich paisley prints with built-in minibars and room safes. The bathrooms are excellent and the courtyard views pleasant. For my hotel money, the suites and larger doubles are the best choices because they have alcove seating with soft armchairs, desk space, larger baths, and loads of out-of-sight storage space. In Suite 604, one window on the pitched roof has a tip-toe view of the Eiffel Tower, and at the other end of the room, the view is of Notre Dame, Beaubourg, and Ste-Chapelle. As you can see, I am sold on this hotel as a wonderful choice for those with more flexible budgets.

FACILITIES AND SERVICES: Air-conditioning, bar, direct-dial phone, elevator, hair dryer, minibar, TV with international reception, laundry service, room safe (50F, 7.62€, per stay)

NEAREST TOURIST ATTRACTIONS (LEFT BANK): St-Michel, St-Germain-des-Prés, Île de la Cité, Île St-Louis, wonderful shopping

HÔTEL LE RÉGENT ★★★ ($, 6)
61, rue Dauphine, 75006
Métro: Odéon

TELEPHONE
01-46-34-59-80
FAX
01-40-51-05-07
EMAIL
Hotel.leregent@wanadoo.fr
INTERNET
www.paris.com
CREDIT CARDS
AE, DC, MC, V
RATES
1–2 persons 780–1,200F
(118.91–182.94€); extra bed
200F (30.49€); lower rates in
off-season; *taxe de séjour* 6F
(0.91€) per person, per day

25 rooms, all with shower or bath and toilet

For Parisian atmosphere in a setting of nonstop activity, it is hard to top the Régent, which offers guests traditional charm in a renovated eighteenth-century building. Fresh flowers and green plants add soft touches to the stone entry and reception areas, which are decorated with antiques and tapestry-covered chairs. A selection of Deux Magots teas, jams, champagne, and dishes is for sale in a display case . . . and why not, both the famed café and this hotel are under the same ownership. The downstairs breakfast room has pink linen cloths and a fresh bouquet on each table. It is a nice place to read the *International Herald Tribune* or *Le Figaro* while enjoying breakfast.

All the rooms are well maintained and have the creature comforts most deem necessary, with the added bonus of terry robes (which are available upon request) and trouser presses. The bathrooms are modern, but the real showstoppers are in the rooms on the highest floors. For one of the prettiest pink-tiled bathrooms in Paris, request Room 52. No. 41, a large twin with three windows, also has an outstanding spacious bathroom with monogrammed towels, a lighted magnifying mirror, and a deep glass-enclosed tub and shower. Just like it is Room 11, which is in green and rust on the first floor; however, because it faces front, guests should expect some street noise. Room 53 is a wood-paneled twin with a view to the top of Notre Dame. If I had to pick a favorite room, I would select No. 62, nestled under the eaves on the sixth floor. From the room, you can see Notre Dame Cathedral. Sitting on the balcony you look over the rooftops to La Tour Montparnasse. The staff, aided by the hotel mascot, a white ball of fluff named Mirabelle, is very pleasant. It should be noted, however, that they are unable to promise specific rooms, but will note special requests and do their best to accommodate them.

FACILITIES AND SERVICES: Air-conditioning, direct-dial phone, elevator from first floor (but not to dining room), hair dryer, laundry service, minibar, TV with international reception, terry robes upon request, trouser press and magnifying mirrors in some rooms, room safe (no charge)

NEAREST TOURIST ATTRACTIONS (LEFT BANK): St-Michel, St-Germain-des-Prés, Île de la Cité, Île St-Louis

BREAKFAST
Continental 65F (9.91€) per person

ENGLISH SPOKEN
Yes

HÔTEL LE RELAIS MÉDICIS ★★★ ($, 37)
23, rue Racine, 75006
Métro: Odéon, Cluny–La Sorbonne
16 rooms, all with shower or bath and toilet

The jury is still out on whether heaven is as divine as a stay at Le Relais Médicis. I will admit it was love at first sight the minute I walked into this picture-perfect dream hotel, where something artistic and imaginative catches your eye at every turn—it might be a humorous bench with black bears carved on each end, or the antique metal toys and Italian Majolica spice jars displayed behind the desk. The total look of the hotel is characteristically French, with the mix of patterns, shapes, sizes, and colors all adding up to a stunning visual effect. In the lush salon, lovely oil paintings are set off by deep red

TELEPHONE
01-43-26-00-60

FAX
01-40-46-83-39

CREDIT CARDS
AE, DC, MC, V

RATES
Single 1,300–1,570F (198.18–239.34€), double 1,360–1,570F (207.33–239.34€), deluxe 1,680F (256.11€); lower rates in off-season; *taxe de séjour* included

BREAKFAST
Continental included, cannot be deducted
ENGLISH SPOKEN
Yes

fabric-covered walls and antique birdcages, which add a light touch. Garden paintings define the springtime feel of the breakfast room, where even the lights reflect the floral theme. Vintage black-and-white photos displayed throughout the halls of the hotel add notes of interest.

Two lifts take guests to the sixteen floral-themed bedrooms, all of which I could live in happily for a long Parisian stay. For instance, in No. 22 you are surrounded by soft greens and corals, with floral dust ruffles complementing the cotton bedspreads. An enviable display of turn-of-the-century colored prints of young women and children are offset by a solo modern painting. The marble bath has reproduction antique chrome fittings and the mirrored wardrobe is large enough to hold everything you brought with you. In Room 36, a deluxe double with twin beds, there is a sofa and a comfortable chair, four windows, and an interesting painting of a bridge scene, divided into four panels. A huge double bookcase occupies one wall, and a dive-drawer marble dresser another. If you occupy the quiet and secluded double-bedded No. 39, the color scheme is a soft orange sorbet, and the view is of the buildings across the way. Frankly feminine, No. 26 is a cheerful, large, beamed room with twin beds, three windows, and an adorable old desk. Colors and fabrics are coordinated in a garden motif; decorative accents include a gold clock and an assortment of old tins. Room 24 is a smaller double with a five-drawer marble-topped dresser. The mirrored wall gives the illusion of more space in this room, which is still big enough to accommodate a round table and two chairs, the perfect place to enjoy a Continental breakfast.

FACILITIES AND SERVICES: Air-conditioning, bar, direct-dial phone, elevator, hair dryer, laundry service, minibar, TV with international reception, room safe (no charge), *peignoirs* (bathrobes) in all rooms, porter

NEAREST TOURIST ATTRACTIONS (LEFT BANK): St-Michel, St-Germain-des-Prés, Luxembourg Gardens, Île de la Cité, Île St-Louis, shopping

HÔTEL LE SAINT-GRÉGOIRE ★★★★ ($, 51)
43, rue de l'Abbé Grégoire, 75006
Métro: St-Placide

TELEPHONE
01-45-48-23-23
FAX
01-45-48-33-95
EMAIL
hotel@saintgregoire.com

20 rooms, all with shower or bath and toilet

Everyone raves about it because on all counts the Hôtel le Saint-Grégoire is a stunning hotel. I will warn you: after one or two nights at this hotel, you will face a dilemma—you will wish you never had to leave Paris.

Though a star has been added since the last edition, making this the only four-star hotel in the book, the prices did not increase significantly. It is, admittedly, on the high side in peak season, but I can assure you it is one of the most popular Big Splurges in the book because so many readers believe it is worth the extra money, not only for the comfort and surroundings, but for the welcome and assistance extended by the staff, skillfully headed by M. François de Béné.

The color scheme is purple, yellow, orange, red, and beige . . . and it works. Decorator David Hicks has created an elegantly intimate atmosphere in this twenty-room hotel by mixing period antiques with handsome modern pieces and sprinkling interesting fabrics, patterned throw rugs, and rich silks throughout a garden setting. As a result, the hotel has a feeling of well-being, from the fireplace in the rose-filled lobby to the linen-clad tables in the *cave* dining room, where freshly squeezed orange juice and yogurt are served with the Continental breakfast.

Please forward all mail to me care of Room 100, a bright yellow, ground-floor double opening onto a small garden. It has a marble-topped coffeetable, a bureau large enough to hold the contents of my suitcase, and two comfortable chairs for lazy late-night reading. The bath has heated towel racks and enough towels to last (almost) forever. If this room is not available, I would be supremely happy in either No. 102, a junior suite, also on a garden—which has its own entryway leading to a large room with a sofa, two easy chairs, and a table at one end—or No. 16, a large room with a terrace on the back of the hotel. No. 14 is a pink double, also with its own terrace, and just perfect if you are alone. Families can request that Rooms 24 and 26 be combined. No. 24 is a small, peach-colored room with a wall hat rack; No. 26 is a larger double with a nice writing table, armoire, and black marble-topped dresser, and it has a light bath with a separate enclosed toilet.

FACILITIES AND SERVICES: Air-conditioning in most rooms, bar, direct-dial phone, elevator, hair dryer, laundry service, TV with international reception, office safe (no charge)

NEAREST TOURIST ATTRACTIONS (LEFT BANK): Luxembourg Gardens, discount shopping, Montparnasse, Bon Marché department store

INTERNET
www.hotelsaintgregoire.com

CREDIT CARDS
AE, DC, MC, V

RATES
1–2 persons: standard 900F (137.20€), superior 1,100F (167.69€); suite and rooms with private terrace 1,500F (228.67€); extra bed 100F (15.24€); dog 80F (12.20€); lower rates in off-season; *taxe de séjour* included

BREAKFAST
Continental 65F (9.91€) per person

ENGLISH SPOKEN
Yes

HÔTEL NOVANOX ★★★ (64)

TELEPHONE
01-46-33-63-60

FAX
01-43-26-61-72

INTERNET
www.hotel-novanox.com

CREDIT CARDS
AE, DC, MC, V

RATES
1–2 persons 580–750F (88.42–
114.34€); extra bed 150F
(22.87€); ask for special
weekend rates; *taxe de séjour*
included

BREAKFAST
Continental 60F (9.15€) per
person

ENGLISH SPOKEN
Yes

155, boulevard du Montparnasse, 75006
Métro: Vavin, Raspail, Port Royal
27 rooms, all with shower or bath and toilet

From the outside it doesn't inspire. But inside, the future beckons at the Novanox, an impressive example of what a sense of style and a great imagination—with a little money thrown in—can do. Hats off to owner Bertrand Plasmans, who, several years ago, gambled everything and took an old hotel and fashioned a modern re-creation with the latest designs and contemporary craftsmanship. The yellow-and-blue lobby, with dangling mobile lights, reminds me of a playful fairyland—everywhere you look the faces of Greek gods and goddesses are softly painted on the walls and depicted on the upholstered chairs and couches. At one end of the lobby is a breakfast area overlooking an enclosed, plant-rimmed sidewalk terrace. Dainty croissants and buttery brioches fill the breakfast baskets and are accompanied by an assortment of jams and a pot of sweet butter. A portion of cheese and fresh fruit complement the meal.

The rooms upstairs have a pastel color scheme, with contemporary furniture specially built to fit the design of each room. The toiletries are from Roger and Gallet, the fresh flowers from the owner's mother's garden, the lamps from Spain, the carpet imported from Germany, and the ideas all from M. Plasmans. The result? Still *magnifique*!

His latest hotel acquisition is the Hôtel Saint-Thomas d'Aquin, a two-star in the seventh arrondissement, which he plans to redo. It's located at 3, rue du Pré-Aux-Clercs; Tel: 01-42-61-01-22.

FACILITIES AND SERVICES: Bar, direct-dial phone, elevator, hair dryer, laundry service, minibar, TV with international reception, room safe (no charge)

NEAREST TOURIST ATTRACTIONS (LEFT BANK): Montparnasse

HÔTEL SAINT-ANDRÉ-DES-ARTS ★ (11)

TELEPHONE
01-43-26-96-16

FAX
01-43-29-73-34

EMAIL
hsaintand@minitel.net

INTERNET
www.france-hotel-guide.com

66, rue St-André-des-Arts, 75006
Métro: Odéon
32 rooms, all with shower or toilet

The Saint-André-des-Arts continues to improve—well, sort of. While some of the airless, trainlike bathrooms with hot red toilet seats are still in use, some more enjoyable stretch tubs have been included in a few of the new bathrooms. Various rooms have also had quickie face-lifts (that is, a coat of paint has been slapped on). Much also stays the same. The carved misericord, which priests used to sit on and lean against during long masses, continues to grace the entry, along with a row of raffia stools under the window, an exhausted black leather sofa, and two folding tables—one of which holds a TV with a stack of CDs on top and another holds the CD player. Most importantly, the friendly manager still stands behind his ruling philosophy, "We are a hotel without extras, including the charges."

The location is strategic, the prices low, and the nonconventional crowd of fashion groupies, hip musicians, budding actors, and starving backpackers is party-loving and carefree. For some people, the rooms are so small that cabin fever sets in immediately. Others may object to the unpleasant symphony of noises drifting through the walls at all hours or to the dim-watt lights dangling from the ceilings. Nonsmokers won't appreciate that maids are allowed to smoke on the job. None of that matters to the devoted regulars, for whom this wrinkled hotel still has a tattered charm they love to romanticize and an attitude by the management they eagerly applaud.

FACILITIES AND SERVICES: Direct-dial phone, no elevator, hair dryer available, TV in most rooms or by request, office safe (no charge)

NEAREST TOURIST ATTRACTIONS (LEFT BANK): St-Michel, St-Germain-des-Prés, Île de la Cité, Île St-Louis

CREDIT CARDS
MC, V

RATES
Single 420F (64.03€), double 510F (77.75€), triple 620F (94.52€), quad 690F (105.19€); *taxe de séjour* included

BREAKFAST
Continental included (no croissants), cannot be deducted

ENGLISH SPOKEN
Yes

HÔTEL SAINT-GERMAIN-DES-PRÉS ★★★ ($, 3)
36, rue Bonaparte, 75006
Métro: St-Germain-des-Prés
30 rooms, all with shower or bath and toilet

The Saint-Germain-des-Prés is the kind of small hotel everyone hopes to find in Paris. Superbly located in the very *coeur* of St-Germain, only a minute or two from two of the most famous cafés—Les Deux Magots and Café Flore—it has a long history of famous guests. It began in 1778 as a Masonic lodge to which Voltaire, Benjamin Franklin, and U.S. Navy captain John Paul Jones belonged. After it became a hotel, it housed philosopher Auguste Comte, American playwright Elmer Rice, and authors Henry Miller and Janet Flanner. Ms. Flanner lived here for years and wrote her "Letters from Paris" column for the *New Yorker* from her top-floor suite.

TELEPHONE
01-43-26-00-19

FAX
01-40-46-83-63

EMAIL
Hotel-Saint-Germain-des-Pres@wanadoo.fr

INTERNET
www.hotel-st-ger.com

CREDIT CARDS
AE, MC, V

RATES
1–2 persons 830–1,070F (126.53–163.12€), deluxe 1,400F (213.43€), suite 1,750F (266.79€); *taxe de séjour* 6F (0.91€) per person, per day

BREAKFAST
Continental included, cannot be deducted

ENGLISH SPOKEN
Yes

The hotel is known for its lovely displays of fresh flowers, which are massed everywhere, from the entryway with its Venetian glass chandelier and hand-painted celestial ceiling to the antique- and tapestry-filled salon overlooking a walled garden filled with blooming hydrangeas and azaleas. The individualized rooms have hand-painted doors and are done in dark woods, with fabric-covered walls, brass beds, and good lighting. The quiet suites face the courtyard. With their separate sitting rooms, they are captivating, especially No. 26, which has Oriental rugs tossed on polished wooden floors, a canopy bed, leaded-glass windows, flower boxes, and a marble bath with Art Nouveau lights and fixtures. Space is well used in No. 25, a double on the back where built-in closets frame the bed; a small desk, chair, and luggage bench offer comfort. Air-conditioning in all the rooms is an added bonus on hot days in this noisy part of Paris.

The hotel's deserved popularity today is due in no small measure to the thoughtfulness of the staff members, who go to great lengths to cater to the needs of their guests. Everyone who stays here agrees that it is definitely worth the Big Splurge.

FACILITIES AND SERVICES: Air-conditioning, bar, direct-dial phone, elevator, hair dryer, laundry service, minibar, modems, robes and slippers in suites and deluxe rooms, room service for light meals, TV with international reception, room safe (no charge)

NEAREST TOURIST ATTRACTIONS (LEFT BANK): Latin Quarter, St-Germain-des-Prés, Île de la Cité, Île St-Louis, wonderful shopping

HÔTEL SAINT-PAUL ★★★ (38)
43, rue Monsieur-le-Prince, 75006
Métro: Odéon, Cluny–La Sorbonne

31 rooms, all with shower or bath and toilet

TELEPHONE
01-43-26-98-64

FAX
01-46-34-58-60

EMAIL
hotel.saint.paule@wanadoo.fr

INTERNET
www.france-hotel-guide.com

CREDIT CARDS
AE, DC, MC, V

In the seventeenth century, this building served as a hostel for Franciscan monks. For the last forty years, it has been a hotel owned by the Hawkins family and is now competently run by their daughter, Marianne, who is ably assisted by an accommodating staff and the black-and-white house cat, Spoutnick. The family's collection of antiques, Oriental rugs, and watercolor paintings has been used in the hotel with elegant results. The seasonal fresh flower bouquets that grace the public areas are grown and arranged by one of the housekeepers, who has been with the hotel for over two decades.

Custom-made curtains, fabric-covered walls, and interesting brass and four-poster beds combine with modern baths to create the pleasing rooms. There are four rooms similar to No. 31, a single overlooking the garden and done in beige grass cloth with a white brass bed. No. 14 has a high ceiling that accommodates a four-poster bed with a tapestry-covered headboard and matching canopy. Twin sleigh beds and plenty of sunshine add to the enjoyment of Room 43, located on the front of the hotel. One of my favorites is No. 51, done in yellow. Situated under the eaves, it has a cozy bedroom with a small sitting room and a bird's-eye view of École de Médecine. For those insisting on total calm, No. 36 on the back is a pretty choice, with its adorable brass bed, big bath, lovely old beams, and open window framing a big tree and rooftop garden across the way.

FACILITIES AND SERVICES: Air-conditioning in some rooms, direct-dial phone, elevator, hair dryer, laundry service, minibar, TV with international reception, room safe (no charge)

NEAREST TOURIST ATTRACTIONS (LEFT BANK): Luxembourg Gardens, St-Germain-des-Prés, St-Michel, Panthéon

RATES
Single 760–860F (115.86–131.11€), double 860–970F (131.11–147.88€), suite (1–4 persons) 1,080–1,390F (164.64–211.90€); *taxe de séjour* included

BREAKFAST
Continental 65F (9.91€), American (two eggs and ham) 85F (12.96€), per person

ENGLISH SPOKEN
Yes

HÔTEL SAINT-PIERRE ★★ (36)
4, rue de l'École de Médecine, 75006
Métro: Odéon, Cluny–La Sorbonne

50 rooms, all with shower or bath and sink, 25 also with toilet

If you want a central Latin Quarter location without spending big bucks to get it, the Saint-Pierre, next to the École de Médecine, is a smart bet. Gone are the usual budget two-star sagging mattresses in the rooms and the garage-sale-reject furniture in the lobby. Here in blazing color are orange halls with simulated stained-glass windows achieved by pasting colored paper over bubbled opaque glass. Twin beds are available and so are stall showers with doors, double-glazed windows appear where necessary, and they provide international television reception. The unexciting bedrooms will inspire you to leave early and return late, spending your time discovering Paris, not snoozing away the afternoon. The rooms pay homage to plain plastics and oddly matched colors, but they are always neat and well maintained and have decent closet and luggage space. Avoid rooms ending in the number 5. They are near the noisy elevator and its slamming door. Management keeps a tight lid on loud voices and carry-in food.

TELEPHONE
01-46-34-78-80

FAX
01-40-51-05-17

CREDIT CARDS
AE, DC, MC, V

RATES
Single 355–480F (54.12–73.18€), double 375–525F (57.17–80.04€), triple 475–610F (72.41–92.99€); *taxe de séjour* included

BREAKFAST
Continental 35F (5.34€) per person

ENGLISH SPOKEN
Yes

FACILITIES AND SERVICES: Direct-dial phone, elevator, hair dryer, minibar in some rooms, TV with international reception, office safe (no charge)

NEAREST TOURIST ATTRACTIONS (LEFT BANK): Latin Quarter, St-Michel, St-Germain-des-Prés, Île de la Cité, Île St-Louis, Luxembourg Gardens

PENSION LES MARRONNIERS (NO STARS, 57)
78, rue d'Assas (first floor on right, stairway A), 75006
Métro: Vavin, Notre-Dame-des-Champs
12 rooms, 1 with shower and toilet

TELEPHONE
01-43-26-37-71

FAX
01-43-26-07-72

EMAIL
o_marro@club-Internet.fr

INTERNET
www.pension-marronniers.com

CREDIT CARDS
None, cash only

RATES
Single 180–400F (27.44–60.98€), double 340–500F (51.83–76.22€); special rates for long stays; *taxe de séjour* 1F (0.15€) per person, per day

BREAKFAST
Included; dinner is also included; neither can be deducted

ENGLISH SPOKEN
Yes

The days of family-run pensions in France, and especially in Paris, are numbered, according to a documentary on the subject filmed here. This *incroyable* cheap sleep, across the street from one of the entrances to the Luxembourg Gardens, is presided over by Marie Poirier, whose family members have been here since the turn of the century. At the Pension les Marronniers, the philanthropically low prices include not only a Continental breakfast but a three-course dinner with cheese. With advance notice, special dietary needs can be catered for. Students, Frenchmen from the provinces doing a work-study program, and smart budgeteers fill this third-floor walk-up home, which has the Laura Ashley decorating seal of approval in the dining and living rooms, complete with Jimi, the house cat asleep in the most comfortable chair or sunniest window ledge, and the two dogs, Mel, a black sheepdog, and Strat, a noisy Yorkie in charge of providing a friendly welcome. The bedrooms might seem primitive to many, but all are cleaned on a regular basis, and the linens changed weekly. Reservations are absolutely essential months in advance, and guests who stay for a long time are preferred. Meals are part of the program and cannot be deducted for any reason.

FACILITIES AND SERVICES: Some direct-dial phones, some minibars, TV and video in lounge, office safe (no charge), no elevator

NEAREST TOURIST ATTRACTIONS (LEFT BANK): Montparnasse, Luxembourg Gardens

WELCOME HÔTEL ★★ (21)
66, rue de Seine, at boulevard St-Germain, 75006
Métro: Odéon, Mabillion, St-Germain-des-Prés
30 rooms, all with shower or bath and toilet

Unpretentious rooms in a fun-filled location are combined with moderate prices to make a stay here more than welcome. Composed of thirty rooms on six floors, this spot on the corner of rue de Seine and boulevard St-Germain is directly across from the picturesque rue de Buci street *marché*. Because many of the rooms are on the small side, and so are the closets, it is an especially suitable stopover for singles. Those wanting more spacious accommodations should ask for a corner room with a view (Nos. 21, 51, or 53). The best is No. 53, done in pink. The plus here is the large bath (for this hotel) with a tub and shower nozzle above. Other popular picks are No. 54, the best single because it has a writing table and a view, and No. 62, an attic nest with beams and a peaked ceiling. The worst is No. 64, with an open closet and windows too high to see out. Despite double windows, quiet is not the rule here. For the least noisy bunks, request rooms that face rue de Seine (Nos. 21 or 51), not on boulevard St-Germain. Top-floor rooms can get hot and stuffy in warm weather, but they are very desirable otherwise.

In the past, the reception staff has been outgoing and helpful. On my last visit, this was definitely not the case. I hope the hotel will not fall victim to an indifferent staff, as two others under the same ownership have, and as a result are no longer mentioned in these pages (Hôtel des Marronniers and Hôtel du Continent).

FACILITIES AND SERVICES: Direct-dial phone, elevator, TV, office safe (no charge)

NEAREST TOURIST ATTRACTIONS (LEFT BANK): St-Michel, St-Germain-des-Prés, Île de la Cité, Île St-Louis, Luxembourg Gardens, shopping

TELEPHONE
01-46-34-24-80

FAX
01-40-46-81-59

CREDIT CARDS
MC, V

RATES
Single 435–510F (66.32–77.75€), double 565–615F (86.13–93.76€); *taxe de séjour* included

BREAKFAST
Continental 50F (7.62€) per person

ENGLISH SPOKEN
Yes

Seventh Arrondissement

Assemblée Nationale, Champ-de-Mars, École Militaire, Eiffel Tower, Invalides, Musée d'Orsay, Rodin Museum, UNESCO

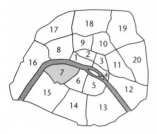

Known affectionately as "Seventh Heaven," this quiet, luxurious residential area is full of stately mansions built before the Revolution and now occupied by embassies, government offices, well-to-do Parisians, and expatriates. The Champ-de-Mars served as the parade ground for the École Militaire and is the backyard of the Eiffel Tower. Les Invalides is the home of four world-famous military museums and is the final resting place of Napoléon Bonaparte. For antique shopping, stroll along the quai Voltaire and rue du Bac. Further west are *les egouts* . . . the sewers of Paris, which date from the Second Empire and were designed by Baron Haussmann. If you are interested in experiencing *les egouts,* the museum at 93, quai d'Orsay runs guided tours.

HOTELS IN THE SEVENTH ARRONDISSEMENT

($) indicates a Big Splurge

GRAND HÔTEL LÉVÊQUE ★★ (13)
29, rue Cler, 75007
Métro: École-Militaire, Latour-Maubourg

50 rooms, 45 with shower and toilet, 5 singles with sink only

Committed cheap sleepers who like the seventh arrondissement love the Lévêque. Located among the colorful food shops that line the rue Cler, it is close to all the things that one often forgets are so important on a trip: banks, a post office, good transportation, do-it-yourself laundries, cleaners, well-priced shops, cafés for a midmorning cup of hot chocolate, a street *marché*, and several exceptional cheese shops and *charcuteries* to tempt picnickers.

The hotel has benefited from yearly improvements and now boasts a glass lift and spiffy, no-nonsense rooms complete with ceiling fan, hair dryer, cable TV, modem, an individual safe, and private shower and toilet in all but five singles. Closets and shelves are spacious enough, but drawer space is nonexistent. Carpets should be upgraded. The owner told me that clients leave behind too many things in drawers, so he just eliminated them altogether. Best rooms definitely face the front. Three on the fifth floor have balconies where you can observe the wonderful street scene below. In Nos. 51 and 52, you can lie in bed and see the Eiffel Tower. The hotel is always busy, and I predict it will be even more in demand thanks to the many improvements. So, if you are interested, book ahead at least one month, and more during peak periods.

FACILITIES AND SERVICES: Direct-dial phone with private number, elevator, fans, hair dryer, modems, TV with international reception, room safe (20F, 3.05€, per stay)

NEAREST TOURIST ATTRACTIONS (LEFT BANK): Champ-de-Mars Park, Eiffel Tower, good shopping, lively street *marché*

TELEPHONE
01-47-05-49-15

FAX
01-45-50-49-36

EMAIL
info@hotel-leveque.com

INTERNET
www.hotel-leveque.com

CREDIT CARDS
AE, MC, V

RATES
Single 325F (49.55€), double 425–500F (64.79–76.22€), triple 650F (99.09€); free showers; *taxe de séjour* 5F (0.76€) per person, per day

BREAKFAST
Continental 45F (6.86€) per person

ENGLISH SPOKEN
Yes

Seine

Pont des Invalides

Quai   d'Orsay

Rue Maubourg

l'Université

Quai   Branly

Rue   de   la   Bourdonnais

Rue   de

R. Monttessuy

Avenue   Rapp

Avenue

Rue Malar

Surcouf

Rue   la   Tour

• 1

▲ 2

3 •

Dominique

Av. Sacy

Av. de la Bourdonnais

Pont d'Iéna

Quai

TOUR
EIFFEL

Av. G. Eiffel

Av. Anatole

Av. Pierre

PARC DU CHAMP DE

Bouvard

R. Sedillot

Rue de l'Exposition

R. Augereau

Rue

R. Amélie

Saint

Rue

Rue   Bosquet

Grenelle

10 •

de

• 11

Latour
Maubourg

M

• 9

12 • • 13

▲ 14

Cler

Av. Gréard

Avenue   Charles

Avenue   de   France

Av. L

Floquet

Av. C. Risier

MARS

Avenue   de   la   Bourdonnais

R. du Champs de Mars

16 •

• 15

17 •

18 • ▲

Rue   Chevert

• 19

Boulevard

HÔTEL
DES
INVALIDES

• 20

École
Militaire   M

Av. de la Motte Picquet

Rue

• 21

• 22

Avenue de Tourville

PL.
VAUBAN

Rue de la   Fédération

Rue Desaix

Rue

Avenue

de

Suffren

Rue Dupleix

PLACE JOFFRE

ÉCOLE
MILITAIRE

Avenue   Lowendal

Rue   Ségur

Av.

de

de   Saxe

Breteuil

d'Estrées

de

Duquesne

Avenue

Dupleix

M

Boulevard

de

Av. de la Motte Picquet

La Motte Picquet
Grenelle   M

Grenelle

Avenue   de

Avenue   de

Av.   de

28 ▲

PLACE
DE
BRETEUIL

Rue

Fondary

Rue

Fremicourt

Nivert

Cambronne

PLACE
CAMBRONNE   M

Boulevard

Suffren   M Ségur

Av. Émile
Zola   M

Rue   de   la   Croix

Garibaldi

Sèvres
Lecourbe

M

Rue

△
N

500 meters

M Métro Station

● R.E.R. Station

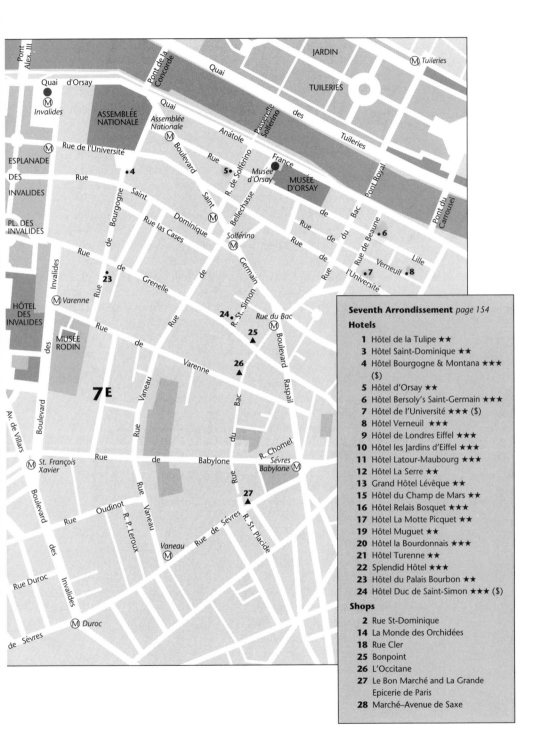

HÔTEL BERSOLY'S SAINT-GERMAIN ★★★ (6)
28, rue de Lille, 75007
Métro: Rue du Bac, St-Germain-des-Prés

16 rooms, all with shower or bath and toilet

TELEPHONE
01-42-60-73-79

FAX
01-49-27-05-55

EMAIL
bersolys@easynet.fr

INTERNET
www.france-hotel-guide.com

CREDIT CARDS
AE, DC, MC, V

RATES
Single 650–750F (99.09–
114.34€), double 700–800F
(106.71–121.96€); pet 100F
(15.24€) per day; *taxe de séjour*
included

BREAKFAST
Continental 55F(8.38€) per
person

ENGLISH SPOKEN
Yes

Bersoly's Saint-Germain continues to be a very good value three-star, which has been owned since the mid-1980s by Mme. Carbonn. The old stone walls and floors in the lobby are clean and polished, and the two breakfast rooms downstairs—one in a bistro style and the other in an Oriental motif—are attractive. Then there is the location: only minutes away from the Musée d'Orsay, the Louvre, serious shopping, and equally serious restaurants (see *Great Eats Paris*).

Every air-conditioned bedroom has been named for a famous French artist. In each case, a reproduction of one of that artist's paintings hangs in the room, and the mood and color scheme of the room are taken from the painting. If you like bold reds and black, request the ground-floor Picasso room, with its entrance off the atrium. If you prefer pastels, the Seurat or Sisley rooms are the ones to ask for. The twin- or king-bedded Gauguin room can communicate with the Turner to form a family suite.

FACILITIES AND SERVICES: Air-conditioning, bar, direct-dial phone, electric teapot, elevator, hair dryer, laundry service, modems, private parking (100F, 15.24€, per day), room service, TV with international reception, room safe (no charge)

NEAREST TOURIST ATTRACTIONS (LEFT BANK): Musée d'Orsay, Louvre, Tuileries, shopping

HÔTEL BOURGOGNE & MONTANA ★★★ ($, 4)
3, rue de Bourgogne, 75007
Métro: Assemblée Nationale, Invalides

32 rooms, all with shower or bath and toilet

TELEPHONE
01-45-51-20-22, toll-free from
U.S., 800-44-UTELL

FAX
01-45-56-11-98

EMAIL
info@bourgogne-montana.com

INTERNET
www.123france.com

CREDIT CARDS
AE, DC, MC, V

RATES
Single 945–1,365F (144.06–
208.09€), double 980–1,365F
(149.40–208.09€), suite
1,890–2,310F (288.13–
352.16€); extra bed 400F
(60.98€); lower off-season rates;
taxe de séjour included

The formal Bourgogne & Montana, facing the Palais Bourbon, is located in a diplomatic neighborhood between Les Invalides and St-Germain. Combining a taste for tradition with a dignified clientele, the hotel is both regal and efficient, with large reception rooms and a historically classified 1924 elevator with lovely old iron work and open fronts that enable you to see the floors you pass as you ascend.

If cost is not too much of a factor, book a room on the fifth or sixth floor. I always hope for No. 67, a junior suite with wonderful views of place de la Concorde, the Madeleine Church, the National Assembly, and the roof of the Grand Palais. When the buildings are illuminated at night, it is pure fairyland. Done in blue and yellow, this twin-bedded room has antiques, a comfortable sofa, large television, built-in closet, luggage space, and a divided bathroom with two sinks. If this is not available, ask for No. 61 with a mansard roofline and a round bathtub. Room 54 has a courtyard view and a gleaming tile bathroom with excellent fittings. No. 42 is a standard choice in simple hotel decor, but it does offer space. Special rates during the off-season make this excellent choice even more affordable for many.

FACILITIES AND SERVICES: Air-conditioning, bar, direct-dial phone, elevator, hair dryer, laundry service, minibar, free parking on the square (if you are lucky), *peignoirs* (bathrobes) in deluxe rooms and suites, TV with international reception, office safe (no charge)

NEAREST TOURIST ATTRACTIONS (LEFT BANK): Musée d'Orsay, Rodin Museum, Invalides, Tuileries, Louvre

BREAKFAST
Buffet included, cannot be deducted

ENGLISH SPOKEN
Yes

HÔTEL DE LA TULIPE ★★ (1)
33, rue Malar, 75007
Métro: Latour-Maubourg, Invalides
22 rooms, all with shower or bath and toilet

For years this former convent was a tired and tattered penny-pincher's choice *sans charme*. Thanks to the efforts of Jean-Louis Fortuit, a French film actor turned hotelier, and his charming wife, Caroline, it is finally a sweet little midrange choice. The twenty-two rooms are tightly snuggled around a tree-shaded garden patio. Bright prints, grass-cloth-covered walls, wrought-iron and wicker furniture, beams galore, ancient stone walls, and peaceful garden views work nicely together, creating the illusion that the small rooms are in a country cottage miles away from Paris. If romance is on your itinerary, book No. 24, which once served as the chapel and still has two of the original stone walls and three windows opening onto the patio. If it's space you need, reserve the two-room, two-bath suite that can sleep five. From the hotel you are in close range for bargain shopping along rue St-Dominique, soaking up the market atmosphere along rue Cler, and trying many of the favored restaurants in *Great Eats Paris*. For tourist endeavors, the Eiffel Tower is within walking distance for most and so is Invalides, the Seine, and the Musée d'Orsay.

FACILITIES AND SERVICES: Direct-dial phone, hair dryer, modems, minibar, parking on request (80F, 12.20€, per day), TV with international reception, office safe (no charge), no elevator (only two floors)

TELEPHONE
01-45-51-67-21

FAX
01-47-53-96-37

INTERNET
www.hoteldelatulipe.com

CREDIT CARDS
AE, DC, MC, V

RATES
Single 600F (91.47€), double 700F (106.71€), suite 1,200F (182.94€); extra bed 150F (22.87€); *taxe de séjour* 5F (0.76€) per person, per night

BREAKFAST
Continental 50F (7.62€) per person

ENGLISH SPOKEN
Yes

NEAREST TOURIST ATTRACTIONS (LEFT BANK): Eiffel Tower, Invalides, Seine, shopping, Musée d'Orsay

HÔTEL DE LONDRES EIFFEL ★★★ (9)
1, rue Augereau, 75007
Métro: École-Militaire, Pont de l'Alma

30 rooms, all with shower or bath and toilet

TELEPHONE
01-45-51-63-02

FAX
01-47-05-28-96

EMAIL
info@londres-eiffel.com

INTERNET
www.londres-eiffel.com

CREDIT CARDS
AE, DC, MC, V

RATES
Single 595F (90.71€), double 695F (105.95€), triple 875F (133.39€); extra bed 110F (16.77€); lower off-season rates; *taxe de sèjour* included

BREAKFAST
Continental 45F (6.86€) per person

ENGLISH SPOKEN
Yes

Realistic prices, a very quiet location in the tony seventh arrondissement, easy walking distance to the Eiffel Tower, colorful shopping, and a good métro connection add up to make this a fine selection. Making it even more attractive is the new, hardworking young owner, Isabelle Prigent, who told me, "I put my heart in this hotel. I want it to be just like my house." After visiting the hotel, I would love to see her home. Isabelle has succeeded well at creating a very cozy hotel where her guests can relax and feel quite at home.

The well-thought-out bedrooms are named after Isabelle's favorite French poets, and they all display her innate good taste: everything matches and is color coordinated. I like her collection, hung throughout, of whimsical prints of old-fashioned makeup cases and beauty supplies. Rooms 52, 54, 62, and 64 have Eiffel Tower views. Nos. 101 (for two) and 103 (a triple) are quiet ground-floor choices overlooking the garden. The six larger rooms in the back building are also quiet, but there is no elevator. Off the reception area is an airy, yellow faux-finished breakfast room with chairs draped in orange fabric anchored by a wheat-colored bow. Isabelle is at the hotel every day, along with her friendly fox terrier, Ketty, to tend to her guests and extend her warm hospitality.

FACILITIES AND SERVICES: Direct-dial phone, elevator to most floors (not in the back building), hair dryer, minibar, TV with international reception, no safe

NEAREST TOURIST ATTRACTIONS (LEFT BANK): Champ-de-Mars Park, Eiffel Tower, Invalides, good shopping, good restaurants (see *Great Eats Paris*)

HÔTEL DE L'UNIVERSITÉ ★★★ ($, 7)
22, rue de l'Université, 75007
Métro: Rue du Bac

27 rooms, 25 with shower or bath and toilet

TELEPHONE
01-42-61-09-39

FAX
01-42-60-40-84

INTERNET
www.hoteluniversite.com

There is a certain vintage charm about this old dowager that is reassuring to her many devoted returnees. This is not a hotel for anyone in the fast track. It is, however, well loved by those who feel most comfortable in older homes where the same chair and sofa have been in place for years . . . and covered in the same fabric, too. All twenty-seven rooms are different, but each is furnished in an antique style with big armchairs, thick beamed ceilings, flocked wallpaper, heavy drapes hanging from brass poles, and fireplaces in most. Rooms have space, a commodity in very short supply in most Parisian hotels. Many of the rooms overlook the Ministry of Finance and a pretty garden. In No. 32, I like the sunny window that lets in the sounds of children playing nearby. The huge antique armoire and mirrored dresser will hold everything you brought to Paris, and all that you buy here as well. In No. 35, nothing really matches, but somehow it all goes together. Two windows overlook the ministry, and the semi-antique furnishings create a certain slipper comfort. From the top-floor Room 52, you can see the tip of the Eiffel Tower. You sleep in a brass bed, shower in a pink marble bathroom, and sit on your own terrace. Two armchairs, a round table, and six-tiered bookshelf lend more homey touches.

Under the hotel is an amazing seventeenth-century crypt that was built with stones dating back to Gallo-Roman times in the first century. The chapel belonged to the Knights of the Temple of Solomon, who fought Pope Clement the fifth. It is now used as a conference room, but it still looks like a massive hall in a feudal castle where the knights of the round table presided.

FACILITIES AND SERVICES: Air-conditioning, direct-dial phone, elevator to fourth floor, hair dryer, laundry service, some minibars, TV with international reception, room safe (no charge), room service for light meals

NEAREST TOURIST ATTRACTIONS (LEFT BANK): Musée d'Orsay, Seine, Tuileries, Louvre, shopping

HÔTEL D'ORSAY ★★ (5)
93, rue de Lille, 75007
Métro: Assemblée Nationale, Solférino
41 rooms, all with shower or bath and toilet

In its past life, the rejuvenated Hôtel d'Orsay was two hotels . . . one of which was the Hôtel Solferino. Run by an owner who believed in deferred maintenance, the hotel quickly became a relic of another age. Now the renovated, side-by-side eighteenth-century buildings are an exercise in quiet elegance and good taste.

The warmly decorated rooms are rich with comforts. Several that overlook a quiet garden are light and cheerful. The largest rooms have twin beds and a bathtub in

CREDIT CARDS
AE, MC, V

RATES
Single (shower, no toilet) 500–750F (76.22–114.34€), double 950F (144.83€), terrace room 1,200–1,300F (182.94–198.18€), triple 1,200–1,500F (182.94–228.67€); *taxe de séjour* included

BREAKFAST
Continental 50F (7.62€) per person

ENGLISH SPOKEN
Yes

TELEPHONE
01-47-05-85-54

FAX
01-45-55-51-16

EMAIL
hotel.orsay@wanadoo.com

CREDIT CARDS
AE, DC, MC, V

RATES
Single 600–700F (91.47–106.71€), double 700–800F (106.71–121.96€), suite 1,500F (228.67€); *taxe de séjour* included

BREAKFAST
Continental 50F (7.62€) per person

ENGLISH SPOKEN
Yes

the bathroom. I like No. 12 because it has extra room and a stylish color scheme in peach, blue, and white. Two windows allow plenty of light and the glass-topped work desk is ample. The maroon-and-blue checkered bedspreads coordinate with the floral draperies in the pitched roof suite (No. 60) to add a contemporary note, as does the double sink in the mirrored bathroom. Two comfortable chairs, twins or a king-size bed, plus a sunny balcony make this choice even more desirable. The sedate location is ideal for walking either to the Louvre via the new Solferino footbrige over the Seine or to the Musée d'Orsay just a few blocks away.

FACILITIES AND SERVICES: Direct-dial phone, elevator to all floors except top-floor suite, hair dryer, laundry service, TV with international reception, room safe (no charge)

NEAREST TOURIST ATTRACTIONS (LEFT BANK): Musée d'Orsay, Louvre, Seine, Tuileries

HÔTEL DUC DE SAINT-SIMON ★★★ ($, 24)
14, rue de St-Simon, 75007
Métro: Rue du Bac

29 rooms, 5 suites, all with shower or bath and toilet

TELEPHONE
01-44-39-20-20,
01-42-22-07-52 (reservations)

FAX
01-45-48-68-25

EMAIL
duc.de.saint.simon@wanadoo.fr

CREDIT CARDS
AE, MC, V

RATES
1–2 persons 1,225–1,600F (186.75–243.92€), suite 1,925–1,975F (293.46–301.09€); extra bed 30 percent of room rate; *taxe de séjour* included

BREAKFAST
Continental 75F (11.43€) per person

ENGLISH SPOKEN
Yes

Everyone has their first hotel in Paris, and this was mine. Of course, in those days it bore about as much resemblance to what it is today as a simple one-star does to the Hotel Ritz. Over the years, and through many changes, my enthusiasm for the hotel has not dimmed, and it still tops my short list of ideal small Parisian hotels.

I am drawn to the Duc de Saint-Simon for many reasons, especially its intimate romantic feeling, wonderful sense of privacy, overall beauty, and high degree of personalized service. Built around a courtyard garden, many of the individually decorated rooms open onto this green view, while several larger rooms and suites open onto their own private terraces. When I first walked into No. 19, a large suite on the first floor, I thought, This is it—I am never leaving! The antique-filled sitting room has comfortable seating, a lovely writing desk, and good lighting. The quiet bedroom has its own television and a double bed where, in the morning, you are wakened by the birds singing outside your garden window. The older style bathroom has all the nice extras: heated towel racks, a magnifying mirror, a tub with a water shield, and a telephone. I like all the other rooms in this very special hotel, but a favorite has always been No. 11, which is decorated in rich fabrics with a corner sitting area and view windows that open onto the gardens, seemingly bringing them inside. Another beautiful room is No. 37. It is a soft, feminine room with a floral theme carried out on the wallpaper, curtains, spread, and lamp shades. I also like the two-drawer antique dresser, framed embroideries, and the roomy bathroom with its inset sink, shelf space, and separate stall shower. No. 34 has a double bed framed by lighted closets and a view overlooking the terraces below. It is elegantly decorated with warm yellow and rose floral colors and furnished with a comfortable armchair, four-drawer marble dresser, and crystal chandelier.

The owners of the hotel, M. and Mme. Lindqvist, have been antiques collectors of note for many years and have used their handsome collection throughout the hotel, from the beautiful grandfather clock in the lobby to the graceful marble-topped dressers in the bedrooms. The downstairs seventeenth-century cellar bar has pillowed niches and quiet corners just big enough for two to sip drinks and talk about life and love.

The prices for a stay here are high, no doubt about it. But for those seeking a quietly elegant, discreet stay in Paris, this should be the hotel of choice.

FACILITIES AND SERVICES: Air-conditioning in some rooms, bar, direct-dial phone, elevator, hair dryer in some rooms, laundry service, TV with international reception in suites (otherwise on request), robes in suites, room safe (no charge), room service for light snacks

NEAREST TOURIST ATTRACTIONS (LEFT BANK): Musée d'Orsay, Tuileries, St-Germain-des-Prés, Rodin Museum, excellent browsing and shopping

HÔTEL DU CHAMP DE MARS ★★ (15)
7, rue du Champ de Mars, 75007
Métro: École-Militaire

25 rooms, all with shower or bath and toilet

Under the competent ownership of Françoise and Stéphane Gourdal (and their fluffy white dog named Chipie), the Hôtel du Champ de Mars is a stylish choice for guests who want to watch their budget but not feel deprived in the process.

The hotel's look reflects the time, talent, enthusiasm, and downright hard work of this delightful couple, who transformed it from stem to stern. The French way with color is often daring. Others might have stopped short of

TELEPHONE
01-45-51-52-30

FAX
01-45-51-64-36

EMAIL
stg@club-Internet.fr

INTERNET
www.hotel-du-champ-de-mars.com

CREDIT CARDS
MC, V

RATES
Single 400F (60.98€), double 440F (67.08€), triple 550F (83.85€); *taxe de séjour* included

BREAKFAST
Continental 40F (6.10€) per person

ENGLISH SPOKEN
Yes

the mix of brightly hued fabrics, but Françoise had both the courage and good taste to pull it off. Her love of flowers is the underlying theme throughout. In the downstairs breakfast room, round tables draped in orange-and-yellow plaid hold bouquets of dried flowers. An old chest with a bowl of potpourri and soft background music create a relaxing place for morning coffee and croissants. The series of golf prints hanging by the elevator are a nod to her husband's enthusiasm for the game.

White doors with big brass doorknobs lead to the yellow-and-blue rooms, all of which are named after French flowers. Tournesol (No. 25) is a pretty yellow-and-blue double with three floral prints over the bed and two windows that let in light from the front of the hotel. Myosotis (No. 55), on the front, is a single with great allure thanks to its small entry, light blue interior, and glimpse of the Eiffel Tower. Mimosa (No. 54) is another pleasant single with a nice view onto the court and rooftops beyond. If it is twin beds you want, ask for Muguet (No. 24). You enter Lilas (No. 4) through a little garden; the striped wallpaper, curtains, bedspreads, and rug are color coordinated in yellow, blue, and white to create a very sweet setting.

Last, but certainly not least, guests will find excellent discount shopping, several banks, a main post office, the métro, a wonderful street *marché* on rue Cler, and lots of favorite *Great Eats Paris* restaurants all close at hand.

FACILITIES AND SERVICES: Direct-dial phone, elevator, hair dryer, TV with international reception, office safe (no charge)

NEAREST TOURIST ATTRACTIONS (LEFT BANK): Champ-de-Mars Park, Eiffel Tower, Invalides, good discount shopping, interesting daily street *marché*

HÔTEL DU PALAIS BOURBON ★★ (23)
49, rue de Bourgogne, 75007
Métro: Varenne

TELEPHONE
01-44-11-30-70

FAX
01-45-55-20-21

EMAIL
HTLBOURBON@aol.com

INTERNET
www.hotel-palais-bourbon.com

CREDIT CARDS
MC, V

32 rooms, 29 with shower, bath, and toilet

The Palais Bourbon has long been a reliable staple for readers of *Great Sleeps Paris* looking for a respectable budget hotel suitable for the entire family. The hotel is in a quiet residential area of Paris that is only a half block from the Rodin Museum, five minutes from Invalides, about ten minutes from the Musée d'Orsay, and just across the Seine from the Tuileries. The Claudon family has owned, managed, and lived in the hotel for more than fifty years, and they keep a steely eye out for anything, or anyone, out of line. Madame Claudon, who is a grandmother with more energy than most people half her age, told me, "I work all the time. I am of another time." It must agree with her, since she has a spring in her step and a twinkle in her eye that could not possibly go unnoticed.

The hotel may not be the snazziest place to sleep in the *quartier,* but it is one of the best budget values, not only in the seventh, but in the entire city. The rooms are very large by Parisian standards and extremely clean, thanks to vigilant housekeeping and an ongoing maintenance program. Continuing improvements include airconditioning in all rooms, the addition of more tiled bathrooms (many with bidets), hardwood floors throughout, and new beds. Popular rooms are No. 3, which can connect with the room next door if larger quarters are needed; No. 4, a quiet double; and No. 1, a twin, also on the back. Reservations are essential as far in advance as possible.

The brick-floored breakfast room, with square and oblong tables surrounding a large round central one, is softened by a tall green plant in the window and an occasional vase of fresh flowers. Black-and-white prints of the Sorbonne and the Palais Bourbon hang on the white stuccoed walls. No, it isn't any more trendy than the rooms, but the breakfast is good if you decide to eat here.

FACILITIES AND SERVICES: Air-conditioning, direct-dial phone (on request, private numbers given at no charge), elevator, hairdryer, some minibars, TV with international reception; room safe in some rooms (no charge)

NEAREST TOURIST ATTRACTIONS (LEFT BANK): Rodin Museum, Invalides, Musée d'Orsay, Tuileries

RATES
Single 300–540F (45.73–82.32€), double 670F (102.14€), triple 770F (117.39€), quad 820F (125.01€), five persons 870F (132.63€); extra bed 60F (9.15€); *taxe de séjour* 5F (0.76€) per person, per day

BREAKFAST
Continental included, cannot be deducted

ENGLISH SPOKEN
Yes

HÔTEL LA BOURDONNAIS ★★★ (20)
111, 113, avenue de la Bourdonnais, 75007
Métro: École-Militaire

60 rooms, all with shower or bath and toilet

Hôtel la Bourdonnais is a personal favorite that over the years has never failed to please. The location could not be better. It is five minutes from the métro and only ten from an RER stop. The area is filled with good shopping, from discount clothing boutiques to a colorful daily street *marché* on rue Cler. There are many inexpensive restaurants within easy walking distance (see *Great*

TELEPHONE
01-47-05-45-42

FAX
01-45-55-75-54

EMAIL
otlbourd@clubInternet.fr

INTERNET
www.hotellabourdonnais.fr

CREDIT CARDS
AE, DC, MC, V

RATES
Single 700F (106.71€), double
800F (121.96€), triple 850F
(129.58€), quad 920F
(140.25€), suite 1,220F
(185.99€); *taxe de séjour*
included
BREAKFAST
Continental 50F (7.62€) per
person
ENGLISH SPOKEN
Yes

Eats Paris). The beautiful Champ-de-Mars Park, with the Eiffel Tower at one end and the impressive École Militaire at the other, is only two blocks away and a great place for a picnic, people-watching, or a morning jog.

The lobby and reception rooms are accented by velvet-covered furniture, soft lighting, and nice paintings. A small breakfast corner and bar overlook a glassed-in garden with a lion fountain where breakfast is served. The traditional rooms and suites are tastefully decorated with excellent reproduction furnishings and soft fabrics. All have very generous closet and drawer space, comfortable chairs, large writing desks, and hidden combination safes to store valuables. The ample marble bathrooms feature big mirrors, hair dryers, laundry drying racks, and plenty of towels. This outstanding hotel is the choice of many international travelers seeking good value, so to avoid disappointment, book way ahead.

FACILITIES AND SERVICES: Air-conditioning, direct-dial phone, elevator, hair dryer, laundry service, some minibars, porter, radio, TV with international reception, pay movies, room safe (no charge)

NEAREST TOURIST ATTRACTIONS (LEFT BANK): Champ-de-Mars Park, Eiffel Tower, Invalides, Trocadéro, good shopping

HÔTEL LA MOTTE PICQUET ★★ (17)
30, avenue de la Motte-Picquet, 75007
Métro: École-Militaire

18 rooms, all with shower or bath and toilet

TELEPHONE
01-47-05-09-57
FAX
01-47-05-74-36
INTERNET
www.france-hotel-guide.com/
h75007mottepicquet.htm
CREDIT CARDS
MC, V
RATES
Single 395–415F (60.22–
63.27€), double 450–515F
(68.60–78.51€), triple 700F
(106.71€), quad 820F
(125.01€); extra bed 100F
(15.24€); *taxe de séjour* included
BREAKFAST
Continental 40F (6.10€) per
person
ENGLISH SPOKEN
Yes

The Hôtel La Motte Picquet features a good location and low-key atmosphere in a revamped hotel where you can settle your account without suffering sticker shock. The two-star hotel is on a busy boulevard within walking distance to Invalides and a jog through the Champ de Mars to La Tour Eiffel. Shophounds will be happy bagging bargains on the nearby rue St-Dominique, and foodies will have a field day with all the nearby choices recommended in *Great Eats Paris*. Around the corner is rue Cler, a lively shopping street lined with cafés, food shops, bakeries, and a post office.

What about the eighteen rooms? The three floors of rooms are decorated in blue, green, and bordeaux with gray walls. They are not lavish, but they are coordinated with matching bed and window treatments and have more than enough closet space, nice new bathrooms, and good towels. The small lobby fronts on the street and has a blue-and-white-checked sofa and chair where you can sit and look out the picture window. Breakfast is served in a mirrored room in back of a coffee bar, which is accented by green plants and bouquets of colorful silk flowers.

FACILITIES AND SERVICES: Direct-dial phone, elevator, hair dryer, TV with international reception, office safe (no charge)

NEAREST TOURIST ATTRACTIONS (LEFT BANK): Invalides, Champ de Mars, Eiffel Tower, Rodin Museum

HÔTEL LA SERRE ★★ (12)
24 bis, rue Cler, 75007
Métro: École-Militaire

29 rooms, 25 with shower or bath and toilet

If time does not allow you to visit other parts of France on this trip, a stay at La Serre will give you a sense of what it would be like to stay in one of the country's beautiful provinces. Each floor has a theme: Brittany on the fifth, Normandy the fourth, Savoie the third, and Alsace on the second. The first floor and lobby are all about Paris. On every floor, the hallways surround you with village scenes, and the rooms evoke their locales through the use of native fabrics, colorful tile insets in the bathrooms, pictures and photographs, flowers and furnishings. At the present time, the fourth and fifth floors are complete and certainly recommended. Those that are on stand-by are not. Admittedly, the ambitious project is an ongoing work in progress, but if you are in a room on a completely redone floor, your stay will be rewarding. The hotel is amid the shops along the colorful rue Cler shopping street. Wife and husband owners Marie-Alice and Philippe make an effort to help their guests enjoy Paris to the fullest.

FACILITIES AND SERVICES: Direct-dial phone, elevator, hair dryer, TV, room safe (no charge)

NEAREST TOURIST ATTRACTIONS (LEFT BANK): Invalides, Champ de Mars, Eiffel Tower, Rodin Museum

TELEPHONE
01-47-05-52-33

FAX
01-40-62-95-66

EMAIL
laserre@easynet.fr

INTERNET
www.123france.com

CREDIT CARDS
AE, DC, MC, V

RATES
Single 300–500F (45.73–76.22€), double 330–530F (50.31–80.80€), triple 650F (99.09€); *taxe de séjour* included

BREAKFAST
Continental 30F (4.57€) per person; complimentary after 3-night stay

ENGLISH SPOKEN
Yes

HÔTEL LATOUR-MAUBOURG ★★★ (11)
150, rue de Grenelle, 75007
Métro: Latour-Maubourg

10 rooms, all with shower or bath and toilet

The Hôtel Latour-Maubourg is a hotel of character with an exceptional, welcoming spirit of friendliness. I hope you will like it as much as I do and the growing number of readers who consider it their home in Paris. For many years it was an elegant pension-hotel that

TELEPHONE
01-47-05-16-16

FAX
01-47-05-16-14

EMAIL
info@latour-maubourg.fr

INTERNET
www.latour-maubourg.fr

CREDIT CARDS
MC, V

RATES
Single 580–750F (88.42–
114.34€), double 850–980F
(129.58–149.40), suite 1,400F
(213.43€); lower rates in
August; *taxe de séjour:* in winter,
included; in summer, 6F
(0.91€) per person, per day

BREAKFAST
Included, cannot be deducted

ENGLISH SPOKEN
Yes, and German

guests never wanted to leave. In fact, one guest arrived when it first opened and was one of the last to leave when it closed in 1993. Facing Invalides across a small park, this townhouse was in the Klein family for more than 150 years, and it was their home until they opened it to paying guests. Now the Klein family is gone, replaced by Victor and Maria Orsenne, their three children, and their dog, Faust. Dog lovers will be interested to know that Faust is 60 percent beagle and a foundling the Orsennes rescued and brought home the day they knew they would have this hotel.

When the Orsennes took over, they closed the hotel in order to totally redo it. They reopened in the spring of 1994, with exceedingly graceful results. They wisely kept the best pieces of furniture, recovering them to give a more up-to-date look. The beautiful wooden staircase was shined and polished, and the gorgeous high ceilings were cleaned and repainted. All of the landscape and Anonymous Ancestor paintings were dusted and rehung. The former dining room, with a large fireplace, now doubles as a sitting room and breakfast area. American guests will especially appreciate the fresh orange juice and daily *Herald-Tribune* that come with the generous Continental breakfast.

The rooms display uniformity and a warm sense of color. The furniture in the bedrooms reflects the 1930s and 1940s and was custom crafted for the hotel. Rooms have soundproof doors, a two-line phone with alarm clock, and an outside line for laptops. Some of the bathrooms are new. I wondered about those that seemed to be older. In talking with a guest, she told me that the 1930s-style tubs are long and deep, so you can stretch out and have the bubbles come right up to your chin. She also appreciated the size and shelf space and was glad they had not been changed. The marble fireplaces are still in place and so are the tall, double French windows that open onto the tiny park across the street, where you can watch pensioners in berets feeding the pigeons or discussing the latest political scandal. Beds are covered with either pillowy duvets or blankets . . . it is your choice, just be sure to state your preference. The first-floor suite and two other rooms facing south are air-conditioned. If you are a nonsmoker, Room 21 is exclusively reserved for nonsmoking guests. Another bonus is this room's nighttime view of the gilded dome of the Invalides.

Victor Orsenne is a busy man. Not only is he a hotelier with an impressive background, but also a chef who owns the Bistro de Montpensier "Chez Victor" near the Palais Bourbon and Louvre (see *Great Eats Paris*).

FACILITIES AND SERVICES: Air-conditioning in a few rooms, electric fans, direct-dial phone, fax and computer hookups, hair dryer, no elevator, laundry service, minibar, TV, office safe (no charge)

NEAREST TOURIST ATTRACTIONS (LEFT BANK): Invalides, Rodin Museum, Musée d'Orsay

HÔTEL LES JARDINS D'EIFFEL ★★★ (10)
8, rue Amélie, 75007
Métro: Latour-Maubourg
80 rooms, all with shower or bath and toilet

Les Jardins d'Eiffel has built a solid reputation as a fine small hotel offering many four-star features at three-star prices. The quiet rooms and suites are simply coordinated and well appointed with wooden built-ins and the latest in modern bathrooms, including lighted magnifying mirrors and telephones. Rooms on the third through the fifth floors have views of the Eiffel Tower. In addition, family communicating rooms have private corridor entrances; nonsmokers can reserve anything on the fourth or fifth floor of the front building and all rooms in the new wing; motorists can park in the private hotel garage (by prior reservation); and sunbathers can work on their tans in the solarium. Should you need a doctor, one is on call twenty-four hours a day. A new wing provides garden and executive rooms done in bright primary colors and bold print fabrics. The competent desk staff will book reservations, organize sightseeing trips, rent a car for you—with or without driver—and confirm airline tickets.

NOTE: Many rooms reserved for nonsmokers.

FACILITIES AND SERVICES: Air-conditioning, bar, baby-sitting, direct-dial phone, dogs allowed, hair dryer, handicapped-accessible rooms, elevator, modems, laundry and cleaning services, minibar, nonsmoking rooms (fourth and fifth floors and new wing), private parking (110F, 16.77€, per 24-hour period), radio, TV with international reception, room safe (no charge), trouser press, concierge, doctor on 24-hour call

NEAREST TOURIST ATTRACTIONS (LEFT BANK): Invalides, Champ-de-Mars Park, Eiffel Tower, shopping

TELEPHONE
01-47-05-46-21

FAX
01-45-55-28-08

EMAIL
eiffel@acom.fr

INTERNET
www.acom.fr/eiffel

CREDIT CARDS
AE, DC, MC, V

RATES
Single 600–850F (91.47–129.58€), double 660–990F (100.62–150.92€), triple 840–1,100F (128.06–167.69€), quad 1,275–1,700F (194.37–259.16€); ask about lower off-season rates; *taxe de séjour* 6F (0.91€) per person, per day

BREAKFAST
65F (9.91€) per person, buffet or Continental in room

ENGLISH SPOKEN
Yes

HÔTEL MUGUET ★★ (19)
11, rue Chevert, 75007
Métro: Latour-Maubourg, École-Militaire
45 rooms, all with shower or bath and toilet

TELEPHONE
01-47-05-05-93
FAX
01-45-50-25-37
EMAIL
muguet@wanadoo.fr
INTERNET
www.hotelmuguet.com
CREDIT CARDS
AE, MC, V
RATES
Single 520F (79.27€), double
580–620F (88.42–94.52€),
triple 800F (121.96€); *taxe de
séjour* included
BREAKFAST
Continental 45F (6.86€) per
person
ENGLISH SPOKEN
Yes

When I revisited the Hôtel Muguet for this ninth edition of *Great Sleeps Paris,* I found that it is still one of the smartest, most stylish two-star values in Paris. Savvy readers obviously agree and are on to this one; they stay here in droves, making it necessary to reserve the view rooms or suite at least six months in advance. Staying here will make anyone feel like a privileged budget traveler, especially in the suite, with its lovely tiled bathroom. The rooms are air-conditioned, which is a rare extra in a two-star, let me assure you. All are outfitted in country-style furniture with different color schemes in either pink, yellow, or blue. Everything is well coordinated; mirrored wardrobes are generous; and from Nos. 61 and 62, on the sixth floor, you can see the Eiffel Tower. From No. 63, your vista is over Invalides. On the fifth floor, ask for No. 51, with a balcony and good Eiffel Tower view. Another room I like is No. 41, a triple with three twin beds. The advantage here is the small sitting room and the large bath with yellow and gray accents. Three new doubles opening onto a garden terrace have been added, two with stall showers and the third with a bathtub.

Thankfully, the parts of the hotel that give it character also remain. The black and gray-green marble facade is intact, and so is the lovely grandfather clock next to the reception desk. No one replaced the colorful flowers and lush green plants in the garden with plastic versions, and more important, the attractive owners, the Pelettier family and their two poodles, Framboise and Mandarine, still live at the hotel and are always ready with their friendly smiles to make their guests feel very special and at home.

The immediate neighborhood could hardly be dubbed "the miracle mile," but it is quiet both day and night. After a nice ten-minute stroll, you can be at Invalides viewing Napoléon's tomb or on a park bench at the Champ-de-Mars Park, admiring the Eiffel Tower while eating a gourmet picnic put together from the food shops that line rue St-Dominique and rue Cler. Good restaurants abound (see *Great Eats Paris*), and so does discount shopping (see "Shopping," page 325).

FACILITIES AND SERVICES: Air-conditioning, direct-dial phone, elevator to five floors, hair dryer, magnifying mirrors, TV with international reception, room safe (no charge)

NEAREST TOURIST ATTRACTIONS (LEFT BANK): Champ-de-Mars Park, Invalides, Eiffel Tower, Rodin Museum

HÔTEL RELAIS BOSQUET ★★★ (16)
19, rue du Champ de Mars, 75007
Métro: École-Militaire

40 rooms, all with shower or bath and toilet

The Relais Bosquet offers guests comfort, space, and peacefulness in a renovated forty-room hotel built around a courtyard. Each room has all the three-star perks as well as an iron and ironing board, an electric fan or air-conditioning, and an assortment of current periodicals. If you are traveling with an infant, the hotel will provide a free baby bath, chair, food warmer, and bed. There are two nonsmoking rooms. Decor is uniform hotel-issue in all the rooms, with creamy wall coverings and nice-quality furnishings. Brass poles, artistically hung with soft pillows covered in the same material as the curtains, are mounted as headboards behind the beds. Baths have three-tiered rolling carts and nice towels. Top room choices are No. 52, a large twin on the back without much personality but with excellent space in both the room and the bathroom, which includes a stretch-out tub and separate enclosed shower; No. 54, which can serve as a small double or generous single; and No. 32, a big room for two with double sinks in the well-lit bathroom. The street is quiet, so consider No. 53 with two windows facing front as a good option. The upscale residential area of the seventh arrondissement offers some great dining choices, casual discount shopping, and easy access by métro or bus to the rest of Paris.

NOTE: Two rooms reserved for nonsmokers.

FACILITIES AND SERVICES: Air conditioning in some rooms, electric fans, direct-dial phone, elevator, free baby equipment (bed, food warmer, bath, and chair), hair dryer, iron and ironing board, minibar, modems, parking (90F, 13.72€, per day), TV with international reception, room safe (no charge), tea and coffee maker, dogs accepted

NEAREST TOURIST ATTRACTIONS (LEFT BANK): Eiffel Tower, Invalides, Champ-de-Mars Park, shopping

TELEPHONE
01-47-05-25-45; toll-free in the U.S., 800-448-8355

FAX
01-45-55-08-24

EMAIL
hotel@relaisbosquet.com

INTERNET
www.relaisbosquet.com

CREDIT CARDS
AE, DC, MC, V

RATES
Single 800–900F (121.96–137.20€), double 850–1,000F (129.58–152.45€); extra bed 100F (15.24€); ask about special rates; *taxe de séjour* included

BREAKFAST
Large Continental 60F (9.15€); coffee, juice, roll 30F (4.57€); per person

ENGLISH SPOKEN
Yes

HÔTEL SAINT-DOMINIQUE ★★ (3)
62, rue St-Dominique, 75007
Métro: Latour-Maubourg

34 rooms, all with shower or bath and toilet

TELEPHONE
01-47-05-51-44

FAX
01-47-05-81-28

CREDIT CARDS
AE, DC, MC, V

RATES
Single 500F (76.22€), double 600–650F (91.47–99.09€), triple 725F (110.53€); extra bed 100F (15.24€); *taxe de séjour* included

BREAKFAST
Continental 45F (6.86€) per person

ENGLISH SPOKEN
Yes

In the 1700s, this building housed Dominican nuns who prayed in a downstairs chapel. Today, it is a quaint hotel on a busy shopping street, and the chapel is the breakfast room. An English country theme begins in the beamed lobby and continues through the tight rooms, which are furnished in pine and wicker and have soft, billowing curtains dressing the windows. Matching spreads, coordinated wall coverings, and a pretty Provençal-style breakfast room, reached via a winding, wooden staircase, are other positive points. My favorite rooms are the two that open onto the terrace, where breakfast is served on warm spring and summer mornings. I also like No. 8, a twin on the back, and although the floors slant a bit, the roomy bedroom and bathroom, with a rolling cart for toiletries, save the day. The rooms do not boast exciting views, the elevator does not service all floors, and not all rooms have a chair (only a backless stool). While these may be deterrents for some, many guests overlook them in favor of a tranquil stay in a hotel with reasonable rates.

FACILITIES AND SERVICES: Direct-dial phone, hair dryer in rooms with bathtubs, TV with international reception, room safe (no charge)

NEAREST TOURIST ATTRACTIONS (LEFT BANK): Invalides, Champ-de-Mars Park, Eiffel Tower, Rodin Museum, discount shopping

HÔTEL TURENNE ★★ (21)
20, avenue de Tourville, 75007
Métro: École-Militaire

34 rooms, all with shower or bath and toilet

TELEPHONE
01-47-05-99-92

FAX
01-45-56-06-04

EMAIL
hotel.turenne.paris7@wanadoo.fr

CREDIT CARDS
AE, MC, V

RATES
Single 375F (57.17€), double 450–525F (68.60–80.04€), family room 620F (94.52€); *taxe de séjour* included

BREAKFAST
Continental 40F (6.25€) per person

It is what it is . . . a sturdy pick for budget watchers who need a dependable place to sleep and regroup for the next day. The halls have been redone, and so have the carpets. It is air-conditioned, has international television reception, and offers a safe in some rooms or in the office, both at no extra charge. Color-coordinated rooms are clean, but have bland furniture compositions of a laminated desk and an armless chair or stool. Bathrooms come with decent towels, two slivers of soap, and square toilet paper. Six leatherette wing-back chairs circle the sitting room. It won't set the world on fire, and neither will its prices burn a hole in your wallet.

FACILITIES AND SERVICES: Air-conditioning, direct-dial phone, elevator, hair dryer, TV with international reception, office or room safe (no charge)

NEAREST TOURIST ATTRACTIONS (LEFT BANK): Invalides, Rodin Museum, Champ de Mars, Eiffel Tower

ENGLISH SPOKE
Yes

HÔTEL VERNEUIL ★★★ (8)
8, rue de Verneuil, 75007
Métro: Rue du Bac, Musée d'Orsay
26 rooms, all with shower or bath and toilet

For museumgoers, the Hôtel Verneuil is ideally located within walking distance to the Musée d'Orsay, the Louvre, and the Rodin Museum. Antique lovers are in heaven, and so are browsers and shoppers, what with all the tantalizing shops and boutiques that line this area. The owner, Sylvie de Latte, is continually full of ideas and plans for her small and charming hotel. In a seventeenth-century building that retains its original cross beams and rough stone walls, it is a haven of peace and comfort where I always feel as though I am a guest in a lovely French home. Madame de Latte is an art collector, and she has skillfully hung many of her favorite pieces throughout the hotel. The black-and-white photos are by her son, who lived in India. The vaulted stone-cellar breakfast room is down a winding spiral staircase with no elevator access.

The room and marble bathroom sizes vary, but the rooms are all personalized with rich fabrics and solid furnishing. Some have canopy beds, most have wood-beam ceilings and ornate doors, and those ending in numbers 2 or 4 have wall murals of Parisian landmarks. The biggest room is No. 302, and the smallest No. 308, which is sold as a double but should be a single.

FACILITIES AND SERVICES: Air-conditioning in some rooms, bar, direct-dial phone, elevator, hair dryer, minibar, modems, TV with international reception, robes in deluxe rooms, room safe (no charge)

NEAREST TOURIST ATTRACTIONS (LEFT BANK): Musée d'Orsay, Rodin Museum, Seine, Tuileries, Louvre

TELEPHONE
01-42-60-82-14

FAX
01-42-61-40-38

EMAIL
verneuil@cybercable.fr

INTERNET
www.france-hotel-guide.com

CREDIT CARDS
MC, V

RATES
Single 760F (115.86€), double 825–910F (125.77–138.73€), deluxe suite 1,140F (173.79€); *taxe de séjour* 6F (0.91€) per person, per day

BREAKFAST
Continental 65F (9.91€) per person

ENGLISH SPOKEN
Yes

SPLENDID HÔTEL ★★★ (22)
29, avenue de Tourville, at 1, avenue Duquesne, 75007
Métro: École-Militaire

48 rooms, all with shower or bath and toilet

TELEPHONE
01-45-51-24-77
FAX
01-44-18-94-60
EMAIL
splendid@club-Internet.fr
CREDIT CARDS
AE, DC, MC, V
RATES
Single 700F (106.71€), double 800–950F (121.96–144.83€), suite 1,300F (198.18€); *taxe de séjour* 6F (0.91€) per person, per day
BREAKFAST
Continental 60F (9.15€) per person
ENGLISH SPOKEN
Yes

Before 1992, the Splendid was anything but—now it lives up to its name on almost every count. Done in an Art Deco theme with soft blond wood and pastel wall colorings, the modernized rooms and serviceable baths offer all the comforts three-star sleepers demand. Balconies on the fifth and sixth floors have views of the École Militaire. While sitting by the window in one of the junior suites (Nos. 507 and 607), you can see *La Tour Eiffel.* If you would rather work, there is a fax and a computer plug. Windows are double glazed to shield against the nonstop traffic at this busy intersection, but on hot nights, better have those earplugs handy or be prepared to swelter behind shut windows.

A large downstairs bar is a good place to go for a relaxing drink, and don't fret over the purple wall covering, green chairs with black accents, and the chrome bar stools . . . they all work to make the room contemporary in an offbeat way. Another colorful spot is the breakfast room: if the strong coffee doesn't wake you up, surely the green armchairs in the bright orange room trimmed with light pink will. The hotel is minutes from rue Cler, a pedestrian market street where well-dressed, basket-toting locals shop for their vegetables, flowers, meats, cheeses, and fresh morning croissants. Close to the hotel are several excellent restaurants (see *Great Eats Paris*), and the métro is a two-minute walk.

FACILITIES AND SERVICES: Bar, direct-dial phone, elevator, hair dryer, laundry service, minibar, parking by reservation only (40F, 6.10€, per day), TV with international reception, robes in suites, room safe (16F, 2.44€, per day), fax and computer outlets in suites

NEAREST TOURIST ATTRACTIONS (LEFT BANK): Eiffel Tower, Champ-de-Mars Park, discount shopping

Eighth Arrondissement

RIGHT BANK
American Embassy, Arc de Triomphe, Étoile, Champs-Élysées, elegant shopping on rue du Faubourg St-Honoré, Petit Palais, Grand Palais, place de la Concorde, Madeleine Church

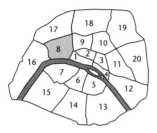

The ten-lane Champs-Élysées, sweeping dramatically from the Arc de Triomphe to the place de la Concorde, is the most famous avenue and parade ground in the world, and it is definitely worth a serious look and stroll. But save the shopping, partying, and eating for less touristy and unspoiled areas. This is the traditional watering hole for show-biz celebrities, glamour girls on the way up or down, tourists in baseball caps, heavy-set men and their young companions, and anyone else who wants to hide behind dark glasses twenty-four hours a day. The flame on the tomb of the unknown soldier burns under the Arc de Triomphe, and the view from the top is inspiring. Twelve avenues radiate from the Arc de Triomphe, forming the world-famous, death-defying traffic circle known as *l'Étoile.*

The place de la Concorde is the largest square in Paris. Two of its most famous occupants are the luxurious Hôtel Crillon and the American Embassy. It is thrilling to stand on this strikingly beautiful square and be surrounded by some of the greatest landmarks in the world: the Tuileries Gardens, the Louvre, and the view up the Champs-Élysées to the Arc de Triomphe, across the Seine to the Palais Bourbon, and up the rue Royale to the Madeleine Church, built as a replica of a Greco-Roman temple by Napoléon I. In the evening, when it is all illuminated and the fountains are playing, it becomes a sight you will never forget.

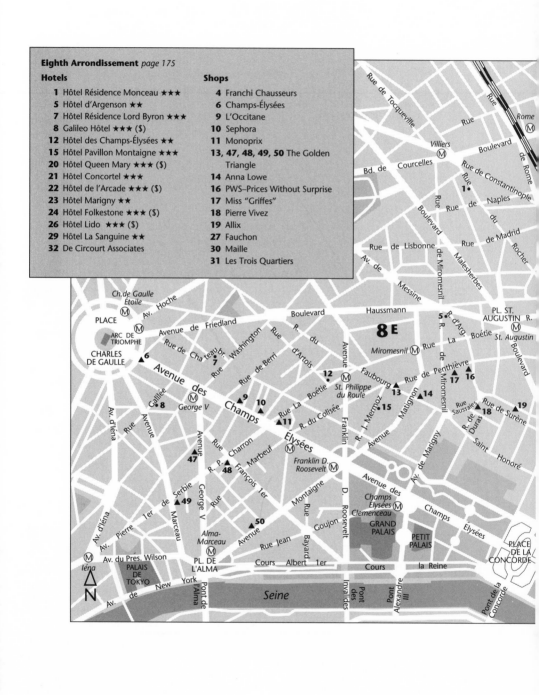

Eighth Arrondissement *page 175*

Hotels

1 Hôtel Résidence Monceau ★★★
5 Hôtel d'Argenson ★★
7 Hôtel Résidence Lord Byron ★★★
8 Galileo Hôtel ★★★ ($)
12 Hôtel des Champs-Élysées ★★
15 Hôtel Pavillon Montaigne ★★★
20 Hôtel Queen Mary ★★★ ($)
21 Hôtel Concortel ★★★
22 Hôtel de l'Arcade ★★★ ($)
23 Hôtel Marigny ★★
24 Hôtel Folkestone ★★★ ($)
26 Hôtel Lido ★★★ ($)
29 Hôtel La Sanguine ★★
32 De Circourt Associates

Shops

4 Franchi Chausseurs
6 Champs-Élysées
9 L'Occitane
10 Sephora
11 Monoprix
13, 47, 48, 49, 50 The Golden Triangle
14 Anna Lowe
16 PWS–Prices Without Surprise
17 Miss "Griffes"
18 Pierre Vivez
19 Allix
27 Fauchon
30 Maille
31 Les Trois Quartiers

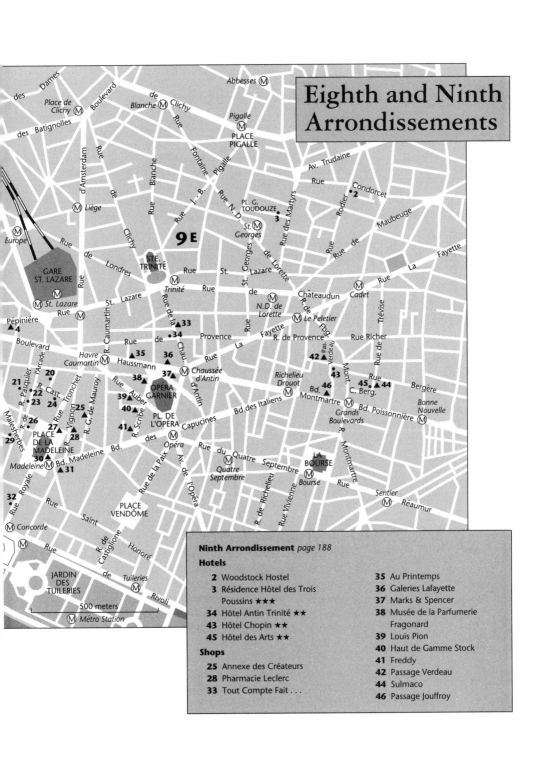

Eighth and Ninth Arrondissements

9E

GARE ST. LAZARE

STE. TRINITÉ

OPÉRA GARNIER

PL. DE L'OPÉRA

PLACE DE LA MADELEINE

PLACE VENDÔME

LA BOURSE

JARDIN DES TUILERIES

500 meters

Ⓜ Métro Station

HOTELS IN THE EIGHTH ARRONDISSEMENT

($) indicates a Big Splurge

GALILEO HÔTEL ★★★ ($, 8)
54, rue Galilée, 75008
Métro: George-V, Charles-de-Gaulle-Étoile
27 rooms, all with shower or bath and toilet

TELEPHONE
01-47-20-66-06
FAX
01-47-20-67-17
CREDIT CARDS
AE, DC, MC, V
RATES
Single 820F (125.01€), double 970F (147.88€); *taxe de séjour* 6F (0.91€) per person, per day
BREAKFAST
Continental 55F (8.38€) per person
ENGLISH SPOKEN
Yes

For years, contented guests with sophisticated, artistic temperaments have flocked to Roland and Elisabeth Buffat's popular hotels on the Île St-Louis: Hôtel de Lutèce and Hôtel des Deux-Îles (see pages 88 and 89). Now they have a third option to tempt them, the Galileo. The Buffat's Right Bank hotel re-creates an elegant French townhome in an oasis of calm, only a few steps from the Champs-Élysées.

Like the flowers in the boutique lobby and garden, guests are beautifully arranged in the elegantly pristine rooms, all fashioned alike in comforting colors of beige, brown, and cocoa. No. 403, a double with two armchairs, a desk, and gray marble bath, has a *Rear Window*–type view onto the life within the nearby apartment building. No. 202, a ground-floor twin with a small sitting area and huge marble bathroom, faces a walled garden. The room size jackpot is shared by two on the fifth floor (Nos. 501 and 502). In addition to being the biggest, their allure comes from their delightful glass-covered, screened verandas with wicker seating that invite year-round usage. Butcher block tables adorn the below-ground, mirrored dining room, and green plants and posters of familiar Paris landmarks and buildings give it interest.

FACILITIES AND SERVICES: Air-conditioning, direct-dial phone, elevator, hair dryer, minibar, TV with international reception, room safe (no charge)

NEAREST TOURIST ATTRACTIONS (RIGHT BANK): Champs-Élysées, Arc de Triomphe

HÔTEL CONCORTEL ★★★ (21)
19–21, rue Pasquier, 75008
Métro: Madeleine
46 rooms, all with shower or bath and toilet

For many years, the conveniences and comforts of the Concortel have appealed to many seeking a midcity location to combine tourism with business. The hotel consists of two blocks of rooms joined by a courtyard. The color-coordinated bed chambers are well arranged, and most offer the space and perks that travelers desire. The desk staff is exceptional, especially Pierre—who has been here more than twenty-five years, speaks wonderful English, and is always ready to help—and Remy, the porter, who has been here a decade and also speaks English. Lower rates in August make this hotel even more attractive.

FACILITIES AND SERVICES: Air-conditioning, bar, conference room, direct-dial phone, elevator in front building (not in two-floor back building), hair dryer, laundry service, modems on request, minibar, parking by reservation (130F, 19.82€, per day), radio, TV with international reception, room safe (no charge), porter

NEAREST TOURIST ATTRACTIONS (RIGHT BANK): Place Vendôme, Madeleine Church, place de la Concorde, Opéra, Galeries Lafayette and Au Printemps department stores

TELEPHONE
01-42-65-45-44
FAX
01-42-65-18-33
EMAIL
concortel@wanadoo.fr
INTERNET
www.hotelconcortel.com
CREDIT CARDS
AE, DC, MC, V
RATES
Single 665–865F (101.38–131.87€), double 710–910F (108.24–138.73€), triple 1,060F (161.60€), quad 1,100F (167.67€); ask about special off-season and business rates; *taxe de séjour* included
BREAKFAST
Continental 45F (6.86€) per person
ENGLISH SPOKEN
Yes

HÔTEL D'ARGENSON ★★ (5)
15, rue d'Argenson, at 111 boulevard Haussmann, 75008
Métro: Miromesnil
28 rooms, all with shower or bath and toilet

Veteran Paris visitors know that the eighth arrondissement is normally Big Splurge territory. Coming to the rescue is this twenty-eight-room, second-floor walk-up, perched above Rene Saint-Ouen, one of the most famous bakeries in Paris. How famous? It was selected to

TELEPHONE
01-42-65-16-87
FAX
01-47-42-02-06
CREDIT CARDS
MC, V

RATES
Single 345–435F (52.59–
66.32€), double 410–470F
(62.50–71.65€), triple 540–
580F (82.32–88.42€); *taxe de
séjour* included

BREAKFAST
Continental in room included,
cannot be deducted

ENGLISH SPOKEN
Yes

provide all the baguettes to the Élysée Palace, and that is *quite* an honor. Those who are familiar with this part of Paris know that noise is part of the deal, and it won't escape you at this hotel. However, if cost is your guiding light, give this one consideration.

You first enter the small wood-paneled salon, which has two chairs. Martine, the owner's daughter, is usually behind the desk, along with her black-and-brown cocker spaniel, Flash. Rooms that once varied from frankly fussy to downright tacky have been toned down to some extent. In most rooms at least the curtains and spreads match, and the wild wallpaper has been removed from the ceilings. I have trouble with the mustard yellow— and beer brown—colored tiles in the bathrooms, which definitely don't go with the plaid towels. There are no twin-bedded rooms, but an extra bed can be added at no additional cost if there are only two of you and you want to sleep separately. If there are three of you, you must pay the triple rate. The hotel is saved because it is cheap and clean, and the rooms are big enough to satisfy almost anyone. Maintenance, performed by Martine's husband, is on top of things.

FACILITIES AND SERVICES: Direct-dial phone, elevator, room fans, hair dryer at desk, TV, room safe (no charge)

NEAREST TOURIST ATTRACTIONS (RIGHT BANK): Champs-Élysées, place de la Concorde, Madeleine Church, shopping at Galeries Lafayette and Au Printemps

HÔTEL DE L'ARCADE ★★★ ($, 22)
9, rue de l'Arcade, 75008
Métro: Madeleine
41 rooms, all with shower and bath and toilet

TELEPHONE
01-53-30-60-00

FAX
01-40-07-03-07

EMAIL
contact@hotel-arcade.com

INTERNET
www.hotel-arcade.com,
www.hotel-arcade.fr

CREDIT CARDS
AE, MC, V

RATES
Single 820–920F (125.01–
140.25€), double 1,040F
(158.55€), triple 1,230F
(187.51€), duplex 1,230F
(187.51€); lower off-season/
summer rates; *taxe de séjour*
included

Good taste is everywhere evident at the Hôtel de l'Arcade, and no wonder when you learn it was decorated by Gerard Gallet, who also did the Orient Express. Thanks to a massive two-year renovation project, the hotel is now one of the smartest three-star addresses in the area. Everything about the hotel is exceptional, and something complimentary can be said about all the soundproofed rooms. The divided lobby, done in celery green and beige, is softened further with fresh flowers and green plants. Wing-back chairs, sofas, and a writing desk are complemented by a decorative stone fireplace. The crowning touch is a beautiful green wrought-iron chandelier with twelve candle lights entwined with white metal flowers. A banquette, black-and-white etchings, and windows shaded by white linen café curtains set the stage for the streetside breakfast room.

All the soundproofed bedrooms have beige walls with wood built-ins, good closets, and appealing bathrooms. They all face front, so there will be no depressing wall views, and the standard rooms connect. No. 602 is a good choice for two. The corner location with three large windows, two closets, armchair seating, and a lovely, light bathroom make it an inviting choice for a longer stay. No. 605 is one of the four duplexes. It is a two-story suite with double televisions, three telephones (including one in the bathroom), and an upstairs bedroom with a small balcony. Lower summer rates make this hotel an even more exceptional value.

FACILITIES AND SERVICES: Air-conditioning, free baby cot, conference rooms, direct-dial phone, elevator, hair dryer, magnifying mirrors, minibar, modems, TV with international reception, room safe (no charge)

NEAREST TOURIST ATTRACTIONS (RIGHT BANK): Madeleine Church, place de la Concorde, Opéra, shopping on rue St-Honoré or at Au Printemps and Galeries Lafayette department stores

BREAKFAST
60F (9.15€) per person, Continental in room or buffet downstairs

ENGLISH SPOKEN
Yes

HÔTEL DES CHAMPS-ÉLYSÉES ★★ (12)
2, rue d'Artois, 75008
Métro: St-Philippe-du-Roule
36 rooms, all with shower or bath and toilet

During World War II, this hotel housed Dutch and American soldiers. It now houses mostly business travelers who want a moderate, reliable nest near the Champs-Élysées and the Arc de Triomphe.

The thirty-six attractive rooms and modern baths have coordinated colors and good space usage, and most importantly, they provide many three-star amenities for two-star prices. Adding to the hotel's popularity is the Art Deco sitting room with a multicolored mural and Erté-style lamp. Behind the inlaid wooden bar is a glass-roofed atrium with a small pool framed by Grecian columns.

FACILITIES AND SERVICES: Air-conditioning, bar, direct-dial phone, elevator, hair dryer, some magnifying mirrors, minibar, modems, TV with international reception, room safe (no charge)

NEAREST TOURIST ATTRACTIONS (RIGHT BANK): Champs-Élysées, Arc de Triomphe, shopping along rue Faubourg du St-Honoré

TELEPHONE
01-43-59-11-42

FAX
01-45-61-00-61

CREDIT CARDS
AE, MC, V

RATES
1–2 persons 500–600F (76.22–91.47€); extra bed 80F (12.20€); *taxe de séjour* included

BREAKFAST
Continental 45F (6.86€) per person

ENGLISH SPOKEN
Yes

HÔTEL FOLKESTONE ★★★ ($, 24)
9, rue de Castellane, 75008
Métro: Madeleine, Havre-Caumartin
50 rooms, all with shower or bath and toilet

TELEPHONE
01-42-65-73-09; toll-free from
the U.S. and Canada,
800-528-1234

FAX
01-42-65-64-09

EMAIL
folkestone@paris-hotels-
opera.com

INTERNET
www.bwfolkestoneopera.com

CREDIT CARDS
AE, DC, MC, V

RATES
Single 800F (121.96€), double
900–950F (137.20–144.83€),
triple or deluxe 1,200F
(182.94€), 4-person suite
1,500F (228.67€); extra bed
150F (22.87€); *taxe de séjour* 6F
(0.91€) per person, per day

BREAKFAST
Buffet 55F (8.38€) per person

ENGLISH SPOKEN
Yes

The Folkestone is part of the Best Western chain in Paris, and it's definitely one of the better choices in an area where prices are usually over the top. A stay here puts you in the middle of the business, high fashion, and entertainment precinct of the city.

An interesting collection of framed French country homes line the hallways leading to the contemporary bedrooms, which are decorated in peach, pale gray, and cream, with polished cotton fabrics on the beds and covering the windows. The smallest doubles, at the back, have miniature bathrooms and no view. The bright rooms on the street have double windowpanes to buffer noise and good space in general. The suites are nice for families because they are naturally larger and have more closet space and better bathrooms.

FACILITIES AND SERVICES: Air-conditioning, bar, direct-dial phone, elevator, hair dryer, minibar, modems in some rooms, radio, TV with international reception, room safe (30F, 4.57€, per stay)

NEAREST TOURIST ATTRACTIONS (RIGHT BANK): Madeleine Church, Opéra, shopping on rue Faubourg du St-Honoré and at Au Printemps and Galeries Lafayette department stores

HÔTEL LA SANGUINE ★★ (29)
6, rue de Surène, 75008
Métro: Madeleine
31 rooms, all with shower or bath and toilet

TELEPHONE
01-42-65-71-61

FAX
01-42-66-96-77

CREDIT CARDS
AE, MC, V

RATES
Single 460–520F (70.13–
79.27€), double 480–650F
(73.18–99.09€); extra bed 100F
(15.24€); *taxe de séjour* 5F
(0.76€) per person, per day

BREAKFAST
Continental 45F (6.86€) per
person

ENGLISH SPOKEN
Yes

The upstairs lobby and reception room promise intimacy in a rather impersonal business district between the Madeleine Church and the Champs-Élysées. Rooms deliver three- and four-star comforts, such as room safes and computer modems in most rooms, private telephone numbers, and telephones in all the bathrooms. Unfortunately, there is no elevator in the four-floor hotel, and back views are nothing short of grim. These are *not* reasons to ignore this good-value place. The neighborhood is tomblike at night and on the weekends when offices are closed, so an uninterrupted night's rest is assured in the front-facing rooms. All the rooms have air-conditioning and pleasing colors and fabrics, and most of the showers have curtains. The Continental breakfast includes orange juice and croissants along with coffee, tea, or rich hot chocolate. The warm welcome and friendliness extended by the staff is the reason many return on a regular basis. During the week, when the hotel caters to businesspeople, it is generally full, but when they go home for the weekend, last-minute reservations are possible.

FACILITIES AND SERVICES: Air-conditioning, private line, direct-dial phone (also in the bathroom), no elevator, hair dryer, some modems, minibar, TV with international reception, room safe (no charge)

NEAREST TOURIST ATTRACTIONS (RIGHT BANK): Madeleine Church, shopping on rue St-Honoré, place de la Concorde, Tuileries, Louvre

HÔTEL LIDO ★★★ ($, 26)
4, passage de la Madeleine, 75008
Métro: Madeleine
32 rooms, all with shower or bath and toilet

For the ultimate center-city location, close to almost everything by foot or métro, the Lido is a stellar choice. Window boxes filled with bright red geraniums set the hotel apart on the little *passage* off place de la Madeleine. An eighteenth-century tapestry dominates the reception and lobby. Exposed beams, magnificent hand-rubbed antiques, a miniature garden, and masses of fresh flowers complete the charming beginning. Even the smallest, red linen–lined room has enough living space. Minibars are hidden in heavy wooden furniture, and delicate lace spreads cover the large beds. Personalized service by the cordial staff and such extras as free parking in front of the hotel, full-length mirrors, sewing kits, and scented soaps make the Lido one of the top selections in the eighth arrondissement.

NOTE: Also under the same family ownership and management is the Hôtel Left Bank Saint-Germain (see page 143).

FACILITIES AND SERVICES: Air-conditioning, bar, direct-dial phone, elevator, hair dryer, minibar, free parking in front of the hotel, TV with international reception, room safe (50F, 7.62€, per stay)

NEAREST TOURIST ATTRACTIONS (RIGHT BANK): Madeleine Church, Fauchon, place de la Concorde, Tuileries, Louvre, Palais-Royal, Opéra, shopping at Galeries Lafayette and Au Printemps department stores, Champs-Élysées

TELEPHONE
01-42-66-27-37; toll-free from the U.S. and Canada, 800-528-1234 (Best Western)

FAX
01-42-66-61-23

EMAIL
lido@paris-hotel-charm.com

INTERNET
www.paris-hotels-charm.com

CREDIT CARDS
AE, DC, MC, V

RATES
Single 830–980F (126.53–149.40€), double 930–1,100F (141.78–167.69€); extra bed 100F (15.24€); lower rates in July, Aug, and Dec; *taxe de séjour* 6F (0.91€) per person, per day

BREAKFAST
Included, cannot be deducted

ENGLISH SPOKEN
Yes

HÔTEL MARIGNY ★★ (23)
11, rue de l'Arcade, 75008
Métro: Madeleine, Havre-Caumartin

32 rooms, 26 with shower or bath and toilet

TELEPHONE
01-42-66-42-71

FAX
01-47-42-06-76

EMAIL
hotelmarigny@wanadoo.fr

INTERNET
www.hotelmarigny.com

CREDIT CARDS
MC, V

RATES
Single 500F (76.22€), double
530F (80.80€); extra bed 150F
(22.87€); *taxe de séjour* included

BREAKFAST
Continental 35F (5.34€) per
person

ENGLISH SPOKEN
Yes

Only a few hundred yards from the Madeleine Church and a bracing ten minutes from Gare St-Lazare and place de la Concorde is this reliable roost owned and aptly run by the Maugars family. The neighborhood is dull as dishwater after 7 P.M. and on weekends, but the prices are right and the métro is close. The spotless rooms are reached by the same antique birdcage elevator that Marcel Proust used when he lived and wrote in the hotel. Most of the rooms are sunny, several connect, and those on the sixth floor, which have double beds only, have balconies where you can step outside and enjoy the view. Renovated rooms are naturally preferred, especially No. 61, a double with a shower. The room is simply decorated in textured white wallpaper, with a matching peach floral fabric on both the bed and curtains. If you like blue, reserve No. 51, a twin on the front that can sleep three, or if you need more room and want everyone to be together, it connects with No. 52, which has a double bed. Back rooms are equal in amenities and will be quiet, but you may find yourself in a room, such as No. 54, with a frosted window that affords absolutely no outlook.

FACILITIES AND SERVICES: Direct-dial phone, elevator, hair dryer available, minibar, TV, office safe (no charge)

NEAREST TOURIST ATTRACTIONS (RIGHT BANK): Madeleine Church, Tuileries, place Vendôme, place de la Concorde, Opéra, shopping at Galeries Lafayette and Au Printemps department stores

HÔTEL PAVILLON MONTAIGNE ★★★ (15)
34, rue Jean-Mermoz, 75008
Métro: St-Philippe-du-Roule

18 rooms, all with shower or bath and toilet

TELEPHONE
01-53-89-95-00

FAX
01-42-89-33-00

CREDIT CARDS
AE, DC, MC, V

RATES
1–2 people 850F (129.58€);
extra bed 140F (21.34€); no
charge for children under 12;
taxe de séjour 6F (0.91€) per
person, per day

What sets the Hôtel Pavillon Montaigne apart from the dozens of other three-star hotels in the *quartier?* Friendly service for one thing, lower rates for another, and attractive rooms that are fusions of traditional and modern. All rooms have adequate closet space and are nicely decorated with a combination of wicker, wood, and mirrors. Contemporary bright colors, campaign desks, matching leather chairs and good lighting make them pleasant places to be, whether for work or just relaxing after a day of seeing Paris. You can hear a pin drop in the evening and on the weekends when all but the sidewalks fold up in this 9-to-5 business area, which is only short walk from the Champs-Élysées, place de la Concorde, and boutique shopping along rue St-Honoré.

FACILITIES AND SERVICES: Air-conditioning, bar, direct-dial phones, elevator to third floor (walk to fourth), hair dryer, laundry service, TV with international reception, room safe (no charge)

NEAREST TOURIST ATTRACTIONS (RIGHT BANK): Champs-Élysées, place de la Concorde, shopping along rue St. Honoré

BREAKFAST
Continental 45F (6.86€) per person

ENGLISH SPOKEN
Yes

HÔTEL QUEEN MARY ★★★ ($, 20)
9, rue Greffulhe, 75008
Métro: Madeleine, Havre-Caumartin
36 rooms, all with shower or bath and toilet

Visitors to Paris who desire a distinguished hotel in the center of the city between the Opéra and the Madeleine Church will have a hard time doing better than the Queen Mary. The hotel's Scottish owner, David Byrne (who also owns Hôtel du Bois in the sixteenth, see page 229), has spared no effort to improve the creature comforts offered. As a result, everytime I am here, I am impressed all over again.

Beautiful ceiling details and thick moldings soften the rooms, which are uniformly done with English carpeting, rich fabrics, and built-in furniture in dark wood tones. Luxury accessories such as air-conditioning, double-glazed windows, twenty-channel TV plus pay-per-view channels, FM radio and alarm clock, two telephones, and beautiful bathrooms add to the appreciation of the rooms. Rooms on the second and fifth floors have balconies; superior rooms and suites face front. Those looking for extra-special accommodations will do well in the sunny, top-floor, beamed suite with its rooftop view, two televisions, private fax, and large gray tile bathroom with its own window. Breakfast is served in a yellow-and-green basement dining room with murals of Tuscany. You have a choice of a regular Continental repast, one for slimmers, or a no-calories-barred American/English breakfast buffet that includes bacon, sausage, eggs, a daily selection of mushrooms, potatoes or tomatoes, and corn flakes, along with your croissants, butter, and jam.

Many thoughtful touches make the difference here: a decanter of sherry in each room, happy hour from 6 to

TELEPHONE
01-42-66-40-50

FAX
01-42-66-94-92

EMAIL
hotelqueenmary@wanadoo.fr

INTERNET
www.hotelqueenmary.com

CREDIT CARDS
AE, MC, V

RATES
Single 795F (121.20€), double 935–1,015F (142.54–154.74€), triple 1,315F (200.47€), suite for 2–3 persons 1,450F (221.05€); extra bed 300F (45.73€); special rates on request; *taxe de séjour* included

BREAKFAST
Continental or American/English buffet 85F (12.96€) per person

ENGLISH SPOKEN
Yes

8 P.M. in the friendly blue-and-white bar off the entry, afternoon tea served in the salon, room service from nine international restaurants or light snacks prepared at the hotel, and drinks served in a tiny fountain garden when weather permits.

Shoppers take serious note: You are in ultra-chic Fashion Country here. The names Lanvin, Yves St-Laurent, Jean-Paul Gaultier, and many more grace boutiques no more than a ten- to fifteen-minute browse from the hotel door.

FACILITIES AND SERVICES: Air-conditioning, bar, direct-dial phone, elevator, private fax in suites, hair dryer, laundry service, minibar, room service, radio, TV with international reception and pay-per-view, room safe (10F, 1.52€, per day), afternoon tea, happy hour (6 to 8 P.M.), trouser press, electric tea kettle, decanter of sherry in room

NEAREST TOURIST ATTRACTIONS (RIGHT BANK): Madeleine Church, Opéra, designer shopping, and shopping at Galeries Lafayette and Au Printemps department stores

HÔTEL RÉSIDENCE LORD BYRON ★★★ (7)
5, rue Chateaubriand, 75008
Métro: George-V, Charles-de-Gaulle-Étoile
31 rooms, all with shower or bath and toilet

TELEPHONE
01-43-59-89-98

FAX
01-42-89-46-04

EMAIL
lord.byron@escapade-paris.com

INTERNET
www.leisureplan.com

CREDIT CARDS
AE, MC, V

RATES
Single 690–880F (105.19–134.16€), double 700–990F (106.71–150.92€), suite 1,400F (213.43€); extra bed 150F (22.87€); children under 12 free; *taxe de séjour* included

BREAKFAST
65F (9.91€) per person

ENGLISH SPOKEN
Yes

The Résidence Lord Byron provides lodgings for half the price of many other hotels in this prestigious, expensive *quartier*. It is on a quiet, winding street less than five minutes from the bright lights and excitement of the Champs-Élysées, and it is so peaceful that it is listed in the *European Guide to Silent Hotels*. Although it has an overall dated and faded feel, the colors are pleasing and the fabrics are coordinated. Most of the larger-than-average rooms overlook a garden courtyard where morning coffee and afternoon tea are served in the summer. In the spring the garden is resplendent with tulips, daffodils, and fragrant narcisis. The hotel was formerly a *hôtel particulière* (privately owned townhome) and is furnished with a wide range of lovingly worn and near-antiques, making no pretenses at modernization or cutting-edge decor. I would avoid No. 18, which is so poorly arranged that you cannot sit at the desk because the beds are in the way. If you are willing to reside on the fifth floor, which is an easy walk up a single flight of stairs, your room will be cheaper.

FACILITIES AND SERVICES: Direct-dial phone, elevator to fourth floor (walk to fifth), fans, hair dryer, minibar, TV, room safe (no charge)

NEAREST TOURIST ATTRACTIONS (RIGHT BANK): Arc de Triomphe, Champs-Élysées

HÔTEL RÉSIDENCE MONCEAU ★★★ (1)
85, rue du Rocher, 75008
Métro: Villiers

51 rooms, all with shower or bath and toilet

Clean lines, bright primary colors, and judicious lighting define the rooms at the Résidence Monceau. Not all bathrooms are high tech, but the new chrome-trimmed bathrooms with freestanding sinks make industrial-quality features look fashionable. The bamboo-furnished lobby suggests the tropics, and so does the little pond and fountain in the garden, but the Art Deco bar with two tables and a row of high gray metal bar stools says this is contemporary Paris. The neighborhood is definitely dull if you are looking for high-stepping nightlife. Frankly, I think that is a real plus—you can always call a cab or take the métro to sample fast-track evening pursuits in other parts of Paris. Who wants to lie awake listening to partygoing revelers when you are trying to sleep at 2 A.M.? The hotel is within an easy walk from Gare St-Lazare if you are planning day trips by train beyond Paris, especially to Giverny.

FACILITIES AND SERVICES: Bar that serves light meals, direct-dial phone, elevator, hair dryer, laundry service, TV with international reception, office safe (no charge)

NEAREST TOURIST ATTRACTIONS (RIGHT BANK): Shopping at Galeries Lafayette and Au Printemps department stores, Parc Monceau, Madeleine Church

TELEPHONE
01-45-22-75-11

FAX
01-45-22-30-88

CREDIT CARDS
AE, MC, V

RATES
1–2 persons 760F (115.85€), suite 920F (140.25€); extra bed for child 100F (15.24€); *taxe de séjour* included

BREAKFAST
Buffet 50F (7.62€) per person

ENGLISH SPOKEN
Yes

Ninth Arrondissement

RIGHT BANK
Grands magazins (Au Printemps and Galeries Lafayette), Opéra, Pigalle

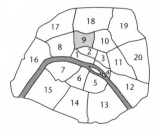

In the southern part of this arrondissement is the beautiful Second Empire Opéra National de Paris Garnier with its famous Chagall ceiling, along with many large banks and shopping at Galeries Lafayette and Au Printemps. At the northern end is the infamous Pigalle, a sleazy neighborhood lined with twenty-four-hour peep shows, bordellos, "ladies of the night"—anything, generally, that constitutes the seamier side of life. Avoid the métro stops Anvers, Pigalle, and Barbès-Rochechouart after dark.

HOTELS IN THE NINTH ARRONDISSEMENT
(see map page 176)

OTHER OPTIONS
Hostels

HÔTEL ANTIN TRINITÉ ★★ (34)
74, rue de Provence, 75009
Métro: Chausée d'Antin–Lafayette, Havre-Caumartin

TELEPHONE
01-48-74-29-07

FAX
01-42-80-26-68

EMAIL
hotel@hotel-antin-trinite.fr

INTERNET
www.paris-antin-trinite.fr;
www.paris-hotel-antin.com

CREDIT CARDS
AE, DC, MC, V

RATES
Single 485–530F (73.94–80.80€), double 545–610F (83.08–92.99€), triple 620–675F (94.52–102.90€); *taxe de séjour* 5F (0.76€) per person, per day

46 rooms, all with shower or bath and toilet

Dedicated shophounds can roll out of bed and into Galeries Lafayette, Au Printemps, Marks & Spencer, and the myriad of other shops and department stores that line the streets of this part of Paris. If shopping is not your *raison d'etre,* you are minutes away from the magnificent Opéra, countless cafés and brasseries, and easy métro and bus connections to take you throughout Paris. The simple, surprise-free rooms are French, and that means small. But they are done in coordinating colors of soft orange and yellow, and they have a desk, chair, luggage rack, and enclosed stall showers. If you want to maintain your budget while staying in this part of Paris, this is a choice that won't disappoint.

FACILITIES AND SERVICES: Direct-dial phone, elevator, hair dryer available, TV with international reception, office safe (no charge)

NEAREST TOURIST ATTRACTIONS (RIGHT BANK): Shopping at all the big department stores, Opéra

HÔTEL CHOPIN ★★ (43)
10, boulevard Montmartre (46, passage Jouffroy), 75009
Métro: Richelieu-Drouot, Grands Boulevards
36 rooms, all with shower or bath and toilet

The Parisians were mall shoppers long before we Americans were. At the turn of the century, Paris had enclosed, skylighted shopping walkways called *passages.* Today these lovely covered areas house a variety of restaurants and shops selling everything from art and antiques to dubious-quality clothing. The Hôtel Chopin is a listed historic monument occupying a unique location at the end of the passage Jouffroy. The door to the hotel was opened the same year as the *passage* (1846), and it has never been locked. Given its longevity, please be prepared for some things that may not be totally *au courant.* Fortunately, the hotel has been redone, and now the rooms have bathrooms; the hallways are uniform and display some pretty painted chests, screens, and chairs; and the rooms, which are all clean and quiet, have better than average two-star decorating. Best rooms are on the top floors because they have skyline views and more natural light, but in No. 409, the tub is under a sloping eave, making upright showering a bit tricky for taller guests.

FACILITIES AND SERVICES: Direct-dial phone, elevator (but some stairs), hair dryer available, TV, office safe (20F, 3.05€, per day; 90F, 13.72€, per week)

NEAREST TOURIST ATTRACTIONS (RIGHT BANK): Shopping at Galeries Lafayette and Au Printemps, Opéra

HÔTEL DES ARTS ★★ (45)
7, Cité Bergère, at 6, rue du Faubourg Montmartre, 75009
Métro: Grands Boulevards (exit Faubourg Montmartre)
26 rooms, all with shower or bath and toilet

The Cité Bergère is a *passage* in central Paris that has eight hotels offering more than four hundred rooms to weary travelers. I have seen them all, and M. and Mme. Bernard's Hôtel des Arts, filled with plants and flowers,

BREAKFAST
Buffet 45F (6.86€) per person
ENGLISH SPOKEN
Yes

TELEPHONE
01-47-70-58-10
FAX
01-42-47-00-70
CREDIT CARDS
AE, MC, V
RATES
Single 405–455F (61.74–69.36€), double 450–520F (68.60–79.27€), triple 595F (90.71€); *taxe de séjour* included
BREAKFAST
40F (6.10€) per person
ENGLISH SPOKEN
Yes

TELEPHONE
01-42-46-73-30
FAX
01-48-00-94-42
CREDIT CARDS
AE, DC, MC, V

RATES
Single 370–390F (56.41–
59.46€), double 390–410F
(59.46–62.50€), triple
530F (80.80€); *taxe de séjour* 5F
(0.76€) per person, per day

BREAKFAST
35F (5.34€) per person

ENGLISH SPOKEN
Yes

is the best of the bunch by far. While it is nothing fancy, the tidy rooms have price tags that appeal to couples on budgets who are happy in a busy city location. The rooms all display a wondrous mixture of period furniture, including some family pieces, such as an old dressing table on the fifth floor that belonged to the owner's *grand-mère*. Flocked and flowered wallpaper, chrome, plastic, fringe, ruffles, and chenille are also used with abandon, but as they redo the rooms, the mix-and-not-match approach gives way to a more coordinated look. There are two small knotty-pine-paneled rooms on the top floor that have mansard windows and are favorites with younger guests. No. 1 is a ground-floor double nicely done in florals with a plain rug, antique bedside tables, and a spotless bathroom with a stall shower.

A lifetime's collection of posters lines the stairs and hallways and now almost reaches the top floor. Postcards and photos sent to the Bernards by their guests cover the top of the reception desk, where Babar, a colorful thirty-year-old parrot, sits in the winter. In the summer he whistles his happy tune in the pretty blue-and-white dining room. While hardly a tourist mecca, the location is within walking distance of the Folies Bergère and a métro stop or two away from Montmartre. Motorists take note: The hotel has four free parking spaces. In any part of Paris, that convenience and savings alone are worth double the price of the room.

FACILITIES AND SERVICES: Direct-dial phone, elevator, hair dryer, TV, office safe (no charge), four free parking spaces

NEAREST TOURIST ATTRACTIONS (RIGHT BANK): Folies Bergère, Opéra, shopping at Galeries Lafayette and Au Printemps department stores

Eleventh Arrondissement

The eleventh and twelfth arrondissements are known as *quartiers populaires* because they are traditional working-class neighborhoods where many foreigners settle. These are not hotbeds of tourist activity, but they do provide interesting glimpses of both the blue-collar Parisian way of life and the new-wave artists. Place de la Bastille joins the third, eleventh, and twelfth arrondissements and still serves as the rallying point for demonstrations, just as it did in the French Revolution. The column in the middle stands where the prison once was. The neighborhoods around the Bastille and the futuristic new Opéra are the city's new bohemia, full of art galleries, lofts, cafés, nightclubs, and boutiques featuring the apparel craze of the moment. Humming night and day, this area is definitely one of the "in" places for anyone who likes to walk on the wild side and stroll on the cutting edge.

RIGHT BANK
Place de la République, Gare du Nord, Gare de l'Est, Bastille, new Opéra, nightlife around rue de Lappe

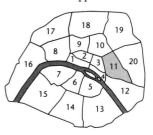

HOTELS IN THE ELEVENTH ARRONDISSEMENT

OTHER OPTIONS

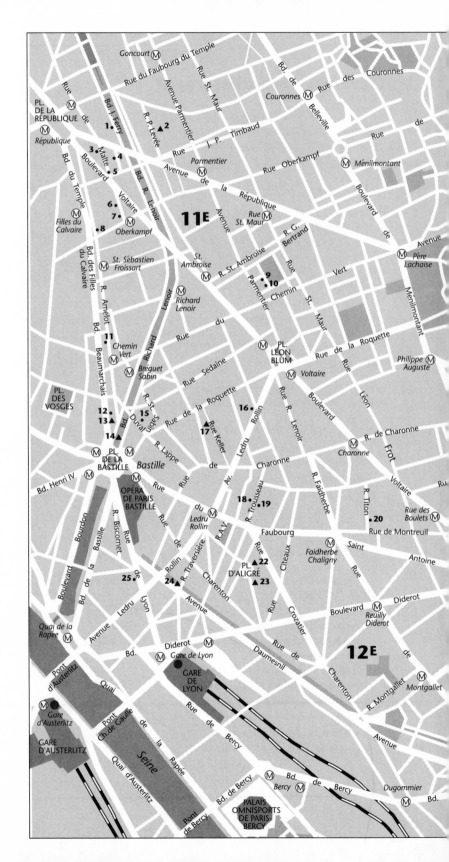

Eleventh and Twelfth Arrondissements

Ménilmontant
Rue
des Pyrénées
Rue Sorbier
Gambetta
Pelleport Ⓜ
Gambetta
Avenue
Gambetta
Ⓜ
PL. GAMBETTA Ⓜ
Rue Belgrand
Porte de Bagnolet Ⓜ
Porte de Bagnolet Ⓜ

Bd. Mortier

Porte de Bagnolet

20 E

CIMETIÈRE DU PÈRE LACHAISE

Rue de Bagnolet
Rue des Pyrénées
Boulevard Davout

Boulevard
Rue
Ⓜ Alexandre Dumas
de Bagnolet
Rue des
PL. DE LA RÉUNION
Orteaux

Av. Philippe
Dumas
de Charonne
R. Buzenval
Buzenval Ⓜ
Rue d'Avron
Maraîchers Ⓜ

A. Auguste
R. de Montreuil
Ⓜ Avron

.21
PLACE DE LA NATION
Av. du Trône
Rue de Lagny
Ⓜ Nation
Ⓜ
Cours de Vincennes
Ⓜ
Porte de Vincennes

Rue
Avenue de
Ⓜ Saint Mandé
Picpus
A. Netter
Av. du Docteur

de
Picpus
de Picpus
Ⓜ Bel Air
Bd.
Bd. Soult

Reuilly
Daumesnil Ⓜ PL. FÉLIX ÉBOUÉ
Reuilly
Bd. Soult
△ N
500 meters
de
Daumesnil Ⓜ
Av. Daumesnil

Ⓜ Métro Station
● R.E.R. Station

DAVAL HÔTEL ★★ (15)
21, rue Daval, 75011
Métro: Bastille, Bréguet Sabin

23 rooms, all with shower or bath and toilet

TELEPHONE
01-47-00-51-23

FAX
01-40-21-80-26

EMAIL
hoteldaval@wanadoo.fr

CREDIT CARDS
AE, DC, MC, V

RATES
Single 385–425F (58.69–
64.79€), double 425F (64.79€),
triple 505F (76.99€), quad
600F (91.47€); *taxe de séjour*
included

BREAKFAST
Continental 50F (7.62€) per
person

ENGLISH SPOKEN
Yes

Monsieur Gonod and his German shepherd dog, Malko, run this Bastille budget hotel with good sense, good humor, and kindness. Valued mainly for its "in" location and conservative prices, the Daval Hôtel occupies a platinum position in the white-hot Bastille area, only a short promenade from the new Opéra and all the cafés, bars, boutiques, and galleries that characterize this popular *quartier*. The beige and white rooms all have the same functional, easy-maintenance style: open closets, compact baths, built-in beds and side tables, blue floral spreads, and industrial-strength carpeting. There are no twin beds, but all rooms are air-conditioned, which is an almost unheard-of luxury in this price range.

FACILITIES AND SERVICES: Air-conditioning, direct-dial phone, elevator, hair dryer, TV with international reception, room safe (no charge)

NEAREST TOURIST ATTRACTIONS (RIGHT BANK): Bastille area, new Opéra

GARDEN HÔTEL ★★ (10)
1, rue du Général-Blaise (facing Square Parmentier), 75011
Métro: St-Ambroise

42 rooms, all with shower or bath and toilet

TELEPHONE
01-47-00-57-93

FAX
01-47-00-45-29

CREDIT CARDS
AE, MC, V

RATES
1–2 persons 370F (56.41€),
triple 470F (71.65€); extra bed
100F (15.24€); *taxe de séjour* 5F
(0.76€) per person, per day

BREAKFAST
Continental 35F (5.34€) per
person

ENGLISH SPOKEN
Limited

Need a neat, clean, safe, and comfortable temporary abode in the eleventh arrondissement? If so, I cannot imagine topping one of Mme. Adams's spotless forty-two rooms, many of which have balconies facing the Square Parmentier, a neighborhood gathering place that defines this corner of Paris. Her antiseptically clean hotel rooms, which are the pride and joy of the sweet housekeeper, Mme. Casablanca, are appointed with light pine built-ins, simple floral wallpaper, and lots of chenille. Color matches do not jar the senses, and bathrooms are functional and have good towels. For breakfast, you can join other guests at a long communal table in a breakfast room accented with a poster of Dutch tulips. Real flowers and potted plants line the reception desk, where you can plot your excursions in Paris by consulting the framed map of the métro.

FACILITIES AND SERVICES: Direct-dial phone, hair dryer available, elevator, TV, office safe (no charge)

NEAREST TOURIST ATTRACTIONS (RIGHT BANK): Bastille area, new Opéra

HÔTEL BEAUMARCHAIS ★★★ (8)
3, rue Oberkampf, 75011
Métro: Filles du Calvaire, Oberkampf

31 rooms, all with shower or bath and toilet

When asked the question, "What wonderful new hotels did you discover on your last trip to Paris?" I always have an answer. This time one of my favorites is the new and modern Hôtel Beaumarchais near the Bastille.

The hotel is owned by four inveterate travelers (a banker, lawyer, architect, and travel agent) who decided to open the kind of hotel they always hope to find, but seldom do. All I can say is that they have certainly succeeded in getting my vote of approval, and judging from their bookings, that of many others as well. The architect partner had his hand in the overall imaginative design, which merges high style with quality materials and classic lines. In the tiled lobby, an Afghan rug defines the seating space, which mixes orange, green, and yellow barrel chairs with clean-lined gray metal tables. A glass display case holds three shelves of various pyramids, including one that looks like a rocket launch. No one tried to camouflage the big metal heat exhaust pipe, which is in full view behind the reception desk. Nevermind, it takes a page from the Centre Georges Pompidou school of decorating and fits right in. Breakfast is served at marble bistro tables with opaque plastic-backed chairs that overlook an interior garden with a central magnolia tree.

The rooms are upbeat and cheerful, each with Italian-designed lighting and a sunburst and a framed modern art print on the walls. In No. 56, a single with a shower, the view is of the dome of the Cirque de l'Hiver (winter circus building). No. 55, a double on the front, has yellow walls, red fruit print bedspreads, and a brightly tiled bathroom. No. 2, a twin on the first floor, is the largest room with two wicker chairs and a Mark Rothko poster over the bed. Before you book this room, be sure the bathroom renovation has been completed. The suites are good buys if more space is a priority, but a bathtub is not . . . they only have showers. I like their sitting areas

TELEPHONE
01-53-36-86-86

FAX
01-43-38-32-86

EMAIL
hotel.beaumarchais@libertysurf.fr

INTERNET
www.hotel.beaumarchais.com

CREDIT CARDS
AE, MC, V

RATES
Single 390–450F (54.96–68.60€), double 550–590F (83.85–89.94€), suite 750F (114.34€); *taxe de séjour* included

BREAKFAST
Continental 40F–50F (6.10–7.62€) per person

ENGLISH SPOKEN
Yes

with cushioned armchairs, more work space, amusing cactus lights, and mirrored wardrobes.

One of the partners is usually on hand to make sure things are going well for all concerned. "We are very friendly," one of them said to me, and that is definitely true.

FACILITIES AND SERVICES: Air-conditioning in most rooms, direct-dial phones, elevator in one building (second building only one floor), hair dryer, TV with international reception, room safe (no charge)

NEAREST TOURIST ATTRACTIONS (RIGHT BANK): Bastille, five-minute walk to place de la République with five métro lines, buses, and taxi stand

HÔTEL DE VIENNE ★ (5)
43, rue de Malte, 75011
Métro: Oberkampf

23 rooms, 4 with shower, none with toilet

TELEPHONE
01-48-05-44-42

FAX
None

CREDIT CARDS
None, cash only

RATES
Single 143–233F (21.80–35.52€), double 176–236F (26.83–35.98€); extra bed for child only 50F (7.62€); *taxe de séjour* included

BREAKFAST
Continental 30F (4.57€) per person

ENGLISH SPOKEN
Yes

For cash-strapped globetrotters beholden to the bottom line, Paris hotel prices usually lead to one of two catastrophes: either of budget or of well-being. Coming to the rescue is this clean little cheapie near place de la République. For twenty years M. and Mme. Arnal have been dispensing their one-star, chenille-clad, mixed-pattern, plebeian-furnished roosts to scores of visitors who don't expect the moon, but who are happy with a bed and not much more . . . not even a shower in the hall if your room is *sans douche*. To get to these time-warped rooms you have to use the stairs, but all complaints are in vain when you get your bill and realize that these are some of the lowest prices in Paris.

FACILITIES AND SERVICES: Direct-dial phone, no elevator, no hall showers

NEAREST TOURIST ATTRACTIONS (RIGHT BANK): None; five-minute walk to place de la République and good public transportation

HÔTEL LYON-MULHOUSE ★★ (12)
8, boulevard Beaumarchais, 75011
Métro: Bastille

40 rooms, all with shower or bath and toilet

TELEPHONE
01-47-00-91-50

FAX
01-47-00-06-31

EMAIL
hotelyonmulhouse@wanadoo.fr

CREDIT CARDS
AE, DC, MC, V

The hotel is named for Lyon and Mulhouse, two stops that stagecoaches made when leaving Paris from the Bastille. This has been a hotel since 1920, and when looking at the early photos, you will see that from the outside nothing has changed, except that the saplings out front are now mature trees whose branches reach the top floor. There is absolutely nothing fancy or pretentious about the plain rooms, but they are very nice . . . not only for their more than ample size but for their spare, coordinated looks, computer hookups, views, and bathrooms with elongated tubs. For views of the Eiffel Tower, the Panthéon dome, and the Beaubourg, request a front room on the fourth, fifth, or sixth floors. Singles should be content in No. 345, a cozy nest under the eaves with vistas of the Eiffel Tower and Montparnasse, Invalides, and the Panthéon. Just once while you are here, take the stairs and notice the pair of pictures hanging in the hallways showing what Paris has lost— that is, the Bastille—and what it has won—that is, the Opéra Bastille.

FACILITIES AND SERVICES: Direct-dial phones, elevator, hair dryer, modems, TV with international reception, office safe (10F, 1.52€, per day)

NEAREST TOURIST ATTRACTIONS (RIGHT BANK): Bastille, nightlife, Marais, place des Vosges

HÔTEL NOTRE-DAME ★★ (3)
51, rue de Malte, 75011
Métro: Oberkampf, République
48 rooms, 31 with shower or bath and toilet

For those who want to spend time exploring Paris and require only a comfortable bed in a decent hotel close to transportation, this family-run hotel run by Joseph and Anne-Marie, a husband-and-wife team, should fill the bill. Both are personally on hand to welcome guests, and Joseph told me he especially likes intellectual clients. The working-class neighborhood is made up of shops that supply residents with life's necessities, but it holds little to capture most tourists' attention. However, the place de la République, with a métro station, taxi stand, and several bus routes crossing it, is only a five-minute walk from the hotel door.

A gray-blue and white interior extends from the reception on one side to the breakfast room, which doubles as a TV lounge and waiting room. It is simple and a bit sterile, but a clean beginning. All rooms have been recently renovated, and they are appealing so long as you don't mind open closets and limited drawer space. Many have balconies, and these are much better than those along the back, which have no view at all. My top choices include No. 64, a pretty yellow room for one with a balcony and stall shower; No. 65, done in soft beige with a balcony, double bed, and a stall shower in

RATES
Single 345–435F (52.59–66.32€), double 375–540F (57.17–82.32€), triple 565–595F (86.13–90.71€), quad 620–660F (94.52–100.62€); *taxe de séjour* included

BREAKFAST
Continental 30F (4.57€) per person

ENGLISH SPOKEN
Yes

TELEPHONE
01-47-00-78-76

FAX
01-43-55-32-31

EMAIL
hotelnotredame@wanadoo.fr

INTERNET
www.fac.fr/hotelnotredame/indexhtml

CREDIT CARDS
MC, V

RATES
Single 210–350F (32.01–53.36€), double 320–400F (48.78–60.98€), triple 430–460F (65.55–70.13€); free shower; *taxe de séjour* 5F (0.76€) per person, per day

BREAKFAST
40F (6.10€) per person

ENGLISH SPOKEN
Yes

the bathroom; and No. 27, a twin on the front with a bathtub, two chairs, and five shelves in addition to the exposed closet. For those in any of the five bathless roosts, there is a free shower on the first floor, and for those in one of the twelve shower-only rooms, there is a toilet on every floor.

FACILITIES AND SERVICES: Direct-dial phone, elevator, hair dryer available, TV in most rooms, office safe (no charge)

NEAREST TOURIST ATTRACTIONS (RIGHT BANK): Not much; five-minute walk to place de la République

HÔTEL PLESSIS ★★ (4)
25, rue du Grand Prieuré, 75011
Métro: Oberkampf, République
50 rooms, 35 with shower or bath and toilet

TELEPHONE
01-47-00-13-38
FAX
01-43-57-97-87
CREDIT CARDS
AE, DC, MC, V
RATES
Single 200–300F (30.49–45.73€), double 225–425F (34.30–64.79€); shower 10F (1.52€); *taxe de séjour* included
BREAKFAST
35F (5.34€) per person, buffet or Continental in room
ENGLISH SPOKEN
Yes

The hotel was built in 1925, and since 1953, it has been run by members of the Montrazat family, who take pride in their well-priced, friendly accommodations that budget travelers from around the globe call home when in Paris. The safe neighborhood is hardly action central for a tourist; it's a place where you will see a mix of old ladies in fuzzy slippers tossing baguettes to the pigeons, children playing, men gathered in cafés, and various shops selling life's necessities.

The six overstuffed Naugahyde armchairs in the faux-wood-paneled lobby and mezzanine bar, also with an upright piano, tell you that no one has called in a decorating team for years . . . if ever. However, you are not sleeping here, but in one of the perfectly adequate, clean chambers where the colors go together, there is space for your luggage, a chair to sit on, and the showers have curtains. Rooms on the fifth floor have balconies. There are good restaurants nearby, nightlife around the Bastille and the Marais are only two métro stops away, and you are a heartbeat from place de la République, where buses, métros, or taxis can take you wherever you want to be in the city.

FACILITIES AND SERVICES: Bar, direct-dial phone, elevator, fans, hair dryer, TV with international reception, office safe (no charge), one sitting room for nonsmokers

NEAREST TOURIST ATTRACTIONS (RIGHT BANK): Not much; short walk to place de la République

HÔTEL RÉSIDENCE ALHAMBRA ★★ (6)
11 bis and 13, rue de Malte, 75011
Métro: Oberkampf

58 rooms, all with shower or bath and toilet

Here is a textbook example of getting what you pay for. Out of the way? Yes, more than a New York minute to get to what's really happening. Close to the métro? Yes, five major lines serve place de la République. A good deal? Yes, a pleasant Parisian nest that would cost much more in tonier parts of the city.

The hotel is better than the neighborhood suggests. Automatic doors lead from the street into the light wood–paneled lobby, which looks onto a country garden. Open closets, no drawers, a built-in desk, and one chair sum up the rooms. Plumbing is of recent vintage in the tiled bathrooms, which have either a stall shower or shower and tub combined. Eight of the rooms overlook what has to be the prettiest hotel garden on the Right Bank—at least of all out-of-the-way two-stars. If you are lucky and secure one of these prime spots, you will overlook rose bushes, seasonal flowers, and trees, all lovingly tended by the owner's sister. Tables and chairs are set outside in the summer, making it an especially nice place to have your morning croissant.

FACILITIES AND SERVICES: Direct-dial phone, TV in twenty-five rooms (20F, 3.05€, extra per day, but free if you mention this book), office safe (no charge)

NEAREST TOURIST ATTRACTIONS (RIGHT BANK): None; short walk to place de la République

TELEPHONE
01-47-00-35-52

FAX
01-43-57-98-75

EMAIL
serviceclient@hotelalhambra.fr

CREDIT CARDS
MC, V

RATES
Single 330F (50.31€), double 365–395F (55.64–60.22€), triple 440–570F (67.08€), quad 650F (99.09€); *taxe de séjour* 5F (0.76€) per person, per day

BREAKFAST
35F (5.34€) extra per person, Continental

ENGLISH SPOKEN
Yes

HÔTEL RHETIA ★ (9)
3, rue du Général-Blaise (near avenue Parmentier), 75011
Métro: St-Ambroise

24 rooms, 16 with shower or bath and toilet

Keep the prices cheap enough and people will come back again and again, and they do—from Sweden, Belgium, Singapore, Australia, England, the United States, and Canada. As one Sydney, Australia, guest put it, "It is neat, clean, tidy, homey . . . all you need." I agree. Not all the rooms have private bathrooms, but they do come with a television. Most are minimally furnished in the usual one-star way, with a well-used collection of furniture. At only 15 francs per person, breakfast can be considered a gift. Grab it! The red hall carpets are worn but clean; the neighborhood is safe and quiet (for Paris); and the rooms along the front face the square Maurice

TELEPHONE
01-47-00-47-18

FAX
01-48-06-01-73

CREDIT CARDS
None, cash only

RATES
1–2 persons 180–240F (27.44–36.59€), triple 250–290F (38.11–44.21€); extra bed 50F (7.62€); shower 10F (1.52€); *taxe de séjour* included

BREAKFAST
15F (2.29€) per person

ENGLISH SPOKEN
Limited

Gardet. You are within reasonable walking distance to all the nightlife the area is known for, and you are a métro ride to everything else that is interesting. Please note, if you are calling or faxing for reservations, the front desk is open for business from 7:15 A.M. to 10 P.M.

FACILITIES AND SERVICES: Direct-dial phone, TV, laundromat on corner

NEAREST TOURIST ATTRACTIONS (RIGHT BANK): Bastille, new Opéra

LIBERTEL CROIX DE MALTE ★★ (7)
5, rue de Malte, 75011
Métro: République, Oberkampf
29 rooms, all with bath or shower and toilet

TELEPHONE
01-48-05-09-36, toll-free in U.S., 800-MERCURE
FAX
01-43-57-02-54
EMAIL
H2760-GM@accor-hotels.com
INTERNET
www.libertel-hotels.com, www.mercure.com
CREDIT CARDS
MC, V
RATES
Single 580F (88.42€), double or duplex 640F (97.57€); extra bed 150F (22.87€); *taxe de séjour* included
BREAKFAST
Buffet 50F (7.62€) per person
ENGLISH SPOKEN
Yes

A stay at this upgraded two-star near the Bastille can satisfy luxury-loving Right Bank natures as well as those with fun-loving Left Bank streaks. Admittedly it is a few degrees from Tourist Central, but transportation is quick and easy from place de la République.

Rooms are well done, baths are modern, and the professional staff congenial. The vivid color palette is taken from the reproduction paintings of Wallasse Ting that hang throughout the hotel. An unusual collection of boxed and acrylic art is displayed in the lobby, which flows into a bright glassed-in dining area with gaily upholstered chair cushions. The hotel has two buildings, one of which has an elevator, and that is the building with the best rooms. For example, in No. 7, the Ting poster of four brightly colored birds sets the turquoise tone for everything in the room: beds, side tables, wardrobe, stool, lampshades, and chair. The other building has duplex two-story rooms with spiral staircases that would not be safe for anyone traveling with children. Otherwise, the only duplex to definitely avoid is No. 207, where guests will have to contend with a painting of a sprawled nude woman over the bed and take a dangerous, winding fire-escape-style staircase to get to the bathroom, where the low roof will force most people to shower on their knees.

FACILITIES AND SERVICES: Bar, direct-dial phone, elevator in one building, TV with international reception, laundry service, office safe (no charge)

NEAREST TOURIST ATTRACTIONS (RIGHT BANK): None; near place de la République

Thirteenth Arrondissement

This large, working-class area is generally thought of as a tourist-free zone. It is the sort of place dedicated Parisian visitors see on their seventh or eighth trip, after they have done everything else they thought important. The area does hold some interesting surprises and should not be totally overlooked. There is the still-functioning Gobelins factory, which is open to the public. A stroll around the winding streets of the Butte aux Cailles district provides a delightful look at one of Paris's oldest yet unknown and untouched parts, but one that is getting renewed attention from insiders who think the eleventh has become passé. The arrondissement also has a huge Asian population, which produces some of the best, and certainly the cheapest, Asian meals to be had on avenue de Choisy, the main street of Chinatown. The Bibliothèque Nationale de France–François Mitterand, designed to replace the Bibliothèque National, is an eight-million-franc project, covering 288,000 square meters along the Seine across from the Ministry of Finance. This enormous new library building, built to resemble four open books, has caused as much controversy as the Opéra Bastille did (and still does).

RIGHT BANK
Gobelins tapestry factory (Manufacture des Gobelins), Butte aux Cailles, Bibliothèque Nationale de France–François Mitterand

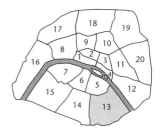

HOTELS IN THE THIRTEENTH ARRONDISSEMENT

LE VERT GALLANT ★★
41–43, rue Croulebarbe, 75013
Métro: Place d'Italie, Gobelins

15 rooms and studios, all with shower or bath and toilet

Balzac said it well: "Paris is an ocean in itself. There is always some spot never seen before, some unknown cavern, flower, pearls, delight hitherto unknown."

A stay at the appealing Le Vert Gallant provides that wonderful feeling of discovery, of finding an unknown corner of Paris for your very own. Located in the Gobelins district in the thirteenth arrondissement, this discreet garden hotel is a charming oasis for those who know Paris well and are looking for something a bit beyond the usual hotel room—and who are willing to sacrifice a dead-center location to get it. Across the street from the hotel is the René Le Gall Square, a green park filled with the sound of children's voices, *mamans* pushing prams,

TELEPHONE
01-44-08-83-50

FAX
01-44-08-83-69

CREDIT CARDS
AE, MC, V

RATES
Single 450F (68.60€), double 500–600F (76.22–91.47€); extra bed 90F (13.72€); *taxe de séjour* 5F (0.76€) per person, per day

BREAKFAST
Continental 40F (6.10€) per person

ENGLISH SPOKEN
Yes

and elderly men and women out for a few minutes of gossip or a quiet moment to read the papers. For anything else, you will need the métro, which is a ten-minute walk. Next door to the hotel is its restaurant, l'Auberge Etchegorry, a Basque retreat that offers hotel guests fantastic prices on prix fixe meals. For more on this special restaurant, see *Great Eats Paris.*

The hotel is made up of fifteen rooms, all of which have windows framing a garden courtyard, which is complete with thirty-seven grape vines. Your morning wake-up call will be the songs of birds in the trees, not the usual rude Parisian awakening from the trash haulers or by furious horn-honking motorists. If you want to cook during your stay, reserve a studio on the ground floor. The rooms above also have kitchens, but because of fire regulations, no actual cooking is allowed on the higher floors. All rooms have an uncluttered, modern look. Colors are soft and pleasing, the accessories appropriate, and the fabrics well coordinated. Bathrooms are small but modern. Maïté and Henri Laborde, your hosts here and at their restaurant, attend graciously to their guests, which further contributes to the overall feeling of well-being one has when staying at this special hotel. A warning is in order: Before arrival, have your affairs in order at home—you may never want to leave.

NOTE: To get there, take the métro to the Les Gobelins stop (at the bottom of the map for the fifth arrondissement, page 98). Walk south on avenue des Gobelins to rue Croulebarbe and take a right. The hotel will be on the left side of the street.

FACILITIES AND SERVICES: Direct-dial phone (each room has its own line), hair dryer, some kitchenettes in ground-floor rooms, minibar, two parking places that must be reserved ahead (40F, 6.10€, a night—an unheard-of bargain!), TV with international reception, office safe (no charge), no elevator (only two floors)

NEAREST TOURIST ATTRACTIONS (LEFT BANK): Nothing; must use public transportation

Fourteenth Arrondissement

In recent years Montparnasse has become the victim of a tragically insensitive redevelopment policy exemplified by the Tour Montparnasse. During the 1920s and 1930s, the fourteenth was well known as the artistic headquarters of the modern art and literary worlds, where Picasso, Modigliani, Chagall, and Léger all had studios. Nostalgia buffs return today and head for the historic brasseries Le Dôme and La Coupole to rekindle memories of the famous who ate and drank there, but they find the spirit is just not the same. Spirits of a different sort can be found at place Denfert-Rochereau, where the "Catacombs" are located. These underground cemeteries, created in 1785 as a hygienic alternative to the aboveground ones, hold the bones of six million Parisians, and during the World War II, they were used as a headquarters by the French resistance.

LEFT BANK
Montparnasse, Les Catecombs

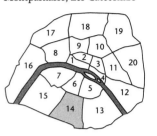

HOTELS IN THE FOURTEENTH ARRONDISSEMENT

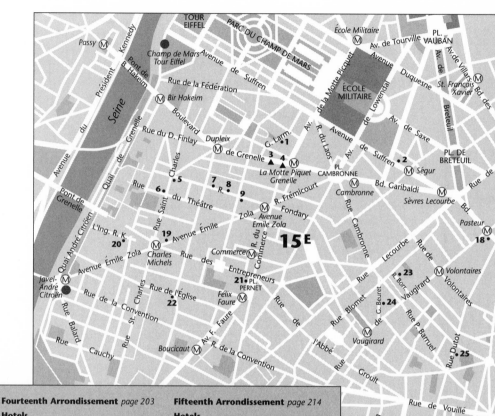

Fourteenth Arrondissement *page 203*

Hotels

11 Hôtel Lenox Montparnasse ★★★
12 Hôtel Raspail ★★★
13 Hôtel Delambre ★★★
14 Hôtel des Bains ★
15 Hôtel l'Aiglon ★★★
16 Hôtel Istria ★★
26 Hôtel Daguerre ★★
27 Hôtel de l'Espérance (NO STARS)
29 Hôtel de Blois ★

Shops

10 Galeries Lafayette
10 Maine-Montparnasse
17 La Boutique de l'Artisanat
    Monastique
28 Rue Daguerre
30 Rue d'Alésia
31 Marché de Vanves

Fifteenth Arrondissement *page 214*

Hotels

1 Hôtel Arès ★★★
2 L'Hôtel du Bailli de Suffren ★★★
5 Hôtel Charles Quinze ★★
6 Hôtel Beaugrenelle St-Charles ★★
7 Pacific Hôtel ★★
8 Family Hôtel
9 Hôtel Fondary ★★
18 Innova Hôtel
19 Hôtel Alize Grenelle Tour Eiffel ★★★
20 Practic Hôtel (NO STARS)
21 3 Ducks Hostel
22 Le Nainville Hôtel (NO STARS)
23 Aloha Hostel
24 Hôtel Délos ★★
25 La Maison

Shops

3 Marché Dupleix
4 Rue du Commerce

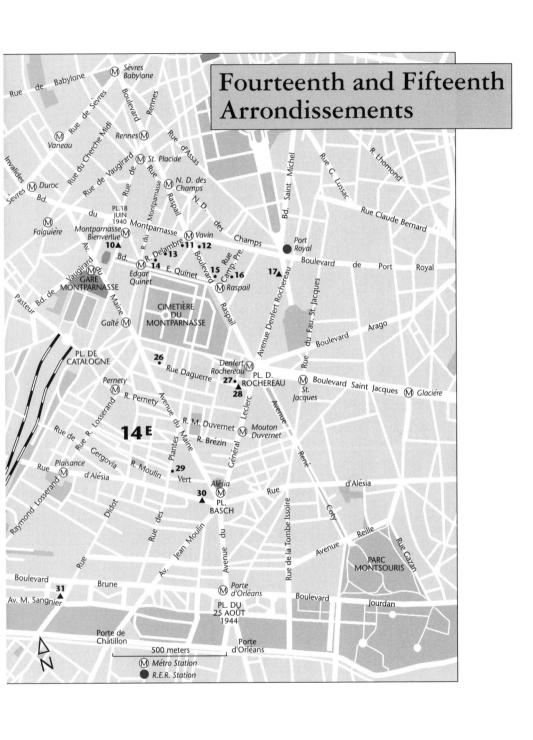

Fourteenth and Fifteenth Arrondissements

Rue de Babylone

Sèvres Babylone Ⓜ

Boulevard Raspail

Rue de Sèvres

Rue du Cherche-Midi

Rennes Ⓜ

Vaneau Ⓜ

Rue d'Assas

Rennes

Invalides

Ⓜ Duroc

Sèvres Bd.

St. Placide Ⓜ

Rue de Vaugirard

Rue de Rennes

N. D. des Champs Ⓜ

N. D. des Champs

Bd. Saint Michel

Rue G. Lussac

R. Lhomond

Rue Claude Bernard

Falguière Ⓜ

PL. 18 JUIN 1940

du

Montparnasse Bienvenüe Ⓜ

Montparnasse

10▲

Raspail

Vavin Ⓜ

•11 •12

Port Royal ●

Champs

Falguière

Av.

Rue du Montparnasse

Bd

R. Delambre •13

•14

E. Quinet

15

Boulevard

Camp. Pre.

•16

17▲

Boulevard de Port Royal

Vaugirard Ⓜ

GARE MONTPARNASSE

Edgar Quinet

Edgar Quinet Ⓜ

Raspail Ⓜ

Avenue Denfert Rochereau

Rue du Fau. St. Jacques

Boulevard Arago

Pasteur Bd. de

Bd. de Maine

Gaîté Ⓜ

CIMETIÈRE DU MONTPARNASSE

Raspail

PL. DE CATALOGNE

26 •

Rue Daguerre

Denfert Rochereau

PL. D. ROCHEREAU

27▲

St. Jacques

Boulevard Saint Jacques

Ⓜ Glacière

Pernety Ⓜ

R. Pernety

Avenue du Maine

28

Leclerc

St. Jacques

Rue de

Rue R. Losserand

Gergovia

R. M. Duvernet

R. Brézin

Mouton Duvernet Ⓜ

Avenue

René

14 E

Plantes

Plaisance Ⓜ

R. Moulin

•29

Vert

d'Alésia

Raymond Losserand

d'Alésia

Didot

Alésia

30▲ Ⓜ

PL. BASCH

Rue

Rue de la Tombe Issoire

d'Alésia

Coty

Reille

Rue Gazan

Rue

Rue des

Jean Moulin

Av.

Avenue du

Avenue

PARC MONTSOURIS

Boulevard

31▲

Brune

Av. M. Sangnier

Porte d'Orléans Ⓜ

PL. DU 25 AOÛT 1944

Boulevard

Jourdan

Porte de Châtillon

△
N

500 meters

Porte d'Orléans

Ⓜ Métro Station

● R.E.R. Station

HÔTEL DAGUERRE ★★ (26)
94, rue Daguerre, 75014
Métro: Gaîté, Denfert-Rochereau
30 rooms, all with shower or bath and toilet

TELEPHONE
01-43-22-43-54,
01-56-80-25-80

FAX
01-43-20-66-84

EMAIL
hotel.daguerre.paris.14@
gofornet.com

INTERNET
www.france-hotel-guide.com/
h75014daguerre.htm

CREDIT CARDS
AE, DC, MC, V

RATES
Single 420–450F (64.03–
68.60€), double 470F (71.65€),
suite 650F (99.09€); extra bed
100F (15.24€); *taxe de séjour*
included

BREAKFAST
Continental 42F (6.40€) per
person

ENGLISH SPOKEN
Yes

For a sleek, modern stay in this neck of the Paris woods, the Hôtel Daguerre is a top-notch two-star choice. Paintings of the *bouquinistes* along the banks of the Seine and a mural of the Louvre accent the small sitting room and stone-walled breakfast area. The standard-issue rooms are comfortably furnished and have more than their share of perks, including heated towel racks. The even-numbered rooms face the street and have showers and more noise. The odd-numbered slots have tubs and are quiet. Two rooms are handicapped-accessible. No room faces a blank wall. The best feature of No. 501, a cheerful twin, is its glassed-in veranda looking toward Montmartre. If this room is booked, ask for No. 601, which has views of Sacré Coeur, or No. 301, with a pleasant view of the garden. If you want your own little terrace, try Nos. 1 or 2.

NOTE: Also under the same ownership is the three-star La Régence Étoile Hôtel in the seventeenth (see page 250).

FACILITIES AND SERVICES: Direct-dial phone, elevator, hair dryer, minibar, TV with international reception, room safe (no charge)

NEAREST TOURIST ATTRACTIONS (LEFT BANK): Montparnasse

HÔTEL DE BLOIS ★ (29)
5, rue des Plantes, 75014
Métro: Alésia, Mouton-Duvernet
25 rooms, 17 with shower or bath and toilet

TELEPHONE
01-45-40-99-48

FAX
01-45-40-45-62

CREDIT CARDS
AE, MC, V

RATES
Single 240–350F (36.59–
53.36€), double 250–375F
(38.11–57.17€), triple 375F
(57.17€); free public shower;
taxe de séjour 3F (9.46€) per
person, per day

BREAKFAST
Continental 30F (4.57€) per
person

ENGLISH SPOKEN
Yes

When I first saw this hotel several years ago, it was my final hotel stop after a long, rainy day, and as I walked I thought, this place is about two blocks east of nowhere, and it better be very, very good. As you can tell, I needed to be impressed, and Mme. Fontange's Hôtel de Blois turned out to be a winner in the one-star hotel sweepstakes. It still is. Cozy, clean, and homey are the words that spring to mind when I think of her cheery sitting room with windows overlooking the street. Breakfast is served here in the morning, and the room is always filled with fresh flowers, never dusty plastic ones (which, as you must know by now, I definitely do not like).

Her overly feminine bedrooms are coordinated, thankfully displaying little of rainbow-palette color schemes and Garage Sale Gothic furniture. Ask for Room 2, with a double bed, polished armoire, tiny floral print wall covering, and a big pink tiled bathroom with new fittings and a shower curtain. Space is at more of a premium in No. 5, but it does have a table and dresser with a mirror and a TV pitched for easy viewing. No. 6 has a shower with doors, a double bed, and no view, but it does have space to live in. I would not want to stay in No. 3, which has a poor layout due to how the shower and toilet were squeezed in. Oriental runners on white painted stairs and a different mural on each of the floors make climbing to your room a pleasant exercise. For those who have been traveling awhile, or are staying more than a few days, a self-service laundromat is right next door. If you need a workout, there is a public swimming pool a hundred meters behind the hotel.

Shopaholics take note: You are within five-minute, bag-toting distance from one of the discount shopping meccas for savvy Parisians: rue d'Alésia. What you save on your room you can spend on a stylish outfit, the likes of which you won't see at home for at least another year, if ever. See "Shopping" for details.

FACILITIES AND SERVICES: Direct-dial phone, no elevator, hair dryer available, TV with international reception, office safe (no charge)

NEAREST TOURIST ATTRACTIONS (LEFT BANK): Discount shopping on rue d'Alésia; otherwise, must use public transportation

HÔTEL DELAMBRE ★★★ (13)
35, rue Delambre, 75014
Métro: Vavin, Edgar-Quinet
30 rooms, all with shower or bath and toilet

I continue to be impressed. Patrick Kalmy's Hôtel Delambre still has my vote for the smartest rehab effort in the fourteenth arrondissement. A few years ago, he took a dog-eared one-star where surrealist André Breton once lived and transformed it from stem to stern into a snazzy three-star and—this is important—kept the prices within reason. In cleaning out the debris from the old hotel, M. Kalmy found some unlikely treasures he incorporated nicely in the lobby and breakfast room. In the streetside dining area, he cleverly displays an old

TELEPHONE
01-43-20-66-31
FAX
01-45-38-91-76
EMAIL
hotel@hoteldelambre.com
INTERNET
www.hoteldelambre.com
CREDIT CARDS
AE, MC, V

RATES
Single 400–550F (60.98–
83.85€), double 470–600F
(71.65–91.47€), suite (1–4
persons) 750F (114.34€); *taxe
de séjour* included
BREAKFAST
Buffet 50F (7.62€) per person
ENGLISH SPOKEN
Yes

metal garden gate, and two original regal columns stand by the elevators.

The rooms are well done in two dominant colors: red and blue or yellow and blue. No. 40, with white walls and enameled doors with wood detailing, is a double with a built-in curved desk and an interesting view over a garden to a block of apartments beyond. No. 50, a two-room minisuite, combines the charm of sloping ceilings with smaller windows. The addition of a skylight, good closet space, and a large bathroom make this a popular choice. For walkers, the hotel is within reach of the Luxembourg Gardens, St-Germain-des-Prés, and the best of Montparnasse. Otherwise, public transportation is easy and close by.

FACILITIES AND SERVICES: Direct-dial phone, elevator to fourth floor, fax and computer lines, hair dryer, laundry service, minibar available, TV with international reception, room safe (no charge)

NEAREST TOURIST ATTRACTIONS (LEFT BANK): Montparnasse, Luxembourg Gardens, St-Germain-des-Prés

HÔTEL DE L'ESPÉRANCE (NO STARS, 27)
1, rue de Grancey, 75014
Métro: Denfert-Rochereau

TELEPHONE
01-43-21-41-04
FAX
01-43-22-06-02
CREDIT CARDS
MC, V
RATES
1–2 persons 200–350F (30.49–
53.36€), triple 360F (54.88€);
shower 20F (3.05€); *taxe de
séjour* 1F (0.15€) per person,
per day
BREAKFAST
Continental 25F (3.81€) per
person
ENGLISH SPOKEN
Yes

17 rooms, 6 with shower, none with toilet

Montparnasse is the neighborhood that made café-hopping famous, so there is no need to spend time in, or money on, your hotel room. You will be doing neither at Jackie Lacourarie's useful seventeen-room address that doesn't pretend to be stylish. It is situated right around the corner from rue Daguerre, a good place to observe the happenings on one of the more active shopping streets in the fourteenth arrondissement. Amenities are lean, but the rooms are *très propre* (very clean), free of cascading patterns and dizzying color schemes, and Jackie bills herself as "the original French mother," which means she will take good care of you. In digs like this, it is always budget-smart to book the cheaper, showerless rooms and use the hall facilities, which in this case are very good.

FACILITIES AND SERVICES: No elevator (two floors), hair-dryer available, TV, office safe (no charge)

NEAREST TOURIST ATTRACTIONS (LEFT BANK): Montparnasse

HÔTEL DES BAINS ★ (14)
33, rue Delambre, 75014
Métro: Edgar-Quinet

41 rooms, all with shower or bath and toilet

Your surroundings are far from the usual lean one-star, especially the formal sitting room decorated with silk flowers in a graceful silver bowl, Oriental rugs, and an oval dining table that would easily seat eight. For a one-star, the prices seem high, but for what you get, they are fair. Late risers will appreciate the set-back location from the street . . . all the rooms are quiet, at least for this part of Paris. The rooms aren't big on decorating frills, but they are free from the Day-Glo colors and frayed-at-the-edges furnishings one usually contends with in one-star abodes. They come equipped with a TV with international reception, hair dryer, room safe, and the possibility of private parking—an unheard-of extra in a one-star hotel.

Even though they lack much storage space, the best deals are the three suites. No. 447 is a two-room selection facing the courtyard. It is open and simply done with hardwood floors, coordinated fabrics, and a corner glass shower in the bathroom. Oddly enough there are no towel racks, and when I asked about their absence, I was told the towels were changed daily. I would hope so. If you are at all claustrophobic, you won't want Suite 227, with only a tiny barred ceiling window in the second bedroom. Some of the doubles (Nos. 111, 112, and 114) are really too small for two, unless you are staying only a night, have very limited luggage, or enjoy very cozy confines with your traveling companion. Better choices are No. 221, overlooking a garden, or No. 71, which can be a double or triple. It is decorated in yellow and has a big bathroom with a glassed-in shower.

FACILITIES AND SERVICES: Direct-dial phone, elevator in front building, hair dryer, parking (70F, 10.67€, per day), trouser press, TV with international reception, room safe (no charge)

NEAREST TOURIST ATTRACTIONS (LEFT BANK): Montparnasse, Luxembourg Gardens, St-Germain-des-Prés

TELEPHONE
01-43-20-85-27

FAX
01-42-79-82-78

CREDIT CARDS
AE, MC, V

RATES
1–2 persons 415–560F (63.27–85.37€), suite 650–700F (99.09–106.71€); *taxe de séjour* included

BREAKFAST
Buffet 45F (6.86€) per person

ENGLISH SPOKEN
Yes

HÔTEL ISTRIA ★★ (16)
29, rue Campagne Première, 75014
Métro: Raspail

TELEPHONE
01-43-20-91-82
FAX
01-43-22-48-45
CREDIT CARDS
AE, DC, MC, V
RATES
Single 580F (88.42€), double 580–600F (88.42–91.47€); extra bed 120F (18.29€); *taxe de séjour* included
BREAKFAST
Continental 45F (6.86€) per person
ENGLISH SPOKEN
Yes

26 rooms, all with shower or bath and toilet

From this address you can wander the tree-lined boulevards and sit in the famous cafés that were the watering holes of Hemingway, Fitzgerald, and Henry Miller when they dominated the Montparnasse literary scene. In the 1920s and 1930s, when this was the *quartier* for artists and writers, the Istria was home to many of them, including Man Ray and his mistress Kiki de Montparnasse, Marcel Duchamp, Josephine Baker, and the Russian poet Vladimir Mayakovsky. Now, under the direction of Philippe Leroux and his delightful wife, Danièle, the hotel is a favorite for those seeking a convenient Montparnasse location. A pretty tiled entry with African art and pieces of country antiques, black-and-white photos of old Paris, and Oriental rugs leads to a postage-stamp-size garden along the back of the hotel. Some of the rooms that overlook the garden are confining for two persons with any luggage. To avoid being cramped, request a third-floor nest. Remember, though, this building is old, and spacious rooms are not its strong suit; history, charm, and friendliness are.

FACILITIES AND SERVICES: Direct-dial phone, elevator for main building, hair dryer, laundry service, TV with international reception, room safe (no charge)

NEAREST TOURIST ATTRACTIONS (LEFT BANK): Montparnasse

HÔTEL L'AIGLON ★★★ (15)
232, boulevard Raspail, 75014
Métro: Raspail

TELEPHONE
01-43-20-82-42
FAX
01-43-20-98-72
EMAIL
hotelaiglon@wanadoo.fr
INTERNET
www.AIGLON.com
CREDIT CARDS
AE, DC, MC, V
RATES
1–2 persons 540–900F (82.32–137.20€), suite (1–4 persons) 1,100–1,550F (167.69–236.30€); extra bed 120F (18.29€); *taxe de séjour* 6F (0.91€) per person, per day

47 rooms, all with shower or bath and toilet

The Hôtel l'Aiglon is a refined choice about a one-minute walk from the Raspail métro stop. A formal tone pervades, from the faux book–lined bar to the beautifully redecorated rooms, all of which have been planned with discretion and good taste. Don't miss the original stained-glass windows over the stairway, which takes guests from the ground floor to a formal dining room with large sideboard and mahogany tables covered in starched white linen.

The rooms all face outward, and many have peaceful views over the Cimetière Montparnasse. They are color-coordinated, with textured fabrics, firm mattresses, good closet and luggage space, and bathrooms with windows.

The eight suites are dreams come true, especially No. 55, with its soft beige walls and carpets. The sitting room is comfortably furnished with a desk, sofa bed, and easy chair, and it has a half bath to one side. Twin beds in the bedroom, with its own balcony, and a double-sink bathroom make up the rest. I also like Suite 19, the only one with a kitchenette. It is handsomely done in kelly green and yellow with a pleasant sitting room, a large bedroom with a walk-in closet, and a beautiful bathroom. In No. 16, bright yellow and green are carried out on the quilted bedspread and curtains. The gray bathroom has gold and beige accents and a floral design in the shower. If you are *tout seul,* it is a perfect choice. Some people may not like the rooms on the top, or sixth, floor because the windows are higher than normal, but I find them quite charming. One of my favorite choices is No. 61. I like the room itself, with a three-drawer chest, a comfortable armchair, and print fabrics, but it is the bathroom that is the real star, with two windows and a view. Motorists will appreciate the private parking, and everyone enjoys the brand of service and hospitality provided by Jacques Rols and his staff.

FACILITIES AND SERVICES: Air-conditioning, bar, direct-dial phone, elevator, hair dryer, kitchenette in one suite, laundry service, minibar, private parking (80F, 12.20€, must request when reserving), TV with international reception, office safe (no charge), laundry service

NEAREST TOURIST ATTRACTIONS (LEFT BANK): Montparnasse

HÔTEL LENOX MONTPARNASSE ★★★ (11)
15, rue Delambre, 75014
Métro: Vavin, Edgar-Quinet
52 rooms, all with shower or bath and toilet

The atmosphere is engaging and the clientele an international blend at the Lenox Montparnasse. The collection of furniture suggests Art Deco and the 1930s in both the lobby and large bar to one side. Green plants bring life to the area, and beautiful sprays of fresh orchids give it wonderful color.

Rooms are nice, with just enough personality to set them apart from other mainstream Montparnasse hotels. If you want more leg room, reserve No. 69, a big twin with a corner sitting room, a tiny fireplace, and a rooftop view. It is softly decorated in blue and light gray. The bathroom has a rolling toiletry cart and blue and green

BREAKFAST
Continental 45F (6.86€) per person
ENGLISH SPOKEN
Yes

TELEPHONE
01-43-35-34-50
FAX
01-43-20-46-64
INTERNET
www.parishotels.com
CREDIT CARDS
AE, DC, MC, V
RATES
1–2 persons: standard 610–660F (92.99–100.62€), club 720–750F (109.92–114.34€); suite for 2–3 persons 1,150–1,400F (175.32–213.43€); *taxe de séjour* included

BREAKFAST
Continental 55F (8.38€) per
person
ENGLISH SPOKEN
Yes

inserts of flowers set against the white tiled walls. No. 56 is a Club Room, which means it is slightly bigger than a standard room, and the bathroom has a tub. No. 60 is a good-value, twin-bedded suite beautifully done in blue and white with hand-painted window shutters and an old tile heater with a marble top. Seating is nicely arranged around a sofa bed and two comfortable reading chairs. The view over a large apartment complex may remind you of *Rear Window*. The top-floor, two-room suite, with its marble fireplace and clock, period furniture, and geometric upholstery, shows that an eclectic combination of styles and patterns can work if done correctly. Amusing etchings of French ladies of leisure with their dogs or coyly wrapped in fur—and not much else—grace the walls. The narrow bathroom has all the extras, including Roger and Gallet products.

FACILITIES AND SERVICES: Bar, direct-dial phone, elevator, hair dryer, laundry service, parking (60F, 9.15€, per day), TV with international reception, office safe (no charge)

NEAREST TOURIST ATTRACTIONS (LEFT BANK): Montparnasse

HÔTEL RASPAIL ★★★ (12)
203, boulevard Raspail, 75014
Métro: Vavin, Raspail
38 rooms, all with shower or bath and toilet

TELEPHONE
01-43-20-62-86
FAX
01-43-20-50-79
EMAIL
raspailm@aol.com
INTERNET
www.123france.com
CREDIT CARDS
AE, DC, MC, V
RATES
Single 560–950F (85.37–144.83€), double 760–950F (115.86–144.83€), junior suite 1,200F (182.94€); extra bed 100F (15.24€); *taxe de séjour* 6F (0.91€) per person, per day
BREAKFAST
Continental 50F (7.62€) per
person
ENGLISH SPOKEN
Yes

Owner Christiane Martinent was in the fashion industry for years before she decided to change careers and become a hotelier. She bought the Hôtel Raspail in the late 1990s, and she has spent a great deal of time, energy, and money bringing it back to its former glory. The hotel's architecture, with arched bay windows and Art Deco ceilings, reflect the era of the 1920s, when painters, musicians, and patrons of the arts made Montparnasse into an international capital of artistic creation and inspiration. Everything in the hotel has either been saved or restored to its original look, including the metallic marquee over the front entrance. Careful attention has also been paid to the needs of guests who need to be plugged in to the digitally demanding world of today.

The rooms are done in a different colors, depending on the floor: peach on the first, champagne beige on the second, biege and green on the third, gray on the fourth, and blue on the top. All thirty-eight soundproofed and air-conditioned rooms face the street, and each honors a famous Montparnasse artist with a print of his or her work hanging on the wall. From some you can see the Eiffel Tower. I like No. 57, a corner room named for Jean Cocteau that has three windows with a direct view of the famous landmark. In addition there is a nice writing desk and a mirrored dressing area, enough closet space, and a white tiled bathroom with a tub. In No. 45, the Pierre Bonnard room, you can see Tour Montparnasse, and if you lean out the window, there is the Eiffel Tower.

FACILITIES AND SERVICES: Air-conditioning, bar, computer adaptors on request, direct-dial phones, elevator, hair dryer, laundry service, TV with international reception, room safe (no charge)

NEAREST TOURIST ATTRACTIONS (LEFT BANK): Montparnasse

Fifteenth Arrondissement

LEFT BANK
Nothing from a tourist's standpoint, but depending on the location, walking distance to La Tour Montparnasse, UNESCO, the Eiffel Tower, Champ-de-Mars

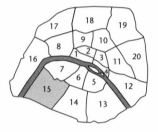

Home to a quarter of a million Parisians, the fifteenth is the biggest arrondissement, but it has few tourist attractions. If you enjoy seeing how the average Parisian lives, this is the perfect vantage point.

HOTELS IN THE FIFTEENTH ARRONDISSEMENT (see map page 204)

OTHER OPTIONS

HÔTEL ALIZE GRENELLE TOUR EIFFEL ★★★ (19)
87, avenue Émile Zola, 75015
Métro: Charles-Michels

TELEPHONE
01-45-78-08-22

FAX
01-40-59-03-06

EMAIL
alize@1sthotel-eiffeltower.com

INTERNET
www.1sthotel-eiffeltower.com

CREDIT CARDS
AE, DV, MC, V

50 rooms, all with shower or bath and toilet

The hotel has been rehabed, rewired, and redecorated, but fortunately not repriced. As a result, it is one of the least expensive three-star buys in the *quartier*. The color scheme is orange and deep rose—from the deep pomegranate-colored sofas and chairs in the sitting room to the hot orange–colored halls—and the same palette continues in the rooms on the first and third floors. The second and fourth floor rooms are done in yellow and either blue or bordeaux, and I personally like them better. You won't find much *vielle charme* or inherent French character in any of the bedrooms, but their motel *moderne* style leaves few surprises. And if you reserve via the Internet or during low-season, the price tags will be slashed. The hotel is owned by Monsieur Colliot, who also has the two-star Hôtel Beaugrenelle St-Charles around the corner (see page 216).

FACILITIES AND SERVICES: Air-conditioning, direct-dial phone, elevator, hair dryer, laundry service, modems, minibar, parking by reservation (80F, 12.20€), TV with international reception, room safe (20F, 3.05€, per day), trouser press

NEAREST TOURIST ATTRACTIONS (LEFT BANK): Fifteen-minute walk to Eiffel Tower; otherwise must use public transportation

RATES
Single 550–570F (83.85–86.90€), double 560–590F (85.37–89.94€); extra bed 160F (24.39€); lower rates on Internet and in off-season; *taxe de séjour* 6F (0.91€) per person, per day
BREAKFAST
50F (7.62€) per person, Continental or buffet
ENGLISH SPOKEN
Yes

HÔTEL ARÈS ★★★ (1)
7, rue du Général-de-Larminat, 75015
Métro: La Motte-Picquet Grenelle
42 rooms, all with shower or bath and toilet

Jean-Pierre and Mirka Seroin's Hôtel Arès is a family-owned and -run choice on a quiet street in a neighborhood of unqualified respectability. For high-scale shopping and dreaming, the Village Suisse antiques showrooms and shops are just around the corner. For dreaming of another kind, in less than ten minutes you can be in the Champ-de-Mars Park admiring the Eiffel Tower, and if you are here on the weekend, stroll through one of the best outdoor *marchés* in Paris on boulevard de Grenelle. The area is also filled with many *Great Eats Paris* restaurants in all price brackets.

The public parts of the 1913 building are attractive, especially the entryway, which has the original colored tile floor intact, and the breakfast area, which is set off by a window garden filled with brightly blooming plants. Each floor features a different painter, and once you get beyond the dubious color schemes of orange sorbet, bright daisy yellow, robin's egg blue, and key lime green that cover the rooms, you will find them to be clean and outfitted with all the conventional comforts. Bathrooms can be dubbed vintage, but functional. The four rooms facing the street have Eiffel Tower views, as do the two top-floor rooms, which have itsy-bitsy bathrooms but are otherwise just fine. My favorite rooms are those on the corners because they have lots of natural light and more space. Quite honestly, I like everything about this hotel and its on-the-ball management except one thing . . . the square toilet paper, which should be outlawed, especially in three-star hotels!

TELEPHONE
01-47-34-74-04
FAX
01-47-34-48-56
EMAIL
aresotel@easynet.fr
CREDIT CARDS
AE, DC, MC, V
RATES
Single 570–740F (86.90–112.81€), double 670–870F (102.14–132.63€), triple 990F (150.92€); extra bed 120F (18.29€); *taxe de séjour* included
BREAKFAST
Continental 50F (7.62€) per person
ENGLISH SPOKEN
Yes

FACILITIES AND SERVICES: Direct-dial phone, elevator, hair dryer, minibar, modems, parking (90F, 13.72€, per day), TV with international reception, room safe (no charge)

NEAREST TOURIST ATTRACTIONS (LEFT BANK): Village Suisse, Champ-de-Mars, Eiffel Tower

HÔTEL BEAUGRENELLE ST-CHARLES ★★ (6)
82, rue St-Charles, at place St-Charles, 75015
Métro: Charles-Michels, Dupleix
51 rooms, all with shower or bath and toilet

TELEPHONE
01-45-78-61-63

FAX
01-45-79-04-38

EMAIL
beaugre@francenet.fr

INTERNET
www.1sthotel-eiffeltower.com

CREDIT CARDS
AE, DC, MC, V

RATES
1–2 persons 540–580F (82.32–88.42€); extra bed 160F (24.39€); children under 12 free; *taxe de séjour* 5F (0.76€) per person, per day

BREAKFAST
50F (7.62€) per person, Continental or buffet

ENGLISH SPOKEN
Yes

This hotel is just as unassuming as its neighborhood, which offers a comfortable look at what everyday life is really all about in Paris, outside of the glittery and artsy *quartiers* that draw most visitors. You can spot the hotel from the place St-Charles . . . just look for the bright red awning and the boxwood bushes framing the entry. The lobby has Art Deco–style leather love seats and armchairs. A modern breakfast room with black laminated tables and chairs is set apart by a bank of green plants. A glassed-in walkway joins the two buildings that make up the fifty-one-room hotel.

Several ground-floor rooms open onto the garden, and these are some of the best. Three rooms on the sixth floor have balconies and Eiffel Tower views, and one on the back, a single, also has a peek of the Eiffel Tower. All the rooms are small, but decent closet space rescues them from feeling too cramped. Light, pastel-colored fabrics and blond furniture lend a modern touch. Peace and quiet prevails at night, as the neighborhood shuts down about 9 or 10 P.M. Owner M. Colliot and his staff work hard to please their guests both here and at his other hotel, the three-star Hôtel Alize Grenelle (see page 214).

NOTE: One of the best Monoprix stores in Paris is right around the corner. See page 323 for a description of this Parisian version of Wal-Mart, Kmart, and a huge supermarket all rolled into one.

FACILITIES AND SERVICES: Air-conditioning, direct-dial phone, elevator in front building only, hair dryer, laundry service, minibar, pets allowed, TV with international reception, room safe (20F, 3.05€, per night), some trouser presses

NEAREST TOURIST ATTRACTIONS (LEFT BANK): Eiffel Tower, shopping at the Centre Beaugrenelle; otherwise, must use public transportation

HÔTEL CHARLES QUINZE ★★ (5)
37, rue St-Charles, at 36, rue Rouelle, 75015
Métro: Dupleix, Charles-Michels
30 rooms, all with shower or bath and toilet

To some, the location of the Charles Quinze might be considered a tourist backwater. For others, it represents a change of pace and is a safe bet for those insisting on peace in noisy Paris. I like it not only because it is well maintained and executed but because it offers an uncongested experience of day-to-day Parisian life. In the place St-Charles, old men sit quietly under the shade of the chestnut trees reading their newspapers and talking about old times. Pretty young girls with long ribbons and smocked dresses roller-skate along the sidewalks, and matrons walk their little dogs. Hurrying housewives carrying brimming shopping baskets go from shop to shop picking just the right ingredients for their evening meal. For trips away from the hotel, the métro stop is only a five-minute walk, and the RER Line C to Versailles is close to the Eiffel Tower, both of which are about a fifteen-minute walk if you window-shop along the way.

The hotel is done simply but with great style. Blue-and-white Chinese porcelain creates an Oriental theme in the small, whitewashed lobby, and each floor of the hotel is coordinated in a different color: blue, pink, or yellow. The concise, spotless rooms have country-style, built-in furniture, and matching draperies and bedspreads. Be sure to notice the framed needlepoint in the reception area. If you look carefully, you will see one done by every member of the family. One dates from 1907, made by the owner's grandmother when she was a little girl. Another by the fireplace was done by her brother-in-law, and her son, Vincent, stitched the one hanging by the door when he was eight.

The hospitable owners, Claire and Martial Fournerie, also own the café/*tabac* next door. Drop in Monday through Friday between noon and 2 P.M. for a typical working-class lunch and order the daily special. They are open for business from 7 A.M. to 8 P.M. weekdays only, and they serve drinks and cold sandwiches when lunch is not in progress.

Mme. Fournerie always takes a personal interest in her guests and their well-being, and she would like know when guests find her through *Great Sleeps Paris . . .* so, please tell her you did.

TELEPHONE
01-45-79-64-15, toll-free in U.S., 800-221-4542

FAX
01-45-77-21-11

INTERNET
www.accorhotel.com

CREDIT CARDS
AE, DC, MC, V

RATES
Single 475F (72.41€), double 590F (89.94€); extra bed 160F (24.39€); children under 12 free; *taxe de séjour* included

BREAKFAST
Continental 55F (8.38€) per person

ENGLISH SPOKEN
Yes

FACILITIES AND SERVICES: Bar (next door), direct-dial phone, elevator, hair dryer, laundry service, minibar, modems, radio, TV with international reception, office safe (no charge)

NEAREST TOURIST ATTRACTIONS (LEFT BANK): A fifteen-minute walk to the Eiffel Tower; otherwise not much

HÔTEL DÉLOS ★★ (24)
7, rue du Général-Beuret, 75015
Métro: Vaugirard
43 rooms, 33 with shower and toilet, none with baths

TELEPHONE
01-48-28-88-32, 01-48-28-29-32

FAX
01-48-28-88-46

EMAIL
hoteldelos@wanadoo.fr

INTERNET
multimania.com/hoteldelos/

CREDIT CARDS
AE, DC, MC, V

RATES
Single 260–420F (39.64–64.03€), double 310–490F (47.26–74.70€); triple, add 100F (15.24€) to double rate; public showers free; lower rates in off-season; *taxe de séjour* included

BREAKFAST
Continental 30F (4.57€), buffet 50F (7.62€), per person

ENGLISH SPOKEN
Yes

Thanks to a Paris pal and born tipster, I discovered the forty-three-room Hôtel Délos. Where is it? Frankly, nowhere if you demand a hot location. On the other hand, it's worth consideration if your eye is on your pocketbook or you want to mix with regular Parisians and see how the salt-of-the-earth live.

The outside is neat and tidy. Inside, there is a miniature garden, a cafeteria-style breakfast room, and in the lobby, a sectional where you can sit and watch the news on a giant TV screen. Rooms are reached via a small elevator. If there are two of you, Nos. 11 and 31 are serviceable choices with open closets and a view of a green tree; No. 15 has twin beds and a window in the bathroom; and No. 16 can be for three, but it would be a tight squeeze. This is a strictly functional hotel offering unadorned, clean rooms devoid of the usual shabby chic one often finds in this price range. Okay, the towels don't always match and the perks are few, but the prices are very friendly, and so is management. And that is what counts for most of us.

Thanks J.B., you were right on.

FACILITIES AND SERVICES: Direct-dial phone, elevator, hair dryer in rooms with shower and toilet, TV with international reception, office safe (no charge)

NEAREST TOURIST ATTRACTIONS (LEFT BANK): None, must use public transportation

HÔTEL FONDARY ★★ (9)
30, rue Fondary, 75015
Métro: Avenue Émile-Zola
20 rooms, all with shower or bath and toilet

TELEPHONE
01-45-75-14-75

FAX
01-45-75-84-42

INTERNET
www.HotelFondary.com

CREDIT CARDS
AE, MC, V

If you do not require much space and won't rebel at an address in a tourist desert, then the Fondary is a quiet budget choice. Were it in a more tourist-inspired setting, the hotel would command higher prices and probably be full all the time with yuppies. The surrounding neighborhood provides a glimpse into Parisian bourgeois life that can be interesting, especially if you want to see more of the "real" Paris. On Wednesday and Sunday there is an enormous outdoor *marché* along boulevard de Grenelle, and every day along rue du Commerce you can watch daily life as shoppers crowd the stores and the open stalls, which sell everything from housedresses, lampshades, and junk jewelry to food, fresh flowers, and car parts. The hotel, owned by the Bosson family since 1920, is actually much better than outward appearances would suggest. On the main floor there is a pretty planked terrace off the dining room and a bar next to reception, where you can buy a soft drink or a beer. Upstairs, the quiet rooms, many of which have a terrace outlook, are decorated in white bamboo, grass cloth, and pastel fabrics. Prices match the size of the hotel: small.

FACILITIES AND SERVICES: Bar (soft drinks and beer), direct-dial phone, elevator, minibar, TV, office safe (no charge); one room is handicapped-accessible

NEAREST TOURIST ATTRACTIONS (LEFT BANK): Twenty-minute walk to Eiffel Tower; otherwise, must use public transportation

RATES
1–2 persons 400–425F (60.98–64.79€); *taxe de séjour* 5F (0.76€) per person, per day

BREAKFAST
Continental 40F (6.10€) per person

ENGLISH SPOKEN
Yes

INNOVA HÔTEL ★★ (18)
32, boulevard Pasteur, 75015
Métro: Pasteur

58 rooms, 55 with shower or bath and toilet

If you like Laurent Cuypers's Hôtel des Mines on boulevard St-Michel (see page 107), you will like the Innova maybe even more. It is a big hotel with fifty-eight rooms and a nice lobby done in the color of the moment: sunny yellow. Breakfast is served in a large room facing the street; tables are covered in Provençal prints and the ladder-back chairs have raffia seats. It is a very welcoming place to begin your Paris day. M. Cuypers's mother is a busy woman. Not only did she make all the curtains and bedspreads for the fifty-one rooms at the Hôtel des Mines, she did all the curtains for the Innova as well. Congratulations are in order for a job beautifully done.

When I visited the hotel, forty rooms had been redone. Eighteen were still waiting for urgent attention, and they are scheduled to be completed by the end of 2000—but just to be on the safe side, ask for a new room. What can you expect? Nonthreatening accommodations, many with ornate ceiling details, luggage space,

TELEPHONE
01-47-34-70-47

FAX
01-40-56-07-91

CREDIT CARDS
MC, V

RATES
1–2 persons 475F (72.41€), triple 575–675F (87.66–102.90€), quad 775F (118.15€); *taxe de séjour* included

BREAKFAST
Buffet 40F (6.10€) per person

ENGLISH SPOKEN
Yes

a hard chair or two, and yellow, blue, white, orange, or lavendar color schemes. Those facing the front of the busy street will be noisy. You can improve your French comprehension by listening to the French-only television channels, or plug in your computer if you need to. Management, under the direction of Jean-Pierre Fromont, is exceptional.

FACILITIES AND SERVICES: Direct-dial phones, hair dryer, lift between every two floors (a new one is planned), parking (70F, 10.67€, per day), TV, office safe (no charge)

NEAREST TOURIST ATTRACTIONS (LEFT BANK): Montparnasse

LE NAINVILLE HÔTEL (NO STARS, 22)
53, rue de l'Église, at 17, rue de la Rosière, 75015
Métro: Charles-Michels, Félix-Faure
37 rooms, 5 with shower or bath and toilet

TELEPHONE
01-45-57-35-80

FAX
01-45-54-83-00

CREDIT CARDS
None, cash only

RATES
1–2 persons 220–375F (33.54–57.17€); public shower 25F (3.81€); *taxe de séjour* included

BREAKFAST
Continental (served in bar) 40F (6.10€) per person

ENGLISH SPOKEN
No

Perched over a bar and café in a pedestrian corner of the fifteenth arrondissement is the budget-lover's Nainville, where prices fall into a prehistoric time warp. Considering the logistics, you would hardly expect it to offer the comforts it does. Let's start with breakfast, which is served in the bar below and includes orange juice and a croissant along with bread and jam. Most no-star hotels wouldn't think of serving breakfast, let alone providing juice as well as croissants and jam. Next, in the fancy rooms (those with a bathtub, that is), you will find a *peignoir* (a bathrobe!). Want to take a break and catch up on the news or sports around the world? Then just flip the TV to CNN or EuroSport and you have it all . . . in English. All this in a no-star hotel?

All right, everything isn't totally a bouquet of roses: there is no elevator, no twin beds, and the toilet paper is square. Then there is the matter of the interior decoration, which in some rooms literally screams at you with wild wallpaper and carpets that were never meant to match anything. But in the end, the good points far outweigh the bad. The semi-antique furniture is comfortably worn but not shabby. The rooms and the bathrooms—both private and those in the hall—are clean. The rooms with private toilets and showers overlook the pretty Square Violet; the neighborhood is quiet all the time; and the owners, Mme. Dupuy and her husband, who runs the bar, are accommodating. I was interested to find out that on April 10, 1938, M. Dupuy was born in the hotel in a second-floor room. It is the one that has a tree in a window box (you can see it well from Room 20). Room 15 belonged to his parents, and it still has their 1937 mirrored armoire. Some other good bets include Nos. 20 and 30 overlooking the park; No. 41, which looks onto a rose garden; No. 10, with a double-beveled-glass armoire; and No. 16, which is on the street, but has the best use of color. Avoid Nos. 13 (too small), 14 (ugly carpet and furniture, no view), 23 (bad shower), and 25 (hideous furry bedspread).

NOTE: The hotel is closed all of July and August

FACILITIES AND SERVICES: Bar; direct-dial phone, no elevator or safe, TV with international reception

NEAREST TOURIST ATTRACTIONS (LEFT BANK): None; must use public transportation

L'HÔTEL DU BAILLI DE SUFFREN ★★★ (2)
149, avenue de Suffren, 75015
Métro: Ségur

25 rooms, all with shower or bath and toilet

The hotel honors the memory of Admiral Pierre André de Suffren, who was appointed Bailli (chief magistrate) of the order of Malta and, in his wake, left a trail of adventures that ranged from Saint Tropez to the Caribbean.

The red carpet at the door suggests the type of first-class treatment you will receive at this dignified hotel owned by M. and Mme. Tardif. Tradition reigns supreme, from the downstairs living room outfitted with comfortable sofas and chairs to the mirrored garden-themed breakfast room and the fabric lined elevator, which delivers guests to the twenty-five individually decorated rooms.

Each one, warmly enhanced by undisputed good taste and harmony, displays a successful mix of reproduction furniture, lush fabrics, and thoroughly modern bathrooms. No. 304 has a ship theme, carried out in the regal colors of gold, blue, and red. The wood-paneled bathroom has a walk-in tiled shower complete with a porthole mirror and a bench for those who prefer to sit while showering. For families, Nos. 403 and 404 can be combined into a two-room apartment. I would be happy in No. 503, a single on the front with a slightly Oriental caste suggested by the grass-cloth-covered walls and the Thai carved woodwork on the closet doors and over the bed. As with all the rooms, toiletries are excellent, towels nice, and mirrors plentiful. After a long day, it is nice

TELEPHONE
01-47-34-58-61

FAX
01-45-67-75-82

EMAIL
bailli.suffren.hotel@wanadoo.fr

INTERNET
www.123france.com/baillidesuffren

CREDIT CARDS
AE, MC, V

RATES
Single 730F (111.29€), double 890F (135.68€), suite 1,600F (243.92€); extra bed 100F (15.24€); ask about special rates and weekend packages; *taxe de séjour* included

BREAKFAST
Continental 45F (6.86€), buffet 75F (11.43€)

ENGLISH SPOKEN
Yes

to join other guests in the living room and share a glass of the hotel's own wine, which comes from vineyards in Aix-en-Provence. The wines (red, rose, and white) are also for sale by whole or half bottles.

FACILITIES AND SERVICES: Air-conditioning, bar, direct-dial phone, elevator, hair dryer, laundry service, some magnifying mirrors, minibar, modems, room safe (no charge), room service for light meals, TV with international reception, *peignoirs* and slippers for VIPs, some trouser presses

NEAREST TOURIST ATTRACTIONS (LEFT BANK): Fifteen-minute walk to Champ-de-Mars, Eiffel Tower, and Invalides; UNESCO

PACIFIC HÔTEL ★★ (7)
11, rue Fondary, 75015
Métro: Avenue Émile-Zola, Dupleix
64 rooms, 43 with shower or bath and toilet

TELEPHONE
01-45-75-20-49

FAX
01-45-77-70-73

CREDIT CARDS
MC, V

RATES
Single 200–316F (30.49–48.17€), double 260–375F (39.64–57.17€); free showers; *taxe de séjour* included

BREAKFAST
Continental 35F (5.34€) per person

ENGLISH SPOKEN
Yes

This hotel and the Family Hôtel (a residence hotel, see page 274) are owned by Michelle, a gracious multi-lingual woman who took them over from her parents and grandmother. Both are on the same street in a blue-collar corner of Paris that is within a brisk fifteen-minute walk to the Eiffel Tower. At the Pacific, the rooms are sparse and spare with blond furniture and neutral colors. Eight in the back building have balconies, and all of those with private facilities have had recent upgrades. Housekeeping is good; you won't see dirt or mold lurking in corners anywhere. Though amenities are lean, so are the prices, which seem so old and behind the times they are almost fossilized.

FACILITIES AND SERVICES: Direct-dial phone, elevator in front building, hair dryer, TV in rooms with facilities, office safe (no charge)

NEAREST TOURIST ATTRACTIONS (LEFT BANK): Fifteen-minute walk to Eiffel Tower; otherwise, must use public transportation

PRACTIC HÔTEL (NO STARS, 20)
20, rue de l'Ingénieur Robert Keller, 75015
Métro: Charles-Michels
34 rooms, 27 with shower or bath and toilet

TELEPHONE
01-45-77-70-58

FAX
01-40-59-43-75

EMAIL
Hotel.Practic.hotel.15E@wanadoo.fr

INTERNET
www.practichotel.wanadoo.fr

For a cheap bed in the fifteenth arrondissement, the Practic Hôtel, just behind the Centre Beaugrenelle shopping complex, attracts a loyal band of regulars who are looking to cut accommodation corners in order to enjoy other aspects of their stay in Paris. While it's definitely not a candidate for those who revel in Louis XV or Madame Pompadour surroundings, the hotel displays few of those depressing, exhausted, faded, and snagged interiors that plague almost every other budget address in Paris. You will be welcomed by one of the sweetest managers this side of heaven, Mme. Agnes Bihan, who has been behind the desk since 1962, and if you are lucky, by Byron, a blond cocker spaniel dog with wonderful, long, curly ears.

The entry—in dull brown with industrial-strength carpeting, a vase of flowers, and old prints of Paris scattered around—definitely is past its due-date and needs a new look. But you don't live in the entry, so just keep going. I am a fan of No. 50, a double with soft gray-and-blue carpet, two desks, a view of the skyscraper apartments that line the Seine, and a beautiful bathroom with a stall shower. Double-glazed windows help to keep the noise levels down. No. 52 is just as nice and has plenty of space. No. 17, in blue with only a sink and bidet, is for one or two people. On the fifth floor is a two-room suite (don't forget we are in a no-star here) with blond furniture. One room has twin beds, the other just one twin. The bathroom comes with soap and shampoo and shower doors . . . all for under $100. What a deal! Eight rooms have *cour* views, but they are not too bad. One thing I noticed on my last visit was that some of the rooms held the smoke smell of their last puffing inhabitants. To avoid this unpleasant situation, be sure to state *when reserving* that you want your room to be thoroughly aired out before your arrive. Breakfast is served in a blue-and-white first-floor dining room and includes cheese, fruit compote, juice, croissants, bread, and jam.

FACILITIES AND SERVICES: Direct-dial phone, elevator, hair dryer available, TV, office safe (no charge)

NEAREST TOURIST ATTRACTIONS (LEFT BANK): None; must use public transportation; nearby is one of the best Monoprix stores in Paris (see "Shopping," page 323)

CREDIT CARDS
AE, MC, V

RATES
1–2 persons 265–385F (40.40–58.69€), triple 525F (80.04€), suite 450F–525F (68.60–80.04€); extra bed 90F (13.72€); free public showers; *taxe de séjour* included

BREAKFAST
Continental 45F (6.86€) per person (includes juice, yogurt, and cheese)

ENGLISH SPOKEN
Generally, yes

Sixteenth Arrondissement

RIGHT BANK
Avenue Foch, Bois de Boulogne, Jardin d'Acclimitation, Marmottan Museum, Musée Guimet, Maison de Balzac, Passy, Palais de Chaillot, Trocadéro, shopping along avenue Victor-Hugo

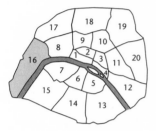

Known as a sedate, posh, and old-moneyed sector, the sixteenth is the home of the BCBG (*bon chic bon genre*) crowd, otherwise known as French yuppies. This is stylish territory, bordered by the Bois de Boulogne and the River Seine. Here you will see luxurious apartments along with prostitutes and transvestites in BMWs on the avenue Foch and at night in the Bois de Boulogne luring customers. Fashionable shops line the rue de Passy and the avenue Victor-Hugo. The Trocadéro, directly across from the Seine and the Eiffel Tower, is the name for the gardens around the Palais de Chaillot, an imposing two-winged building that houses four museums. The spectacular view from the steps of the Trocadéro at night, across the Seine to the Eiffel Tower, with the illuminated pools, fountains, and statues between, is one you must not miss. Neither do you want to miss the Marmottan Museum, which houses a magnificent display of Claude Monet's water lily canvases; the Guimet, which has a collection of Oriental and Asian art; or the Maison de Balzac, the home where Honoré de Balzac lived and worked.

HOTELS IN THE SIXTEENTH ARRONDISSEMENT

OTHER OPTIONS
Camping Out

($) indicates a Big Splurge

AU PALAIS DE CHAILLOT HÔTEL ★★ (13)
35, avenue Raymond Poincaré, 75016
Métro: Trocadéro, Victor-Hugo

28 rooms, all with shower or bath and toilet

For up-to-the minute appeal in an area not known for budget anything, look no further than this hotel. Two brothers, Cyrille and Thierry Pien, who received their masters in business administration in the United States, joined forces and completely gutted and revamped the twenty-eight room hotel, which is nicely situated between the Trocadéro and the Champs-Élysées. The results are impressive. And so are the prices. A 5 percent discount is given throughout the year to readers who mention the book, and a whopping 15 percent is given from July 15 to August 31 on the price of any room. Reserve now, and don't forget to say who sent you!

From beginning to end, the hotel is a model of postmodern, casual French chic. Two potted trees frame the red awning entrance. To one side is a little summer terrace where breakfast can be served; otherwise, breakfast takes place in a yellow marbleized room with a half-mirrored wall reflecting five tables and armchairs. The bright bedrooms combine wicker with bold colors and have flashy bathrooms that include tubs and/or showers with corner shelves for shampoo and soap. All doubles face the street, and from Nos. 61, 62, and 63 you can see the tip of the Eiffel Tower. There are five rooms similar to No. 34, which is on the back. I like the walk-in closet, the small sitting area with red detailing around the ceiling, and the Dufy print over the bed. These rooms also have twin beds that can be adapted to a king. In addition to the usual amenities, the hotel offers room service for drinks, laundry service, and PC compatible plugs. For the area, it is impossible to imagine a better value.

FACILITIES AND SERVICES: Direct-dial phone, elevator, hair dryer, laundry service, PC compatible plugs, room service for drinks, TV with international reception, office safe (no charge)

NEAREST TOURIST ATTRACTIONS (RIGHT BANK): Palais de Chaillot, Trocadéro, shopping along avenue Victor-Hugo and in Passy, Arc de Triomphe, and Champs-Élysées

TELEPHONE
01-53-70-09-09

FAX
01-53-70-09-08

EMAIL
hapc@club-Internet.fr

INTERNET
www.chaillotel.com

CREDIT CARDS
AE, DC, MC, V

RATES
Single 490F (74.70€), double 590 (89.94€), junior suite 660F (100.62€); extra bed 150F (22.87€); 5 percent discount anytime for *Great Sleeps Paris* readers, and 15 percent July 15–Aug 31; *taxe de séjour* 5F (0.76€) per person, per day

BREAKFAST
Continental 45F (6.86€) per person

ENGLISH SPOKEN
Yes

Sixteenth Arrondissement

Bd. R. Wallace

Allée de Longchamp

Porte
Dauphine

PL. DU
M. DE LATTRE
DE TASSIGNY

Route   de   Suresnes

Rue   de la Faisanderie

Allée de Longchamp

Rue

Avenue   de

BOIS

Boulevard   Lannes

DE

Porte de la
Muette

Av.   Henri   Martin

Bd.   Rue

BOULOGNE

PL. DE
COLOMBIE

Émile   R. de la Pompe

Allée de la Reine Marguerite

Augier   **16**

Boulevard   Suchet

Avenue   Raphaël

CARREFOUR
DES
CASCADES

La Muette   Av.

Avenue   de   l'Hippodrome

Ch. Muette (M)

24

Cloud

Av. de   Ingres   Beauséjour

Saint

Bd.   Rue   du   Av. Mozart

de

Rue   (M)

de Ranelagh   Ranelagh

HIPPODROME
D'AUTEUIL

R. Jasmin   Mozart   l'Assomption

Rue

Boulevard   Suchet   de   Montmorency

(M) Jasmin

Avenue

La Fontaine   Gautier

Bd.   de

Rue   Théophile

Porte
d'Auteuil

Av.   PL. DE

Avenue de la Porte d'Auteuil

PL. DE LA
PORTE DE
D'AUTEUIL

Rue d'Auteuil (M) Michel Ange
Auteuil

Église
d'Auteuil

BARCELONE   Versailles

Murat   (M) Porte d'Auteuil

(M)
Michel Ange   Chardon
Molitor   Lagache   R. Mirabeau Mirabeau

Pont
Mirabeau

Boulevard

Porte
Molitor

Rue   (M) Molitor   (M)

Rue Balard

d'Auteuil

Michel   Chardon

Boulevard

Rue du Château

Avenue   Robert   Schuman

Bd.

Lagache

Avenue   de   Quai Louis Blériot

de   Exelmans (M) Exelmans

Versailles

Rue

PARC
ANDRÉ CITROËN

R. C. Farrère

PARC
DES
PRINCES

Rue

de

△
N

500 meters

(M) Métro Station

● R.E.R. Station

Route de la Reine

Avenue

Pont de
Garigliano

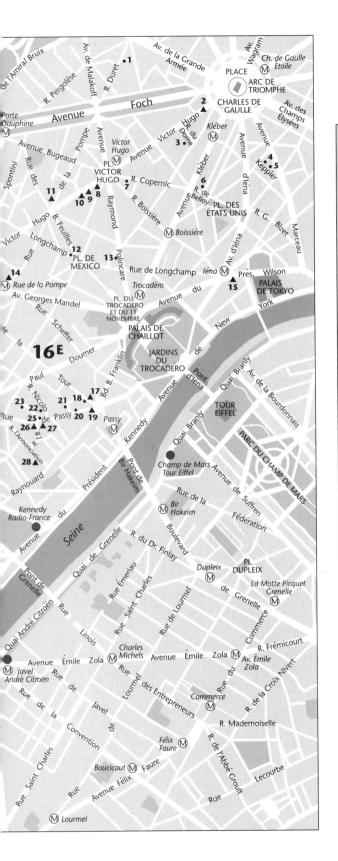

CHAMBELLAN MORGANE ★★★ (5)
6, rue Keppler, 75016
Métro: George-V, Charles-de-Gaulle-Étoile
20 rooms, all with shower or bath and toilet

TELEPHONE
01-47-20-35-72
FAX
01-47-20-95-69
INTERNET
www.france-hotel-guide.com/
h77116chambellan.htm
EMAIL
chambellan.morgane@
gofornet.com
CREDIT CARDS
AE, DC, MC, V
RATES
1–2 persons 800–1,000F
(121.96–152.45€); *taxe de séjour*
6F (0.91€) per person, per day
BREAKFAST
Buffet 60F (9.15€) per person
ENGLISH SPOKEN
Yes

In 1984, when I began writing my Paris hotel guide, I fell in love with a little hotel in the sixteenth arrondissement called Résidence Morgane. It was run by a *petite grand-mère* who pampered her guests beyond the call of duty. She would make an omelet at midnight, keep your messages, forward your mail, and do your laundry and ironing if asked. When I returned a year later, Madame had left and the hotel had been taken over by a gruff, noncaring owner. Five years later, on a hunch, I decided to recheck the hotel. I am so glad I did. Although Madame had not come back, new owners had masterminded a renovation that turned the hotel into the epitome of three-star elegance and classic luxury. Things have not changed since: they still do their utmost to please their international clientele.

The stage is set by the entrance and lobby, done in yellow and blue with white enamel woodwork and beautifully upholstered Louis XV–style antiques. The only holdover from the past is the old, copper Morgane nameplate by the front doorstep. Well lighted halls lead to stylishly outfitted bedrooms with silk wall coverings, matching quilted spreads and curtains, a comfortable chair, and efficient mirrored and marbled bathrooms. Lower rates in July and August and on weekends, subject to availability, make this more attractive to wider audience.

FACILITIES AND SERVICES: Bar; conference room, direct-dial phone, elevator, hair dryer, minibar, radio, room service, laundry service, TV with international reception, office safe (no charge)

NEAREST TOURIST ATTRACTIONS (RIGHT BANK): Champs-Élysées, Arc de Triomphe

HÔTEL DE SÉVIGNÉ ★★★ (6)
6, rue de Belloy, 75016
Métro: Bossière, Kléber
30 rooms, all with shower or bath and toilet

TELEPHONE
01-47-20-88-90
FAX
01-40-70-98-73
EMAIL
hotel.de.sevigne@wanadoo.fr
INTERNET
www.hotel-sevigne.fr
CREDIT CARDS
AE, DC, MC, V

"My sole occupation is the immense joy of receiving you into my home." These words, written by the Marquise de Sévigné in a letter to her daughter on February 5, 1674, echo the welcome extended today by the owner of this hotel, Mme. Boileau, and her professionally trained staff.

Who was the Marquise de Sévigné? Marie de Rabutin-Chantal, Marquise de Sévigné (1626–1696), was a prolific letter writer who shed light on the political, social, and literary aristocratic life of high society and the nobility of the seventeenth century during the reign of Louis XIV. Orphaned at an early age, she was educated by her grandmother, who began a convent in Paris. The street, rue de Belloy, was on the edge of the convent's fields. Madame de Sévigné lived an elegant life in castles around France, but from 1677 to 1696, when she was in Paris, she held court in her townhouse, the Hôtel Carnavalet near the place des Vosges.

The hotel is an excellent three-star value and loaded with extras. The five floors of the hotel are named after people and places of significance in Madame Sévigné's life. The first floor is named after her husband's castle, Les Rochers; the second, Carnavalet, her home in Paris; third, Bourbilly, her grandmother's castle; fourth, Le Comte Roger Bussy-Rabutin, her cousin; and the fifth, Le Chateau de Grignan, her daughter's castle where Madame died. All thirty rooms are designed to cater to the comfort and well-being of their guests. In each you will find a large desk with both fax and computer connections, balconies on the second and fifth floors, plenty of closet and luggage space, and bathrooms with magnifying mirrors, space for toiletries, and good lighting. The hotel is across from the place des Etats-Unis, a quiet green square only a few minutes from all the pomp and circumstance awaiting you along the Champs-Élysées.

FACILITIES AND SERVICES: Direct-dial phones, elevator, hair dryer, laundry service, minibar, modems, parking (200F, 30.49€, per day), TV with international reception, room safe (no charge)

NEAREST TOURIST ATTRACTIONS (RIGHT BANK): Champs-Élysées, Trocadéro, Palais de Chaillot, Eiffel Tower

RATES
1–2 persons 700–800F (106.71–121.96€); extra bed 250F (38.11€); *taxe de séjour* 6F (0.91€) per person, per day

BREAKFAST
55F (8.38€) per person, buffet or Continental

ENGLISH SPOKEN
Yes

HÔTEL DU BOIS ★★★ (3)
11, rue du Dome, at 29, avenue Victor-Hugo, 75016
Métro: Charles-de-Gaulle-Étoile, Kléber
41 rooms, all with shower or bath and toilet

For a stay on the exclusive avenue Victor-Hugo, just ten boutiques down from the Arc de Triomphe and place d'Étoile, many consider the Hôtel du Bois to be a reasonable choice. However, while it was a two-star last edition, it has now upgraded to a three-star, and the hotel doesn't quite live up to such lofty aspirations. In fact, it really remains an adequate two-star hotel with some

TELEPHONE
01-45-00-31-96

FAX
01-45-00-90-05

EMAIL
hoteldubois@wanadoo.fr

INTERNET
www.hoteldubois.com

CREDIT CARDS
AE, MC, V

RATES
Single 560–595F (85.37–
90.71€), double 625–790F
(95.28–120.43€); extra bed
250F (38.11€); lower off-season
rates; *taxe de séjour* 6F (0.91€)
per person, per day

BREAKFAST
Continental 60F (9.15€) per
person

ENGLISH SPOKEN
Yes

drawbacks. The entrance to the hotel is in a passageway reached by steep steps from street level or, if you come by car, on an upper level through one-way streets from behind. You will recognize the hotel by the pretty planter boxes under each window. Owner David Byrne (see Hôtel Queen Mary, page 185) has shined, polished, and gradually redone the tired rooms, refitted the reception area, and given the old bathrooms quickie face-lifts. These improvements meet the technical criteria of a three-star, but it's otherwise worthy of the designation in name only. Aside from reasonable rates for the high-rent area, the rooms are on two floors with no elevator. Some bathrooms still have exposed pipes, curtainless showers, and almost no shelf space; rooms for two and three have seating for one; and those on the back side of both floors of the hotel face an ugly, depressing, blank gray wall. To get to the safe, you have to lie on the floor and pay for the privilege. The bottom line: This makes an affordable choice in an otherwise pricey neighborhood, but choose your room carefully.

FACILITIES AND SERVICES: Direct-dial phone, no elevator, hair dryer, minibar, TV with international reception and pay-per-view movies, room safe (10F, 1.52€, per day)

NEAREST TOURIST ATTRACTIONS (RIGHT BANK): Champs-Élysées, Arc de Triomphe, shopping along avenue Victor-Hugo

HÔTEL DU ROND-POINT DE LONGCHAMP ★★★ ($, 12)

TELEPHONE
01-45-05-13-63

FAX
01-47-55-12-80

INTERNET
www.rd-pt-longchamp.fr

CREDIT CARDS
AE, DC, MC, V

RATES
Single 520–2,006F (79.27–
305.81€), double 812–2,012F
(123.79–306.73€), triple
2,018F (307.64€); ask about
off-season rates; *taxe de séjour*
included

BREAKFAST
70F (10.67€) per person, buffet
or Continental in room

ENGLISH SPOKEN
Yes

86, rue de Longchamp, at place de Mexico, 75016
Métro: Trocadéro, Victor-Hugo
57 rooms, all with shower or bath and toilet

The area around the hotel dates back to the thirteenth century, when Longchamp was an austere abbey surrounded by fields and meadows belonging to a few farms. One of them was located right next to the hotel, and there is a plaque to commemorate Boileau and La Fontaine, two great French writers who came here to buy their fresh milk. Today the area is one of the most prestigious residential areas in the capital.

The owner of this wonderful hotel, Gerard Dumontant, served as the president of the independent hoteliers in France, so you can imagine that his hotel reflects only the best . . . and let me assure you it does. The hotel appeals to traditionalists looking for exceptional value, classic service, and a multitude of facilities.

The ground floor consists of a plant-filled lounge, a bar, and a billiards room with soft leather armchairs. Some of the rooms are decidedly Louis XIV, with four-poster beds and heavy curtains swooping from floor to ceiling. Others reflect more modern tastes. Views of the Eiffel Tower can be seen from rooms ending with the number 2. Several are superbly planned for businesspeople. These rooms double as an office and sitting room during the day and have a comfortable pull-down Murphy bed at night. All rooms have international television reception, air-conditioning, computer modems, and fabulous marble bathrooms.

FACILITIES AND SERVICES: Air-conditioning, bar, business facilities, conference room, direct-dial phone, elevator, hair dryer, laundry services, minibar, modems, radio, room service, TV with international reception, room safe (no charge)

NEAREST TOURIST ATTRACTIONS (RIGHT BANK): Palais de Chaillot, Trocadéro, Eiffel Tower, shopping on avenue Victor-Hugo

HÔTEL ÉTOILE MAILLOT ★★★ (1)
10, rue de Bois-de-Bologne, at rue Duret, 75016
Métro: Argentine
28 rooms, all with shower or bath and toilet

It is happening throughout Paris: hotel owners who have been in business for years are cashing out and retiring to the South of France, and new owners, loaded with fresh ideas backed by big bank loans, are taking over. Such is the case at the Étoile Maillot. For years, the hotel appeared in this book, until its shabby sense of genteel poverty was just too much for me. Now it has been rescued from the graveyard of good taste by its new owner, M. Delfau, and it is once again on my three-star list of recommendations for travelers wanting to be near the Champs-Élysées, the Palais des Congrès convention center, and all the business going on at La Defense.

The plan is to redo eight rooms a year, and these are the ones you want. These rooms are uniform in their Gallic charm and judicious use of antiques. No. 17, softly decorated in a medley of beige fabrics, has framed profile silhouettes of fancy French ladies decorating the walls. Two lighted closets guarantee plenty of hanging and shelf space, but there is limited desk space. No. 16 is smaller but just as appealing thanks to its two armchairs and marble-topped dresser. Mirrors and fresh flowers

TELEPHONE
01-45-00-42-60

FAX
01-45-00-55-89

EMAIL
paris@reservethebest.com

CREDIT CARDS
AE, DC, MC, V

RATES
Single 600–800F (91.47–121.96€), double 630–880F (96.04–134.16€), suite 850–900F (129.58–137.20€); 2-night weekend specials that include breakfast 510–760F (77.75–115.86€); *taxe de séjour* included

BREAKFAST
Continental 45F (6.86€), buffet 65F (9.91€), per person

ENGLISH SPOKEN
Yes

add to the reception area, where you are invited to enjoy a drink from the bar or to sit by the faux fireplace.

FACILITIES AND SERVICES: Air-conditioning in some rooms, bar, direct-dial phone, elevator, hair dryer, laundry, minibar, some modems, TV with international reception, office safe and some room safes (no charge)

NEAREST TOURIST ATTRACTIONS (RIGHT BANK): Champs-Élysées, Arc de Triomphe, Bois de Boulogne

HÔTEL GAVARNI ★★ (21)
5, rue Gavarni, 75016
Métro: Passy

30 rooms, all with shower or bath and toilet

TELEPHONE
01-45-24-52-82

FAX
01-40-50-16-95

EMAIL
reservation@gavarni.com

INTERNET
www.gavarni.com

CREDIT CARDS
AE, DC, MC, V

RATES
Single 430–485F (65.55–73.94€), double 530F (80.80€), extra bed 100F (15.24€); *taxe de séjour* 5F (0.76€) per person, per day

BREAKFAST
Continental 40F (6.10€) per person

ENGLISH SPOKEN
Yes

The Hôtel Gavarni is one of the top two-star choices in Passy, one of Paris's most sought-after residential and shopping *quartiers*. The hotel is on a quiet little street off rue de Passy and is run by the lovely Nelly Rolland, who realized her dream come true when she bought this hotel from the Mornands, who owned it for years. Nelly is a graduate of the Hotel Management School in Lausanne, Switzerland, and she is young and full of life and new ideas. Her charm and innate sense of style are evident the minute you meet her, and it is clear they have carried over into her hotel.

The reception has smart yellow and white wall treatments, accented by a sofa and two armchairs covered in warm coral. A small breakfast room holds four tables and modern wicker and chrome chairs. The rooms have been redecorated in contemporary colors and materials. The cozy singles on the back side of the hotel have corner marble fireplaces and are popular with many repeat visitors. Bathrooms are behind folding doors and are small, but functional, with good towels. No. 603 is a favorite because both windows have a view of the Eiffel Tower, which is especially beautiful when illuminated at night. Other rooms with various Eiffel Tower views include Nos. 502, 503, 504, and 602 (which also has a fireplace).

FACILITIES AND SERVICES: Direct-dial phone, elevator, hair dryer, laundry service, modems, TV with international reception and free movie channel, office safe (no charge)

NEAREST TOURIST ATTRACTIONS (RIGHT BANK): Passy, shopping, Palais de Chaillot, Trocadéro, Eiffel Tower

HÔTEL KEPPLER ★★ (4)
12, rue Keppler, 75016
Métro: George-V, Kléber

49 rooms, all with shower or bath and toilet

For a two-star, family-run hotel, the Keppler offers much more than just a cheap sleep in a tony location. The lobby shows off a pretty fireplace and a small corner bar. The large dining room has mahogany upholstered chairs, blue walls, and Levelor blinds along the streetside windows. For the price, you cannot expect luxurious rooms with deep pile carpeting and designer fabrics. They do, however, offer good value. The charmless surroundings have efficiently modern desks and chairs and ample closet and drawer space. Four rooms have balconies. A team of uniformed maids wearing beepers keeps everything shipshape, and management keeps an ear tuned to inappropriate noise. There are many repeat guests, and it is easy to understand their loyalty to this hidden Parisian value, where reservations (and a deposit) are required far, far in advance of your stay.

FACILITIES AND SERVICES: Bar, direct-dial phone, elevator, hair dryer available, some modems, TV with international reception, room safe (no charge)

NEAREST TOURIST ATTRACTIONS (RIGHT BANK): Arc de Triomphe, Champs-Élysées, Guimet Museum, Palais de Chaillot, and Trocadéro

TELEPHONE
01-47-20-65-05

FAX
01-47-23-02-29

EMAIL
hotel.keppler@wanadoo.fr

INTERNET
www.france-hotel-guide.com/ h75116hotelkeppler.htm

CREDIT CARDS
AE, MC, V

RATES
1–2 persons 500F (76.22€); baby cot 50F (7.62€); extra bed 30 percent of room rate; *taxe de séjour* included

BREAKFAST
Continental 35F (5.34€) per person

ENGLISH SPOKEN
Yes

HÔTEL MASSENET ★★★ (23)
5 bis, rue Massenet, 75016
Métro: Passy, La Muette

41 rooms, all with shower or bath and toilet

For a beautiful stay in Paris on a tranquil street in Passy, I like the formal Massenet, a family-owned hotel since the 1930s. The well-heeled French executive clientele appreciate the serene neighborhood close to the *bon ton* Passy shopping district; the professional services of the uniformed hotel staff—especially Thay, the courteous receptionist, who has worked the desk for almost two decades—and, above all, the prices. These travelers know that if the Massenet were in a more mainstream location, the prices would be nearly doubled.

Downstairs, the public rooms are paneled in rich walnut. Soft seating and a small library along one wall create an appealing English intimacy. Morning croissants are served in a little alcove overlooking a colorful patio. All the comfortable rooms are well furnished and impeccably maintained. No. 70, a corner double, has its

TELEPHONE
01-45-24-43-03

FAX
01-45-24-41-39

EMAIL
hotelmassenet@wanadoo.fr

CREDIT CARDS
AE, DC, MC, V

RATES
Single 555–735F (84.61– 112.05€), double 840F (128.06€); extra bed 150F (22.87€); baby bed 100F (15.24€); *taxe de séjour* 6F (0.91€) per person, per day

BREAKFAST
Continental 45F (6.86€) per person

ENGLISH SPOKEN
Yes

own balcony looking out to the Eiffel Tower and La Tour Montparnasse and a walk-in closet that is almost as large as some hotel rooms I have stayed in. If traveling alone, request No. 71, a top-floor single with an Eiffel Tower view terrace, or No. 51 with a small balcony, double closet with shelves, and a large bathroom. If quiet and space are top priorities, No. 25, a back twin, has a triple-drawer marble dresser, workable desk, three chairs, double luggage rack, and a bathroom with two sinks, a large tub, and oversize towels.

FACILITIES AND SERVICES: Air-conditioning (except on the third floor), bar, direct-dial phone, elevator, hair dryer, laundry service, minibar, TV with international reception and pay-per-view movies, office safe (no charge)

NEAREST TOURIST ATTRACTIONS (RIGHT BANK): Passy, shopping, twenty-minute walk to Palais de Chaillot, Trocadéro, and the Eiffel Tower

HÔTEL NICOLO ★★ (22)
3, rue Nicolo, 75016
Métro: Passy, La Muette
28 rooms, all with shower or bath and toilet

TELEPHONE
01-42-88-83-40

FAX
01-42-24-45-41

CREDIT CARDS
AE, DC, MC, V

RATES
Single 475F (72.41€), double 530–600F (80.80–91.47€), triple 760F (115.86€), suite 800F (121.96€); lower prices in Aug; *taxe de séjour* 5F (0.76€) per person, per day

BREAKFAST
Continental 40F (6.10€) per person

ENGLISH SPOKEN
Yes

Join diplomats visiting their nearby embassies, delegates to the European Organization for Economic Co-operation and Development, and other savvy travelers by staying at the discreetly hidden Hôtel Nicolo in the center of Passy. Because the hotel is set back off the street, your room will be blissfully free from the usual symphony of Parisian street noises. Now, it is even more alluring because a new owner is gradually sweeping out the funky furnishings, flocked wallpaper, dated colors, and woebegone bathrooms. The results, and the prices in the renovated rooms, can be summed up in one word: *Wow!*

Check into No. 5, where the bed is backed by an Asian screen and the wall decorated by a colorful parrot print. Green and soft beige fabrics blend well with the overall Oriental feeling in this room. In addition to a chest of drawers, a comfortable armchair, and excellent workspace, you will have a fabulous new bathroom with double sinks and an Indonesian hand-painted floral frame around the mirror. Red-hot red is the color of choice in the dynamic No. 1, which is offset by a sparkling white tiled bathroom. The Art Deco suite, No. 21, sleeps four and is done in yellow with a collection of parrot prints decorating the walls. A sunken oval bathtub is the highlight of the lovely bathroom, which also has an Indonesian frame around the mirror.

At press time, only five rooms had been redone, but the project is scheduled for completion in 2001. Quite honestly, if you are unable to stay in one of the stunning new rooms, I would suggest going elsewhere. So when reserving, be certain that your room is one of the brand-new models, not one of the creaky accommodations that are as out of date as the bustle.

FACILITIES AND SERVICES: Direct-dial phone, elevator to fifth floor (walk to sixth), hair dryer, laundry service, TV with international reception, room safe (no charge)

NEAREST TOURIST ATTRACTIONS (RIGHT BANK): Passy, shoppping, twenty-minute walk to Palais de Chaillot, Trocadéro, and the Eiffel Tower

HÔTEL PASSY EIFFEL ★★★ (20)
10, rue de Passy, 75016
Métro: Passy, La Muette
50 rooms, all with shower or bath and toilet

The Hôtel Passy Eiffel, on the main street in Passy, provides a first-hand look at one of Paris's most exclusive neighborhoods, which has some of the best shopping you can find. The marble-lined foyer and lobby open onto a garden courtyard with six rooms facing it. Two salons are positioned along each side: one has a grand piano and inviting seating; the other is an airy, glass-enclosed breakfast room. Wood-beam ceilings add a sense of dimension to the variety of rooms, which are tasteful, clean, and very comfortable with pleasing views. I think No. 51, a suite with a spacious bathroom and four windows opening onto a balcony, is a good deal, as is No. 50, with soft pink damask tissue on the walls and a bathroom with corner mirrors and a large enclosed shower. If you are traveling solo, No. 61 on the back has good space, but for a view, balcony, bathtub, and more light, request No. 54. From the top floor on the side street, guests can watch the elevator scale the Eiffel Tower as it takes tourists to the top. For breakfast, be sure to sample some of the honey bottled directly from the owner's beehives.

FACILITIES AND SERVICES: Air-conditioning in most rooms, direct-dial phone, elevator to fifth floor, hair dryer, minibar, modems, TV with international reception, office safe (no charge)

NEAREST TOURIST ATTRACTIONS (RIGHT BANK): Passy, shopping, Palais de Chaillot, Trocadéro

TELEPHONE
01-45-25-55-66

FAX
01-42-88-89-88

EMAIL
passyeiffel@wanadoo.fr

INTERNET
www.passyeiffel.com

CREDIT CARDS
AE, DC, MC, V

RATES
Single 737F (112.31€), double 790F (120.43€), triple 910F (138.73€); *taxe de séjour* included

BREAKFAST
Continental 55F (8.38€) per person

ENGLISH SPOKEN
Yes

HÔTEL REGINA DE PASSY ★★★ (18)
6, rue de la Tour, 75016
Métro: Passy

TELEPHONE
01-55-74-75-75
FAX
01-40-50-70-62,
01-45-25-23-78
EMAIL
regina@gofornet.com
CREDIT CARDS
AE, DC, MC, V
RATES
1–2 persons 800–900F
(121.96–137.20€), apartments
900–1,600F (137.20–243.92€);
extra bed 250F (38.11€); *taxe de
séjour* included
BREAKFAST
Buffet 85F (12.96€) per person
ENGLISH SPOKEN
Yes

64 rooms, all with shower or bath and toilet

Built in 1930 for the International Exhibition, this hotel is high on the Right Bank of the Seine across from the Eiffel Tower. The almost-grand lobby has a staircase framed by signed stained-glass windows. Half of the hotel rooms have been restyled, and they are sophisticated and ultra-modern with geometric prints, chrome-and-leather furniture, and modern bathrooms. The older rooms are still in excellent condition and retain a benign elegance from their past . . . as well as lower price tags. Fifteen rooms have small balconies where you can step out and look over the Passy neighborhood with the Eiffel Tower in the distance. The two penthouse apartments with private rooftop terraces boast impressive furnishings, marble bathrooms (one with a sunken tub), small bars, fully equipped kitchens, and enough wardrobe space for most of us to unpack and stay a year. These apartments would be the answer for a small family or anyone on an extended stay. The hotel would score much better on my tally sheet were it not for the poor image created by the desk staff, most of whom need a refresher course in cordiality and customer service.

FACILITIES AND SERVICES: Air-conditioning in one apartment and some rooms, bar, direct-dial phone, elevator, hair dryer, minibar, modems, TV with international reception and video, room safe (no charge)

NEAREST TOURIST ATTRACTIONS (RIGHT BANK): Passy, shopping, twenty-minute walk to Palais de Chaillot, Trocadéro, and Eiffel Tower

HÔTEL VICTOR HUGO ★★★ (7)
19, rue Copernic, 75016
Métro: Victor-Hugo

TELEPHONE
01-45-53-76-01
FAX
01-45-53-69-93
EMAIL
victor.hugo@escapade-
paris.com
INTERNET
escapade-paris.com
CREDIT CARDS
AE, DC, MC, V

75 rooms, all with shower or bath and toilet

The hotel has been a stalwart in the sixteenth arrondissement for years. For a long time, it seemed to be resting on its laurels and mired in the past. Despite that, I have always liked the garden breakfast room, with its flagstone floor and fruit and vegetable vendor cart that is used for the buffet. Adding to the outdoor theme are the green lattice walls, Villeroy and Boch fruit basket china, and Parisian poster–wrapped pillars that look just like those you see on all the city streets. Some of the rooms are still somewhat matronly, but if you land in one of the fifteen redone rooms on the sixth and seventh floors, which overlook the vast reservoir behind the hotel, you should be happy. Nos. 75 and 77 are good examples. Both are large doubles with a balcony and reservoir views, large windows, and big new bathrooms. Harmonious, pastel colors in cream and rose with lavender accents add to their peaceful ambience.

FACILITIES AND SERVICES: Air-conditioning, bar, direct-dial phone, elevator, hair dryer, laundry service, TV with international reception and pay-per-view movies, room safe (no charge)

NEAREST TOURIST ATTRACTIONS (RIGHT BANK): Champs-Élysées, Arc de Triomphe, shopping along avenue Victor-Hugo, Trocadéro

LE HAMEAU DE PASSY ★★ (25)
48, rue de Passy, 75016
Métro: Passy, La Muette
32 rooms, all with shower or bath and toilet

Hidden in a garden walkway off the busy rue de Passy, Le Hameau de Passy is a snappy two-star in this posh pocket of Paris. All the rooms face the garden and are done in the same style, with stark white walls, open closets, soft sheer curtains at the windows, and harmonizing fabrics and carpets. Ground-floor rooms in the three-story buildings lack security, so I suggest asking for something on a higher floor. If you are lucky and land in Building 4, the elevator takes the strain out of climbing up several flights to your room. Otherwise, in Buildings 1, 2, and 3, you will pay the same price and still have to hike up a winding outdoor metal stairway to get to your room. If this sort of exercise does not bother you, and you want to be only a whisper away from all the great shopping in Passy—including the designer discount and consignment clothing stores along rue de la Tour and rue de la Pompe—then consider this hotel. For details about this special shopping niche in Paris, see "Shopping," page 293.

FACILITIES AND SERVICES: Direct-dial phone, elevator in Building 4 only, hair dryer, modems, TV with international reception, office safe (50F, 7.62€, per day)

NEAREST TOURIST ATTRACTIONS (RIGHT BANK): Passy, shopping, twenty-minute walk to Palais de Chaillot, Trocadéro, and the Eiffel Tower

RATES
Single 775–880F (118.15–134.16€), double 925–990F (141.01–150.92€), triple 1,320F (201.23), suite 1,550F (236.30€); *taxe de séjour* included

BREAKFAST
Continental 55F (8.38€), buffet 70F (10.67), per person

ENGLISH SPOKEN
Yes

TELEPHONE
01-42-88-47-55

FAX
01-42-30-83-72

EMAIL
hotel@hameaudepassy.com

INTERNET
www.hameaudepassy.com

CREDIT CARDS
AE, DC, MC, V

RATES
Single 560F (85.37€), double 610–630F (92.99–96.04€), triple 715F (109€); extra bed 100F (15.24€); *taxe de séjour* included

BREAKFAST
Included, cannot be deducted

ENGLISH SPOKEN
Yes

Seventeenth Arrondissement

The better half of the seventeenth arrondissement extends west from boulevard Malesherbes to the Arc de Triomphe. To the east and toward Gare St-Lazare, it is full of questionable characters dealing in the shadier side of life and residentially challenged *clochards* relaxing in doorways, guzzling beer or cheap wine. This is an area to avoid. The main attraction is the Palais des Congrès, a convention center with restaurants, movie theaters, and the pick-up and drop-off point for passengers going to and from Roissy–Charles-de-Gaulle Airport. There are many fine hotels in the better section of the arrondissement, and the areas around them are safe. Bus and métro connections to more tourist-inspired parts of Paris are excellent.

HOTELS IN THE SEVENTEENTH ARRONDISSEMENT

OTHER OPTIONS
Residence Hotels

($) indicates a Big Splurge

CENTRE VILLE ÉTOILE ★★★ (15)
6, rue des Acacias, 75017
Métro: Argentine
16 rooms, all with shower or bath and toilet

Original, smart, and stylish are three words that well describe this Art Deco–inspired hotel close to the Arc de Triomphe and the Champs-Élysées. A three-story glass atrium joins the two buildings, which house only sixteen sleeping slots. An interesting collection of American cartoon prints enlivens the lobby and hallways. The small masculine rooms, which haven't a ruffle in sight, display a judicious use of space and employ hard-edge colors of red, black, blue, and white along with black lacquered furnishings. Tiled and mirrored bathrooms are modern, with shelf space for toiletries and stretch tubs for leisurely bathing. The personable staff goes beyond the call of duty in welcoming guests and pampering them in the evening by closing the curtains, turning down the beds, and putting a chocolate on the pillow. Nonsmokers will be happy to know there are five rooms exclusively reserved for you.

FACILITIES AND SERVICES: Air-conditioning, direct-dial phone, elevator, hair dryer, laundry service, minibar, modems, *peignoirs,* TV with international reception, room safe (no charge)

NEAREST TOURIST ATTRACTIONS (RIGHT BANK): Arc de Triomphe, Palais de Congrès

TELEPHONE
01-58-05-10-00

FAX
01-47-54-93-43

EMAIL
hcv@centrevillehotels.com

INTERNET
www.centrevillehotels.com

CREDIT CARDS
AE, DC, MC, V

RATES
Single 600–800F (91.47–121.96€), double 700–950F (106.71–144.83€); extra bed 100F (15.24€); lower off-season rates; *taxe de séjour* 6F (0.91€) per person, per day

BREAKFAST
Continental 55F (8.38€) per person

ENGLISH SPOKEN
Yes

Seventeenth Arrondissement

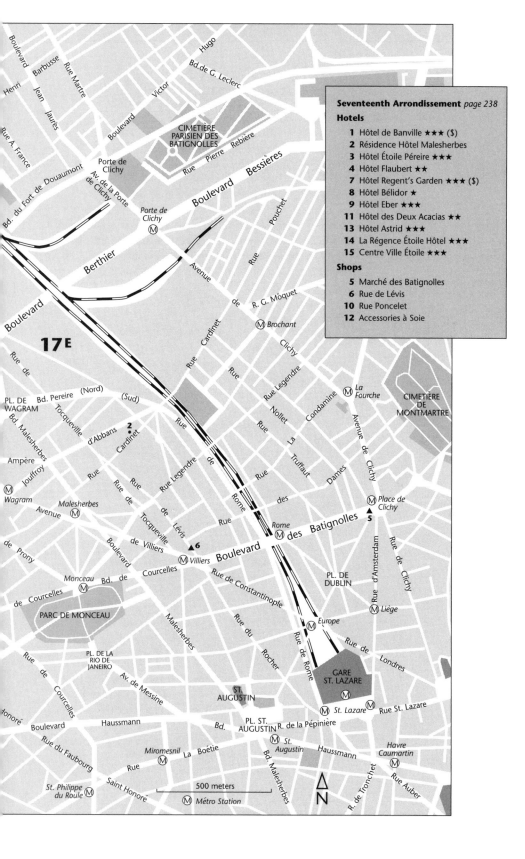

Seventeenth Arrondissement *page 238*

Hotels

1 Hôtel de Banville ★★★ ($)
2 Résidence Hôtel Malesherbes
3 Hôtel Étoile Péreire ★★★
4 Hôtel Flaubert ★★
7 Hôtel Regent's Garden ★★★ ($)
8 Hôtel Bélidor ★
9 Hôtel Eber ★★★
11 Hôtel des Deux Acacias ★★
13 Hôtel Astrid ★★★
14 La Régence Étoile Hôtel ★★★
15 Centre Ville Étoile ★★★

Shops

5 Marché des Batignolles
6 Rue de Lévis
10 Rue Poncelet
12 Accessories à Soie

HÔTEL ASTRID ★★★ (13)
27, avenue Carnot, 75017
Métro: Charles-de-Gaulle-Étoile, Argentine

41 rooms, all with shower or bath and toilet

TELEPHONE
01-44-09-26-00
FAX
01-44-09-26-01
EMAIL
paris@hotel-astrid.com
INTERNET
www.hotel-astrid.com
CREDIT CARDS
AE, DC, MC, V
RATES
Single 570–620F (86.90–94.52€), double 680–800F (103.67–121.96€), triple 895F (136.44), quad 950F (144.83€); extra bed 100F (15.24€); lower off-season rates; *taxe de séjour* included
BREAKFAST
Buffet included, cannot be deducted
ENGLISH SPOKEN
Yes

Florence Guillet heads one of the best family-run hotels in Paris. Started by her grandfather in 1937, the Hôtel Astrid provides comfortable, moderately priced accommodations in this top-drawer part of the city. The colors throughout the hotel are cheerfully appropriate and blend well with the furnishings. Each floor is themed. Starting from the top you have nature and birds, then Paris bridges, Impressionists, and old Paris. Two of the nicest bedrooms have small balconies for viewing the Arc de Triomphe. The rooms are upgraded continually, and each one has its own individual ambience. No. 21, pictured on the hotel's brochure, is a nice choice because it is bigger. It has two armchairs, a marble fireplace, twin brass beds, and good closets; the bathroom has a tub, but no shower. I also like No. 25, which is done in pastels and has desk and luggage space, two chairs, and a double bed. The spotless bathroom has a stall shower, hooks, and a shelf for toiletries. No. 42, done in florals, has a new bath; and No. 36, a large, two-bedroom triple, also comes with a new tile-and-granite bathroom.

Finally, the hotel is only about a five-minute walk from the Air France bus stop for Roissy–Charles-de-Gaulle Airport, so if you're traveling light, you can save money on cab fare.

FACILITIES AND SERVICES: Conference room, direct-dial phone, elevator, hair dryer, laundry service, TV with international reception, room safe (no charge)

NEAREST TOURIST ATTRACTIONS (RIGHT BANK): Arc de Triomphe, Champs-Élysées

HÔTEL BÉLIDOR ★ (8)
5, rue Bélidor, 75017
Métro: Porte Maillot (see note)

47 rooms, 18 with shower or bath and toilet

TELEPHONE
01-45-74-49-91
FAX
01-45-72-54-22
CREDIT CARDS
None, cash only, paid in advance
RATES
Single 205–318F (31.25–48.48€), double 205–390F (31.25–59.46€); public shower 30F (4.57€); *taxe de séjour* included

No serious economy-minded traveler in Paris can afford to overlook the Bélidor. It is an old-fashioned sort of hotel that has been in the same family for fifty years. Their furniture fills the first of two breakfast rooms; it is not only the prettiest but is nonsmoking. In the second, there is a marble-and-brick fireplace, an upright piano, and you can smoke, but the ambiance just isn't there. The owner is just as sweet as ever, the room colors and patterns are just as mixed, and all the electrical switch boxes are openly displayed over the radiator by the reception desk. A stay here provides you with a clean bed in a decent area just around the corner from the Palais des Congrès. The rooms are neat as pins, and those with bathtubs are larger than many two- and three-star rooms costing twice the price. Don't let the orange chenille and nontouristy location deter you. After only a ten- or fifteen-minute métro journey, you can be standing under the pyramid at the Louvre, floating down the Seine on a *bateau mouche,* or strolling through the most romantic streets in St-Germain-des-Prés. It is crucial to remember to plan ahead for this one because it is booked weeks in advance all during the year.

NOTE: The métro station at Porte Maillot is enormous, so look for these directions in French for the correct exit: *sorti côté Paris, bd. Gouvion-Saint-Cyr côté impair.* (In other words, exit on the Paris side of the métro station, on the odd-numbered side of boulevard Gouvion St-Cyr.)

FACILITIES AND SERVICES: Direct-dial phone, no elevator or TV, office safe (no charge)

NEAREST TOURIST ATTRACTIONS (RIGHT BANK): Palais des Congrès exhibition and convention center; otherwise, must use public transportation

BREAKFAST
Continental 30F (4.57€) per person
ENGLISH SPOKEN
Yes

HÔTEL DE BANVILLE ★★★ ($, 1)
166, boulevard Berthier, 75017
Métro: Péreire, Porte-de-Champerret
37 rooms, all with shower or bath and toilet

The classic Hôtel de Banville is my idea of a wonderful, personalized Parisian hotel. It was built in 1928 by architect Jerome Bellat, who designed many of the magnificent buildings the seventeenth arrondissement is famous for. From the beautiful lobby to the rooms filled with family antiques and heirlooms, you can tell immediately that this is a hotel where the owners know and care very much about what they are doing. The hotel has developed a large following of appreciative guests who applaud the efforts of owner Mme. Lambert, her daughter, Marianne Lambert-Moreau, and their right-hand man, Jean-Pierre, who is also the talented artist who did all the paintings that hang throughout the hotel. A portrait of their dog, Charlie, the hotel mascot, is displayed over the reception desk. Charlie is very popular; in fact, he even receives mail from guests who have grown to love him during their repeated visits. Mme.

TELEPHONE
01-42-67-70-16
FAX
01-44-40-42-77
EMAIL
hotelbanville@wanadoo.fr
INTERNET
www.hotelbanville.fr
CREDIT CARDS
AE, MC, V
RATES
Single 810F (123.48€), double 950F (144.83€); all the following rates are for 1–2 persons: *La Chambre de Julie* 700F (106.71€), *L'appartement de Marie* 1,550F (236.30€), *La Chambre d'Amélie, La Chambre Théodore de Banville,* and *Les Pastourelles* 1,150F (175.32€); *taxe de séjour* included

BREAKFAST
Continental 70F (10.67€),
Dietetique 80F (12.20€),
Pleinform 95F (14.48€), per
person
ENGLISH SPOKEN
Yes

Lambert grew up in the hotel business, and all of her family is involved in the industry in some way. Her background and expertise, combined with her impeccable good taste, are evident everywhere you look. Mme. Lambert told me, "I want this hotel to be like a private house, and I think I have realized my wish." I agree without question.

Every time I visit the hotel, I think, This is it. What more can be done to improve on perfection? . . . and each time I find wonderful new additions. On one visit, a new sitting room and piano bar featuring live music had been added next to the lobby and dining area, which displays hand-painted murals. This time it was the stunning new bathrooms and a series of superior rooms, each with its own name and something outstanding and unique to recommend it. If someone had told me before I saw these absolutely fabulous bathrooms that an open bathroom (with separate, enclosed toilets, of course) subtly incorporated into the main room itself would work, I would have had my doubts. I can assure you that they work magnificently . . . and I predict once you see these, you will be devising ways to remodel your own. I know I am.

L'appartement de Marie is a suite aptly subtitled, "an invitation to dream." It is true. I cannot imagine a dream more romantic or wonderful that this fabulous two-room suite, with a wrought-iron canopy bed surrounded in soft, white gauze netting. The large, sunny sitting room, done in contemporary brick and beige colors, has a sweeping view from the Arc de Triomphe to the Tour Montparnasse. If the view does not capture your attention, the imaginative open bathroom surely will. Located within the suite—not behind closed doors—it features a double antique marble sink and huge bathtub, with an enclosed toilet to one side. Honeymooners should reserve the captivating *La Chambre d'Amélie,* where glass doors open onto a terrace filled with sunshine all day long. Seated in a comfortable chair, your vista includes Montmartre, the Eiffel Tower, Arc de Triomphe, Montparnasse, and more. In the open marble bathroom, you can float in the huge footed tub and see the Eiffel Tower. The Théodore de Banville room incorporates wood found in country farms to separate the bedroom from its walk-through marble bathroom. Here you see the tip of the Eiffel Tower from your balcony, and sleep in a bed covered with a snowy white quilt. *Les*

Pastourelles are also a series of superior rooms. It is impossible to select a favorite, but No.1, with its red bathtub on legs, is very appealing. I also like the antique lamps, good desk space, and the red painted-wood backdrop behind the bed. Even the smallest room in the hotel, *La Chambre de Julie,* has its own sunny terrace and is done with elegance and gentle charm. Each year five new rooms are created. Notice I did not say redone—because they are true works of art worthy of a feature article in *Architectual Digest.* Even if you do not stay in one of the superior rooms, it would be impossible to be disappointed in any of the rooms at this outstanding hotel.

Breakfast is also special at the Banville. You can order a basic Continental, the *Dietetique* (which features wheat bread and yogurt), or go all out and have the *Pleinform,* which means sausage, eggs, and fruit juice along with your croissants and coffee.

The hotel is located on a busy boulevard lined with plane trees. The métro is close, and you can take the RER to the Musée d'Orsay and St-Michel. For buses, the No. 92 puts you at Étoile and the No. 84 drops you at place de la Concorde.

FACILITIES AND SERVICES: Air-conditioning, bar, direct-dial phone, elevator, hair dryer, parking can be arranged, some *peignoirs* and magnifying mirrors, all rooms with second telephone line (modems on request), twenty-four-hour room service for light meals, TV with international reception, room safe (no charge)

NEAREST TOURIST ATTRACTIONS (RIGHT BANK): None; must use public transportation

HÔTEL DES DEUX ACACIAS ★★ (11)
28, rue de l'Arc-de-Triomphe, 75017
Métro: Charles-de-Gaulle-Étoile, Argentine
31 rooms, all with shower or bath and toilet

Never mind its rather plain atmosphere—this choice will please visitors wanting to stay within a certain budget and still be conveniently close to the Champs-Élysées. It is owned by members of the Roubache family, who have fluffed and dusted it since taking over a few years ago from Mme. Delmas—who ran it for seventy years and resisted change with an iron-willed determination. In back of the reception desk you will notice a huge map of the Paris métro system that dates back to the time that Mme. Delmas's parents owned the hotel. Fortunately the Roubaches kept it for posterity . . . if not for nostalgic reasons.

TELEPHONE
01-43-80-01-85
FAX
01-40-53-94-62
INTERNET
www.123france.com
CREDIT CARDS
AE, MC, V
RATES
1–2 persons 450–500F (68.60–76.22€), triple 600–650F (91.47–99.09€), quad 800F (121.96€); extra bed 150F (22.87€); *taxe de séjour* 5F (0.76€) per person, per day

BREAKFAST
35F (5.34€) per person
ENGLISH SPOKEN
Yes

Upstairs, new paint, carpets, bedspreads, and a few new bathrooms have perked up the rooms. No one could ever call this modest place modern, but now one can certainly call it much improved. The cheapest rooms are Nos. 52, 54, 56, and 58. These top-floor perches are not only cheap, they are sunny and cheerful. Bathrooms are elfin, but at these rates you are lucky to have a shower and toilet to call you own. On the opposite end of the value scale is No. 1, an encapsulated twin that has a great bathroom, but also a view of the kitchen and the hotel trash bins. No. 12 is a better bet, if you don't mind fifties furnishings and tile work. For a new bathroom in a room on the back, ask for No. 10.

NOTE: Enclosed public parking is available across the street for motorists.

FACILITIES AND SERVICES: Direct-dial phone, elevator, hair dryer available, TV with international reception, office safe (no charge)

NEAREST TOURIST ATTRACTIONS (RIGHT BANK): Champs-Élysées, Arc de Triomphe

HÔTEL EBER ★★★ (9)
18, rue Léon-Jost, 75017
Métro: Courcelles

TELEPHONE
01-46-22-60-70
FAX
01-47-63-01-01
CREDIT CARDS
AE, DC, MC, V
RATES
1–2 persons 690–850F
(105.19–129.58€), suite
1,200–1,500F (182.94–
228.67€); extra bed 100F
(15.24€); *taxe de séjour* 6F
(0.91€) per person, per day
BREAKFAST
Continental 65F (9.91€) per
person
ENGLISH SPOKEN
Yes

18 rooms, all with shower or bath and toilet

Travelers longing for peace and quiet have at their disposal a group of French hotels whose owners have taken a vow of silence. The Hôtel Eber is one of the 275 members of Relais du Silence, an association of individually owned hotels dedicated to providing a silent and calm atmosphere where guests can feel at home. At the Eber, the entrance along a tiled walkway opens onto a beamed salon centered around a Henri II carved wooden fireplace. To the left of the reception desk is an inviting bar and breakfast area with comfortable armchairs. In the back is a green patio, where metal tables and chairs are set out on warm days for al fresco breakfasts. The rooms tend to be small and are decorated in light beiges with good-looking American art prints and posters on the walls. The family rooms feature not only two rooms but two bathrooms. In Room 55 guests have a lovely terrace that's shaded by an awning in the summer. There is no view, but there is plenty of light . . . and of course, peace and quiet. Many of the hotel clientele are from the world of fashion or entertainment, not a group known for its introverted behavior. However, owner Jean-Marc

Eber says that those who want nonstop excitement should stay in St-Germain-de-Prés.

You will need public transportation for most things on a tourist agenda, but it might be interesting to walk by 25, rue de Chazelles, about two blocks away, to see where the Statue of Liberty was originally built. There is a photo of it under construction hanging by the hotel elevator. Also on display around the hotel are photos of the statue in varying stages of development and the signatures of those who attended the completion ceremonies.

FACILITIES AND SERVICES: Air conditioning, direct-dial phone, elevator, hair dryer, laundry service, minibar, modems, TV with international reception, office safe (no charge), room service from area restaurants

NEAREST TOURIST ATTRACTIONS (RIGHT BANK): Arc de Triomphe, Champs-Élysées, Parc Monceau

HÔTEL ÉTOILE PÉREIRE ★★★ (3)
146, boulevard Péreire, 75017
Métro: Péreire

26 rooms, all with shower or bath and toilet

The Étoile Péreire, a member of the Relais du Silence (see Hôtel Eber above), is a sophisticated hotel offering modern luxury at affordable prices. Occupying a distinctive building that is hard to identify as a hotel, it benefited from a long-overdue remodeling project in 1987, when the 1900s-style rooms and claw-foot bathtubs were tossed out, and again in 1999, when all the rooms and the lobby received face-lifts. Not lost in the changes are the tranquillity and character of the accommodations and the dedicated services of the staff, headed for many years by Ferruccio Pardi and his wife, who, in her white starched apron, rigorously oversees daily room maintenance.

The rooms all overlook a courtyard and are individually decorated around a specific color or theme. The result is mixture of modern touched with the fanciful. The best selections are the two-story duplexes with air-conditioning, ceiling fans, and skylights. In No. 409, Beardsley-type prints set the masculine tone carried out in black laminate furnishings, soft beige linen-covered walls, and gray-and-black speckled carpets. In No. 205, a double, the green walls and latticework create a gardenlike feeling. No matter where you land, your bathroom will be modern and well supplied with Roger

TELEPHONE
01-42-67-60-00

FAX
01-42-67-02-90

EMAIL
info@etoiceleper.com

INTERNET
www.etoileper.com

CREDIT CARDS
AE, DC, MC, V

RATES
Single 620–720F (94.52–109.76€), double 810F (123.48€), duplex 1,120F (170.74€); no charge for extra bed; *taxe de séjour* 6F (0.91€) per person, per day

BREAKFAST
60F (9.15€) per person

ENGLISH SPOKEN
Yes

and Gallet products. M. Pardi prides himself on his breakfasts, which are served in a white-and-gray basement dining room that displays the art of Jean Marais. Diners have a choice of twenty of the best quality jams, jellies, or honeys to accompany their croissants and fresh orange or grapefruit juice. If you want more, ham or bacon and eggs are available.

While hardly in the tourist mainstream, the hotel is close to Porte Maillot and the Air France air terminal. A large city park with tennis courts and plenty of picnic benches is across the street, as well as several old dining favorites listed in *Great Eats Paris.*

NOTE: The second floor is exclusively nonsmoking, as are the superior rooms and most of the duplexes.

FACILITIES AND SERVICES: Air-conditioning in four duplexes, bar, direct-dial phone, elevator, hair dryer, laundry service, minibar in all rooms except singles with showers, modems, parking can be arranged, TV with international reception, room safe (no charge)

NEAREST TOURIST ATTRACTIONS (RIGHT BANK): None; must use public transportation

HÔTEL FLAUBERT ★★ (4)
19, rue Rennequin, 75017
Métro: Ternes, Péreire

TELEPHONE
01-46-22-44-35
FAX
01-43-80-32-34
CREDIT CARDS
AE, DC, MC, V
RATES
Single 495–510F (75.46–77.75€), double 590–620F (89.94–94.52€), triple 765F (116.62€); extra bed 100F (15.24€); *taxe de séjour* 5F (0.76€) per person, per day
BREAKFAST
Buffet 50F (7.62€) per person
ENGLISH SPOKEN
Yes

41 rooms, all with shower or bath and toilet

One of the most attractive features of this hotel is its lush garden overflowing with cascading vines and colorful seasonal plants. Bamboo furniture in the dining room and rooms lends a light tropical air. Singles or couples with scanty luggage, or who don't mind close quarters, can reserve one of the rooms opening onto the garden. For a degree more space and better lighting, I like the top-floor *chambres.* New owners, Françoise and Patrick Schneider, have removed the chirping birds and thinned out the jungle that had been allowed to almost overtake the breakfast room, and they have added four new rooms. They couldn't make the existing ones bigger, but they did improve bathrooms and polished the general decor. They kept the most important aspect of the hotel: moderate prices that are good for this part of Paris, which is not known for much in the budget range.

FACILITIES AND SERVICES: Direct-dial phone, elevator, hair dryer, minibar, TV, no safe

NEAREST TOURIST ATTRACTIONS (RIGHT BANK): Ten-minute walk to Champs-Élysées and Arc de Triomphe

HÔTEL REGENT'S GARDEN ★★★ ($, 7)
6, rue Pierre-Demours, 75017
Métro: Charles-de-Gaulle-Étoile (exit rue Carnot), Ternes

39 rooms, all with shower or bath and toilet

TELEPHONE
01-45-74-07-30; toll-free in the U.S. and Canada, 800-528-1234 (Best Western)

FAX
01-40-55-01-42

EMAIL
hotel.regents.garden@ wanadoo.fr

INTERNET
www.bestwestern.fr

CREDIT CARDS
AE, DC, MC, V

RATES
Single 730–1,100F (111.29–167.69€), double 800–1,450F (121.96–221.05€); *taxe de séjour* 6F (0.91€) per person, per day

BREAKFAST
Buffet 65F (9.91€) per person

ENGLISH SPOKEN
Yes

Originally built by Napoléon III for his personal physician, this building is now a refined garden hotel. Hidden behind a high brick wall, it seems a little far from the hub of activity, but in fact, rue Pierre-Demours is only a few minutes' walk from the Champs-Élysées and the Arc de Triomphe.

The cavernous, high-ceilinged rooms have crystal chandeliers, decorative moldings, marble fireplaces, brass bedsteads, floor-to-ceiling mirrors, and authentic period furnishings. Most have been redone to reflect their former Second Empire glory. Many rooms connect for convenient family use, and several have large walk-in closets with built-in shelves and shoe racks. The bathrooms are thoroughly twentieth century and luxuriously fitted with fluffy terry robes, scented bubble bath and soaps, and plenty of light and mirrors for applying makeup. Most rooms overlook the garden, which is landscaped with large trees, two gazebos, stone statues, flowering walkways, and a terrace with tables for summer breakfasts or afternoon teas. Despite the fact that the hotel still has a tired sitting area with saddly worn chairs and a drooping velvet sofa, everyone who has ever stayed here, and I include myself, loves it, and you will, too. We all know to smile gently at this lapse because we do not come here for the sitting area, but for the rooms, which offer affordable elegance with an ambiance of bygone days in Paris.

FACILITIES AND SERVICES: Air-conditioning, direct-dial phone, elevator, hair dryer, minibar, modems, parking in front (65F, 9.91€, per space on a first-come basis), TV with international reception, office safe (no charge)

NEAREST TOURIST ATTRACTIONS (RIGHT BANK): Champs-Élysées, Arc de Triomphe

LA RÉGENCE ÉTOILE HÔTEL ★★★ (14)
24, avenue Carnot, 75017
Métro: Charles-de-Gaulle-Étoile, Argentine

38 rooms, all with shower or bath and toilet

TELEPHONE
01-58-05-42-42

FAX
01-47-66-78-86

EMAIL
hotelregenceetoile-paris@
gofornet.com

INTERNET
www.globe-market.com/h/
75017regenceetoile.htm

CREDIT CARDS
AE, DC, MC, V

RATES
Single 525–630F (80.04–
96.04€), double 820–890F
(125.01–135.68€); *taxe de séjour*
6F (0.91€) per person, per day

BREAKFAST
Continental 55F (8.38€) per
person

ENGLISH SPOKEN
Yes

The hotel is on the jacaranda-lined avenue Carnot, one of the spokes of the famed Étoile that radiates from the Arc de Triomphe. Because the prices are reasonable for a three-star, it is a good choice if you are a budget-minded business traveler in Paris and your work takes you to La Defense or the Palais des Congrès convention center. It is new, dependably decorated, and only a stone's throw or two from the bright lights and crowds along the Champs-Élysées.

A lighted nymphette statue in pristine alabaster greets guests as they enter the Directoire-style sitting area, where comfortable velvet-covered armchairs and sofas flank a marble fireplace. A sparkling mirrored elevator takes you to the predictably acceptable rooms, which are in yellow and blue. Everything you need is here: air-conditioning, television with CNN, two chairs, a desk, a mirrored armoire, and heated towel racks in a twenty-first-century bathroom. Breakfast is served downstairs in a room that has Turner-like murals wrapping around three of the walls, and the glass-topped metal tables and chairs have gold-painted bows and garlands.

FACILITIES AND SERVICES: Air-conditioning, bar, direct-dial phone, elevator, hair dryer, laundry service, minibar, TV with international reception, room safe (no charge)

NEAREST TOURIST ATTRACTIONS (RIGHT BANK): Arc de Triomphe, Champs-Élysées

Eighteenth Arrondissement

Montmartre is a rambling *quartier* full of contrasts, combining picture-postcard quaintness and razzle-dazzle. It was here that Toulouse-Lautrec drew the can-can girls dancing at the Moulin Rouge, and Picasso and Braque created Cubism at the Bateau-Lavoir. The panoramic view from the steps of the Sacré Coeur at dawn or sunset, the many artists, and the intimate village atmosphere that prevails along the narrow streets—many of which are the same as when Utrillo painted them—continue to evoke the dynamic spirit and colorful past of this vibrant part of Paris, and it is a must-stop for any visitor. A walk down rue Lepic or rue des Abbesses, lined with bars and shops, leads to Pigalle. East of Montmarte is La Goutte d'Or, where many North Africans live, and to the north is the famed flea market at Clignancourt.

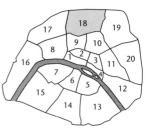

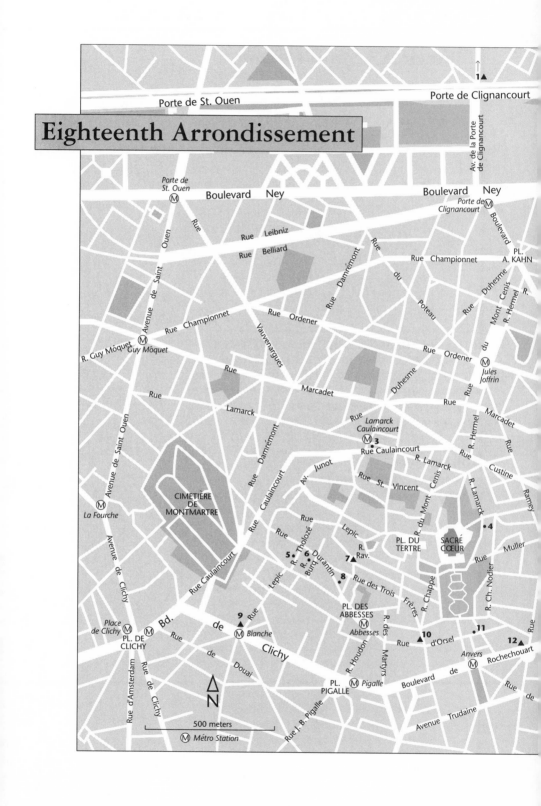

Eighteenth Arrondissement

Porte de St. Ouen

Porte de Clignancourt

Av. de la Porte de Clignancourt

Porte de St. Ouen

Boulevard Ney

Boulevard Ney

Porte de Clignancourt

PL. A. KAHN

Rue Championnet

Boulevard

Ⓜ

Rue Leibniz

Rue Belliard

Rue Damrémont

du

Rue

Duhesme

R.

Avenue de Saint Ouen

Rue

R. Guy Môquet

Ⓜ Guy Môquet

Rue Championnet

Vauvenargues

Rue Ordener

Poteau

Rue Ordener

Mont Cenis

R. Hermel

Ⓜ Jules Joffrin

Rue

Rue

Marcadet

Duhesme

Rue

Marcadet

Rue

Lamarck

Rue

du

Rue Lamarck Caulaincourt

Ⓜ •3

Rue Caulaincourt

R. Hermel

Custine

Rue Damrémont

Av. Junot

Rue St. Vincent

R. Lamarck

R. du Mont Cenis

R. Lamarck

Ramey

Avenue de Clichy

CIMETIÈRE DE MONTMARTRE

Rue Caulaincourt

Rue

Rue

Lepic

PL. DU TERTRE

SACRÉ CŒUR

•4

Muller

Ⓜ La Fourche

Rue

R. Tholozé

5 • • 6 Durantin

R.

R. Rav.

7 ▲

Rue

Rue des Trois

Rue

R. Ch. Nodier

Rue Caulaincourt

Lepic

R. Burq

8 •

Frères

R. Chappe

de

Place de Clichy Ⓜ

PL. DE CLICHY

Bd.

Rue

9 ▲

Rue

PL. DES ABBESSES

Avenue de Clichy

de

Ⓜ Blanche

Clichy

Ⓜ Abbesses

R. des

10 ▲ d'Orsel

•11

12 ▲

Rue d'Amsterdam

Rue de Clichy

de

Douai

Martyrs

Rue

Anvers Ⓜ

Rochechouart

Rue de

△ N

PL. PIGALLE

R. Houdon

Ⓜ Pigalle

Boulevard de

Rue

500 meters

Ⓜ Métro Station

Rue J. B. Pigalle

Avenue Trudaine

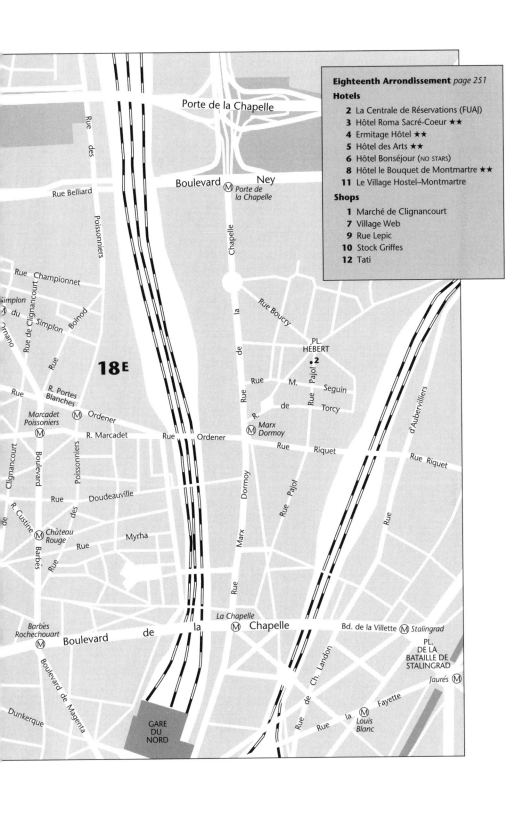

Porte de la Chapelle

Rue des

Rue Belliard

Boulevard Ney
Porte de
la Chapelle

Chapelle

Poissonniers

Rue Championnet

implon

du Simplon

Rue de Clignancourt

Boinod

rnano

18E

Rue Boucry

la

de

PL.
HÉBERT

.2

Rue

Rue Pajol

M.

Seguin

Rue

R. Portes
Blanches

Rue

de

Torcy

Marcadet
Poissoniers

Ordener

R.

Marx
Dormoy

Clignancourt

Boulevard

Poissonniers

R. Marcadet

Rue Ordener

Rue

Riquet

Rue Riquet

d'Aubervilliers

R. Custine

Rue des Doudeauville

Dormoy

Rue Pajol

Rue

Château
Rouge

Rue

Myrha

Barbés

Marx

Rue

La Chapelle

Barbés
Rochechouart

Boulevard

de

la

Chapelle

Bd. de la Villette

Stalingrad

PL.
DE LA
BATAILLE DE
STALINGRAD

Boulevard de Magenta

Ch. Landon

Jaurés

Dunkerque

de

Rue

la

Fayette

Louis
Blanc

GARE
DU
NORD

Rue

ERMITAGE HÔTEL ★★ (4)
24, rue Lamarck, 75018
Métro: Lamarck–Cauliancourt, or bus 80 or 85
12 rooms, all with shower or bath and toilet

TELEPHONE
01-42-64-79-22

FAX
01-42-64-10-33

CREDIT CARDS
None, cash only

RATES
Single 460F (70.13€), double 520F (79.27€), triple 660F (100.62€), quad 770F (117.39€); *taxe de séjour* included

BREAKFAST
Included, cannot be deducted

ENGLISH SPOKEN
Yes, also German and Italian

Close your eyes and imagine waking up in Paris in an antique-filled hotel high atop Montmartre with magical views over the entire city. Sound wonderful? It does, and it is all possible at the Ermitage, a poetic refuge run for many years by the engaging Maggie Canipel and her husband. Now they have retired, and their lovely daughter, Sophie, is in charge. However, Maggie still comes back now and then, and she fills in completely when Sophie and her family go on vacation. In the late 1970s, M. and Mme. Canipel sold everything they had and bought the Ermitage. They updated the plumbing, filled the old mansion with their collection of fine furniture, and began welcoming guests, continually outdoing themselves with their boundless energy and engaging smiles in order to make everyone feel at home. They succeeded beautifully and are now one of the favorite hotels for readers of *Great Sleeps Paris*. If this sounds appealing, book the Ermitage the minute you know the dates for your trip.

Any one of the twelve rooms could steal your heart, but my favorites are still Nos. 6 and 10—on the top floor, with tall French windows opening onto the morning sun and views of all Paris—and Nos. 11 and 12, which open onto their terrace garden. No. 2 is beautiful, with a magnificent set of nineteenth-century reproduction Louis XV bedroom furniture: a carved bed, two side tables, and a mirrored armoire. A crystal chandelier completes the picture.

True, you need strong legs and lungs to walk up the hill from the métro, but once there, you will be richly rewarded not only by the warmth and hospitality of Sophie and her family but by being in the center of one of the most picturesque parts of Paris. You can wander the streets once painted by Utrillo, peek into artists' ateliers, and have your portrait painted by one of the pseudo-artists lining the touristy place du Tertre. Undiscovered restaurants in all price ranges are within easy walking distance (see *Great Eats Paris*).

FACILITIES AND SERVICES: Direct-dial phone, no elevator or TV, hair dryer in ten rooms, office safe (no charge)

NEAREST TOURIST ATTRACTIONS (RIGHT BANK): Montmartre

HÔTEL BONSÉJOUR (NO STARS, 6)
11, rue Burq, 75018
Métro: Abbesses, Blanche

34 rooms, 5 with shower, none with bath or toilet

Attention tightwads! If money is your first concern, this old—but very clean—hotel should be one of your first picks. Occupying a hillside corner location, it is well protected from the low life and tourist mania that plagues Montmartre and its underbelly, Pigalle. New this time around are five private showers, a fax, bright blue paint in the hallways, blackout curtains in the rooms, stair carpeting, and an adorable baby girl named Miriam.

It is run by Paul Bellart, who checks you in, and his hard-working wife, Amina, who is in charge of housekeeping. The rooms appeal to a young, intellectual, and sometimes impoverished crowd of international guests, who cheerfully ignore the mishmash of furniture and do not mind using hall facilities. The cheapest rooms face walls. If you can swing just a little more money, ask for one with a balcony (Nos. 23, 33, 43, or 53, which is the best because it has a nice Parisian view) or No. 51, a triple with a tiny peek of the tip of the Sacré Coeur. The balcony rooms come with double beds. If you need twins, ask for No. 41 on the street, which also has more space and better bedspreads than some others. Breakfast is not part of the plan here, but you can save money and feel more Parisian by walking a block or two to one of the many Montmartre bakeries and cafés that line rue des Abbesses and rue Lepic.

FACILITIES AND SERVICES: None; no elevator (five floors)

NEAREST TOURIST ATTRACTIONS (RIGHT BANK): Montmartre

TELEPHONE
01-42-54-22-53

FAX
01-42-54-25-92

CREDIT CARDS
None, cash only

RATES
Single 120–200F (18.29–30.49€), double 180–230F (27.44–35.06€), triple 270F (41.16€); extra bed 70F (10.67€); shower 10F (1.52€); *taxe de séjour* included

BREAKFAST
Not served

ENGLISH SPOKEN
Yes

HÔTEL DES ARTS ★★ (5)
5 rue Tholozé, 75018
Métro: Abbesses, Blanche

50 rooms, all with shower or bath and toilet

The Lemeyre family works as an honest, hard-working team, intent on providing good value for money, which is my unwavering bottom line. The attractively furnished lobby and breakfast rooms are especially appealing, with textured walls, fresh flowers, and a growing collection of local artwork depicting scenes and aspects of life in Paris and the village of Montmartre. The rooms are redecorated on a revolving basis using bright colors, good quality furnishings, and nicely coordinated fabrics. If

TELEPHONE
01-46-06-30-52

FAX
01-46-06-10-83

EMAIL
hotel.arts@wanadoo.fr

INTERNET
www.france-hotel-guide.com

CREDIT CARDS
AE, MC, V

RATES
Single 360F (54.88€), double
450F (68.60€); extra bed for
child only 45F (6.86€); *taxe de
séjour* included

BREAKFAST
Buffet 35F (5.34€) per person

ENGLISH SPOKEN
Yes

you don't mind walking up a flight of stairs, the sixth floor rooms have rooftop views of the white tip of Sacré Coeur, and in Nos. 60 and 62, you will see the tip of La Tour Eiffel and La Defense. The street is quiet, so at night you won't be wakened by wild, cruising party animals out on the town.

FACILITIES AND SERVICES: Direct-dial phone, elevator to fifth floor (walk to sixth), hair dryer, TV with international reception, office safe (no charge)

NEAREST TOURIST ATTRACTIONS (RIGHT BANK): Montmartre

HÔTEL LE BOUQUET DE MONTMARTRE ★★ (8)
1, rue Durantin, 75018
Métro: Abbesses

TELEPHONE
01-46-06-87-54

FAX
01-46-06-09-09

CREDIT CARDS
MC, V

RATES
Single 415F (63.27€), double
420F (64.03€), triple 485F
(73.94€), quad 510F (77.75€);
taxe de séjour included

BREAKFAST
Continental 35F (5.34€) per
person

ENGLISH SPOKEN
Limited

36 rooms, all with shower, 22 with bath and toilet

If you have a fondness for Montmartre, and you want to experience the fun and the village atmosphere of the area and still stay under budget, the Bouquet de Montmartre is a little honey of a hotel. Its second-floor lobby may be difficult to find, but the search is worth it.

The Gibergues family works hard to keep their Victorian hotel as nice as it is for the price. They are on duty from Monday to Saturday, 9 A.M. to 6 P.M., so when calling for reservations, bear this in mind. If you can wear blinders or dark glasses in your room, or do not mind living in a kaleidoscope of colors and patterns, then read on. Most of the bedrooms fall into the "cute and confusing" category; in No. 43, you have a view. In all the rooms, lacy curtains, velvet chairs with plastic covers, floral rugs, and busy wallpaper march along with brightly tiled bathrooms in purple, lavender, royal blue, and aqua. All are positively spotless and tear-free. Breakfast is served in an ornate dining room with red velvet chairs, lacquered furniture, and globe lights—all of which serves to remind you that this is Montmartre, after all.

From the hotel you can stroll in any direction and see something interesting. You can climb up to Sacré Coeur or crawl down the hill to Pigalle, where Paris's seedy side is on full display. For longer trips, jump on the Montmartobus, a minibus service that plies the winding streets snaking around the Butte. You can ride from the bottom at Pigalle to the end of the line at Jules Joffrin métro station. Stop along the route if something intrigues you and get back on; it is one of the most pleasurable rides you can take in Paris.

FACILITIES AND SERVICES: Direct-dial phone, office safe (no charge), no elevator or TV

NEAREST TOURIST ATTRACTIONS (RIGHT BANK): Montmartre

HÔTEL ROMA SACRÉ-COEUR ★★ (3)
101, rue Caulaincourt, 75018
Métro: Lamarck–Caulaincourt

57 rooms all with shower or bath and toilet

Frankly, this place is a bit of a gamble because its location is way out of the mainstream and does require some walking up and down hills. Still, it has cachet: Room 701 was where Georges Braque had his studio when Montmartre was in its artistic heyday in the 1920s. It is easy today to picture the artist standing on the wraparound balcony, gazing at northern Paris on the horizon, and turning out his canvases. Other rooms of note are Nos. 506 and 507, with views to Sacré Coeur, and No. 704 with a balcony. Singles do not fare well: the rooms are meager and the outlooks discouraging, so if you are a lone voyager, pay a little more and get a small double. The innocuous rooms are in nonclashing colors of soft peach, simple browns, and white. Management is agreeable, and the neighborhood is pretty in that it reflects a real part of Paris that is untouched by the maddening tourist crowds.

FACILITIES AND SERVICES: Direct-dial phone, elevator to all but the top floor, hair dryer, minibar, radio, TV, office safe (no charge)

NEAREST TOURIST ATTRACTIONS (RIGHT BANK): Montmartre

TELEPHONE
01-42-62-02-02

FAX
01-42-54-34-92

CREDIT CARDS
AE, DC, MC, V

RATES
Single 400F (60.98€), double 450 (68.60€), triple 570F (86.90€); lower rates subject season and availability; *taxe de séjour* 5F (0.76€) per person, per day

BREAKFAST
Continental 40F (6.10€) per person

ENGLISH SPOKEN
Yes

Other Options

If hotel life is not for you, there are other reasonable, inexpensive options that make sleeping sense in Paris. For the cheapest choice of all, consider a return to nature—that is, camping, which you can do just outside of Paris in the Bois de Boulogne. If you are a student, or can go the hostel route, there are many excellent low-priced accommodations awaiting you. Other cost-saving possibilities are to stay in a residence hotel in a unit with a kitchenette, or to become truly Parisian and rent your own studio or apartment. The benefits of these last two choices are numerous, from having more space to spread out to the adventure of interacting with merchants while shopping for life's necessities in your own Parisian neighborhood.

Apartment Rental Agencies

If you want to live in Paris, not just be a visitor during your stay, then the best way to experience Paris *comme les Parisiens* is to rent a short-term apartment. Believe me, once you do it, you will not want to return to the confines of hotel living in the City of Light for any of your future visits. If you are going to be in Paris for more than a few days, extra space begins to matter. A stay in a Parisian apartment not only gives you more elbow room than a hotel, and for less money in the long run, it makes you feel less frantic about seeing and doing absolutely everything. You are caught up instead with the fun adventure of exploring and getting to know your own Paris *quartier,* which you will soon come to think of as your own, becoming a little Parisian in the process.

During the years I have researched Paris apartments, I have seen just about every nightmare possible—including total dumps that were not only filthy and unattractive but in terrible areas that have absolutely nothing to offer a tourist. Many are operated by huge firms, or are let by absentee owners who are on the scene to collect your money but then vanish, leaving you high and dry when maintenance problems arise, which they generally do. Just as with all of the hotels and shops listed in this book, I have personally visited every apartment agency listed and viewed a large sampling of what they offer before I considered recommending them to you.

Even though I mention it as the number-one tip in apartment renting, it bears repeating here: If you rent an apartment, be sure you clearly understand the payment, cancellation, and refund policies. It is beyond the scope of *Great Sleeps Paris* to detail the various policies you will encounter, but they are *never* in your favor. Therefore, it is absolutely essential that you purchase cancellation insurance, which is available through many state automobile associations, travel agents, and in some cases through the apartment agency itself. This small investment will pay off tenfold if you have to change dates, cancel altogether, or must suddenly cut short your stay.

Tips on Renting a Paris Apartment

1. Most important: Know the deposit, payment, and cancellation policies, and buy cancellation insurance.

2. Get a guaranteed rate and find out about extra charges such as linens, cleaning (whether weekly maid service is included or extra, and what the final cleaning fee is), telephone, heating, and so on.

3. Ask for photographs of the apartment you are considering.

4. Be very specific when stating your needs: size of flat and number of occupants; whether you want a stall shower rather than a hand-held shower nozzle in a half tub with no shower guard or curtain; and what sort of kitchen equipment you'd like—do you need only

a microwave, do you want pots and pans for major cooking events, or are you just going to drink wine and eat baguettes and French cheese at the dining room table? Don't forget to consider the beds. Will a sofa bed do, or does your back demand something better, and if so, will you require a double bed or twin beds?

5. Is a television important for you—one that includes CNN, BBC, and Euro-Sport? Don't discount a TV, as it's a great way to improve your French comprehension. Is there a phone and how much are calls? Can you make both local and long-distance calls? Is there an answering machine, fax, and Internet hookup?

6. How far is the apartment from *your* center of interest? Where is the nearest market, laundry and dry cleaner, pharmacy, métro and bus stop, best café, and *pâtisserie?* Ask for a good local map with your address and the nearest métro stop pinpointed on it.

7. Is the apartment suitable for children? Is there a park or playground nearby?

8. Noise. Paris operates on a twenty-four-hour basis and *is* noisy. If you must have the most quiet possible, ask for an inside location *sur la cour,* where you will sacrifice view and possibly light, but gain some solitude.

9. Is there an elevator to your apartment? Many buildings in Paris do not have them. While that penthouse apartment with a dynamic view is romantically wonderful, consider carrying groceries, shopping purchases, and your luggage up and down. Think about this one carefully . . . stairs can get to be a problem, *fast*.

10. Upon arrival, will someone meet you at the apartment and show you the ropes, or do you have to go to an office in Paris to get the keys? This is very important after a long international flight: dragging luggage and tired children through Paris in search of the keys to your Paris kingdom is not an attractive option.

11. What other services does the apartment rental company offer? Ask about drivers; itinerary planning throughout France and in other parts of Europe; ongoing reservations; and air travel arrangements and concierge services in Paris.

12. Check with your homeowner's or renter's insurance policy to see if it covers you for any damage that may occur while you are renting a foreign apartment. Many of these policies do cover you. If so, fax the information to the agency in question. Many times hefty deposits are taken, and unfortunately, *you* can be blamed for damages caused by another renter. To avoid this, upon arrival, go over the apartment very carefully and point out any damages or potential problems, no matter how small they may seem. When you leave, get a written statement that the apartment was in good condition when you left it.

APARTMENT RENTAL AGENCIES

CHEZ VOUS
1001 Bridgeway, Suite 245
Sausalito, CA 94965

Chez Vous apartments offer you a Paris address in several of the best areas of the city, not in marginal, out-of-the-way *quartiers* that some apartment owners or agencies will try and convince you are interesting. The possibilities are in the fourth, fifth, sixth, and seventh arrondissements. None of the apartments are owner-occupied. All are on long-term lease to Chez Vous, who maintains and decorates them. The catalog listing the Paris properties is called *Bonjour Paris!!!*, and it not only gives you good information about their apartments but leaves nothing to chance in explaining the payment or cancellation policies. If you are venturing outside of Paris, and this type of stay appeals to you, ask about their other rental properties throughout France and in London.

TELEPHONE
415-331-2535

FAX
415-331-5296

EMAIL
bonjour@chezvous.com

INTERNET
www.chezvous.com

CREDIT CARDS
None, U.S. checks only

RATES
From $185 per night for two people (three-night minimum) and up; better rates for longer stays ; linen fee $25 per person; end-of-stay cleaning fee varies

ENGLISH SPOKEN
Yes

DE CIRCOURT ASSOCIATES (32)
11, rue Royale, 75008
Métro: Concorde

De Circourt Associates was founded by Claire de Circourt to assist those people moving to Paris, either for professional reasons or for a stay of at least two months. Madame de Circourt is a very savvy businesswoman who has lived and worked in New York City, so she knows the type of living accommodations most Americans want and the services they expect. Her customer service is superb because she always provides back-up, or intermediary help, if any client ever has a problem. She has computerized listings of thousands of apartments and homes in Paris and the suburbs, which are updated every fifteen days. Thanks to this sophisticated computerized search system, she or one of her exceptionally competent English-speaking staff will find you the place of your

TELEPHONE
01-43-12-98-00

FAX
01-43-12-98-08

EMAIL
circourt@homes-paris.com

INTERNET
www.homes-paris.com

CREDIT CARDS
AE, DC, MC, V

RATES
From $1,000 per month and up; minimum stay at least two months; prefer six-month or one-year lease

ENGLISH SPOKEN
Yes

dreams at a price you can afford. The possibilities range from a romantic, beamed, one-bedroom walk-up on Île de la Cité, to a zany artist's studio done in black and white with a bird-shaped chair, to the to-die-for apartment occupied by Robert Altman while he was on location in Paris filming *Prêt à Porter.* It is all up to you and your budget—whatever you want, chances are excellent De Circourt Associates will have it.

NOTE: There is a two-month minimum stay, but six months to a year is preferred.

GUEST APARTMENT SERVICES (51)
5, quai d'Anjou, 75004
Métro: Sully-Morland

TELEPHONE
01-44-07-06-20

FAX
01-46-33-37-73

EMAIL
info@guestapartment.fr

INTERNET
www.guestapartment.fr

CREDIT CARDS
MC, V

RATES
Per day: from 650F (99.09€) for small studio to 3,500F (533.57€) for luxurious apartment; fabulous townhouse 7,000F (1,067.14€); lower rates for longer stays

ENGLISH SPOKEN
Yes

Guest Apartment Services specializes in short-term rentals of some of the most beautiful Parisian apartments I have seen. Each property is carefully chosen for its innate charm and authentic character, and it has been decorated in a comfortable Parisian style with beautiful period furnishings, nicely equipped kitchens, and modern bathrooms. I can assure you they are wonderful . . . nothing is faded, out-of-date, or displays even a hint of that shabby-chic decor one often finds in French rental properties. All are located either on the beguiling Île St-Louis or in other lovely areas of central Paris. Some have quiet garden views, others have sweeping, panoramic picture-postcard outlooks. From the smallest studio on a quiet courtyard with a lovely magnolia tree to an elegant townhouse near place des Vosges, complete with indoor swimming pool and garden—and the staff to maintain them—you can be assured that Christophe Chastel and Philippe Pée and their staff will provide you will a memorable Parisian stay. All apartments include weekly maid and linen service (daily maid service is available), cable television, stereo with CD, private telephone and fax, and all major appliances. Arrangements can be made for airport transfers, a car and driver during your stay or for trips out of Paris, a personal chef, baby-sitting . . . whatever is needed to enhance your stay.

INSIGHTFUL TRAVELERS
57 Rutland Square, #4
Boston, MA 02118

TELEPHONE
617-859-0702

FAX
617-267-4794

EMAIL
IT@latoile.com

Insightful Travelers, which operates out of Boston, is owned by Susan Fox and Rick Hill. This dynamic duo work with several purveyors of Paris apartments to find their clients the accommodation that is best suited to their needs, interests, tastes, and budget. They have no allegiance to any special purveyor and can therefore give clients unbiased accounts of the properties they offer. They also provide color photos whenever possible. Susan and Rick make frequent trips to Paris to revise and update their inventory to insure that the apartments they represent continue to meet their stringent standards. Apartment choices range from the "cheap and cheerful" to "big splurge/luxurious" and can accommodate up to six. On-site Paris representatives are always available to help with any emergencies. There is a minimum five-night stay.

PANACHE
141 South Main Street
Cohasset, MA 02025

Connie Afshar specializes in short-term apartment rentals in Paris that are centrally located in the Marais, Île St-Louis, Île de la Cité, les Halles, and near the Louvre. The properties range from basic-budget to lovely and lavish and are equipped accordingly. It all depends on your pocketbook and your needs. Properties are inspected regularly, and detailed descriptions are available on their Internet site.

PARIS VACATION APARTMENTS
86, boulevard de Clichy, 75018

In the U.S.: Erica Berman
37 Somerset Road
Lexington, MA 02420-3519

If you saw the Woody Allen film *Everyone Says I Love You,* you will remember the Montmartre *pied-à-terre* he rented to impress his would-be lover, played by Julia Roberts, and the spectacular view it had of the Sacré Coeur. For the film actors it was just a temporary on-site set location. For you, an apartment with the same fabulous view can be your home in Paris.

American Erica Berman and her French business partner, Alex Mony, are young, energetic, artistic, and full of great ideas. They have taken several Montmartre apartments, and two right on the Palais Royale, and renovated them into smart, stylish, uncluttered wonderful accommodations that all say, "This *is* Paris!" Being

INTERNET
www.insightfultravelers.com

CREDIT CARDS
AE for some apartments, otherwise personal checks

RATES
From $150–$400 per day; prices vary according to size, location, and amenities as well as length of stay (5-day minimum)

ENGLISH SPOKEN
Yes

TELEPHONE
781-383-6006

FAX
781-383-6087

EMAIL
afshar@medione.net

INTERNET
www.panacherental.com

CREDIT CARDS
Depends on apartment, otherwise cash or check

RATES
From $125–$500 per night; lower rates for stays over one month

ENGLISH SPOKEN
Yes

TELEPHONE
France: 01-44-92-06-55, 01-42-59-37-11
U.S.: 718-862-3304

FAX
France: 01-42-64-20-03, attn: Alex and Erica

EMAIL
eberman95@aol.com, or pva@wfi.fr

INTERNET
www.parisvacationapartments .com

CREDIT CARDS
MC, V; also accepts wire transfer, bank draft, money order, or personal checks

RATES
Small studios from $600 per
week; average price around
$1,000–$2,000 per week; lower
rates for longer stays and in
off-season
ENGLISH SPOKEN
Yes

American, Erica knows the mind-set of her compatriots
and has designed the apartments to appeal to American
visitors. She has used simple colors, sprinkled the rooms
with antiques, and fitted the kitchens and baths to
American standards and tastes. Erica and Alex live in
Montmartre and are accessible to their clients. Upon
arrival, they meet you on-site and provide you with the
necessary details, and they provide ongoing advice to
make sure you feel at home during your stay. Weekly
maid service along with major appliances, television,
utilities (except telephone and fax charges) are included.
Prices are fair, and my recommendation is high.

RENTVILLAS.COM
1742 Calle Corva
Camarillo, CA 93010

TELEPHONE
800-726-6702, 805-987-5278
FAX
805-482-7976
EMAIL
mail@rentvillas.com
INTERNET
www.rentvillas.com
CREDIT CARDS
MC, V
RATES
Starting around 1,150F
(175.32€) per week
ENGLISH SPOKEN
Yes

Rentvillas.com has an enviable track record of being
one of the most customer-focused rental companies in
the industry. Founded by Suzanne Pidduck, it has grown
from covering only Italian properties to being a thoroughly computerized operation with properties all over
Europe, including Paris and the French countryside.
Every time I have used Suzanne to help me organize a
long-term stay I have been very pleased, and I have been
impressed with the back-up provided in several emergency
situations. Everyone on staff has extensive travel experience, and you will be matched with a travel advisor who
has expertise in your area of interest. The Website is an
easy way to find just the property you want.

ROTHRAY (14)
10, rue Nicolas-Flamel, 75004
Métro: Châtelet

TELEPHONE
01-48-87-13-37
FAX
01-40-26-34-33
EMAIL
lampard@worldnet.fr
CREDIT CARDS
None; cash or personal checks
in your currency
RATES
From $95–$210 per day (less
by month); prices vary
according to size and location as
well as length of stay (7-day
minimum, prefer stays of one
month or more)
ENGLISH SPOKEN
Yes

There is no contest. It is an undisputed fact that
RothRay apartments are tops . . . the *best* in Paris.
Period. This opinion is shared not only by all of their
loyal and contented clients but by the rest of the competition! I absolutely agree—after one stay, I vowed to
always let competent Ray Lampard and his capable partner, Roth, arrange my living accommodations anytime I
am in Paris. Some short-term private apartment rentals
in Paris can be potluck affairs: you find unwelcome
surprises on arrival, and during your stay you must
contend with strange decor, varying amenities and levels
of cleanliness, and haphazard services by the agency in
charge, who shows little interest in you after they have

your money . . . up front. You will find none of these problems in any apartment rented through RothRay.

Their apartments are located in interesting *quartiers,* where a stroll around a corner will put picturesque Paris at your fingertips. After a few days you will discover what fun it is to actually be a part of Paris, and you'll probably spend a good deal of your time trying to make more permanent arrangements, or figuring out how to return again more often. It will be love at first sight when you walk into one of their tastefully furnished and beautifully equipped studios and apartments. In addition to attractive furnishings, most have cable televisions, stereo systems, washers and dryers, dishwashers, and American-style kitchens beautifully equipped with nice china, crystal, and utensils. You can only fully appreciate the quality of their kitchens if you have ever tried to prepare a meal in a French closet-style kitchen with a mishmash of "rental" pots and pans and chipped, unmatched dishes for serving. Their own apartments are constantly being improved to meet the exacting standards of Roth, who will spend days locating just the right knobs for new kitchen cabinets, or will move a wall a few centimeters to allow for a washer/dryer to be installed. Before guests arrive, he personally inspects the apartment to make sure everything is in order, and both he and Ray are available in Paris for problem-solving. This is an important point: you are not dealing with a local representative of the person or company you rented from. With RothRay you are dealing with the two people who are the owners and who are in charge of, and responsible for, everything. Weekly maid service, linen changes, and a refrigerator stocked with fruit juices, wine, and beer are included. As one guest happily told me, "There is RothRay, and then everyone else, just trying to catch up." How very true that is.

NOTE: RothRay Apartments are so in demand that they are booked sometimes a year in advance. *Please* make your reservation the minute you know your dates in Paris. There is a seven-day minimum, and they prefer one-month rentals.

Camping Out

LES CAMPINGS DU BOIS DE BOULOGNE

Allée du Bord de l'Eau, Bois de Boulogne, 75016
Métro: Porte-Maillot, then take bus 244 (see note)

TELEPHONE
01-45-24-30-00

FAX
01-42-24-42-95

CREDIT CARDS
AE, DC, MC, V

RATES
All rates are per night: Two-person tent without electricity 85F (12.95€), with electricity 165F (25.15€); RV hookups 150F (22.87€); mobile home (up to 4 persons) 370F (56.41€), each additional person 25–35F (3.81–5.34€); lower rates in Sept–June

BREAKFAST
Not available

ENGLISH SPOKEN
Yes

While Coleman stoves, tents, inflatable mattresses, and citronella candles are not on everyone's packing list for a trip to Paris, they might be on yours if you are a camper. Yes, it *is* possible to pitch a tent in Paris! Les Campings in the Bois de Boulogne is on the far edge of the park and provides the only true rustic opportunity for those who like to make a tent of the stars. Geared to students and hearty international travelers, or those with RVs, the campground is located four kilometers away from the nearest métro, making it almost essential that you have your own set of wheels. Otherwise, there is a camp bus, but its schedule may not match yours (either going to or coming from the city) and then you'll be forced to walk. The bus service exists only from April to October, and it's free in July and August. A convenience store, money changer, hot showers, a coin-operated washer and dryer, and a restaurant are open to campers. The office is open from 7 A.M. until 10 P.M. and accepts *no* reservations for campsites, but it does accept them for mobile-home bookings and large camping groups. Everything is always on a first-come, first-served basis.

NOTE: Here are directions from the Porte-Maillot métro station, which is four kilometers from the campground. Exit the station and take shuttle bus no. 244; get off at route des Moulins, and walk down the path to the right. Do not follow misleading signs to the left on main road.

FACILITIES AND SERVICES: Open year-round, coin-operated washing machines and dryers, convenience store, information office, money changer, free hot showers, bus service and restaurant from April to October

NEAREST TOURIST ATTRACTIONS: None

Hostels

Hostels appeal to travelers with youth on their side and wanderlust in their hearts. Only one of the hostels listed here has an age limit, but otherwise they all follow the same general guidelines: shared rooms, public facilities, lockouts in the afternoon, and sometimes a sheaf of other rules and restrictions regarding drinking, smoking, guests, curfews, and so on. However, they often make up in camaraderie what they lack in luxury, and you are almost certain to meet like-minded budget travelers who will be more than willing to share their tales of Parisian adventures.

If you are serious about hosteling, then you should consider becoming a member of Hosteling International/American Youth Hostel (HI/AYH), which runs forty-five hundred hostels in seventy countries. There is no age limit (13 percent of members are senior citizens), and they offer other services as well. If you are not already a member when you arrive at an affiliated hostel, you will be charged a supplement per night for six nights, which will then qualify you as a member. Auberge Jules Ferry, listed below, is the best located HI hostel in Paris, and for general information on Hosteling International and a list of their other Paris hostels, see La Centrale de Réservations below.

HOSTELS

ALOHA HOSTEL (23)
1, rue Borromée, 75015
Métro: Volontaires

TELEPHONE
01-42-73-03-03

FAX
01-42-73-14-14

EMAIL
friends@ aloha.fr

INTERNET
www.cheaphostel.com,
www.friends@aloha.fr

CREDIT CARDS
None, cash only

RATES
Communal rooms are 117F
(17.84€) per person per night;
lower rates in off-season;
showers are free; towel 6F
(0.91€); sheets 30F (4.57€); *taxe
de séjour* included

BREAKFAST
Included

ENGLISH SPOKEN
Yes

60 beds, 8 rooms with showers, none with toilets

The Aloha Hostel, along with five other hostels in Paris, are owned by two brothers. These are the Aloha, La Maison, Le Village Hostel–Montmartre, 3 Ducks Hostel, Woodstock Hostel, and Young & Happy Hostel. While each hostel is has its own personality, they have many similarities in rates, services, and amenities. Unless otherwise stated, the following information applies to all six hostels. They are open year-round, and there is no age limit (only stamina and spirit), but during summer high-season between April and October, all stays are limited to two weeks. Every day there is a cleaning lockout between 11 A.M. and 4 or 5 P.M. and a strict 2 A.M. curfew, though reception is open daily from 8 A.M. to 2 A.M. No booze is allowed and no credit cards are accepted—it is cash only. There are lower rates in winter from November through March. Breakfast, which consists of bread and coffee, is included, and so are showers and the *taxe de séjour*. If you do not BYO sheets and towels, count on spending 30F (4.57€) for sheets and 6F (0.91€) for a towel. You can surf the Internet or send and receive emails for 10F (1.52€) for ten minutes. Don't ask for a refund, they don't exist. Extensions must be made by 10 P.M. the day before. There are kitchen privileges, a TV in the lounge, and always a friendly atmosphere and helpful, English-speaking staff.

At the Aloha Hostel in particular, guests can mingle in the backpack-laden reception area, comparing cheap travel tips gleaned from years of surviving on the edge. Rooms benefit from a redecoration project; beams were added and so were new showers. There are no singles. The working-class neighborhood is full of bakeries, supermarkets, banks, and other survival-type shopping. Otherwise, it's at least twenty minutes to tourist destinations.

FACILITIES AND SERVICES: Safe in office (no charge), communal kitchen, Internet access

NEAREST TOURIST ATTRACTIONS (LEFT BANK): None; must use public transportation

AUBERGE INTERNATIONAL DES JEUNES (19)
10, rue Trousseau, 75011
Métro: Ledru-Rollin

190 beds

It is clean, you can book ahead, and you can pay by credit card. When you arrive, you will have a spartan clean room that is shared with two to six people. Private facilities are in rooms for five or six, sinks are in all the others, and showers are free. There is no curfew, no age limit, and no ban on groups, but you will have to observe a cleaning lockout from 10 A.M. to 3 P.M.

FACILITIES AND SERVICES: Locked luggage area, office safe (no charge)

NEAREST TOURIST ATTRACTIONS (RIGHT BANK): Bastille, nightlife

TELEPHONE
01-47-00-62-00
FAX
01-47-00-33-16
EMAIL
aij@aijparis.com
INTERNET
www.aijparis.com
CREDIT CARDS
AE, MC, V
RATES
March–Oct, 95F (14.48€) per person; Nov–Feb, 85F (12.96€) per person; *taxe de séjour* included
BREAKFAST
Included
ENGLISH SPOKEN
Yes

AUBERGE JULES FERRY (1)
8, boulevard Jules Ferry, 75011
Métro: République

99 beds

No curfew, no age limit, no reservations, no groups, and no stays over one week in this sanctioned Hosteling International choice near place de la République. Rooms sleep from two to six, and the price includes breakfast, showers, and sheets. Cleaning lockout is from noon to 2:30 P.M.; office hours are from 8 A.M. to 1 A.M.

FACILITIES AND SERVICES: Internet facilities, lockers (10F, 1.52€, per day)

NEAREST TOURIST ATTRACTIONS (RIGHT BANK): Not much; must use public transportation

TELEPHONE
01-43-57-55-60
FAX
01-43-14-82-09
EMAIL
Paris.Jules-Ferry@fuaj.org
INTERNET
www.fuaj.org
CREDIT CARDS
MC, V
RATES
115F (17.53€) per person; *taxe de séjour* included
BREAKFAST
Included
ENGLISH SPOKEN
Yes

LA CENTRALE DE RÉSERVATIONS (FUAJ) (2)
27, rue Pajol, 75018
Métro: Marx Dormoy

La Centrale de Réservations (FUAJ), run by Hosteling International, is a good place to go to get a cheap student bed in Paris, or anywhere else in Europe. Membership in Hosteling International is required; it costs 70F (10.67€) if you are twenty-six years old or younger, or 100F (15.24€) if you are over twenty-six. Cards are good for one year from date of purchase. A trip to one of their Paris offices will provide you with a same-day reservation in any of their affiliated hostels or budget

TELEPHONE
01-44-89-87-27
FAX
01-44-89-87-10
EMAIL
fuajidf@micronet.fr
INTERNET
www.fuaj.org
CREDIT CARDS
MC, V

hotels. Not only can you book a bed, but you can make on-going travel arrangements by bus, boat, or air; book tours to other parts of the world; or nail down an excursion in Paris. There will be a reservation fee, payable at the time of booking, but it is deducted from the cost of your bed. The office is open Monday to Friday from 9:30 A.M. to 5 P.M., Saturday 10 A.M. to 4 P.M.

If you can't get to the office in the eighteenth arrondissement, a more convenient office is near the Centre Georges Pompidou at 9 rue Brantôme, 75003; Métro: Rambuteau; Tel: 01-48-04-70-40; Fax: 01-42-77-03-29. Offices hours are Monday to Friday 10 A.M. to 6 P.M., Saturday 10 A.M. to 1 P.M., 2 to 6 P.M.

LA MAISON (25)
67 bis, rue Dutot, 75015
Métro: Volontaires, Pasteur
27 rooms, all with shower and toilet

La Maison is a good hostel for families and senior citizens hell-bent on spending as little as possible to sleep cheap in paris. There are single rooms, if you want to spend the double rate to get them, in addition to twins and quads. All rooms have their own showers and toilets. It is located in a safe but touristically dull area, next to the Ministère de l'Éducation, where you will find a supermarket, laundromat, post office, and plenty of bakeries. For a complete description of rules, regulations, and perks, see Aloha Hostel, page 268.

FACILITIES AND SERVICES: Elevator, Internet access, kitchen privileges, TV in lounge, office safe (no charge)

NEAREST TOURIST ATTRACTIONS (LEFT BANK): None; must use public transportation

LE VILLAGE HOSTEL–MONTMARTRE (11)
20, rue d'Orsel, 75018
Métro: Anvers
75 beds in rooms for 2–6 persons, all with shower and toilet

At this hostel, all the rooms have private facilities, and six rooms (Nos. 201, 205, 302, 305, 401, and 406) have views of Sacré Coeur and the gardens surrounding it. If these rooms are not available, you can enjoy the view from the small hostel terrace. The hostel is located on a street lined with fabric shops, and the famed bargain bin department store Tati is at the corner. Montmartre can be fun if you don't mind the hikes around the *butte,* and if you revel in the laid-back party atmosphere that permeates the more tourist-saturated parts of this special area of Paris. Note that for you, anyway, partying can't go on forever because of the 2 A.M. curfew. For a complete description, see Aloha Hostel, page 268.

FACILITIES AND SERVICES: Fitness room, Internet access, kitchen privileges, TV in lounge, office safe (no charge)

NEAREST TOURIST ATTRACTIONS (RIGHT BANK): Montmartre

RÉSIDENCE BASTILLE (16)
151, avenue Ledru-Rollin, 75011
Métro: Voltaire, Ledru-Rollin
150 beds

The rules are the same as in most hostels, including no drinking, no smoking, no eating, and no outside visitors allowed in the institutional rooms. Cleaning lockout is from noon to 4 P.M., but the desk is open between 7 A.M. and 12:30 P.M. and from 2 P.M. to 1 A.M. To stay here you have to be thirty years old or younger, you can stay for only five nights, and you must pay for your full stay upon arrival. No-shows or late cancellations are penalized the cost of a room for one night. All rooms have a sink and a few of the four-bedded cells have toilets and showers.

FACILITIES AND SERVICES: Elevator, Internet facilities, TV with international reception in lounge, office safe (20F, 3.05€, per day)

NEAREST TOURIST ATTRACTIONS (RIGHT BANK): Bastille

TELEPHONE
01-43-79-35-86
FAX
01-43-79-35-63
CREDIT CARDS
MC, V
RATES
Single 175F (26.68€); all other rooms 125F (19.06€) per person; 10 percent student discount (with ID card); *taxe de séjour* included
BREAKFAST
Included
ENGLISH SPOKEN
Yes

3 DUCKS HOSTEL (21)
6, place Étienne Pernet, 75015
Métro: Commerce
70 beds in shared rooms; 6 rooms also have showers only

This youthful hangout is not the sort of place moms and dads would check into—nor is it one you would want them to check out on your behalf. Its rugged appeal draws backpackers and other wanderers who value camaraderie along with wild and ribald fun over esthetics or a peaceful night's rest. The relaxed management requires shirts and shoes to be worn at all times and provides cooking facilities, hot showers, summer barbecues, a TV in a casual bar with cheap beer, and rooms for two, three, or four persons. Future guests should remember that there are no lockers, only a storage room. The reception and bar are open all day. For a complete description, see Aloha Hostel, page 268.

TELEPHONE
01-48-42-04-05
FAX
01-48-42-99-99
EMAIL
backpack@3ducks.fr
INTERNET
www.3ducks.fr
RATES
Also has doubles for 137F (20.89€) per person

NOTE: 3 Ducks Hostel is on the right side of Jean Baptiste de Grenelle Church, at the end of rue de Commerce.

FACILITIES AND SERVICES: Bar with beer and soft drinks, TV in bar, office safe (no charge), kitchen privileges, Internet access

NEAREST TOURIST ATTRACTIONS (LEFT BANK): Far from everything, must use public transportation

WOODSTOCK HOSTEL (2)
48, rue Rodier, 75009
Métro: Anvers, Poissonnière
58 beds

TELEPHONE AND FAX
01-48-78-87-76
EMAIL
flowers@woodstock.fr
INTERNET
www.woodstock.fr
RATES
Also has doubles for 117F (17.87€) per person; dorm rooms 107F (16.31€) per person

Woodstock Hostel is about a ten-minute walk from the Gare du Nord and Gare de l'Est train stations and across the street from a pretty park where you can enjoy a picnic lunch or watch the children playing. Also close by are bakeries, a grocery, and a laundromat. Even though it is close to Pigalle and all the sleaze of that area, the hostel is in a safe pocket. For a complete description, see Aloha Hostel, page 268.

FACILITIES AND SERVICES: Office safe (no charge), kitchen privileges, Internet access, luggage storage room

NEAREST TOURIST ATTRACTIONS (RIGHT BANK): Not much; must use public transportation

YOUNG & HAPPY HOSTEL (Y & H HOSTEL) (30)
80, rue Mouffetard, 75005
Métro: Place Monge, Censier-Daubenton
65 beds

TELEPHONE
01-45-35-09-53
FAX
01-47-07-22-24
EMAIL
smile@youngandhappy.fr
INTERNET
www.youngandhappy.fr
RATES
Also has doubles for 137F (20.89€) per person

The Young & Happy Hostel is so named because it's friendly and everyone who stays here has such a good time. It is located on rue Mouffetard, a famous *marché* street with loads of cheap eats—everything from crêpes and croissants to pizza slices and dripping Greek sandwiches. It is also close to the Latin Quarter. You can reserve with a one-night advance deposit, or arrive when they open and hope for the best. For a complete description, see Aloha Hostel, page 268.

FACILITIES AND SERVICES: Kitchen privileges, TV in lounge, Internet access, office safe (no charge)

NEAREST TOURIST ATTRACTIONS (LEFT BANK): Rue Mouffetard, Jardin des Plantes, Latin Quarter

Residence Hotels

Residence hotels are a very European concept, and I personally often choose to stay in them because they combine many of the services and amenities you find in regular hotels with the advantages of renting your own apartment. They generally come with a fully equipped kitchen, are usually roomier and have closet space, and often include some sort of maid service. They are nice options for travelers staying for longer periods of time, and they bear absolutely no resemblance to the down-and-out accommodations that often go by the name "residence hotels" in the States.

Note that residence hotels in France can choose whether or not to apply for a star rating, and many do not. If a place listed below possesses no stars, that does not mean it is a "no star"; it could be luxurious and expensive, it just doesn't have the stars to prove it.

CENTRE PARISIEN DE ZEN (25)
35, rue de Lyon, 75012
Métro: Gare de Lyon, Bastille
6 studios with kitchenettes

Peace and serenity are the by-words of this calming alternative to a stressful hotel stay. Graznya and Jacob Perl, both Polish and both Zen masters, have opened six studio apartments and a meditation center in an old school building. When I first heard about it, I definitely had my doubts. Once I saw the amazingly low prices for the sparkling clean, whitewashed, wood-floor studios surrounding a leafy, cobbled courtyard, doubts flew out the window and I was ready to check in. Each bright, sunny, Ikea-furnished unit sleeps two on a low-to-the-ground mattress with a duvet cover. In addition to a private bath and shower, there is a kitchen corner with two burners, refrigerator, sink, and all the utensils and

TELEPHONE
01-44-87-08-13

FAX
01-44-87-09-07

EMAIL
perlzen@yahoo.com

CREDIT CARDS
None, cash only

RATES
Rates are per week: Single 1,750F (266.79€), double 2,450F (373.50€); *taxe de séjour* included

BREAKFAST
Not served

ENGLISH SPOKEN
Yes, fluently, and Polish

dishes you will need to set up housekeeping. Closet and drawer space is certainly adequate. Nice touches include Graznya's framed paintings and a few paperback books. The only television and telephone are in the common room, but if you are staying a month or more, you can get your own telephone line and private number. Once-a-week maid service and linen change is included. The meditation room is open to everyone, whether or not you are a Buddhist.

The neighborhood is a ten-minute walk from the Bastille, where you can hop on a métro or bus for safaris throughout Paris. The Marais, place des Vosges, and Picasso Museum are all under a twenty-minute stroll. If you are a night owl, there is the fun and frivolity along rue de Lappe to keep you partying until dawn. On Thursday and Sunday there is a huge open-air market at Bastille, and for shopping needs in between, plenty of little food shops are tucked around. A minimum stay of one week is required, and longer stays are welcomed.

FACILITIES AND SERVICES: Coin-operated washer and dryer, meditation room; no elevator, phone, TV, or safe

NEAREST TOURIST ATTRACTIONS (RIGHT BANK): Bastille, Marais, Place des Vosges

FAMILY HÔTEL (8)
23, rue Fondary, 75015
Métro: Dupleix, Émile-Zola, La Motte Picquet–Grenelle

21 studios, all with kitchenette, shower, and toilet

TELEPHONE
01-45-75-20-49
FAX
01-45-77-70-73
CREDIT CARDS
MC, V
RATES
1–2 persons 220–400F (33.54–60.98€); lower prices for longer stays: 20 percent discount after 7 nights, 30 percent discount after 15 nights; *taxe de séjour* included
BREAKFAST
Not available
ENGLISH SPOKEN
Yes

These plain-as-a-pin studios in the middle of the working-class fifteenth arrondissement put the B in Basic. The twenty-one bargain sites are geared for economizers who are in for the long haul and want *only* a clean place to cook, eat, sleep, and take a shower. Nothing more. Fifteen have a TV, some have sofa beds, and some have proper double or twin beds. The low-maintenance floors are white tile, bathrooms are reminiscent of train compartments, and the closets are designed for those who travel light and never shop. The colors match and so does the simple furniture. Kitchens are stocked with the barest essentials you will need to do simple cooking. The units are kept clean, thanks to the maids who swoop through three times a week. The operation is run by the Pacific Hôtel just down the street (see page 222), and from what I could see, the staff is available only to check people in and out and render crisis management.

NOTE: All reservations and check-ins are handled

through the Pacific Hôtel at the telephone and fax provided here.

FACILITIES AND SERVICES: Direct-dial phone with separate line for each studio, elevator, kitchenettes, maid service three times a week, TV in fifteen rooms, office safe at Pacific Hôtel (no charge)

NEAREST TOURIST ATTRACTIONS (LEFT BANK): Eiffel Tower, Seine; otherwise, must use public transportation

HOME PLAZZA RÉSIDENCE HÔTELS: BASTILLE AND SAINT-ANTOINE

The two Home Plazza residences are located in a part of Paris, the eleventh arrondissement, that until a few years ago was considered a tourist wilderness. Now they are close to the thick of things. The two residence hotels offer equipped studios and flats furnished in a modern style that holds up well under hard use. While the Bastille résidence has the edge on location and amenities offered, the Saint-Antoine site is less impersonal and sterile. At both, impressive discounts can be negotiated during the low season and for longer stays, but during the fashion shows, the Paris Air Show, and any other internationally publicized events, fairs, or conferences, there are outrageous supplements.

NOTE: The following information is the same for both Bastille and Saint-Antoine.

CREDIT CARDS: AE, DC, MC, V

RATES: From one-person singles, 850F (129.59€), to 6-person rooms, 1,750F (266.79€); lower rates on request, in low season, and for long stays; *taxe de séjour* included

BREAKFAST: Buffet 80F (12.20€), American 135F (20.58€), per person

ENGLISH SPOKEN: Yes

HOME PLAZZA BASTILLE ★★★ (11)
74, rue Amelot, 75011
Métro: St-Sebastien-Froissart, Chemin Vert
290 studios and apartments, fully furnished with equipped kitchens

FACILITIES AND SERVICES: Air-conditioning, bar, conference room, direct-dial phone, elevator, hair dryer, iron, laundry and cleaning service, parking (100F, 15.24€, per day), room safe (5F, 0.76€, per day), TV with international reception, restaurant

NEAREST TOURIST ATTRACTIONS (RIGHT BANK): Marais, place des Vosges, Bastille

TELEPHONE
Central reservations: 01-40-21-22-23; reception at hotel: 01-40-21-20-00
FAX
01-47-00-82-40
EMAIL
resabastille@home-plazza.com
INTERNET
www.1st-paris-hotelsplazza.com

HOME PLAZZA SAINT-ANTOINE ★★★ (21)
289 bis, rue du Faubourg St-Antoine, 75011
Métro: Nation

TELEPHONE
Central reservations:
01-40-21-22-23; reception
at hotel: 01-40-09-40-00

FAX
01-40-09-11-55

EMAIL
resanation@home-plazza.com

INTERNET
www.1st-paris-
hotelsplazza.com

89 studios and apartments, fully furnished with equipped kitchens

From a security standpoint, I would avoid the rooms on the garden level.

FACILITIES AND SERVICES: Air-conditioning, conference room, direct-dial phone, elevator, hair dryer, iron, laundry and cleaning service, parking (100F, 15.24€, per day), TV with international, office safe (no charge), room safe (5F, 0.76€, per day)

NEAREST TOURIST ATTRACTIONS (RIGHT BANK): Nothing; must use public transportation

HÔTEL RÉSIDENCE DES ARTS ($, 13)
14, rue Gît-le-Coeur, 75006
Métro: Odéon, St-Michel

TELEPHONE
01-55-42-71-11

FAX
01-55-42-71-00

EMAIL
RDesarts@aol.com

INTERNET
www.residence-des-arts.com

CREDIT CARDS
AE, MC, V

RATES
Studio 825–1,045F (125.77–
159.31€), suite 1,320–1,650F
(201.23–251.54€), apartment
1,980F (301.85€), studio &
suite combined 2,090–2,530F
(318.62–385.70€); *taxe de séjour*
included

BREAKFAST
Continental 55F (8.38€) per
person

ENGLISH SPOKEN
Yes

5 studios, 5 suites, 1 large penthouse apartment

If you are looking for the ease of independent living combined with the full services of a hotel, the posh Résidence des Arts is for you. Pivotally located in the very core of St-Germain-des-Prés, the fifteenth-century private residence hotel offers five beautiful studios, five suites, and one stunning penthouse apartment, each one combining luxurious touches with the convenience of a kitchen and individual service. Starting from the top, No. 6, the penthouse, is a large one bedroom choice with mansard windows. The sitting room, in rich plum and gold, has a desk, large-screen television, and comfortable seating. The bedroom has a spacious bath with a separate bathtub and enclosed stall shower. The corner kitchen is well stocked for light cooking. As with all of the units, there is also a private telephone line, modem connection, and air-conditioning. Next in size are the suites. I like No. 22, with a king-size bed and two windows looking toward the street. The studios are small, but they are certainly comfortable for one, or for two for a short stay. The bathroom comes with a stall shower, and all the other comforts are here. One benefit of the studios and suites is that they can be combined into large two-bedroom apartments, which is convenient for families. Lower rates are available in the off-season and for longer stays.

FACILITIES AND SERVICES: Air-conditioning, direct-dial phone with private line, hair dryer, elevator, kitchen with microwave, laundry service, modems, parking on request, TV with international reception, office safe (no charge), daily maid service, daily towel and linen change

NEAREST TOURIST ATTRACTIONS (LEFT BANK): Seine, Île de la Cité, Île St-Louis, St-Germain-des-Prés, St-Michel

RÉSIDENCE HÔTEL DES TROIS POUSSINS ★★★ (3)
15, rue Clauzel, 75009
Métro: St-Georges
40 rooms: 24 studios with kitchens, 16 hotel rooms, all with bath or shower and toilet

In its former life, the Résidence Hôtel des Trois Poussins was a fleabag bunker for young, hard-partying backpackers who were more interested in the earthly activities around Pigalle than in a decent place to stay. To say the place has been renovated is an unjustice. It has been totally transformed and is now a very smart-looking address geared toward a discriminating clientele who are accustomed to the better things in life. The hotel is a combination of regular hotel rooms and studios with kitchenettes, allowing you to choose whichever style of accommodation suits your needs. Finally, its location in a small, nice neighborhood enclave is light-years away in spirit from the seamier neighborhood next to it.

Everything in the hotel has been well conceived, from the small, fitted kitchens, to the coordinated checks and prints that decorate the pretty rooms, to the garden where summer breakfasts are served. Many of the sixth-floor rooms have views that stretch from the Panthéon and Notre Dame to L'Eglise Notre Dame de Lorette. One of the most popular, especially for honeymooners, is No. 602, which has large windows encompassing this wide view and a lovely new bathroom. Those on the fourth floor are bathed in sunshine. The staff has a sense of what personal service is . . . and they deliver it. Nearby is an interesting market street, and you are within brisk walking distance to Montmartre. Special rates during the low season and for stays that include Friday, Saturday, and Sunday nights are available on request and depend on the season.

FACILITIES AND SERVICES: Direct-dial phone with private line, elevator, hair dryer, kitchens in all the studios, laundry service, daily maid service in studios, modems, two handicapped-accessible rooms, TV with international reception, room safe (no charge)

NEAREST TOURIST ATTRACTIONS (RIGHT BANK): Montmartre

TELEPHONE
01-53-32-81-81

FAX
01-53-32-81-82

EMAIL
h3p@clup-Internet.fr

INTERNET
www.les3poussins.com

CREDIT CARDS
AE, MC, V

RATES
Hotel: single 750F (114.34€), double 850–1,050F (129.58–160.07€), triple or quad 1,250F (190.56€); studio with kitchenette: single 850F (129.58€), double 950–1,150F (144.83–175.32€), triple or quad 1,350F (205.81€); *taxe de séjour* included

BREAKFAST
Buffet 55F (8.38€) per person

ENGLISH SPOKEN
Yes

RÉSIDENCE HÔTELIÈRE TROUSSEAU ★★ (18)
13, rue Trousseau, 75011
Métro: Ledru-Rollin

TELEPHONE
01-48-05-55-55

FAX
01-48-05-83-97

EMAIL
tr@hroy.com

INTERNET
www.hroy.com/trousseau

CREDIT CARDS
AE, MC, V

RATES
Hotel plan: from 1–2 person studio, 580F (88.42€), to 6–8 person duplex, 1,600F (243.92€), per night; daily cleaning and linen change, sheets changed every two days. Residence plan (3-night minimum): from 1–2 person studio, 550F (83.85€), to 6–8 person duplex, 1,350F (205.81€); daily maid service, weekly change of sheets and towels; Kitchen Kit 100F (15.24€), or free after third week; lower rates for longer stays; *taxe de séjour* included

BREAKFAST
Buffet 50F (7.62€) per person

ENGLISH SPOKEN
Yes

66 studios and suites, all with fully fitted kitchens, bath, shower, and toilet

To tell you the truth, I never expected to find such a nice residence hotel a fifteen-minute walk *east* of the Bastille. If it was almost any place else in Paris, it would be close to twice the price and jam-packed year-round. The Trousseau is part of a small chain that deals mainly in four-star addresses in Paris and along the French Riviera, so demanding, exacting guests are nothing new to management. The sixty-six studio flats and duplex suites have fully equipped kitchens with microwaves and satellite television reception. Disciples of Sister Parish and Billy Baldwin were not called upon to be decorating consultants, but the no-surprise rooms have excellent bathrooms with lots of shelf space, a medicine cabinet, and a drying rack. No. 710 is a large, two-story duplex with a mezzanine bedroom and a ship theme, which is carried out in a variety of ways: with photos of yachts on the walls, in the bunk-bedded sleeping cabins—which give you the illusion of being underwater because you can't see anything out of the port-hole—and in the bathrooms, or "Captain's Quarters," which have port-hole mirrors and wooden slat shower floors. Just so you know, in the studios the sofa doubles as the bed, the closets have no doors, and some floors are tiled, not carpeted. You can choose between two rate plans: the hotel plan has no minimum night stay and includes daily maid and linen service, while the residence plan has a three-night minimum stay, daily maid service, and weekly linen service.

The overall popularity of this selection is due in no small measure to the list of amenities offered: private car parking, conference room, office space, fax capabilities, a golf practice cage with minigolf—no kidding!—along with coin-operated laundries and shopping carts in the garage to help you lug your loot. Also, the proprietors own wineries in Bordeaux and sell their wines at this hotel, and they have named the rooms after a wine-producing chateau.

FACILITIES AND SERVICES: Bar, conference room, direct-dial phone, elevator, hair dryer, fitted kitchen, private parking (80F, 12.20€, per day), TV with international reception, trouser press, office safe (no charge), golf range (no charge), weekly or daily maid service (depending on accommodation), coin-operated washer and dryer

NEAREST TOURIST ATTRACTIONS (RIGHT BANK): None; must use public transportation

RÉSIDENCE HÔTEL MALESHERBES (2)
129, rue Cardinet, 75017
Métro: Malesherbes

21 studios, all with equipped kitchens, shower or bath, and toilet

The location is more than a few heartbeats away from Tourist Central, but the prices are interesting for those who want to be able to make a cup of tea or prepare a sandwich, and who do not require much living space in which to do it. These twenty-one way-above-average, soundproofed studios have been decorated with provincial prints, quilted spreads, and antiqued furniture. Kitchenettes are mini in size and scope—they are not geared for preparing banquets or experimenting with Julia Child's most complicated recipes, but they are big enough to fix something purchased from the tempting outdoor *marché* held along rue Levis, just a few minutes' walk from here. There is also no getting around the small bathrooms and limited drawer space, but the showers are good and everything works. Once-a-week maid service is included.

FACILITIES AND SERVICES: Private telephone line for each studio, elevator, equipped kitchenettes, hair dryer, laundry service, parking (75F, 11.43€, per day), dogs accepted (75F, 11.43€, per day), TV, office safe (no charge)

NEAREST TOURIST ATTRACTIONS (RIGHT BANK): None; must use public transportation

TELEPHONE
01-44-15-85-00

FAX
01-44-15-85-29

CREDIT CARDS
AE, MC, V

RATES
Studio for 1–2 persons 470–550F (71.65–83.85€), triple 680F (103.67€), per day; lower rates for longer stays; extra bed 80F (12.20€), baby bed 30F (4.57€); *Taxe de séjour* 3F (.46€) per person, per day

BREAKFAST
40F (6.10€) per person, served in studio

ENGLISH SPOKEN
Yes

Student Accommodations

There are more than ten thousand student beds in Paris. The following list of both public and private sources offers help in finding low-cost student accommodations year-round. Where applicable, only main reservation offices are listed. Most sites have a minimum stay in the summer, and curfews are not uncommon. All will give you the rules of the road *before* you get your bed, so there will be no excuses for improper conduct or pleading ignorance. It is critically important to remember that often *only* cash is accepted, and that most times you must either be an enrolled student or within a certain age bracket.

Any student can take advantage of the French government–run and/or –subsidized student lodgings as well as a wide range of other student discounts. To qualify for the *tarif étudiant,* you are required to show proof of full-time student status, in addition to your university or college ID, or if you are not a student, prove you are between the ages of twelve and twenty-five. The best way to show this additional proof is with the International Student Identity Card (ISIC) or with the Go-25 card (if you are between twelve and twenty-five years old and not a student). Both cards entitle you to savings on selected museum entry fees, film and theater tickets, transportation costs, meals at certain student dining halls, and of course, lodgings. The ISIC card is only valid in France if you are under twenty-six. Teachers can get some of the same discounts and all of the benefits by purchasing the International Teacher Identity Card (ITIC). In the United States the cards costs $20 (and require a one-inch-size passport photo) and are available through Council Travel (see below). One of the best benefits of these cards is the heath insurance, which provides you with the following coverage at no additional cost: hospital coverage (sixty-day maximum stay), accident, accidental death, emergency evacuation, and repatriation of remains. In addition, an ISIC card will save on airfares, transportation, attractions, and accommodations in more than ninety countries. It also provides users with a twenty-four-hour emergency help line and worldwide voice mail, fax messaging, and phone card service through its ISIConnect feature. It is an unbelievable bargain. You can buy both cards in Paris from CROUS (see page 283), but you won't qualify for the health or accident insurance. If you send for the card, allow three weeks; if you go to your local office, it will be issued on the spot. For more information, log onto www.isic.org.

For information about work-study programs, contact the Council Travel Office at the Council on International Education Exchange (CIEE) headquarters, 205 East 42nd Street, 16th floor, New York, NY 10017, or call 888-2-COUNCIL. For worldwide reservations or the CIEE location nearest you, contact them at 6 Hamilton Place, fourth floor, Boston, MA 02108, or call 800-2-COUNCIL. Hours are Monday to Friday 9 A.M. to 9 P.M. and Saturday 10 A.M. to 6 P.M. For information about their educational programs, call 888-COUNCIL; hours are Monday to Friday

10 A.M. to 6 P.M., Saturday 11 A.M. to 3 P.M. You can also visit their Website at www.counciltravel.com, or for more information on the work-study programs abroad, email them at info@ciee.org. Council Travel has branches in most major U.S. cities and you can call the 800-number above for the location nearest you.

In Paris, CIEE is located at 1, place de l'Odéon, 76006, Telephone: 01-44-41-74-74, Fax: 01-43-26-97-45, Métro: Odéon.

Finally, if none of the above work, try the Office du Tourisme at 127, Champs-Élysées, 75008; Métro: Charles-de-Gaulle-Étoile; Tel: 01-36-68-31-12, or for recorded information in English, 01-49-52-53-56. It's open in winter Monday to Saturday from 9 A.M. to 8 P.M., Sunday 11 A.M. to 6 P.M., and in summer daily from 9 A.M. to 8 P.M. Lines are long and selections are not always the cheapest. Count on paying a supplement for the reservation service.

STUDENT ACCOMMODATIONS

ASSOCIATION DES ÉTUDIENTS PROTESTANTS DE PARIS (AEPP) (48)
46, rue de Vaugirard, 75006
Métro: Mabillon, St-Sulpice, Rennes
45 dormitory beds, no private facilities

Centrally located by the Luxembourg Gardens, the facility is open to students who are between eighteen and thirty. Maximum stay is five weeks in dormitory-style accommodations, which must be paid for in advance. From June through August there are a few rooms for one or two. Breakfast is included in the daily rate, and cooking facilities are also available. On arrival, a refundable key deposit (200F, 30.49€) and a one-year membership fee (10F, 1.52€) will be charged.

Office hours are Monday to Friday from 8:45 A.M. to noon, 3 to 7 P.M. (in summer 5 to 7 P.M.); Saturday from 8:45 A.M. to noon, 6 to 8 P.M.; and Sunday from 10 A.M. to noon.

TELEPHONE
01-43-54-31-49,
01-46-33-23-30

FAX
01-46-34-27-09

EMAIL
aepp.resa@worldnet.fr

CREDIT CARDS
None

RATES
All rates are per person: single 120F (18.29€), double 110F (16.77€), dorm room (4–8 persons) 95F (14.48€); *taxe de séjour* included

BREAKFAST
Included

ENGLISH SPOKEN
Yes

FACILITIES AND SERVICES: Cooking privileges, office safe (no charge), TV downstairs

NEAREST TOURIST ATTRACTIONS (LEFT BANK): Luxembourg Gardens, St-Michel, St-Germain-des-Prés, Montparnasse

BUREAU DES VOYAGES DE LA JEUNESSE (BVJ)

Paris/Louvre location (40):
20, rue Jean-Jacques Rousseau, 75001
Métro: Louvre–Rivoli
280 beds, none with shower, bath, or toilet

Quartier Latin location (12):
44, rue des Bernardins, 75005
Métro: Maubert-Mutualité
110 beds, none with shower, bath, or toilet

TELEPHONE
Paris/Louvre: 01-53-00-90-90
Quartier Latin: 01-43-29-34-80
Group reservations (both locations): 01-53-00-90-95

FAX
Both locations: 01-53-00-90-91

INTERNET
Both locations:
www.bvjhotels.com

CREDIT CARDS
MC, V (only at Paris/Louvre)

RATES
All rates are per person: single 155F (23.63€), double 130F (19.82€), dorm 120F (18.29€); *taxe de séjour* included

BREAKFAST
Included

ENGLISH SPOKEN
Yes

There are 390 beds for young people (ages eighteen to thirty-five) available in the heart of Paris, either on the Right Bank near the Louvre (called Paris/Louvre) or on the Left Bank in the Latin Quarter (at Quartier Latin). Most of the clientele travel light with only a backpack and don't mind sharing dorm rooms with up to seven other weary travelers. The good news is that the prices are reasonable, and there are some single and double accommodations in addition to the shared dorm rooms (for up to eight). The key is to land in a room with as few roommates as possible. No towels or soap are provided with the free showers at Paris/Louvre, but at Quartier Latin, all rooms have a shower; lockers cost only 10F (1.52€) and are worth it; there is no daytime lockout; and at the Louvre location, there is a subsidized restaurant. Individual travelers usually need a two- or three-day advance reservation, but groups should reserve as far ahead as possible. Both are under the umbrella of UCRIF Étapes Jeunes (see page 284).

FACILITIES AND SERVICES: Elevator at Paris/Louvre, lockers (10F, 1.52€), Internet facilities, meals at Paris/Louvre are 40–55F (6.10–8.38€) for lunch or dinner, TV at Quartier Latin, no towels or soap provided, no daytime lockout, no safe

NEAREST TOURIST ATTRACTIONS: Paris/Louvre location (Right Bank): Louvre, Palais Royal, Centre Georges Pompidou (Beaubourg), Les Halles; Quartier Latin location (Left Bank): St-Michel, Latin Quarter, Seine, Île de la Cité, Île St-Louis

CROUS ACADÉMIE DE PARIS (37)
39, avenue Georges-Bernanos, 75005
Métro: Port-Royal

TELEPHONE
01-40-51-36-00

CROUS is mainly known for providing students with inexpensive meals in its Restos-U (see *Great Eats Paris*). It also is in charge of all university student accommodations in Paris, and it has beds available during French university vacations. It is also a source of cheap trips and discount tickets for theater and cultural events, and the ISIC card is sold here. The address above is the main office where you should start your search, whether it be for meal tickets, a bed for your stay, or a trip outside of Paris. Hours are Monday to Friday from 9 A.M. to 5 P.M. English is spoken most of the time.

MAISON INTERNATIONALE DE LA JEUNESSE ET DES ÉTUDIANTS (MIJE) (39)
6, rue de Fourcy, 75004
Métro: St-Paul

TELEPHONE
01-42-74-23-45

FAX
01-40-27-81-64

EMAIL
mije@wanadoo.fr

INTERNET
www.jije.com/

CREDIT CARDS
None, cash only

RATES
All rates are per person: single 220F (33.54€), double 170F (25.92€), triple 150F (22.87€), dorm (4 to 8 persons) 140F (21.34€); restaurant: lunch or dinner 50F (7.62€) and 60F (9.15€); *taxe de séjour* included

BREAKFAST
Included

ENGLISH SPOKEN
Yes

MIJE offers some of the best student beds in Paris in two converted seventeenth-century historic mansions and a former convent. Each room holds from two to eight people; all rooms have a sink and shower. The address given above (Le Fourcy) is also the main office where all reservations are made. There is also a dining room here that is open to anyone staying in the three hostels. Sheets are provided, but not towels or soap. There is a 15F (2.29€) one-year membership fee, the maximum stay is seven nights, no one accepted over thirty (unless in a single room), no smoking is allowed, and there is a room lockout from noon to 3 P.M.. Advanced reservations by telephone or fax are accepted from 7 A.M. to 1 A.M. daily. Do it! These are very popular accommodations.

NOTE: The other two locations are Fauconnier, 11, rue Fauconnier (4th), Métro: St-Paul; and Maubuisson, 12, rue des Barres (4th), Métro: Hôtel-de-Ville.

FACILITIES AND SERVICES: Internet facilities at Fourcy and Fauconnier; restaurant at Fourcy, office safe (no charge)

NEAREST TOURIST ATTRACTIONS (RIGHT BANK): Marais, Bastille, the islands, St-Michel, St-Germain-des-Prés

MAISON INTERNATIONALE DES JEUNES (MIJCP) (20)
4, rue Titon, 75011
Métro: Faidherbe-Chaligny
170 beds, no private facilities

TELEPHONE
01-43-71-99-21
FAX
01-43-71-78-58
EMAIL
muj.cp@wanadoo.fr
CREDIT CARDS
None, cash only
RATES
1150F (17.53€) per person; free
shower; sheet 15F (2.29€);
towel 6F (0.91€); *taxe de séjour*
included
BREAKFAST
Included
ENGLISH SPOKEN
Yes

Open to people age eighteen to thirty (older if with a group), the MIJCP offers clean rooms with two to eight basic bunks and not much else. Length of stay is between three and four nights. Breakfast and a free shower are included in the daily rate; everything else is extra. Facilities are nil: no safes, lockers, laundry, TV, or even bed lights, and you must bring your own sheets, soap, and towels or rent them here. There is a 2 A.M. curfew and a daily cleaning lockout from 10 A.M. until 5 P.M. The office is open from 8 A.M. to 1 A.M. This is one to keep in mind when all else fails.

FACILITIES AND SERVICES: None

NEAREST TOURIST ATTRACTIONS (RIGHT BANK): Bastille (long walk)

OTU VOYAGE (7)
119, rue St-Martin, Parvis de Beaubourg, 75004
Métro: Rambuteau

TELEPHONE
01-40-29-12-12
FAX
01-40-29-12-25
INTERNET
www.otu.fr
CREDIT CARDS
MC, V
ENGLISH SPOKEN
Yes

Located across the square from the Centre Georges Pompidou (Beaubourg), OTU provides discount travel help and information on accommodations and many other related items of interest to anyone age eighteen to thirty. Office hours are Monday to Saturday 10 A.M. to 5 P.M. They also sell the ISIC card, which every student should have in their possession (see page 280).

UNION DES CENTRES DE RECONTRES INTERNATIONALES DE FRANCE (UCRIF) (21)
27, rue de Turbigo, 75002
Métro: Étienne-Marcel

TELEPHONE
01-40-26-57-64
FAX
01-40-26-58-20
EMAIL
info@ucrif.asso.fr
INTERNET
www.ucrif.asso.fr
ENGLISH SPOKEN
Yes

UCRIF welcomes and accommodates young travelers in several lodgings in Paris and throughout the rest of France. While geared mainly toward groups, solo sleepers are welcome. For descriptions of two of their Paris locations, see BVJ Paris/Louvre and Quartier Latin, page 282. For the complete listing, contact the Maison de L'UCRIF. Office hours are Monday to Friday from 9 A.M. to 6 P.M.

Shopping: Great Buys and Savvy Chic

Paris is wrenchingly beautiful, and so are many of its people. If you use your eyes and take in everything, you can learn more about true style in a weekend than in a lifetime's perusal of fashion magazines.

—Lucia Van der Post

A museum is a museum, but a bargain is forever . . .

—Suzy K. Gershman, Born to Shop Paris

Paris is a shopper's dream world. Even those who claim to dislike shopping are bound to be attracted by the unending selection of shops with beautiful window displays. The *haute couture,* open air *marchés* overflowing with beautiful foods, extravagant toy shops, and the dazzling displays of jewelry, antiques, and collectibles tempt everyone from the serious buyer to the casual browser. There has always been something very stylish about the French. Just the addition of the word French to everyday objects such as jeans, silk, perfume, bread, wine, cheese, and toast lifts them out of the ordinary. For many of us, going to Paris is a dream come true, but it isn't quite enough . . . we want to bring something of Paris home with us. However, a recent study showed Paris to be the most expensive city in Europe for buying clothes and shoes. What are we to do—those of us who cannot afford to pay the astronomically high prices that come with such glorious merchandise? The answer is: Become a Parisian smart shopper.

After you have been in Paris for a day or so, you will realize that style counts: the French do not just get dressed, they get turned out, many in *couturière* battle dress. You will no doubt wonder how a modest shop clerk manages to look so elegant, considering his or her low wages and the high price tags for clothing. The answer is simple: savvy Parisian shoppers know where to go for the best quality and value, and they never pay full price.

Shopping the secondhand clothing stores was once reserved for a minority who seldom admitted frequenting used clothing outlets, but it has now become a mainstream activity in Paris. Buying cheap has been given a new cachet. Determined discount bounty hunters shop with a vengeance for vintage clothing, which has become so "in" that designers have based entire collections on specific retro looks. As a life-long, dedicated discount shopper with a black belt in the art, I know that bargain shopping of any kind can be both frustrating and exhausting—until you find that fabulous designer suit in your size and favorite color for half price. Any type of discount shopping in Paris takes a good eye, limitless patience, endurance, and comfortable shoes. In Paris, of all places, it should be more than just a quest to track down the cheapest items available . . . it should be fun. Finding something *très à la mode* at below retail in Paris is not that difficult once you know how. The trick is in knowing when and where to shop to get the most for your money. That is what "Great Buys and Savvy Chic" will help you to do: transform your T-shirt into a significant outfit, with just the right pair of pants, a sassy jacket, and perfect accessories for the moment—all for reduced prices and, more importantly, for less than you would pay at home.

With all discount shopping, especially clothing stores, the selections will vary from day to day and season to season. Shops also come and go. What is here today and very "in" may be gone tomorrow. Not all shops take credit cards, so be prepared with extra francs. The comfort of the customer is seldom a top priority if you are on the designer discount beat. As a result, many of these places do not have proper dressing rooms, most are jammed with merchandise, there is limited individual attention, and in many cases only fragmented English is spoken. And never mind the ice-maiden *vendeuse* who has an innate knack for sizing you up and pricing everything you are wearing in one glance. Believe me, it is all worth it because nothing is more satisfying than being clad in designer labels at knockdown prices.

In addition to leading you to fabulous clothing, "Great Buys and Savvy Chic" guides you to a gamut of great shopping: from the best English-language bookstores, children's toys and clothes, cosmetics, kitchen supplies, and jewelry to flea and antique markets, produce markets, museum shops, historic *passages,* and department stores. Armed with "Great Buys," you are bound to find great gifts and clothes, save money, and come home with unique discoveries your friends will die over. *Bon chance!* And please, if you uncover something wonderful, let me know.

Tips for Great Shopping

> **Nobody who has not lived in Paris can appreciate the unique savor of that word *femmes*.**
>
> —*Arnold Bennett,* Paris Nights *(1913)*

1. Know the prices at home so you will be able to spot a bargain when you see it in Paris. Carry a calculator to be sure you are getting the bargain you think you are.

2. When you enter a store, you will be greeted with *Bonjour Madame* (or *Monsieur*), and when you leave, *Au revoir Madame* (or *Monsieur*). Please respond in kind, with *Bonjour Mademoiselle,* and so on. It is considered extremely bad form not to acknowledge the salespeople when entering or leaving a store.

3. If you like something, can get it home, and can afford it, buy it when you see it. If you wait until later, it probably will not be there when you go back, or you will see it later or when you get home for twice the price.

4. Look for these signs in the windows—they mean lower prices:

Soldes	a sale in progress
Fin de Séries	end of collection
Dégriffés	labels cut out
Stock	overstock
Dépot Vente	resale
Fripes	used clothing
Troc, brocante	secondhand

5. Very seldom will you be able to return something, and if you manage to do so, the hassle will probably not be worth it. To avoid this time-consuming headache, be sure when you buy something that it does not have flaws, that it fits, and that it's what you want.

6. Never change money at a shop. The rate will not be in your favor. Go instead to a bank or use a credit card.

7. If you are shopping at one of the flea markets, you can definitely bargain. The asking price is not the price you are expected to pay. You should be able to get the price down by 15 to 30 percent. Also, bring cash: plastic is not part of a bargaining discussion, and most sellers do not take credit cards of any type.

8. Pharmacies marked with a green cross on a white background are upscale and expensive. They are the places to go if you need a prescription filled or advice on cold remedies. Many pharmacies also carry excellent hair and skin products. But everyday toiletries and cosmetics will be cheaper in supermarkets or at Monoprix.

9. Pack an empty, soft-folding suitcase in your luggage so you can transport your treasures without the extra bother and expense of mailing. An extra bag on an airline (over the limit of two, plus a carry-on) will cost around a hundred dollars, and that will be less than you will have to pay at the store or at the post office to have it sent.

10. Be sure to get the 10 percent discount card issued to all foreigners who shop at the major department stores (with the exception of Bon Marche and Marks & Spencer). If you add this savings to the *détaxe* (which is 13 percent), the savings can be considerable (see "Department Stores," page 291).

11. If you are eligible for a tax refund, take the time to fill out the *détaxe* form, and remember to turn it into the customs officials at the airport before you relinquish your luggage or go through customs or passport control (see "Tax Refund: *Détaxe,*" page 289).

12. When returning to the United States, remember these points when going through customs:

- You and every member of your family, regardless of age, can bring back $400 worth of purchases duty-free. Family members can pool their duty-free purchases (see "Customs," page 290).

- Don't cheat, don't smuggle, and above all, don't do drugs.

- Be nice.

Shopping Hours

Generally speaking, shop hours are Monday through Saturday from 10 A.M. to 7 P.M. Large department stores are open later one night a week. Small shops sometimes close Monday morning, for lunch, and often for all or part of August. Food markets are usually open Sunday morning but closed on Mondays. With the exception of the heavily touristed areas, all stores are closed on Sunday and holidays.

Size Conversion Charts

Many French off-the-rack manufacturers have their own cuts, and sizes are not always uniform. Whenever possible it is important to try on clothing before you buy. Because that is not always possible, bring your measurements and carry a tape measure with both inches and centimeters. Be careful with men's shirt sleeves, as the length is not always given; be prepared to measure. Table and bed linen sizes are also different from those in the States.

Women's dresses: To change French dress sizes to U.S. sizes, subtract 28 from the French dress size. To change U.S. dress size to French, add 28 to the U.S. dress size.

French	32	34	36	38	40	42	44
U.S.	4	6	8	10	12	14	16

Women's sweaters and blouses: To change French sizes to U.S., subtract 8 from the French blouse or sweater size. To change U.S. sizes to French, add 8 to the U.S. blouse or sweater size.

French	38	40	42	44	46	48	50
U.S.	30	32	34	36	38	40	42

Men's suits: To change French suit sizes to U.S. sizes, subtract 10 from the French suit size. To change U.S. suit size to French, add 10 to the U.S. size.

French	46	48	50	52	54	56	58
U.S.	36	38	40	42	44	46	48

Men's shirts: To change French shirt sizes to U.S., subtract 8 from the French size and divide by 2. To change U.S. shirt size to French, multiply the U.S. size by 2 and add 8.

French	36	37	38	39	40	41	42	43
U.S.	14	14.5	15	15.5	16	16.5	17	17.5

Shoes: To change French shoe size to U.S., subtract 32 from the French size. To change U.S. shoe size to French, add 32 to the U.S. shoe size.

French	36	37	38	39	40	41	42	43	44
U.S.	4	5	6	7	8	9	10	11	12

Children's clothing: French children's clothes are sized according to the child's age. Look for the abbreviations "m" and "a," which stand for month and year (in French, "m" stands for *mois,* or "month," and "a" stands for *ans,* or "years"). Thus: 2m means 2 months, 16m means 16 months, 2a means 2 years, 6a means 6 years, and so on.

Tax Refund: *Détaxe*

Every tourist visiting France is entitled to a *détaxe* (tax rebate) for purchases totaling 1,200F (182.94€) or more on the same day in the same store. The refund averages about 13 percent. If shopping with a friend, combine your purchases to reach the total and share the proceeds when they arrive. The simple paperwork is filled out by you and the store. You will need to have your passport available for identification. On the *détaxe* form, you will be asked to state whether you want the refund mailed to you in a French franc or euro check or to have it credited to your credit card. Getting your refund by check is not recommended because it is hard to deal with in the United States and getting it can take forever. Get it on your credit card, since your credit card company will credit the refund to you in U.S. dollars. Expect a delay of two to three months. For items shipped directly from the store, the *détaxe* is automatically deducted without any paperwork.

At your point of exit from France, present your tax refund form. A customs official will stamp your documents, which you then mail back to the store in the self-addressed, stamped envelope the store will give you at the time of purchase. There is even a post office mailbox next to customs at the airport. That's it. Sometimes an eager official will ask to see your purchases, so keep them handy just in case. At the airport, look for the window that says *douane de détaxe* and allow an extra half hour to accomplish the mission. Generally, when you are making your purchase, you must ask for the *détaxe* forms because most smaller shopkeepers do not volunteer the information. In the large department stores there are special offices that take care of the paperwork. Yes, it all does take some extra time and effort, but the savings do add up, so persevere.

NOTE: The *détaxe* does not apply for food, drink, medicine, unset gems, antiques, works of art, automobiles or their parts, or commercial purchases.

Customs

Each United States citizen, even a week-old baby, is entitled to bring back $400 worth of duty-free goods acquired abroad. Families can pool their duty-free purchases, so you can use what your spouse and children do not. After the $400 point, there will be a 10 percent charge on the next $1,000, and more as the amount increases. Have your receipts ready and make sure they coincide with what you filled out on the landing card. Don't cheat or lie, as you will invariably be caught. Then you and your luggage will undergo exhaustive searches, and that will just be for openers. Any purchase worth less than $50 can be shipped back to the States as an unsolicited gift and is considered duty-free, and it does not count in your $400 limit. You can send as many of these unsolicited gifts as you wish, but only one unsolicited gift per person for each mailing, and don't mail anything to yourself. If your package worth exceeds $50, you will pay duty.

Antiques must be over one hundred years old to be duty-free.

A work of art is duty-free, and it does not matter when it was created or who the artist was.

If you have expensive cameras, piles of imported luggage, fancy watches, or valuable jewelry, carry the receipts for them, or you could be questioned about them and even end up paying duty on them.

Finally, it's simply a fact of customs: people who look like hippies get stopped and have their bags searched. The same goes for bejeweled and bedecked women wrapped in full-length furs and carrying expensive designer luggage.

For more information on U.S. Customs rules and regulations, send for the free brochure "Know Before You Go," available from the Department of the Treasury, U.S. Customs Service, Washington, D.C., 20229; Tel: 202-927-6724; Internet: www.customs.ustreas.gov.

Consignment Shops: *Dépôts-Ventes*

Consignment shops sell previously owned items at a fraction of original cost. Some people balk at the idea of wearing "used" clothing, but please try to shed this reluctance. Keep in mind that many of the items are barely worn; they are being consigned so that their owner will have more money to spend in the designer boutiques . . . only to recycle them again after one wearing. In Paris, it is considered very fashionable to resurrect something from oblivion and incorporate it into your wardrobe, or to outsmart retail buyers by finding a fabulous Armani suit for a fraction of what they paid for it. Believe me, this is big business in Paris and you would be surprised at the number of very sophisticated and well-known fellow bargain-inspired shoppers you may recognize standing next to you searching the racks for just the perfect "previously owned" outfit.

For a complete list of all the consignment shops in this book, see page 347.

Department Stores

Bargain shoppers take note: Most of the department stores listed here will issue a 10 percent discount shopping card upon presentation of your passport. Just go to the Welcome Desk; someone who speaks English will be there to issue you the card. When paying, you will have to go to a special *caisse* (a cashier's desk) to pay, and then take your paid receipt back to the department where you initially found the item. It's a bit of a drag . . . but it is 10 percent, and that can add up. The exceptions are Tati, Monoprix, Bon Marché, and Marks & Spencer.

On top of that, don't forget that you will qualify for the 13 percent *détaxe* if you spend 1,200F (182.94€) or more. Unfortunately, that amount is not cumulative over several shopping trips; it is per day. But if you plan accordingly and combine it with your 10 percent discount card, you can save 23 percent. Keep this in mind especially if you are shopping for items that may be sold elsewhere in Paris in specialty boutiques. For example, many Americans have a love affair with Mephisto and Arche shoes, and know that they are cheaper in Paris. Both Galeries Lafayette and Au Printemps carry these shoes . . . so, why buy them someplace else if you can buy them here and save an additional 10 percent plus the *détaxe?* In addition, Au Printemps you can purchase Lora Lune cosmetics, and they have scented candles and toilet waters from the Diptyque Boutique. La Samaritaine has a l'Occitane, and the same savings applies.

For a complete list of all the department stores in this book, see page 348.

Designer Discount Boutiques

Anyone can pay retail. . . . It takes talent, dedication, and hard work to get a good deal.

—Diana Withee, art historian and
veteran shopper

These boutiques sell designer label stock at well below the retail prices you will pay elsewhere in Paris for exactly the same items, but you will be looking at last season's collections. Sometimes the labels have been cut out.

For a complete list of all the designer discount boutiques in this book, see page 348.

Sales: *Soldes*

During most of the year, when you venture into one of the designer shops, they are quiet enough for you to hear the rustle of money being spent by wealthy customers. However, we less-affluent mortals also have a chance in these stores. It is hard to imagine the U.S. government dictating to stores the dates on which they can hold sales . . . but that is exactly what happens in France. As it now stands, during the first three weeks in January and July, the French *ministre de shopping* has declared that *toute* Paris will be on sale. In addition, Galeries Lafayette, Au Printemps, and many other large department stores have special offers throughout the rest of the year. But the real bargains are found during the January and July sales, when the crowds of shoppers move with dizzying swiftness, all zeroing in on the considerable savings. If you can brave these shopping pros, this is the time to go to the designer boutiques and pick up a little number for about one-third the U.S. retail price. In October, Hèrmes has its once-yearly sale. The line forms the night before, with shoppers eager to pay 50 percent less for the famous signature scarves (currently retailing for over $250), ties, leather goods, and conservative line of clothing. Again, if you do not mind standing in line and fighting crowds packed in ten-deep, then this sale is a must for Hèrmes fans.

Shopping Areas

PLACE DES VICTOIRES, FIRST ARRONDISSEMENT
Métro: Étienne Marcel, Palais-Royal–Musée du Louvre
This is a smart shopping section nestled behind Palais-Royal. After going around the place des Victoires, branch out down the side streets. This is an area of many fashion innovators and well worth serious time just to see what you will be wearing two years from now. The prices are not in the bargain department, unless you happen to hit a sale.

PLACE VENDÔME, FIRST ARRONDISSEMENT
Métro: Tuileries, Opéra
Cartier, Van Cleef & Arpels, Trussardi, and international banks cater to the needs of the guests at the Hôtel Ritz around place Vendôme.

MARAIS AND PLACE DES VOSGES, THIRD AND FOURTH ARRONDISSEMENTS
Métro: St-Paul
The Marais is the oldest *quartier* in Paris. The kosher food shops along rue des Rosiers, the trendy boutiques along rue Francs Bourgeois, and the avant-garde designers make shopping in the Marais an excellent off-beat adventure. The place des Vosges, built between 1605 and 1612 by Henri IV, was the first planned square to be built in Paris. Today, the symmetrical, soft pink stone square is lovely. Be sure to include a stroll through the stone arcades and sit in one of the cafés (see *Great Eats Paris*).

VILLAGE ST-PAUL, RUE ST-PAUL, AND RUE DU PONT LOUIS PHILIPPE, FOURTH ARRONDISSEMENT
Métro: St-Paul
The Village St-Paul is a collective name for the antique and *brocante* dealers who line rue St-Paul and the courtyard squares surrounding it. One of the most interesting is Baïkal, at 24, rue St-Paul, specializing in Asian artifacts and antiques. It is run by Michael Monlaü and his partner, Thierry de la Salmoniere. Their shop has an interesting past. For almost

seventy years it was a local bar run by the same woman, and by her parents before that. When Michael and Thierry took it over, they saved and restored the old bar and countertop, which had stood in the same place for a century. Today it stands in the middle of the shop, where for all those years the locals spent part of their lives, and left part of their souls, standing against it, tossing down their daily quotas. The bar is not for sale, but everything else is. On the rue du Pont Louis Philippe, you will find calligraphy and paper shops and stores selling perfumed candles.

ST-GERMAIN-DES-PRÉS, SIXTH AND SEVENTH ARRONDISSMENTS
Métro: St-Germain-des-Prés

Sensational shopping can be found on the rue de Sèvres, rue Bonaparte, rue de Four, rue St-Sulpice, rue Jacob, and the rue de Seine, to mention only a few of the streets that line this *quartier,* which is literally packed with fashion boutiques, antique shops, art galleries, and bookshops. In fact, if you have only a short time to devote to shopping and browsing, this is where you should go.

CHAMPS-ÉLYSEES, EIGHTH ARRONDISSEMENT
Métro: Charles-de-Gaulle-Étoile

The day has passed when the Champs-Élysées was considered the finest address a retailer could have. Today there are waves of tourists flowing up one side and down the other of the most famous avenue in the world. Movie theaters, airline offices, banks, car dealers, fast-food outlets, mini-malls, and outdoor cafés—all charging top prices for everything— line each side of the majestic avenue. Pickpockets also work both sides of the street and they are pros . . . watch out! Of course, you are going to walk along the Champs-Élysées, but reserve your time for sipping an afternoon drink at a café and for fascinating people-watching. Do your shopping elsewhere.

THE GOLDEN TRIANGLE, EIGHTH ARRONDISSEMENT
Métro: Alma-Marceau

When cost is not an object, come to the Golden Triangle, which is formed by Avenue George-V, avenue Marceau, avenue Montaigne, rue du Faubourg St-Honoré, and rue François 1er. For window-shopping and dreaming of the highest order, these five premier shopping streets are to designer fashion and *haute couture* as the Louvre is to priceless art. The boutiques and shops are not to be missed, even if you only stroll by the elegant window displays.

RUE DE PASSY AND AVENUE VICTOR HUGO, SIXTEENTH ARRONDISSEMENT
Métro: Passy, Victor Hugo

Walking down either of these streets in the sixteenth arrondissement will give you an idea of what it is like to be upper-middle-class and living in Paris. You will see few tourists, no razor-shaved haircuts, and certainly no hawkers waving T-shirts or plastic replicas of the Eiffel Tower. This is the land of the BCBGs (French yuppies), old money, and tradition. There are several cafés if someone in your party would rather sit and have a beer while watching the world wander by.

Discount Shopping Streets

Just as Paris has its high-priced shopping streets, it also has its discount shopping streets. No dedicated discount shopper will want to miss a trip to one of these streets where, if you are lucky, you will bring home something marvelous that your friends would kill for . . . even at three times the price you paid.

Note that acceptance of credit cards and hours vary with each shop; however, in general stores are open Monday 2–7 P.M., and Tuesday to Saturday 10 A.M.–7 P.M.

RUE MESLAY, 75003 (2) (see map page 78)
Métro: République

One entire street devoted to shoes—one store after the other—with everything from clodhoppers to four-inch red-satin sling pumps. Prices are good. The best advice is to browse first, then go back and do serious buying. Finding the perfect pair of shoes takes time and energy, not to say patience. Don't try to squeeze this one in . . . allow time and leave nonshopping pals at the hotel. If all else fails here, you can run by Tati at 13, place de la République (see page 309).

RUE ST-PLACIDE, 75006 (42) (see map page 124)
Métro: Sèvres-Babylone

Bargain fever has hit Paris in a cluster of boutiques along rue St-Placide. Start at Bon Marché department store and work both sides of the street. This can be frustrating if the crowds are out in force, especially at lunchtime when the office workers surge through and on Saturday when housewives leave *les enfants* at home and make the pilgrimage. Best buys are in casual sportswear and teenage "must-haves" of the moment. There are a limited number of top-name designers, but everything is *au courant*. Windows are often more appealing than the stuffy, cramped interiors. Sharpen your elbows for this—and watch your handbag carefully.

RUE ST-DOMINIQUE, 75007 (2) (see map page 156)
Métro: Latour-Maubourg

From avenue Bosquet to boulevard de Latour-Maubourg, shops sell clothing for men, women, and children from designer *dégriffés* (labels cut out) to bins of last season's T-shirts. Affordable.

RUE DE PARADIS, 75010
Métro: Château d'Eau, Gare de l'Est
This is the best area in Paris for china and crystal, in one crowded shop after another. Be sure to look at the magnificent Baccarat crystal store, and check their back table with the red dots on end-of-the-line designs, which sell for up to half regular price. Baccarat is at 32, rue de Paradis; it's open Monday to Friday 9 A.M.–6 P.M., Saturday 10 A.M.–noon, 2–5 P.M. Other worthwhile stops are at Aurelia Paradis, 21 bis, rue de Paridis, for Lalique and Lumicristal, 22 bis, rue de Paradis. Staff at both shops speak English; the *détaxe* is available after spending 1,200F (182.94€), and they ship.

RUE D'ALÉSIA, 75014 (30) (see map page 204)
Métro: Alésia
Both sides of rue d'Alésia are home to an assortment of outlet shops carrying last season's lines of designers, some you have heard of and some you never will. The best line of attack is to go up one side and down the other to get an overview, then come back to those that seem promising. Worse time to go is on Saturday. Some of the better shops are the following: SR (Sonya Rykiel), No. 64; Evolutif, No. 72; Dorothée Bis, No. 74; Stock 2, No. 92; Stock System, Tout Compte Fait, No. 103, Nos. 110–112; Kookaï, No. 111; L.A. City, No. 113; Cacharel, No. 114; Daniel Hechter, Nos. 116–118; Philippe Salvert, No. 122; Alésia Discounts, No. 139.

WARNING: The numbering system is crazy, but these are close.

Passages

Long before anyone heard of shopping malls, Paris had *galeries* and *passages*—skylighted, decorated, tiled, and beautiful. Built in the early nineteenth century for wealthy shoppers, they are a reflection of the prosperity and flamboyance of the Belle Epoque era. Tucked away off major commercial streets, mainly in the second and ninth arrondissements, they are easy to miss if you are not looking for them. Unfortunately, in a few, commercialism has taken over and there are some low-end shops. On the other hand, the occupants of the spaces come and go, and it is still fun to stroll through one or two if only to see a sampling of the old-fashioned shops selling handmade dolls, fancy pipes, old books, 78-rpm records, model trains, and toys.

In general, you can count on most shops being open from Monday to Saturday, 10 A.M. to 7 P.M. Most shops will take some credit cards, but policies vary.

GALERIE VÉRO-DODAT (37)
19, rue Jean-Jacques Rousseau, 75001 (see map page 56)
Métro: Palais-Royal–Musée du Louvre
This *passage* opened in 1826 and has an ornate interior and some interesting shops, including an old toy shop.

GALERIE COLBERT (10)
6, rue des Petits-Champs, 75002 (see map page 56)
Métro: Bourse
Built in 1826, it is next to the Bibliothèque Nationale and restored to all of its nineteenth-century glory.

GALERIE VIVIENNE (11)
4, rue des Petits-Champs, 75002 (see map page 56)
Métro: Bourse
The most beautiful passage of all opened in 1823.

PASSAGE DES PANORAMAS (3)
11, boulevard Montmartre, 75002 (see map page 56)
Métro: Grands Boulevards
One of the oldest, dating from 1800, its name is taken from the panoramas of Rome, Jerusalem, London, Athens, and other world capitals.

PASSAGE DU GRAND-CERF (18)
145, rue Saint-Denis, 75002 (see map page 56)
Métro: Étienne Marcel
Paved in marble, the *passage* has a high glass roof, wrought-iron walkways, and wood-framed windows in shops devoted to contemporary design.

PASSAGE JOUFFROY (46)
10, boulevard Montmartre, 75009 (see map page 176)
Métro: Grands Boulevards
Built in 1846, this was the first *passage* to be heated. It also contains the Hôtel Chopin (see page 189) and the Musée Grevin, the hundred-year-old Paris wax museum inspired by Madame Tussaud's in London.

PASSAGE VERDEAU (176)
31 bis, rue du Faubourg-Montmartre and 6, rue de la Grange-Batelière, 75009 (see map page 176)
Métro: Richelieu-Drouot, Grands Boulevards
Shops have been here since 1847, and some of the merchandise in the collectibles shops looks it; check out books, records, and more.

Shopping Malls

Indoor shopping complexes are popping up all over Paris. They are not my favorite shopping venues, but if you need several items and only have a short time to shop, they are useful.

CARROUSEL DU LOUVRE (41) (see map page 56)
99, rue du Louvre, 75001
Metro: Palais-Royal–Museé du Louvre

Combine your visit to the Louvre with a shopping stroll through the tempting boutiques here, which range from Limoges and Lalique to a Virgin Megastore, from clothing boutiques and to a post office . . . you name it, and they have it. One of the best all-purpose shopping destinations in Paris, and it is open on Sunday!

See *Great Eats Paris* for details on the Carrousel du Louvre food court.

TELEPHONE: 01-43-16-47-15

CREDIT CARDS: Depends on shop, but always MC, V

OPEN: Daily 10 A.M.–8 P.M.

FORUM DES HALLES (42) (see map page 56)
Main entry: rue Pierre Lescott, 75001
Métro: Les Halles

This is the result of filling the hole left after the wholesale food market Les Halles was moved to Rungis. The Forum des Halles is the largest commercial project in France and has the largest métro station beneath it. When it opened, the multilevel complex attracted 40 million shoppers a year. Even though the area has lost some of its original luster and allure, those youthful in mind, body, and spirit still gravitate to this covered shopping wonderland to check out the general scene, cruise the shops, eat in the fast-food joints, and try the hair salons offering sculpted cuts or dye jobs in glowing pink, green, or yellow. If you don't feel like doing any of the above, you can watch a film in the Cine Cité multiplex (which has over thirty theaters), swim in the public swimming pool, or just hang out. The largest métro station in the world lies under it, but please be careful: this is not considered a safe place to wander late at night.

TELEPHONE: 01-40-39-38-74

CREDIT CARDS: Depends on shop, but usually MC, V

OPEN: Mon–Sat 10:30 A.M.–7:30 P.M. for the shops

LES TROIS QUARTIERS (31) (see map page 176)
23, boulevard de la Madeleine, 75008
Métro: Madeleine

At this shopping mall you'll find seventy-five boutiques and a sports store to behold. Prices are high, but stroll through anyway to get an idea of how much you will save by shopping at the other shops listed in this book. The quality is better than at Forum des Halles, but the spirit is really dead.

TELEPHONE: 01-42-97-80-12

CREDIT CARDS: Depends on boutique, but usually MC, V

OPEN: Mon–Sat 10 A.M.–7 P.M.

MAINE-MONTPARNASSE (10) (see map page 204)
Tour, Maine-Montparnasse, 75014
Métro: Montparnasse–Bienvenüe

Round up the usual chain stores, stick them in a mundane indoor mall at the Montparnasse-Bienvenüe métro and train station, and you have this shopping mall. It does have a small Galeries Lafayette, but it is certainly not worth a special trip. If you are here, fine; otherwise, never mind.

TELEPHONE: Not available

CREDIT CARDS: MC, V (depends on store)

OPEN: Mon–Sat 10 A.M.–7 P.M. (stores vary)

PASSY PLAZA (26) (see map page 226)
Corner rue Jean Bologne and rue de Passy, 75016
Métro: Passy, La Muette

This shopping mall has middle-of-the-road boutiques with lots of clothes for the junior set or for something to knock around in and still feel fashionable. Also a very good supermarket.

TELEPHONE: Not available

CREDIT CARDS: Varies with each shop

OPEN: Shops, Mon–Sat 10 A.M.–7:30 P.M.; supermarket, Mon–Sat 8:30 A.M.–8 P.M.

Store Listings by Arrondissement

FIRST ARRONDISSEMENT (see map page 56)

BOUTIQUE PARIS-MUSÉES (42)
Forum des Halles
1, rue Pierre Lescott, 75001
Métro: Les Halles

There are three of these museum boutiques in Paris offering reproductions of items from the various permanent collections of the city's big museums. This boutique specializes in contemporary design reproductions, the other two in classic. Here you will find a wonderful selection of jewelry and household goods. While the address is Forum des Halls, it is located on your left as you enter the Forum from rue Pierre Lescott.

The other two locations are in the third and fourth arrondissements (see pages 309 and 311).

TELEPHONE: 01-40-26-56-65
CREDIT CARDS: AE, V
OPEN: Mon 2–7 P.M., Tues–Sat 10:30 A.M.–7 P.M.

CATHERINE PERFUMES AND COSMETICS (23)
6 and 7, rue de Castiglione, 75001
Métro: Tuileries

Jacques Levy, his wife, and their two daughters run these two boutiques across the street from each other on rue de Castiglione. They offer an excellent selection of perfumes, cosmetics, scarves, hair ornaments, jewelry, and ties. They speak English, and don't employ "hard sell" tactics. You will receive a tax-free price of 20 percent off if you purchase over 1,200F (182.94€) worth of merchandise, which translates into a savings of up to 35 percent when combined with the *détaxe*. If you buy less than 1,200F (182.94€), you will get a 25 percent discount. For mail orders, which you can do by fax, the same discounts are offered.

TELEPHONE: 01-42-61-02-89, 01-42-60-48-17
FAX: 01-42-61-02-35
CREDIT CARDS: AE, DC, MC, V
OPEN: Mon–Sat 9:30 A.M.–7 P.M.; closed 15 days in Aug, dates vary

COLETTE (26)
213, rue St-Honoré, 75001
Métro: Tuileries

Colette bills itself as *styledesignartfood*. It is one of the "hot" addresses in Paris, but frankly I think it is a shopping experience best characterized as "overpriced boutique chic meets designer kitsch," which the customer is supposed to consider *la dernier cri* in cutting-edge fashion—that is, a frisbee for your dog in its own Gucci carry-bag for only 260F (39.64€). The band of ohhh, so cool *vendeuses,* dressed in skin-tight designer (of course!) jeans and spray-on sleeveless T-shirts, cruise the aisles trying to look busy. Models wander around dressed in over-the-top outfits no one would ever wear . . . even if they could afford them. The shop has three levels, and downstairs is a stylized food and designer water bar with prices as high as the noses of the diners and drinkers. Go to Colette, don't miss it in fact, because it is the city's only Museum of the Outrageous.

TELEPHONE: 01-55-35-33-90
FAX: 01-55-35-33-99
CREDIT CARDS: AE, DC, MC, V
OPEN: Mon–Sat 10:30 A.M.–7:30 P.M.

CYBERCAFÉ DE PARIS (47)
11-15, rue des Halles, 75001
Métro: Châtelet

All your cyber needs can be met here everyday from 11 A.M. until 11 P.M. There is no food, only sodas.

TELEPHONE: 01-42-21-11-11
FAX: 01-42-21-15-15
EMAIL: info@cybercafedeparis.com
CREDIT CARDS: AE, MC, V
OPEN: Daily 11 A.M.–11 P.M.

DU PAREIL AU MÊME (42)
Forum des Halles, Niveau-2 (second level), 75001
Métro: Les Halles

Finally, adorable French children's clothing we all can afford. If you have shopped for children in Paris before, you know how prohibitive the prices are . . . a little play outfit could cost $100, and a tiny bikini, $50. Take heart, and take your credit card to this mecca for mommies: Du Pareil au Même. If you have anyone on your list between the ages of one and twelve years, you absolutely *must* include one of these shops on your Paris A-list of things to do. At last count, there were twenty shops well positioned throughout Paris. There are also shops in every major French city. If France is not on your travel map, don't worrry, you can shop with Du Pareil au Même on the Internet and have your purchases sent. This a major breakthrough in French merchandizing for children, and it has captured everyone's attention. Don't miss it. Consult their Internet site, or pick up a card, which lists all of their many locations throughout Paris and France.

TELEPHONE: 01-40-13-95-29

INTERNET: www.dpam.fr

CREDIT CARDS: AE, MC, V

OPEN: Generally Mon–Sat 10 A.M.–7 P.M.; hours vary slightly at each location

DU PAREIL AU MÊME BÉBÉ (53)
1, rue Saint-Denis, corner avenue Victoria, 75001
Métro: Châtelet

Du Pareil au Même has created a shop exclusively for babies, with eight locations around Paris. The discount clothing for the tiny ones is just as adorable as what the other stores sell for the older children. This one is not far from the Du Pareil au Même in Forum des Halles

TELEPHONE: 01-42-36-26-53

INTERNET: www.dpam.fr

CREDIT CARDS: AE, MC, V

OPEN: Generally Mon–Sat 10 A.M.–7 P.M.; hours vary slightly at each location

FORUM DES JEUNES CRÉATEURS (42)
Forum des Halles
Entrance on rue Pierre Lescott or rue Berger, 75001
Métro: Les Halles

Fifty young designers have joined forces to display their creations in the Forum des Halles. Aimed at a young, buffed, fashion-conscious audience, this is the place to check out what new talent is around, and to spot that which has an edge on the future. The designers are located at Porte Berger, Niveau-1 (Berger gate, Level-1)

TELEPHONE: Not available

CREDIT CARDS: Depends on designer

OPEN: Mon–Sat 11 A.M.–7 P.M.

HERBORISTERIE DU PALAIS ROYAL (8)
11, rue des Petits-Champs, 75001
Métro: Pyramides

The shop stocks between five and six hundred types of herbal teas and makes their own plant-based soaps and cosmetics (try the carrot face oil). They also sell nutritionally correct cereals, cookies, bottled juices, honey, essential oils, herbal remedies, and vitamins. But you had better know what you want, since you can't count on too much English.

TELEPHONE: 01-42-97-54-68

CREDIT CARDS: MC, V

OPEN: Mon–Fri 8:30 A.M.–7 P.M., Sat 10:30 A.M.–6:30 P.M.

LA DAME BLANCHE (31)
186, rue de Rivoli, 75001
Métro: Palais-Royal–Musée du Louvre

You will soon become dizzy and confused walking along the tourist trail that leads from place de la Concorde down rue de Rivoli. The area has one of the highest concentrations of tourist merchandise in the city. You know the type: plastic Eiffel Towers, T-shirts with the Mona Lisa and a smart remark, gaudy scarves, and wild ties your husband would blush wearing. However, dedicated shophounds know that with a little digging, treasures are here. Where? At Michael and Suzanne's La Dame Blanche, which was started by their mother in 1969 as a small glove boutique. The windows of their side-by-side shops are jam-packed with Limoges boxes that collectors will go mad over, Le Faïence de Quimper, leather gloves, authentic French berets, silk scarves, small and large tapestries, and more. Do not let this confusing clutter deter you from exploring the best shop along this stretch. Not only is the selection the best, so are the prices. If you want a special Limoges box, ask Michael and he can have it made for you. Both Michael and his sister, Suzanne, speak English, offer excellent service, and are delightful besides. They ship worldwide. Don't forget to fill out the paperwork for the *détaxe* if you spend 1,200F or more.

TELEPHONE: 01-42-96-31-56

FAX: 01-42-96-02-11

CREDIT CARDS: AE, DC, MC, V

OPEN: Mon–Sat 10 A.M.–6:30 P.M.

LA DROGUERIE (33)
9–11, rue du Jour, 75001
Métro: Les Halles (exit Turbigo-Rambuteau)

It doesn't look like much when you walk by it, but once inside it is an Ali Baba's cave of glorious ribbons, yarn, trim, buttons, feathers, and glitter, plus the glue to put it all together. If you are into jewelry making, beading, knitting, making your own purses—or any other creative DIY hobby—this is a treasure trove you will love.

TELEPHONE: 01-45-08-93-27

FAX: 01-42-36-30-80

CREDIT CARDS: MC, V (150F, 22.87€, minimum)

OPEN: Mon 2–6:45 P.M., Tues–Sat 10:20 A.M.–6:45 P.M.

LA SAMARITAINE (50)
19, rue de la Monnaie, 75001
Métro: Pont-Neuf

The view of Paris from the top floor of La Samaritaine on rue de la Monnaie, which is building two, is justly famous. At an altitude of 243 feet, you have a 360-degree panoramic view of Paris, with a table to help you pick the main sights . . . and it costs you nothing. Four buildings make up this block-long department store, which has the biggest toy department in Paris at Christmas. The perfume and cosmetics department on the ground floor has a small l'Occitane stand, often with special promotions. I always cruise by the stalls set up around the outside of the store. Alot of it is pure junk, but I have found silk pajamas and clever waterproof watches for only 50F (7.62€).

TELEPHONE: Welcome Service: 01-40-41-22-68; Store: 01-40-41-20-20

FAX: 01-40-41-21-70

CREDIT CARDS: AE, DC, MC, V

OPEN: Mon–Sat 9:30 A.M.–7 P.M. (Thurs until 10 P.M.)

LE PRINCE JARDINIER (29)
117–121 Jardins du Palais Royal, Arcade Valois, 75001
Métro: Palais-Royal–Musée du Louvre

The Palais Royal gardens are known and loved as some of the most beautiful in Paris. Now, in addition to admiring the palace built by Cardinal Richelieu in 1632, you have another enchanted garden to visit. Prince Louis-Albert de Broglie, a young Paris banker, has opened Le Prince Jardinier, a charming garden boutique along the arcades of the Palais Royal. Not only does he sell seeds and spades, he has handcrafted garden tools, brass buckets and stainless steel watering cans, and tools that fit into custom-made aprons and sacks. On the main floor are displays of garden attire—aprons, bags, hats, smocks, and coats—along with gardening tools, plants, herbal teas, and spices. Upstairs are botanical prints, books, and farm implements made into sculptures. One titled customer has found Prince Broglie's wares irresistable, and he uses them on his Highgrove estate: Prince Charles.

TELEPHONE: 01-42-60-37-13

FAX: 01-42-60-76-75

CREDIT CARDS: MC, V

OPEN: Tues–Sat 10:30 A.M.–7 P.M.

MARÉCHAL (25)
232, rue de Rivoli, 75001
Métro: Tuileries

If you cannot find a Limoges box here to suit you, they will have one custom designed for you and shipped anywhere you like. In addition to a fabulous selection of well-displayed boxes, they have every size teapot imaginable, dolls from Provence, and quality Paris souvenirs. They also have a mail-order service.

There is a second, much smaller location at 5, avenue de l'Opéra, 75001; Tel: 01-42-60-10-23; Métro: Opéra.

TELEPHONE: 01-42-60-71-83
FAX: 01-42-60-33-76
CREDIT CARDS: AE, MC, V
OPEN: Mon–Sat 10:30 A.M.–6 P.M., Sun 11 A.M.–6:30 P.M.

OLIVER B (35)
21, rue Pierre Lescot, 75001
Métro: Étienne Marcel, Les Halles

At Oliver B you will find inexpensive separates that are easy to wear and cheap enough to toss out after a season or two. Lots of small sizes and nothing too far out. The clothes are poorly displayed, but at least they are organized by color. They have good sales in January and July.

TELEPHONE: 01-40-26-26-26
CREDIT CARDS: AE, MC, V
OPEN: Mon–Sat 10:30 A.M.–7 P.M.

SCOOTER (34)
10, rue de Turbigo, 75001
Métro: Étienne Marcel

Scooter specializes in jewelry, accessories, and clothing of the moment that are young, fun, and inexpensive.

TELEPHONE: 01-45-08-50-54
CREDIT CARDS: MC, V
OPEN: Mon 2–7 P.M., Tues–Sat 11 A.M.–7 P.M.

W. H. SMITH (24)
248, rue de Rivoli, 75001
Métro: Concorde

If you forgot to bring along a book to read, long for an English-language magazine, or need a travel guide (especially one on Paris or France), W. H. Smith will come to your rescue. The British-based bookstore has two floors filled to the brim with English-language books, newspapers, magazines, and videos. It also has a wonderful travel book section that stocks the books in the *Great Sleeps* and *Eats* series.

TELEPHONE: 01-44-77-88-99
FAX: 01-42-96-83-71
EMAIL: whsmith.france@wanadoo.fr
CREDIT CARDS: AE, MC, V
OPEN: Mon–Sat 9 A.M.–7:30 P.M., Sun 1–7:30 P.M.

SECOND ARRONDISSEMENT (see map page 56)

A. SIMON (13)
36, rue Etienne Marcel, and 33, 38, rue Montmartre, 75002
Métro: Étienne Marcel

Calling all chefs, gourmets, and gourmands—whether past, present, or budding—as well as anyone with a love of cooking and good food: In these two A. Simon shops (located across the street from each other and separated into tablewares and cooking equipment), you will find all the French cooking and dining essentials you will ever need. With its vast inventory of cooking utensils of every known type and variety and its fascinating array of tableware, this is the Rolls Royce in its field. Prices are geared for the volume buyer, but anyone is welcome, and you will be graciously treated whether you outfit a restaurant or buy a tiny *pichet* for your *vin du table*.

TELEPHONE: 01-42-33-71-65
FAX: 01-42-33-68-25
CREDIT CARDS: AE, MC, V
OPEN: Mon 1:30–6:30 P.M., Tues–Sat 9 A.M.–6:30 P.M.

ANTHONY PETO (14)
56, rue Tiquetonne, 75002
Métro: Étienne Marcel

Hats off to these fabulous *chapeaux!* I love hats and wear them often, especially when traveling. Anthony Peto runs his shop in conjuction with Marie Mercié, who has her own location and her own hats in the sixth arrondissement (see page 322). Between the two stores, their hats run the gamut from frankly fanciful to downright sane and sensible. If you need a hat for any occasion, or, like me, just enjoy wearing—or admiring—them, please make a point of seeing some of the best hats in Paris.

Anthony's shop is more for men, though he carries some things for women. I like his summer Panama hats you can roll up in your suitcase; they just pop back into shape when ready to wear.

TELEPHONE: 01-40-26-60-68

CREDIT CARDS: AE, DC, MC, V

OPEN: Mon–Sat 11 A.M.–7 P.M.; closed middle of Aug

ET VOUS STOCK (20)
17, rue de Turbigo, 75002
Métro: Étienne Marcel

They offer up to 50 percent off on the simply styled, Et Vous brand of men's and women's clothing, which almost anyone can wear.

TELEPHONE: 01-40-13-04-12

CREDIT CARDS: AE, MC, V

OPEN: Mon–Sat noon–7 P.M.

EXPLORA (16)
46, rue Tiquetonne, 75002
Métro: Étienne Marcel

I was first drawn to the beautifully colored line of clothing and accessories—geared toward active, eclectic women—before I knew about the store. The Explora line is designed in Paris and uses only high-quality fabrics such as pima cotton, cashmere, and alpaca. You will see the Explora label in all the major Parisian department stores, and in Neiman Marcus in the United States, but for the best selection and prices, come to the source.

TELEPHONE: 01-40-41-00-33

FAX: 01-42-33-79-96

EMAIL: expl46@aol.com

INTERNET: www.explora-paris.com

CREDIT CARDS: AE, MC, V

OPEN: Mon–Fri 10 A.M.–2 P.M., 3–7 P.M., Sat 3–7 P.M.; closed 2 weeks in Aug

GIANNI D'ARNO PUR RÉVE DE SOIE (2)
17, rue St-Marc, 75002
Métro: Richelieu-Drouot, Bourse

Come here for the best-priced washable silk blouses in Paris in a rainbow of colors, patterns, and styles. No Chinese imitation imports . . . all are French or Italian silk. Scarves are by Erre, the same quality as Hermès, but for much less money. Custom-made orders are the same price and take fifteen days for delivery in Paris, or they will send.

TELEPHONE AND FAX: 01-42-36-98-73

CREDIT CARDS: MC, V

OPEN: Mon–Fri 11 A.M.–6 P.M.; closed one week around Aug 15 (call to check)

MENDÈS–YSL (YVES ST-LAURENT) (4)
5, rue d'Uzès, 75002
Métro: Grands Boulevards

Every plugged-in Parisian shopper knows Mendès, where fashion-conscious shoppers pick up discountedYves St-Laurent prêt-à-porter and Rive Gauche collections that are at least one season out of date. Collections arrive in July and January, and in December and June they have a sale and take off an additional 20 to 30 percent. In addition to the YSL label on clothes and accessories, look for the occasional Christian Lacroix outfit. About two years ago they moved into this new location, which is bigger and better organized, and *les vendeuses* are actually helpful. There are no dressing rooms, so you must change and try on in public, but no one cares. If you hit this one right, it is a gold mine.

To find it, enter rue Uzès from rue Montmartre. The shop is on the right side of the street, and as you face number 5, it is the first door on your left . . . the glass one with black wrought-iron grillwork.

TELEPHONE: 01-42-36-83-32
CREDIT CARDS: AE, MC, V
OPEN: Mon–Sat 10 A.M.–6:30 P.M.; closed three weeks in Aug

STOCK KOOKAÏ (17)
82, rue Réaumur, 75002
Métro: Réaumur-Sebastapol

There are Kookaï boutiques worldwide, but this is the only showroom devoted to permanent sale items from the line. There are two sections, with the newer, regularly priced clothing toward the back. You can tell which section is which easily: the clothing in front is last season's collection, and it is where fellow savvy shoppers are plying the goods.

TELEPHONE: 01-45-08-93-69
INTERNET: www.kookai.fr
CREDIT CARDS: AE, DC, MC, V (80F, 12.20€, minimum)
OPEN: Mon 11:30 A.M.–7:30 P.M., Tues–Sat 10:30 A.M.–7:30 P.M.

TATI OR (6)
19, rue de la Paix, 75002
Métro: Opéra

What!? A Tati jewelry store four doors down from Cartier and only a block or two from place Vendôme, home of Van Cleef & Arpels and the Ritz Hotel!! *Quelle horreur.* As you are walking down rue de la Paix, you can't help but notice the Tati awning covering the sidewalk from the door to the street . . . just like Alain Figaret's does, the expensive men's store next door. The Tati stores, the biggest and lowest-priced stores in Paris, are known for promoting volume, never quality (see page 309 for more on these retail wonders). If Cartier and the like are beyond your budget, now you have Tati Or, a ninety-square-meter boutique selling discount gold jewelry, with prices starting around 29F (4.42€) for gold earrings, 35F (5.34€) for a little gold heart, and 150F (22.87€) for a wedding band and going up to 9,000F (1,372€) for an ostentatious bauble set with precious stones. Engraving is free.

The chairman of Bucheron jewelers was quoted as saying, "You have Lasserre and Taillevent restaurants, but there is also McDonald's." This is definitely the McDonald's of jewelry stores. Obviously, owner Fabien Ouaki knew what he was doing when he signed the original lease requiring a monthly rent in excess of $25,000 (which is a lot of gold hearts). Now there are Tati Or shops in almost every arrondissement in Paris and in at least a dozen cities throughout France. In addition, you now have Tati Optique to fit you with glasses, and Tati Voyage to assist you with all your travel needs. Who knows what is next in store for Tati devotees?

TELEPHONE: Not available
CREDIT CARDS: MC, V (100F, 15.24€, minimum)
OPEN: Mon–Sat 10 A.M.–6 P.M.

THIRD ARRONDISSEMENT (see map page 78)

ADECTA—ACCESSORIES DE LA MODE (5)
6, rue du Grenier–St-Lazare, 75003
Métro: Rambuteau (exit rue du Grenier-St-Lazare)

The sign over door says it all: Manufacture de Chapeaux. This is really a wholesale operation featuring children's accessories, hats for every member of the family, scarves, belts, umbrellas, and ties (including the snap-on variety). If you are tactful and don't ask questions, and spend around 500F (76.22€), they will let you buy. Admittedly, you will need help toting home your loot when you can find baby hats here for 25F (3.81€) a piece—the same ones that sell for three and four times the price in baby shops.

TELEPHONE: 01-42-71-79-88, 01-42-77-31-33
CREDIT CARDS: MC, V
OPEN: Mon–Fri 8:30 A.M.–1 P.M., 2–6 P.M.; closed holidays, mid-July to mid-Aug

BOUTIQUE MAJOLIQUE (9)
79, rue Vieille-du-Temple 75003
Metro: Rambuteau

For a description, see Boutique Majolique on page 319.

TELEPHONE: 01-42-78-58-81

FAX: 01-42-78-05-15

BOUTIQUE PARIS-MUSÉES (27)
Musée Carnavalet, 23, rue de Sévigné, 75003
Métro: St-Paul

For a full description of this museum shop, see page 299. This location is inside Musée Carnavalet, which explores the history of Paris.

TELEPHONE: 01-42-74-08-00

LAURENT GUILLOT (10)
48, rue de Turenne, 75003
Métro: Chemin Vert, St-Sebastien–Froissart

Laurent Guillot's crystal and Plexiglas jewelry trimmed in gold and silver is shown on the pages of *Elle, Vogue,* and almost every other fashion magazine on the stands. This is his display/boutique in Paris, and it is worth seeing if you like beautifully handcrafted, contemporary jewelry at surprisingly reasonable prices. He is planning to add furniture and flower containers to his repertoire.

TELEPHONE: 01-48-87-87-69

FAX: 01-48-87-87-53

CREDIT CARDS: MC, V

OPEN: Mon–Sat 11 A.M.–12:30 P.M., 1:30–7 P.M.

TATI (3)
13, place de la République, 75003
Métro: République

Attention shoppers! If you love swap meets, garage sales, and basement fire sales, then Tati is for you. The crowds are impossible, especially on Saturday, but for truly amazing bargains hidden among some real junk, join the diverse crowd at a Tati. Prices defy the competition on stock that ranges from bridal wear to linen slacks, cheap silk shirts, cheaper shoes, baby gear, and kitchen equipment, and now separate jewelers, opticians, and travel agencies. Be sure to check each item carefully because quality control is not a priority when this much volume is concerned. And what volume. The Tati empire grosses in excess of $3 billion per year—and is growing daily.

TELEPHONE: 01-48-87-72-81

CREDIT CARDS: MC, V

OPEN: Mon–Sat 10 A.M.–7 P.M

WEB BAR (4)
32, rue de Picardie, 75003
Métro: Filles du Calvaire

This is one of the best all-around cyber cafés in Paris. It not only is a place to handle your email and Internet business, but it's a place to eat, listen to music, partake in a poetry reading, see a short film, and generally hang out.

TELEPHONE: 01-42-72-66-55
FAX: 01-42-72-66-75
EMAIL: webbar@webbar.fr
INTERNET: www.webbar.fr
CREDIT CARDS: MC, V
OPEN: Mon–Fri 8:30 A.M.–2 A.M., Sat 11 A.M.–2 A.M., Sun noon–midnight

---

FOURTH ARRONDISSEMENT (see map page 78)

A LA BONNE RENOMMEE (20)
20, rue Vieille du Temple, 75004
Métro: St-Paul

A la Bonne Renommee became famous for their multifabric and multicolored handbags. Now they have expanded into clothing and accessories, both to wear and to use in the home. Some of the colors and fabric mixes leave me wondering, and so do most of the prices, but if you can find something you like on sale, it will be a good buy . . . and probably last a long time.

TELEPHONE: 01-42-72-03-86
CREDIT CARDS: AE, DC, MC, V
OPEN: Mon–Sat 11 A.M.–7 P.M.

BAZAR DE L'HÔTEL DE VILLE (BHV) (17)
52–64, rue de Rivoli, 75004
Métro: Hôtel de Ville

This is a shopping experience no do-it-yourselfer should miss, except on Saturday when an estimated twenty-five thousand shoppers stream through the store. It is famous for its basement hardware department, which is a Parisian DIY experience in itself—with vast kitchen and automotive sections, not to mention paints, electrical goods, furnishings, and even clothes and accessories.

TELEPHONE: 01-42-74-90-00
INTERNET: www.bhv.fr
CREDIT CARDS: AE, MC, V
OPEN: Mon–Sat 9:30 A.M.–7 P.M. (Wed until 10 P.M.)

BOUTIQUE PARIS-MUSÉES (26)
29 bis, rue des Francs-Bourgeois, 75004
Métro: St-Paul

For a description of this museum store, see page 299.

TELEPHONE: 01-42-74-13-02

C & P (38)
16, rue du Pont Louis-Philippe, 75004
Métro: Pont-Marie, St-Paul

Marie Chaumette and Patrick Poirier design fluid, wearable clothing that never seems to go out of style. These are the clothes you always reach for in your closet when you are dressing for the day or packing for a trip. The colors are simple: black, blue, gray, beiges, and white. Fabrics are excellent and the prices affordable when you think how long you are going to enjoy the outfit.

TELEPHONE: 01-42-74-22-34
CREDIT CARDS: MC, V
OPEN: Mon 2–7 P.M., Tues–Sat 11 A.M.–7 P.M.

FAÏENCERIES DE QUIMPER (12)
84, rue St-Martin, 75004
Métro: Hôtel de Ville, Rambuteau

Here you can get everything for the Quimper collector, including paper napkins. The display is excellent, but I found it strange that nothing has a price tag. They will ship.

TELEPHONE: 01-42-71-93-03
CREDIT CARDS: MC, V
OPEN: Mon–Sat 11 A.M.–7 P.M.

FRANCK FANN COIFFEUR (36)
5, rue d'Ormesson, 75004
Métro: St-Paul

Where to get your hair cut? It is always a problem in a strange city, especially if you cannot communicate very well. Relax, now you have Franck to do your hair. He is wonderful at cutting, coloring, and styling both men's and women's hair, and he speaks English. In fact, he has given me the best hair cuts I have ever had. I only wish I could convince him to move to the States so I could go to him on a regular basis. He likes Miami, Florida . . . so there is hope! I haven't had any of the other operators, but I have watched them at work, and they are competent and professional: Jean-Christophe is exceptional with long hair; Virginie does everything well, especially highlighting; and Flora gives therapeutic and relaxing massages, manicures, and facials in the *hammam* (or spa).

In French salons, all services are individually priced and tipped, from the shampoo to the blow dry. At Franck's, it should run around 200–250F (30.49–38.11€), plus tip, and that is very reasonable. Appointments are not necessary. However, it doesn't hurt to call ahead to let them know you are coming, especially if you want Franck; he is only here on Wednesdays and Saturdays, when you will see his snazzy sports car parked illegally in front of the shop. Whenever you go, please say hello to everyone for me . . . and encourage Franck to open a second salon in the States very soon.

TELEPHONE: 01-48-04-50-62
CREDIT CARDS: MC, V
OPEN: Mon–Sat 10 A.M.–7 P.M.

LE WEB 46 (23)
46, rue du Roi de Sicile, 75004
Metro: St-Paul

Another place for computer junkies to keep in touch with their world. Prices are slightly less than elsewhere: 15F (2.29€) for fifteen minutes, 30F (4.57€) for twenty-five minutes, and 45F (6.86€) for an hour. You can send a fax anywhere in France for under 10F (1.52€) and worldwide for under 20F (3.05€).

TELEPHONE: 01-40-27-02-89
FAX: 01-40-27-03-89
CREDIT CARDS: MC, V
OPEN: Mon–Fri 11:30 A.M.–midnight, Sat noon–9 P.M., Sun noon–midnight

L'OCCITANE
18, place des Vosges, 75004 (33)
17, rue des Francs-Bourgeois, 75004 (29)
55, rue St-Louis-en-l'Île, 75004 (50)
Métro: St-Paul, Pont-Marie

For the best in natural, vegetable-based cosmetics, go to l'Occitane. All the products are from Provence and include cosmetics, essential oils, soaps, creams, perfumes, and bath accessories. It is worth a trip to the shop just to smell the aromas and admire the beautiful displays. Whatever you buy will be beautifully gift wrapped. These three shops in the fourth arrondissement are my favorites, but there are branches all over Paris. At last count, the company had shops in Europe, America, Asia, the Middle East, Oceania, and Africa. But you are lucky . . . the prices in France are up to one-third less than elsewhere. All of the l'Occitane stores are closed on Sunday with the exception of the shops listed above on rue des Francs Bourgeois and place des Vosges, which are also open noon to 7 P.M. on that day. There is a L'Occitane in the first arrondissement in the Carrousel du Louvre shopping mall (see page 297), and I've noted several other convenient L'Occitanes throughout this section.

TELEPHONE: 01-40-46-81-71 (l'Île St-Louis)
CREDIT CARDS: MC, V
OPEN: Mon–Sat, 10:30 A.M.–7 P.M.

LORA LUNE (22)
22, rue de Bourg-Tibourg, 75004
Métro: Hôtel de Ville

If you like Lush in London, you are going to like Lora Lune in Paris. Both natural beauty products companies are based on the same appealing concept: natural body care products for beauty and well-being sold by weight. You are encouraged to try the products, and the sales force is helpful if you need to ask questions before deciding just how much soap, body lotion, bath oil, or face cream you want, and in which scent: lavender, honey, oats, musk, or sandalwood. They also have a boutique in the Au Printemps department store (see page 330).

TELEPHONE: 01-48-04-31-24
EMAIL: infor@loralune.com
CREDIT CARDS: V
OPEN: Mon 2–7:40 P.M., Tues–Sat 11 A.M.–8 P.M., Sun 1–7 P.M.

MARKS & SPENCER (15)
88, rue de Rivoli, at rue St-Martin, 75004
Métro: Châtelet

This is the Parisian branch of the London standby, which has a good selection of basic clothes that are not in the trendy fast track. The silk lingerie is well priced. The food hall in the basement is a good place to buy prepared snacks or a jar of real English bitter marmalade. There is another store in the ninth arrondissement (see page 332).

TELEPHONE: 01-41-61-08-00
CREDIT CARDS: MC, V
OPEN: Mon–Sat 9:30 A.M.–8 P.M.

MATIÈRE PREMIERE (30)
12, rue de Sévigné, 75004
Métro: St-Paul

Baubles, bangles, and beads—either assemble your own or buy ready-made necklaces, earrings, and pins at decent prices. There is another shop in the sixth arrondissement (see page 322).

TELEPHONE: 01-42-78-40-87
FAX: 01-40-27-91-85
CREDIT CARDS: MC, V
OPEN: Mon–Sat 10 A.M.–7 P.M.

MOUTON À CINQ PATTES (24)
15, rue Vieille du Temple, 75004
Métro: St-Paul, Hôtel de Ville

For a description of this discount store, see page 323.

TELEPHONE: 01-42-71-86-30

PORCELAINE DE PARIS (43)
4, rue de la Bastille, 75004
Métro: Bastille

For a description, see page 334.

TELEPHONE: Not available

PWS–PRICES WITHOUT SURPRISE (31)
13, rue de Sévigné, 75004
Métro: St-Paul

Owner Claude Windisch got the idea for his discount store (which has another location in the eighth arrondissement) after visiting the United States and seeing all the cut-price stores. Although he has women's apparel, he is better for men. He stocks everything for the man in your life, from top-name to no-name designer clothing. Prices are 30 percent off this season's clothing. Manager Miriam Benarroche speaks English and is very helpful.

TELEPHONE: 01-44-54-09-09
CREDIT CARDS: AE, DC, MC,V
OPEN: Mon 2–7 P.M., Tues–Sat 10 A.M.–7 P.M.

SIDNEY CARRON (8)
37, rue des Archives,75004
Métro: Hôtel de Ville, Rambuteau

The window displays of unusual jewelry caught my eye . . . and then I looked at the prices charged by this talented designer in her workshop/boutique. For the beautifully crafted silver and gold jewelry, the prices are amazing bargains. Most of the artistic pieces sell between 150–350F (22.87–45.73€).

TELEPHONE: 01-48-87-27-70
FAX: 01-48-87-32-77

CREDIT CARDS: None, cash only
OPEN: Mon–Fri 9:30 A.M.–7 P.M., Sat 2–7 P.M.

STOCK GRIFFES (19)
17, rue Vieille du Temple, 75004
Métro: Hôtel de Ville, St-Paul

It is not my first choice for low-cost duds, but if you are nearby, swing through, you might get lucky. The general selection is good, but keep an eye on quality. There is another location in the eighteenth arrondissement (see page 340).

TELEPHONE: 01-48-04-82-34
CREDIT CARDS: MC, V
OPEN: Tues–Sat 10:30 A.M.–7:30 P.M.

FIFTH ARRONDISSEMENT (see map page 98)

Shops

THE ABBEY BOOKSHOP (6)
29, rue de la Parcheminerie, 75005
Metro: St-Michel, Cluny–La Sorbonne

Canadian Brian Spence stocks new and used English books, takes special orders, and holds special literary events in his bookshop near the Cluny Museum. Check his Website for the events schedule.

TELEPHONE: 01-46-33-16-24
FAX: 01-46-33-03-33
EMAIL: abparis@compuserve.com
INTERNET: www.ourworld.compuserve.com
CREDIT CARDS: AE, MC, V
OPEN: Mon–Sat 10 A.M.–7 P.M., sometimes also on Sun

ARTISANS DU RÊVE (31)
33, rue Gay-Lussac, 75005
Métro: Luxembourg

All things from Brittany . . . and the genuine articles: pea coats for adults and children, wool sweaters, authentic striped Breton T-shirts, BZH (a powerful Breton apéritif), and a few pieces of old Quimper. You can also order new, individual Quimper-like pottery bowls and have them personalized with your own name. They also carry Celtic jewelry.

TELEPHONE: 01-43-29-47-82

CREDIT CARDS: AE, DC, MC, V

OPEN: Mon 1–7 P.M., Tues–Sat 10 A.M.–7 P.M.; hours vary in July and Aug

CLICKSIDE (7)
14, rue Domat, 75005
Métro: Maubert-Mutualité, Cluny–La Sorbonne

Computer nerds can click on daily to surf the net, check emails, and play network games. It is slightly less congested than many cyber cafés, but they blast annoying music at a deafening volume. They are Mac friendly and have black-and-white or color laser printing. Coffee and sodas are available if you need a jolt of caffeine to keep you going.

TELEPHONE: 01-56-81-03-00

EMAIL: info@clickside.com

INTERNET: www.clickside.com

CREDIT CARDS: MC, V

OPEN: Mon–Sat 10:30 A.M.–midnight, Sun 1–11 P.M.

CYBER CAFÉ–LATINO (21)
13, rue de l'École Polytechnique, 75005
Métro: Maubert-Mutualité

A cyber space with a Latin twist, where you can down tapas or empanadas while working on the computer. It is a friendly place, with Latino music going all day long and a list of services that includes a two-month, personal email account that includes one hour of free connection time (50F, 7.62€).

TELEPHONE: 01-40-51-86-94

EMAIL: webmaster@cybercafelatino.com

INTERNET: www.cybercafelatino.com

CREDIT CARDS: MC, V (100F, 15.24€, minimum)

OPEN: Mon–Sat 11:30 A.M.–2 A.M., Sun 3–9 P.M.

DIPTYQUE (13)
34, boulevard St-Germain, 75005
Métro: Maubert-Mutualité

Join Puff Daddy, Elton John, and scores of other celebrities who light scented candles from Diptyque. The seven-ounce glass containers hold every wonderful scent you have heard of . . . and plenty you haven't. Traditionalists can buy rose, lilac, cinnamon, or hyacinth, but why not experiment with something unusual: fig tree, new mown hay, tea, or myrrh? Room sprays that match the candle scents enhance the experience. Go one step further and wear a matching eau de toilette in the same fragrance. Don't leave without a bottle of *vinaigre de toilette* (literally, toilet vinegar). Based on a nineteenth-century recipe using plants, woods, and spices, this elixir has many uses. In the bath it revives and refreshes; as an aftershave or face spray, it tones and refreshes; and a capful in a bowl of boiling water will remove cooking and tobacco smells in a room.

TELEPHONE: 01-43-26-45-27
FAX: 01-43-54-27-01
EMAIL: diptyque@diptyque.tm.fr
INTERNET: www.diptyque.tm.fr
CREDIT CARDS: AE, MC, V
OPEN: Tues–Sat 10 A.M.–7 P.M.

LA LIBRAIRIE DES GOURMETS (33)
98, rue Monge, 75005
Métro: Censier-Daubenton

If it is about food and wine, chances are that Catherine Jouvin or Paule Caillat at the La Librairie des Gourmets stocks the book . . . or can order it for you. For more about Paule Caillat and her popular down-to-earth cooking classes, and gourmet tours in France, see page 21.

TELEPHONE: 01-43-31-16-42
FAX: 01-43-31-60-32
INTERNET: librairie-des-gourmets.com
CREDIT CARDS: AE, MC, V
OPEN: Mon–Sat 10:30 A.M.–7 P.M.; closed Aug 15–21

L'OCCITANE (35)
130, Rue Mouffetard, 75005
Métro: Monge

For a description, see page 312.

TELEPHONE: Not available

VILLAGE WEB (4)
18, rue de la Bûcherie, 75005
Métro: Maubert-Mutualité, St-Michel

Village Web has two locations that offer every Web service currently out there. The one in the fifth is two minutes from Notre Dame, the other in the heart of Montmartre. At either one, you can also fax, Xerox, and order hot and cold drinks. Unfortunately they don't take credit cards.

TELEPHONE: 01-44-07-20-15
FAX: 01-44-07-20-18
EMAIL: Infos@village-web.net
INTERNET: www.village-web.net
CREDIT CARDS: None, cash only
OPEN: Daily 10 A.M.–10 P.M.

SIXTH ARRONDISSEMENT (see map page 124)

A LA BONNE RENOMMEE (4)
1, rue Jacob, 75006
Métro: St-Germain-des-Prés

This is a second, smaller location. For a complete description, see page 310.

TELEPHONE: 01-46-33-90-67

ARZAT (43)
6, rue St-Placide, 75006
Métro: Rennes, St-Placide

Silver collectors might find just the thing they have been searching for at this narrow shop sandwiched in among all the discount clothing stores that line both sides of rue St-Placide. None of it is new, and neither are the assorted pieces of china and crystal. If you have a piece that needs restoring, here is where to bring it.

TELEPHONE: 01-42-84-20-66
CREDIT CARDS: AE, DC, MC, V
OPEN: Mon 2–7 P.M., Tues–Sat 11 A.M.–7 P.M.; closed Aug 10–20

BOUTIQUE MAJOLIQUE (5)
42, rue Dauphine, 75006
Métro: St-Germain-des-Prés

All the beautifully embroidered linens and cottons you see in this boutique will require some ironing. If you love beautiful table linens and accessories, it will be worth the effort.

TELEPHONE: 01-55-42-93-55
CREDIT CARDS: AE, MC, V
OPEN: Mon–Sat 10 A.M.–7 P.M.

CARTES D'ART (17)
9, rue du Dragon, 75006
Métro: St-Germain-des-Prés

If postcards or stationery are what you want, this is *the* store. In addition to literally thousands of postcards, you will find greeting cards and other stationery products that make nice gifts or souvenirs for you. Madame Leroux is usually behind the cash register, so if you don't see what you want, just ask her and she will probably have it someplace.

TELEPHONE: 01-42-22-88-15
FAX: 01-45-44-21-35
CREDIT CARDS: AE, DC, MC, V
OPEN: Mon–Sat 11 A.M.–7 P.M.

CHRISTIAN LU (52)
86, rue de Vaugirard, 75006
Métro: St-Placide

Christian Lu designs all the silks you see in her colorful shop and waits on you herself. Everything is made in China, but the quality and craftsmanship are very high. She has large, hand-rolled scarves; mix-and-match skirts, blouses, and trousers; and some dresses. The scarves make great gifts. Everything is hand washable.

TELEPHONE: 01-45-44-93-37
FAX: 01-46-71-53-43
CREDIT CARDS: V
OPEN: Mon–Sat 10:30 A.M.–7 P.M.

COUTURIERS DE LA NATURE (31)
23, rue St-Sulpice, 75006
Métro: St-Sulpice, Odéon

Brigi Hettall makes the most beautiful dried floral arrangements I have ever seen. And I don't like dried or fake flowers . . . but I make an exception with hers because they are works of art. The topiary bouquets come in all sizes and are made with real roses, lilacs, other blooms, and greenery that have be specially treated to retain their true, natural color. I bought my first arrangement five years ago hoping it would retain its color and last through the summer. I am now wondering if it ever will fade or look tired because it is still just as pretty as the day I bought it. Don't worry about getting your flowers home. She ships all over the world, or will wrap them in such a way that nothing will be damaged. Even if you don't buy a thing, her little shop is lovely to look at.

TELEPHONE AND FAX: 01-56-24-06-08
EMAIL: couturiers@couturiers-nature.com
CREDIT CARDS: MC, V
OPEN: Mon–Sat 10 A.M.–7:30 P.M.

DU PAREIL AU MÊME (45)
14, Rue St-Placide, 75006
Métro: St-Placide

For a description of this discount children's clothing store, see page 301.

TELEPHONE: 01-45-44-04-40

DU PAREIL AU MÊME (20)
168, boulevard Saint-Germain, 75006
Métro: St-Germain-des-Prés

For a description of this discount children's clothing store, see page 301.

TELEPHONE: 01-46-33-87-85

DU PAREIL AU MÊME BÉBÉ (58)
17, Rue Vavin, 75006
Métro: Vavin

For a description of this discount baby clothing store, see page 301.
TELEPHONE: 01-43-54-12-34

GILBERT JOSEPH PAPETERIE (26)
30, boulevard St-Michel, 75006
Métro: St-Michel, Odéon

Gilbert Joseph is omnipresent in this part of Paris. What started out as a bookstore over a hundred years ago has grown into a conglomerate of stores selling books, art supplies, and every type of stationery known to civilized humanity. The bookstores are not of as much interest to most Parisian shoppers as this stationery store, where the merchandise is spread out over three floors.

TELEPHONE: 01-44-41-88-66
CREDIT CARDS: MC, V (50F, 7.62€, minimum)
OPEN: Mon–Sat 10 A.M.–7:30 P.M.

GRAPHIGRO (55)
133, rue de Rennes, 75006
Métro: St-Placide

No artist should miss this three-level emporium dedicated to the needs of artists of all types and levels of ability.

TELEPHONE: 01-42-22-51-80

CREDIT CARDS: MC, V

OPEN: Mon–Sat 10 A.M.–7 P.M.

LA BOUTIQUE À BOUTONS (49)
110, rue de Rennes, 75006
Métro: Rennes, St-Placide

Need a button? There are more than eight thousand types of buttons in stock. Are you a needlepoint enthusiast or know someone who is? Then put Madame Grall's charming boutique on your shopping list. All the kits you see are French designed, and many are exclusive to this shop. There are even starter kits for children ages six to ten that contain everything you will need to complete the project. In addition to the overwhelming selection of buttons and needlepoint supplies, the store has decorative ribbons and tapes, a huge thimble collection, and Limoges needle cases.

TELEPHONE: 01-45-48-34-85

CREDIT CARDS: MC, V

OPEN: Tues–Sat 10 A.M.–7 P.M.

LA DERNIÈR GOUTTE (8)
6, rue de Bourbon-le-Château, 75006
Métro: St-Germain-des-Prés

Juan Sanchez is the multidimensional American owner of this wine shop near the St-Germain-des-Prés Church and the famous Les Deux Magots café. He features lesser known estate-bottled regional French wines at prices that are 30 to 40 percent less than you would pay elsewhere. Tastings are usually held on Saturday, and often the winemaker is present to talk about his wines. If you are close by, stop in, have a taste, and you will probably leave with several bottles to sample in Paris or to take home.

TELEPHONE: 01-43-29-11-62

FAX: 01-40-46-84-47

EMAIL: goutte@club-internet.fr

CREDIT CARDS: AE, MC, V

OPEN: Mon 4–9 P.M.; Tues–Fri 9:30 A.M.–1:30 P.M., 4–9 P.M.; Sat 9:30 A.M.–9 P.M.; Sun 10:30 A.M.–2 P.M., 3–6:30 P.M.; wine tastings Sat 11 A.M.–1:30 P.M., 4–9 P.M.; closed part of Aug, dates vary

LA MAISON DES THÉIÈRES
17, rue de l'Odéon, 75006 (33)
13, rue de Vaugirard, 75006 (39)
Métro: Odéon

It is more a museum dedicated to the art of tea making rather than a store selling twelve hundred types of teapots in twenty-five different colors and all the tea to put into them. The best teapots are metal with enamel lining. This is because the enamel does not hold flavors, so the type of tea can be changed often. These pots also stay hot for two hours and can be put directly on the stove. The owner, M. Lang, is a gentleman and always helpful in explaining what is necessary in making proper tea. His selection and expertise are so well known that even Japanese tourists shop here for their tea needs. This is the only shop in Europe that imports biologic tea from Vietnam, which is considered to be the best, and it is the most reasonable. A second shop at 13, rue de Vaugirard (Tel: 01-46-34-15-90), is devoted to Japanese porcelain.

TELEPHONE: 01-46-33-98-96
FAX: 01-46-34-25-97
CREDIT CARDS: AE, MC, V
OPEN: Mon–Sat 10:30 A.M.–1 P.M., 2–7 P.M.

L'OCCITANE (56)
26, rue Vavin, 75006
Métro: Vavin

For a description, see page 312.
TELEPHONE: Not available.

MARIE MERCIÉ (31)
23, rue St-Sulpice, 75006
Métro: Odéon, St-Sulpice

Marie Mercié runs her amazing hat shop in conjunction with Anthony Peto, who has his own store in the second arrondissement (see page 305). Marie makes theatrical hats exclusively for women, and her creations are almost museum quality—suitable for a day at Ascot, the wardrobe department of a film studio, or the most elaborate fashion event imaginable.

TELEPHONE: 01-43-26-45-83
CREDIT CARDS: AE, DC, MC, V
OPEN: Mon–Sat 11 A.M.–7 P.M.; closed middle of Aug

MATIÈRE PREMIERE (24)
89, rue de Seine, 75006
Métro: Odéon

For a complete description, see page 314.
TELEPHONE: 01-44-07-39-07

MONOPRIX (16)
50, rue de Rennes, 75006
Métro: St-Germain-des-Prés

A complete renovation has transformed this once grubby Monoprix into a contemporary shopping experience, befitting its neighbor, Emporio Armani, which occupies the corner location we all knew and loved as Le Drug Store. Upstairs is a small women's ready-to-wear department plus an Express Manicurist, free "flash" makeup services, and a free skin diagnostic. Downstairs is an enormous grocery, deli, coffee bar, café, and bakery. You'll almost forget this is a Monoprix . . . until it's time to check out, and then you'll be snaked behind ten or fifteen other frustrated customers waiting for your turn to pay. Some things never change, and the lines at Monoprix are one of them.

Monoprix stores are all over Paris. Another central location is in the eighth arrondissement (see page 328).

TELEPHONE: Not available
CREDIT CARDS: AE, MC, V
OPEN: Mon–Sat 9 A.M.–10 P.M.

MOUTON À CINQ PATTES (44)
8, 10, 18, 48, rue St-Placide, 75006
Métro: St-Placide, Sèvres-Babylone

With numerous addresses in Paris, these bargain-bin clothing stores have the corner on the discount shopping market. Fellow shoppers are ferocious and the places are messy. I also think the overall quality is poor and the service almost nonexistent. So, why bother? Well, for real discount diggers who are near one of the locations, it is worth a quick look for the once-in-a-blue-moon find.

There is another location in the sixth arrondissement: 19, rue Grégoire-de-Tours, 75006 (22); Tel: 01-43-29-73-56; Métro: Odéon. There is also another store in the fourth arrondissement, page 314. All stores have the same hours as the rue St-Placide location.

TELEPHONE: 01-45-48-86-26
CREDIT CARDS: AE, MC, V
OPEN: Mon–Fri 10:30 A.M.–7:30 P.M., Sat 10:30 A.M.–8 P.M.; some locations close between 1–2 P.M.

THE SAN FRANCISCO BOOK COMPANY (35)
17, rue Monsieur-le-Prince, 75006
Métro: Odéon

It is messy, cluttered, and the second-hand English-language books are stacked two deep, so finding something you are looking for literally resembles looking for a needle in a haystack. Then again, if you don't want to pay retail, it sometimes takes a little extra effort, and you will expend it here. Actually it is a nice place to while away an hour or so just rummaging, and the good part is that you will usually run across something of interest.

TELEPHONE: 01-43-29-15-70
FAX: 01-43-29-52-48
EMAIL: sfbooks@easynet.fr
CREDIT CARDS: None, cash only
OPEN: Mon–Sat 11 A.M.–9 P.M., Sun 2–7 P.M.

SCOOTER (19)
19, rue du Dragon, 75006
Métro: St-Germain-des-Prés
For a description, see page 304.
TELEPHONE: 01-45-49-48-28

SOULEIADO (28)
78, rue de Sienne, and 3, rue Lobineau, 75006
Metro: Odéon, Mabillon
For the best in prints and products from Provence, Souleiado is the name everyone knows. No one said anything about it being cheap, but the quality is superb and the selection runs all the way from a lavender sachet to outfitting your entire home and wardrobe á la Souleiado. There are two storefronts right around the corner from each other; the rue de Sienne store emphasizes tablewares, and the rue Lobineau store has fabrics and ready-to-wear.
TELEPHONE: 01-43-54-62-25 (rue de Sienne), 01-44-07-33-81 (rue Lobineau)
FAX: 01-44-07-33-78 (both locations)
CREDIT CARDS: AE, DC, MC, V
OPEN: Mon–Sat 10:30 A.M.–7 P.M.

TEA AND TATTERED PAGES (53)
24, rue Mayet, 75006
Métro: Falguière, Duroc
Owned by vivacious expatriate Kristi Chavane, Tea & Tattered Pages promises hours of contented browsing through an enormous sea of used English-language books. If you need a little sustenance, tea, coffee, lunch Monday to Friday, weekend brunch, and brownies are served. The staff is friendly and plugged into the English-speaking Paris scene, and I guarantee you will not regret a visit to this well-organized two-level shop.
TELEPHONE: 01-40-65-94-35
CREDIT CARDS: None, cash only
OPEN: Daily 11 A.M.–7 P.M.

TOUT COMPTE FAIT . . . (46)
31, rue St-Placide, 75006
Métro: St-Placide
For children's clothes that don't cost an arm and a leg, Tout Compte Fait . . . runs a close second to Au Pareil du Même (see page 301). Stores are all over Paris.

TELEPHONE: 01-42-22-45-64
CREDIT CARDS: MC, V
OPEN: Mon–Sat 10 A.M.–7 P.M.

SEVENTH ARRONDISSEMENT (see map page 156)

Shops

BONPOINT (25)
82, rue de Grenelle, 75007
Métro: Rue du Bac

If you can afford to shop at Bonpoint for your children's clothes, then you don't need this book, since this is probably the most expensive store for outfitting babies and children in Paris. However, this Bonpoint discounts last season's collections and anything else the other stores can't sell. While it still doesn't qualify as cheap, the quality is superb, and the clothes last for generations. Even better prices during the sales in January and July.

TELEPHONE: 01-45-48-05-45
CREDIT CARDS: V
OPEN: Mon–Sat 10:30 A.M.–6:30 P.M.; closed in Aug

LA MONDE DES ORCHIDÉES (14)
65, avenue Bosquet, 75007
Métro: École Militaire

If you need a thank-you gift for someone in Paris, or just want to surprise the love of your life with a beautiful French orchid, Jacqueline Augnet's orchid boutique is the place to go. You can buy one large bloom in a clear transparent bag for under $20. It is a striking gift that will last for several weeks. Also available are orchid potted plants, orchid jewelry, and books in French about orchids.

TELEPHONE: 01-45-56-08-75
FAX: 01-45-50-23-28
CREDIT CARDS: AE, MC, V
OPEN: Mon 3:30–8 P.M., Tues–Sat 10:30 A.M.–8 P.M.; closed 3 weeks in Aug

LE BON MARCHÉ and LA GRANDE EPICERIE DE PARIS (27)
38, rue de Sèvres, at rue du Bac, 75007
Métro: Sèvres-Babylone

The first department store in Paris, and still my favorite, this show-place store has balustrades and balconies designed by Gustave Eiffel. It combines the elegant and the practical, and is easy to manage. Be sure to see La Grande Epicerie de Paris, their excellent grocery and fresh food store—a fairyland for the gourmet.

TELEPHONE: 01-44-39-80-00

CREDIT CARDS: AE, DC, MC, V

OPEN: Department store, Mon–Sat 9:30 A.M.–7 P.M.; Food store, Mon–Sat 8:30 A.M.–9 P.M.

L'OCCITANE (26)
90, rue du Bac, 75007
Métro: Rue du Bac

For a description, see page 312.

TELEPHONE: Not available

EIGHTH ARRONDISSEMENT (see map page 176)

ALLIX (19)
6, rue de Surène, 75008
Métro: Madeleine

The two owners, Felix Gomez and Aline Rodriguez, make simple, unusual handbags that are sold throughout the world at three or four times the prices you will pay here. They also stock selected items of jewelry. The merchandise is very well displayed, and English is spoken.

TELEPHONE: 01-42-65-10-79

FAX: 01-40-07-05-11

CREDIT CARDS: MC, V

OPEN: Mon–Fri 11 A.M.–2:30 P.M., 3:30–6:30 P.M.; closed Aug

ANNA LOWE (14)
104, rue du Faubourg du St-Honorè, 75008
Métro: Miromesnil, St-Philippe-du-Roule

Anna Lowe is one of the best designer discount stores in Paris. The location is great, next door to the famous Hôtel Bristol and in the midst of many top fashion houses and designers. You will find all the top-name French and Italian designers, including Chanel, and a fabulous selection of evening wear at reduced prices. All labels are left in. Sensational July and mid-December sales and fast alterations.

TELEPHONE: 01-42-66-11-32, 01-40-06-02-42

FAX: 01-40-06-00-53

EMAIL: AnnaLowe@sollers.fr

CREDIT CARDS: AE, DC, MC, V

OPEN: Mon–Sat 10 A.M.–7 P.M.

FAUCHON (27)
30, place de la Madeleine, 75008
Métro: Madeleine

Fauchon is to grocery shopping as the Ritz is to hotels . . . *le ne plus ultra!* A trip to the famed shop and amazing *charcuterie* epitomizes gourmet grocery shopping. A jar of *herbes de provence,* fancy honey, or tin of cookies with the Fauchon label is a very much appreciated gift.

TELEPHONE: 01-47-42-95-40

FAX: 01-47-42-89-25

CREDIT CARDS: AE, DC, MC, V

OPEN: Mon–Sat 9:30 A.M.–7 P.M.

FRANCHI CHAUSSEURS (4)
15, rue de la Pépinière, 75008
Métro: St-Augustin

They have lots of Charles Jourdan shoes at half price, but the styles are a bit dated. They also have end-of-series shoes and Italian designs at good prices, but there's no place to really sit to try on unless you count the one stool by the door. Remember, this is discount and comfort is not part of the price you are paying.

There is another location in the eighth: 10, rue de Rome, 75008; Tel: 01-43-87-42-59; Métro: Saint-Lazare; same hours, but closed in July, open August.

TELEPHONE: 01-42-94-28-88

CREDIT CARDS: AE, DC, MC, V

OPEN: Mon–Fri 10:30 A.M.–7 P.M.; closed Aug

L'OCCITANE (9)
Galerie des Champs Élysées, 84, avenue Champs-Élysées, 75008
Métro: Franklin-D-Roosevelt

For a description, see page 312.

TELEPHONE: Not available

MAILLE (30)
6, place de la Madeleine, 75008
Métro: Madeleine

The Maille boutique is devoted to products from the best and most famous name in mustards. There are over twenty varieties, many of which are attractively gift packaged with recipes included (in French, but if you speak any French, simple enough to follow). In addition, the boutique stocks vinegars, mustard pots, pickles, and olives. Prices start as low as 25F (3.81€), and the more unusual mustard varieties make great gifts: *moutarde aux fruits rouges, moutarde au cognac, moutarde au champagne, moutarde à la framboise,* and *moutarde aux noix.*

TELEPHONE: 01-40-15-06-00

CREDIT CARDS: MC, V

OPEN: Mon–Sat 10 A.M.–7 P.M.

MISS "GRIFFES" (17)
19, rue de Penthièvre, 75008
Métro: Miromesnil

The shop has been in business for more than a half century, and it is now run by its third owner, Mme. Vincent, who has been here for twenty years. I think it is one of the best in the discount hunt for women's clothing, shoes, handbags, and accessories from all the top names, including Chanel, Armani, Ungaro, and Valentino. Prices are high at first glance, but not when you consider what you would pay retail in the boutiques. Also available are prototype collections of last season's models, a few of Mme. Vincent's own designs, and wonderful custom-made blazers. Free alterations are ready in two days. A 10 percent discount will be given to readers who show her *Great Sleeps Paris.*

TELEPHONE: 01-42-65-10-00

CREDIT CARDS: AE, DC, MC, V

OPEN: Mon–Fri 11 A.M.–7 P.M., Sat noon–7 P.M.; closed middle 2 weeks in Aug

MONOPRIX (11)
52, avenue des Champs-Élysées, at rue La Boëtie, 75008
Métro: Franklin-D-Roosevelt

If you are a Kmart or Target shopper, you will be a Monoprix shopper in Paris. Stores dot the landscape and vary in size and atmosphere, but this is the one that has the longest hours and is the one most tourists will see. All Monoprix stores are good to keep in mind for quick-fix cosmetic buys (including Bourjois, which all smart discount shoppers know is the prototype for Chanel, and sold at a fraction of cost of the designer brand), cotton underwear, fashion accessories of the moment, toothbrushes, and housewares. Here there is a tourist souvenir corner, basement grocery, and thousands of other daily shoppers in addition to you. Because of the inadequate ratio of cash registers to shoppers, you may feel as if you are in the checkout line behind them all.

Another location is in the sixth arrondissement (see page 323).

TELEPHONE: 01-42-25-27-60
CREDIT CARDS: AE, MC, V
OPEN: Mon–Sat 9 A.M.–midnight

PIERRE VIVEZ (18)
6, rue des Saussaies, 75008
Métro: Champs-Élysées, Miromesnil

A large collection of traditional, lightweight, pure wool sweaters in all the classic designs, plus seasonal outfits and cotton T-shirts for women and sweaters for men. Everything is guaranteed washable.

TELEPHONE: 01-42-65-26-54
CREDIT CARDS: AE, MC, V
OPEN: Mon–Sat 10 A.M.–7 P.M.

PWS–PRICES WITHOUT SURPRISE (16)
1, rue de Penthiévre, 75008
Métro: Miromesnil

For complete details, see the fourth arrondissement location, page 314. This branch has only menswear.

TELEPHONE: 01-47-42-64-30

SEPHORA (10)
70, avenue des Champs-Élysées, 75008
Métro: Georges-V

Bouncers guard the front doors of the Champs-Élysées Sephora, probably to try to stem the virtual sea of people who stream through here to revel in the absolutely mind-boggling collection of cosmetics, perfumes, and miscellaneous beauty accessories. All the big name lines are here, including Bourjois (the prototype for Chanel). No *détaxe,* but competitive prices make them worth a look. Sephora is now opening in the States, so it may not be the experience it once was, but if you are by this flagship store, take a look.

There is also a location in the first arrondissement in the Forum des Halles (see page 297), and there is one in the sixteenth at 50, rue de Passy; Métro: Passy. However, there is no air-conditioning in the rue de Passy store, so avoid on hot days.

TELEPHONE: 01-53-93-22-50
FAX: 01-53-93-22-51
INTERNET: www.sephora.com
CREDIT CARDS: AE, MC, V
OPEN: Mon–Sat 10 A.M.–midnight, Sun noon–9 P.M.

NINTH ARRONDISSEMENT (see map page 176)

Shops

Passages and Shopping Malls

ANNEXE DES CRÉATEURS (25)
19, rue Godot-de-Mauroy, 75009
Métro: Madeleine, Auber

No Chanel or Yves St-Laurent, but they have last season's fashions for women from French, Italian, and Japanese manufacturers. Labels are left in, and quality varies. There are two shops next to each other, one for dressy, the other for sportswear and separates. They also have hats, jewelry, coats, bags, and wedding gowns. Sales are in January and July.

TELEPHONE: 01-42-65-46-40

CREDIT CARDS: AE, MC, V

OPEN: Mon–Sat 10:30 A.M.–7 P.M.

AU PRINTEMPS (35)
64, boulevard Haussmann, 75009
Métro: Havre-Caumartin

This is known as "The Most Parisian Department Store." Famous designer boutiques, a separate men's store, and an excellent leather and cosmetic department are on the ground floor. Also, there's a fabulous umbrella section, which sells thirty thousand *parapluies* per year! Don't miss the beautiful views of Paris from a window perch in the cafeteria or outdoor terrace; have a coffee if you must while you're here, but don't waste time or money on the dismal food.

TELEPHONE: 01-42-82-50-00

INTERNET: www.printemps.fr

CREDIT CARDS: AE, DC, MC, V

OPEN: Mon–Sat 9:30 A.M.–7 P.M. (Thur until 9 P.M.)

FREDDY (41)
3, rue Scribe, 75009
Métro: Opéra

Freddy specializes in perfumes, but also stocks scarves, ties, cosmetics, and costume jewelry. Forty percent is taken off if you spend 1,200F (182.94€); if you spend less, you will get a 30 percent discount. Prices are marked with the discount already taken off. If you show a copy of *Great Sleeps Paris,* you will receive a small gift.

TELEPHONE: 01-47-42-63-41
FAX: 01-40-06-03-14
CREDIT CARDS: AE, DC, MC, V
OPEN: Mon–Sat 9 A.M.–7 P.M.

GALERIES LAFAYETTE (36)
40, boulevard Haussmann, 75009
Métro: Chaussée d'Antin–Lafayette

Galeries Lafayette carries the top names in fashion, featuring seventy-five thousand brand names, including their own label. It also boasts a record number of daily shoppers. More than a hundred thousand people per day stream through their Haussmann store, and of course they want you to be one of them during your Parisian stay. In addition to a huge perfume and cosmetic section, they have one floor devoted to lingerie, another to home decorating, and everything else you can imagine—including a one-hour photo service, *bureau de change,* car park, restaurants (including McDonald's in the toy department, naturally), travel and theater agencies, and a watch and shoe repair department. Gourmets and gourmands will want to visit their grocery department (Gourmet Lafayette), which borders on the inspirational: its dazzling array of delicacies features everything a gastronome could possibly want, including food stations where you can stop for a plate of just-made pasta, a sampling of sushi, a quick cappuccino, or a pastry (see *Great Eats Paris*). Even dedicated noncooks will want to see this beautiful section of Galeries Lafayette.

TELEPHONE: 01-42-82-36-40
FAX: 01-42-82-80-18
INTERNET: www.galerieslafayette.com
CREDIT CARDS: AE, MC, V
OPEN: Mon–Sat 9:30 A.M.–6:45 P.M. (Thur until 9 P.M.)

HAUT DE GAMME STOCK (40)
9, rue Scribe, 75009
Métro: Opéra

The shop is located in a courtyard and features two sections of designer clothing for men and women at discounted prices. Not always the top names, but usually Armani or Versace has-beens.

TELEPHONE: 01-40-07-10-20
FAX: 01-40-07-10-21

CREDIT CARDS: AE, DC, MC, V
OPEN: Mon–Sat 10 A.M.–7 P.M.; closed Aug 15–31

LOUIS PION (39)
9, rue Auber, 75009
Metro: Opéra, Auber

Watches for everyone on your list at prices starting at 60F (9.15€) for an alarm clock and 100F for a watch (15.24€). Several locations throughout Paris.

TELEPHONE: 01-42-65-40-33
CREDIT CARDS: AE, DC, MC, V
OPEN: Mon–Sat 9:30 A.M.–7 P.M.

MARKS & SPENCER (37)
35, boulevard Haussmann, 75009
Métro: Havre-Caumartin

For a complete description, see page 313.

TELEPHONE: 01-47-42-49-91

MUSÉE DE LA PARFUMERIE FRAGONARD (38)
9, rue Scribe, 75009
Métro: Opéra, Auber

In the museum you will see displays showing the perfume-making process according to Fragonard and a collection of their perfume bottles. This part is free, then you exit through the boutique, where a patient multilingual sales force is available to help you decide on just the right fragrance. I think the best buy is the box of five perfumes, which you can divide into five separate gifts. It isn't all perfume. The boutique stocks beautifully packaged soaps, cosmetics, and candles. If you are having trouble making up your mind, remember the words of Coco Chanel: "A woman who doesn't perfume herself has no future!"

TELEPHONE: 01-42-60-37-14, 01-47-42-93-40
FAX: 01-42-60-32-29
INTERNET: www.fragonard.com
CREDIT CARDS: AE, DC, MC, V
OPEN: Mon–Sat 9 A.M.–5:30 P.M.

PHARMACIE LECLERC (28)
10, rue Vignon, at rue de Sèze, 75009
Métro: Madeleine

Leclerc is a one-hundred-year-old pharmacy stocking their own line of cosmetic products, called *Poudre Leclerc*. You will see some of their products in other pharmacies, but here they have the full line. I like their face powders, which are packaged in twenty different tints, including banana, apricot, and orchid. The clerks are helpful, and they will let you try before you buy.

TELEPHONE: 01-47-42-04-59
FAX: 01-47-42-75-13

CREDIT CARDS: AE, MC, V

OPEN: Mon–Sat 8:30 A.M.–7:30 P.M.

SULMACO (44)
13, rue de Trévise, 75009
Métro: Grands Boulevards

English-speaking owner Philippe Madar offers an excellent selection of designer men's fashions and accessories at below retail. In addition to off-the-rack clothing, it is possible to order custom-made clothes. The detail in the double-lined tailor-made suits is superb. Ready-made suits start around 2,900F (442.€), and tailor-made, with your initials inside, begin around 5,000F (762.25€). These are good prices when you consider you can deduct the 13 percent *détaxe* after spending only 1,200F (182.94€). A master tailor is also employed to do alterations, which are included in the price of the garment except during sales. Tailor-made suits are guaranteed ready in twenty days for a first fitting, and delivery in the next three days. If a French tailor-made suit appeals to you, make Sulmaco your first shopping stop in Paris. Sales are held at the end of December and January and during the first part of July.

TELEPHONE: 01-48-24-89-00

CREDIT CARDS: AE, DC, MC, V

OPEN: Mon–Sat 10 A.M.–7 P.M.; in Aug, Mon–Sat noon–6:30 P.M.; closed middle 10 days of Aug

TOUT COMPTE FAIT . . . (33)
62, rue de la Chaussée d'Antin, 75009
Métro: Chaussée d'Antin–Lafayette

For a description of this store, see page 324.

TELEPHONE: 01-48-74-16-54

ELEVENTH ARRONDISSEMENT (see map page 192)

ALLICANTE (13)
26, boulevard Beaumarchais, 75011
Métro: Bastille, Chemin Vert

Allicante specializes in oils from France, but it also carries Italian and Greek varieties, all bottled on site by the grower. The selection is daunting, but you can sample to your heart's content before deciding which to buy. Not all the oils are olive. You can purchase sesame, raisin, or pistachio oil, aromatic oils, essential oils, and therapeutic oils. It is quite an interesting learning and tasting experience.

TELEPHONE: 01-43-55-13-02
INTERNET: www.allicante.com
CREDIT CARDS: MC, V
OPEN: Mon noon–7:30 P.M., Tues–Sun 10 A.M.–7:30 P.M.

ANNE WILLI (17)
13, rue Keller, 75011
Métro: Ledru-Rollin, Bastille

Anne Willi is a talented young designer who makes and sells her line of clothes for active young women in this workshop/boutique. Her clothing is not expensive. Many of the separates are reversable, which makes mixing and matching a way to maximize an outfit.

TELEPHONE: 01-48-06-74-06
FAX: 01-48-06-74-04
CREDIT CARDS: MC, V
OPEN: Mon 2–8 P.M., Tues–Sat 11:30 A.M.–8 P.M.; closed 2 weeks in Aug

PORCELAINE DE PARIS (2)
8, rue de la Pierre-Levée, 75011
Métro: Parmentier

Porcelaine de Paris is the second-oldest Porcelaine manufacturer in France (after Sèvres) and the last porcelain manufacturer still actively working in Paris. It is interesting to note that only women work here, with the exception of the production manager. I don't have to tell you about the high quality of this magnificent china, which includes everything from a small pin dish to complete kitchens, bathrooms, and countless table settings. You will see Porcelaine de Paris proudly displayed in every fine department or home furnishing store. However, you do not have to pay these retail prices. End of series and seconds are available, and special promotions are held. Shipping is available. Before you buy a complete dinner set, be sure to inquire about the lead count, as some of the patterns will not meet the strict U.S. guidelines. If you can't get to the depths of the eleventh arrondissement to visit this combination factory, warehouse, and salesroom, then go to their boutique in the fourth arrondissement (see page 314).

TELEPHONE: 01-43-57-40-35, 01-49-29-99-20
FAX: 01-43-57-99-80
INTERNET: www.porcelainedeparis.com
CREDIT CARDS: MC, V
OPEN: Mon–Fri 10 A.M.–6 P.M.; closed in Aug

TWELFTH ARRONDISSEMENT (see map page 192)

BETTY (22)
10, place d'Aligre, 75012
Métro: Ledru-Rollin

Probably the best time to check Betty is early Sunday morning; combine it with a trip to the flea market at place d'Aligre. Betty is not worth a separate journey, but it is worth a quick look. Upstairs they say they have designer labels, but not many on most top-ten lists. The prices are low, and if you want something French and don't care about famous designer labels, you might find this interesting.

TELEPHONE: 01-43-07-40-64

CREDIT CARDS: None, cash only

OPEN: Tues–Sun 9 A.M.–12:30 P.M., also Thur and Sat 2:30–7 P.M.; closed Mon

VIADUC DES ARTS (24)
9–129, avenue Daumesnil, 75012
Métro: Bastille, Gare de Lyon, Daumesnil

The railway tracks on top of the stone viaduct carried the suburban railway from Bastille. Now the vaulted archways are enclosed and house a variety of artists' workshops, galleries, boutiques, and a café. The rail tracks have been replaced by a walkway with trees and gardens that goes all the way to the Bois de Vincennes.

TELEPHONE: Not available

CREDIT CARDS: Depends on shop

OPEN: Tues–Fri noon–7 P.M., Sun 11 A.M.–7 P.M. (some stores may differ)

FOURTEENTH ARRONDISSEMENT (see map page 204)

GALERIES LAFAYETTE (10)
Centre Commercial Montparnasse, Tour Montparnasse Complex, 212, rue du Départ, 75014
Métro: Montparnasse–Bienvenüe

For a complete description, see page 331.
TELEPHONE: 01-45-38-52-87

LA BOUTIQUE DE L'ARTISANAT MONASTIQUE (17)
68 bis, avenue Denfert-Rochereau, 75014
Métro: Denfert-Rochereau, Port Royal

Doting *grand-mères,* beware! What a find for adorable children's clothing (including christening outfits that are destined to become family heirlooms), layettes, handicrafts, embroidered linens, cosmetics, food products, and beautiful robes and nightgowns . . . all made by French priests and nuns in monasteries throughout France. The quality is beautiful, and whatever you buy will show the name of the monastery where it was made, and it will be hand signed by the sister or priest who made it. A volunteer staff of sweet, gray-haired ladies graciously assist you, wrap your purchase, and take your money. Even if you only buy a candle or a bar of soap, it is worth a visit.

TELEPHONE: 01-43-35-15-76

CREDIT CARDS: MC, V

OPEN: Mon–Fri noon–6:30 P.M., Sat 2–7 P.M.; closed holidays, last week of July, and all Aug

FIFTEENTH ARRONDISSEMENT (see map page 204)

SIXTEENTH ARRONDISSEMENT (see map page 226)

DÉPÔT–VENTE DE PASSY (17)
14–16, rue de la Tour, 75016
Métro: Passy

This is one of the best consignment shops, offering a super selection of clothing in mint condition featuring all the biggies for women, from Chanel and Hermès accessories to Dior, Gucci, and Prada. It has a nice staff, fair prices of about 40 to 50 percent off regular retail (only 20 percent for Chanel), and good dressing rooms. This is one of the favorites of smart French discount denizens.

TELEPHONE: 01-45-20-95-21
CREDIT CARDS: AE, MC, V
OPEN: Mon 2–7 P.M., Tues–Sat 10 A.M.–7 P.M.; closed Aug

DU PAREIL AU MÊME (9)
97, avenue Victor Hugo, 75016
Métro: Victor-Hugo

For a description of this discount children's clothing store, see page 301.

TELEPHONE: 01-47-37-06-31

DU PAREIL AU MÊME BÉBÉ (9)
111, avenue Victor Hugo, 75016
Métro: Victor-Hugo

For a description of this discount baby's clothing store, see page 301.
TELEPHONE: 01-47-27-48-10

FRANCK ET FILS (24)
80, rue de Passy, 75016
Métro: La Muette, Passy

This small, elegant department store sells traditional clothing to the women of Passy, one of Paris' most expensive neighborhoods. You will get a 10 percent discount on anything you buy, plus the *détaxe,* if you spend 1,200F (182.94€).

TELEPHONE: 01-44-14-38-00
CREDIT CARDS: AE, DC, MC, V
OPEN: Mon–Sat 10 A.M.–7 P.M.

L'AFFAIR D'UN SOIR (11)
147, rue de la Pompe, 75016
Métro: Victor-Hugo

The shop is located in one of the poshest neighborhoods of Paris, so this tells you another secret of the well-dressed French woman—maybe she leases! If you have been invited to the Élysée Palace and "haven't a thing to wear," don't worry, call l'Affair d'Un Soir for your dress rental appointment. For women *soirée*-goers, silk dresses, ball gowns, hats, and elegant accessories are available. They will also rent just one necklace, or a hat, if that is all you need to complete an ensemble. For the men, tuxedos and everything to go with them are also here. Sophie de Mestier designs two original collections each year that she rents to her elegant clientele. Many customers rent an outfit and cannot bear to part with it, so they end up buying it. Prices for rentals start from 500F to 2,500F (76.22–381.12€). There is a 3,000F (457.35€) deposit; cleaning and alterations are included. To rent something, it is better to make an appointment.

TELEPHONE: 01-47-27-37-50
CREDIT CARDS: AE, MC, V
OPEN: Mon 2–7 P.M., Tues–Sat 10:30 A.M.–7 P.M.

L'OCCASERIE
19 and 30, rue de la Pompe, 75016 (16)
14, rue Jean Bologne, 75016 (27)
16 and 21, rue de l'Annonciation, 75016 (28)
Métro: Rue de la Pompe, La Muette

At these three locations in the upmarket sixteenth arrondissement, men and women can find gently worn designer togs, furs, shoes, accessories, and vintage luggage for less. These consignment shops are all within walking distance of each other, but none stocks children's wear.

TELEPHONE: 01-45-03-17-99
CREDIT CARDS: MC, V
OPEN: Tues–Sat 11 A.M.–7 P.M.; Aug closing varies with each shop

L'OCCITANE (8)
109, Avenue Victor Hugo, 75016
Métro: Victor-Hugo

For a description, see page 312.

TELEPHONE: Not available

RÉCIPROQUE (14)
88, 89, 92, 93, 95, 97, 101, 123, rue de la Pompe, 75016
Métro: Rue de la Pompe

The grande dame of formerly worn designer fashions for a fraction of their original retail price, this is the largest consignment shop in Paris. It has everything from gifts and antiques to estate jewelry, shoes, bags, clothes, furs, evening wear, and men's clothing. The sheer volume is staggering, so allow plenty of time if this type of *haute* thrift shopping is your forte. Sales are held in January, July and August. The staff is helpful.

TELEPHONE: 01-47-04-30-28
CREDIT CARDS: AE, MC, V
OPEN: Tues–Sat 11 A.M.–7:30 P.M.

TOUT COMPTE FAIT . . . (10)
115, avenue Victor Hugo, 75016
Métro: Victor-Hugo

For a description of this discount children's clothing store, see page 324.

TELEPHONE: 01-47-55-63-36

SEVENTEENTH ARRONDISSEMENT (see map page 240)

Shops	
Accessories à Soie	**339**
Food Shopping	
Marché des Batignolles	**345**
Rue de Lévis	**343**
Rue Poncelet	**343**

ACCESSORIES À SOIE (12)
21, rue des Acacias, 75017
Métro: Argentine

Scarves by Nini Ricci, YSL, pretty silk sweaters, ties and shirts for the man in your life—all at discount prices. The scarves are beautifully wrapped in the designer box they came in. Sales in January and July.

TELEPHONE: 01-42-27-78-77
CREDIT CARDS: AE, DC, MC, V
OPEN: Mon–Sat 10:30 A.M.–2 P.M., 3–7:30 P.M.

STOCK GRIFFES (10)
1, rue des Trois Frères, 75018
Métro: Pigalle, Abbesses

For a description of this discount clothing store, see page 315.
TELEPHONE: 01-42-55-42-49

TATI (12)
4-30, boulevard Rouchechouart, 75018
Métro: Barbes-Rochechouart, Anvers

For a complete description, see page 309. However, at this location, watch out for pickpockets, especially children.
TELEPHONE: 01-55-29-50-00

VILLAGE WEB (7)
6, rue Ravignan, 75018
Métro: Abbesses

For a complete description of this cyber café, see page 317.
TELEPHONE: 01-42-64-77-70

Flea Markets: Les Marchés aux Puces

What to do on a Saturday or Sunday morning? Go early to the flea market. Wear old clothes and comfortable shoes, beware of pickpockets, and bring cash. You will have a good time even if you don't buy a thing. The days of finding a fabulous antique for a few centimes are gone, but you will probably find a keepsake or two. If you have nothing special on your list, just people-watch; the wildlife at the *puces* beats that at the zoo.

MARCHÉ D'ALIGRE (23)
Place d'Aligre, 75012 (see map page 192)
Métro: Ledru-Rollin

Marché d'Aligre is an Arab market with bottom-of-the-barrel prices. That's also where most of the quality is, especially for the produce. Wear a concealed money belt and go on a Sunday morning when it is really jumping. Prowl through the little shops, which have the lowest prices on baskets, tea glasses, *couscousières,* teapots, and Middle Eastern kitsch. You can bargain a little and probably save 30 or 40 percent over what you would pay in an uptown shop. In the center of it all is a small flea market selling little objects, antique buttons, bric-a-brac, and tacky clothes. Fashion mavens might want to swing through Betty, a designer discount shop that at times has something interesting (see page 335).

OPEN: Tues–Sun 7:30 A.M.–1 P.M.

MARCHÉ DE VANVES (31)
Avenue Georges-Lafenestre, 75014 (see map page 204)
Métro: Porte de Vanves

This is a good place for small antiques and collectibles that tuck easily into a suitcase. Start by walking along avenue Marc-Sangier, and in a morning you will be able to browse and bargain your way through it and come away with a treasure or two. The locals know to come way before noon, when most of the serious sellers fold up their stalls. Every Sunday morning from March to October, the Square Georges-Lafenestre is an open-air art gallery where you can buy directly from the artists.

OPEN: Sat–Sun 7:30 A.M.–6 P.M.

MARCHÉ DE CLIGNANCOURT (1)
Avenue Michelet, at rue des Rosiers, 75018 (see map page 252)
Métro: Porte de Clignancourt

Clignancourt is the largest flea and antique market in the world—too big to conquer in only a day. More than 11 million bargain hunters come every year, making this the number four tourist site in France. Once you get past the piles of jeans and the Indians selling cheap beads, head for the Marché Biron on the corner of 85, rue des Rossiers. It has the most expensive sellers, but it's the most serious for furniture and art. The Paul Bert Marché, at 110, rue des Rosiers and 18, rue Paul Bert, has an unusual collection of Art Deco pieces and antiques from the late 1890s. The Marché Jules-Valles, 7, rue Jules-Valles, has the least expensive items, and lots of 1920s and 1930s lace and postcards. For vintage clothing, the Marché Malik at 53, rue Jules-Valles, is the place. Bring cash, expect to bargain, and wear a moneybelt. Pickpockets are pros here.

NOTE: When you exit the métro station, simply head north, following the crowds and the signs, to find the flea market. Cross boulevard Ney onto avenue de la Porte de Clignancourt, and you can't miss it.

INTERNET: www.antikita.com
OPEN: Sat 8 or 9 A.M.–6 P.M., Sun–Mon 10 or 11 A.M.–6 P.M.

MARCHÉ DE MONTREUIL
Place de la Porte de Montreuil, 75020
Métro: Porte de Montreuil

The huge market begins once you get through the long line of vendors hawking cheap trash on the bridge, but even then you will wonder why you came. Basically cheap junk of little value or interest for most of us unless you are looking for tools, domestic appliances, and beat-up furniture.

OPEN: Sat–Mon 9 A.M.–5 P.M.

Food Shopping Streets and Outdoor Roving Markets

There are two types of markets in Paris (in addition to the growing number of *supermarchés*): *rue commerçantes*—stationary indoor/outdoor markets along certain streets that are open six days a week, including Sunday morning, but not on Monday—and the *marchés volants*—outdoor roving markets of independent merchants who move from one neighborhood to another on Tuesday to Sunday mornings only, never in the afternoon. A visit to one of these markets provides a real look at an old, unchanging way of daily Paris life. When you go, take your camera, don't touch the merchandise, and watch your wallet. I guarantee you that a trip or two to a Paris market will spoil you for your hometown supermarket. In Paris markets, fruits and vegetables of every variety are arranged with the skill and precision usually reserved for fine jewelry store windows. Equal care and attention is given to the displays of meats, fish, cheese, and fresh flowers. Everyone has a favorite vendor for each item on their shopping list, and vendors respond with very personal service. It is not unusual for a fruit seller to ask you not only what day you want to eat your melon or peaches, but at what time, and to select the fruit accordingly. A few favorites are listed here.

Food Shopping Streets–Rues Commerçantes

Generally, these are open Tuesday to Sunday 8 A.M.–1 P.M. and 4:30–7 P.M.; closed Monday all day and Sunday afternoon. You can usually use credit cards for larger purchases at wine shops and the like, but it's strictly cash only for produce and most other fresh food.

RUE MONTORGUEIL, 75002 (15) (see map page 56)
Métro: Étienne Marcel, Sentier

Rue Montorgueil is crowded with dogs, children, motor scooters, and people of all ages and persuasions, who create a great, lively Parisian ambience on one of the best shopping streets in Paris. The street is lined with three supermarkets, five *boulangeries/pâtisseries,* four produce stands, meat (including horse) markets, fish mongers, cheese and wine shops, three florists, pharmacies, cleaners, phone and photo shops, a hardware store, bars and cafés galore, and a nice hotel.

OPEN: With the exception of the bakeries, most of the food shops are closed Mon, but open Tues–Sat 8:30 A.M.–7 P.M., Sun 8:30 A.M.–1 P.M.

RUE MOUFFETARD, 75005 (36) (see map page 98)
Métro: Censier-Daubenton, Place Monge

One of the most photographed and colorful steet markets in Paris, but the quality is suspect and the prices high.

RUE DE BUCI AND RUE DE SEINE, 75006 (9) (see map page 124)
Métro: Odéon

Loud, colorful, and tourist-infested—and it has high prices if you were going to shop here daily. It's sociologically interesting to sit at one of the outdoor cafés and watch the crowd.

RUE CLER, 75007 (18) (see map page 156)
Métro: École-Militaire

The gathering place for aristocratic shoppers in the tony seventh arrondissement.

RUE DAGUERRE, 75014 (28) (see map page 204)
Métro: Denfert-Rochereau

Lots of cafés filled with people-watchers, there's a Monoprix on the corner, and the markets have good quality products.

RUE DU COMMERCE, 75015 (4) (see map page 204)
Métro: Commerce, La Motte-Picquet–Grenelle

This provides an interesting look at blue-collar Paris.

RUE DE LÉVIS, 75017 (6) (see map page 240)
Métro: Villiers

There is plenty here to tempt you—from bakeries to wine shops and a Monoprix.

RUE PONCELET, 75017 (10) (see map page 240)
Métro: Ternes

A popular shopping destination with good cheese shops and colorful food hawkers.

RUE LEPIC, 75018 (9) (see map page 252)
Métro: Abbesses, Blanche

It runs up the hill from boulevard de Clichy and merges into the heart of this side of the Butte Montmartre.

Outdoor Roving Food Markets–*Marchés Volants*

These are open on the days listed, unless otherwise noted, from 7:30 A.M. to 1:30 P.M. only. At the markets, look for the sign *producteur,* which usually hangs along the back of the stall. It means the merchant is selling foods or products he or she grew or produced and the quality is usually better.

CARMES (10)
Place Maubert, 75005 (see map page 98)
Métro: Maubert-Mutualité

A small market with the usual food stalls, but also those selling foie gras, clothing, rugs, quilts, and Provençal prints.

OPEN: Tues, Thur, Sat, 8 A.M.–1 P.M.

MONGE (29)
Place Monge, 75005 (see map page 98)
Métro: Place Monge

Smaller than most, so it's easy to look it all over before deciding what looks the best.

OPEN: Wed, Fri, Sun, 8 A.M.–1 P.M.

RASPAIL (41)
Boulevard Raspail, between rue du Cherche-Midi and rue de Rennes, 75006 (see map page 124)
Métro: Rennes, Sèvres-Babylone

On Sunday the products are from local growers and producers offering excellent organic fruits and veggies, even sulfate-free wines. If you are a health foodie, you will love it.

OPEN: Tues, Fri, Sun (organic), 9 A.M.–1 P.M.

AVENUE DE SAXE (28)
Avenue de Saxe, from place de Breteuil to place de Fontenoy, 75007 (see map page 156)
Métro: Sèvres-Lecourbe, Duroc

The Eiffel Tower serves as a beacon between the lines of food sellers.

OPEN: Thur, Sat

RICHARD-LENOIR (14)
Boulevard Richard-Lenoir, at rue Amelot, 75011 (see map page 192)
Métro: Bastille, Richard-Lenoir

Not far from the Bastille, and very local.

OPEN: Thur, Sun

DUPLEIX (3)
Boulevard du Grenelle, between rue de Lourmel and rue de Commerce, 75015 (see map page 204)
Métro: Dupleix, La Motte-Piquet–Grenelle

This is considered one of the best roving markets in Paris because it's so big and has everything, and it's well worth an hour or so on a Sunday morning. In addition to food you can buy suitcases, smocked dresses, violins, and much more. Despite its proximity to the Eiffel Tower, it's not touristy; in fact, Parisians love to live in the fifteenth arrondissement simply because of this market.

OPEN: Wed, Sun

COURS DE LA REINE (15)
Avenue Président Wilson, 75016 (see map page 226)
Métro: Alma Marceau, Iéna

Big, beautiful with lots of luxurious foodstuffs befitting the exclusive neighborhood.

OPEN: Wed, Sat

MARCHÉ DES BATIGNOLLES (5)
Boulevard des Batignolles, between rue de Rome and place de Clichy, 75017 (see map page 240)
Métro: Place Clichy, Rome

Mostly organic products directly from the growers.

OPEN: Sat

A Shopper's Glossary

These are a few words and phrases to help you during your shopping adventures. For a larger glossary, see page 350.

Ça coute combien?	How much does this cost?
Acceptez-vous les cartes de crédit?	Do you accept credit cards?
affiche	poster
à la mode	in style
atelier	workshop
bas	stockings
bleus de travail	blue cotton worker's uniform
bricoleurs	do-it-yourselfers
brocanteur	second-hand dealer
caleçons	boxer shorts
Carte Bleu	Visa charge card
ceinture	belt
chaussures	shoes
cravate	tie
dégriffés	labels cut out
dépôt vente	resale shop
détaxe	tax refund
duvet	down comforter
écharpe	scarf
espèces	cash
Eurocard	MasterCard charge card
faience	hand-painted pottery
fermé	closed
fin de series	end of the collection
fripes	second-hand clothes (à la thrift shops)
gant	glove
grand magasin	large department store

haute couture	expensive custom-made designer clothing
jupe	skirt
magasin	large department store
manteau	coat
marché	market
marché aux puces	flea market
ouvert	open
pantalons	pants
parfumerie	perfume store
peignoir	dressing gown, robe
premier étage	first floor above ground (second floor in U.S.)
prêt-a-porter	ready-to-wear
pull	sweater
rez-de-chausée	ground floor (first floor in U.S.)
sac	purse
soldes	sales
stock	overstock
tablier	apron
taille	size

Shops by Type

Glossary of French Words and Phrases

The French are surprisingly tolerant of foreigners who make an attempt to speak a few words. If you combine that with a smile and some sign language, and liberal use of *Madame* and *Monsieur, s'il vous plaît,* and *merci beaucoup,* you will be surprised how far you will get. Before your trip, buy some French language tapes, or check them out from the library, and listen to them whenever you can. You will be amazed at how much you will absorb. For a list of shopping terms, see page 345.

At the Hotel

a room for one/two persons	*une chambre pour une/deux personnes*
a double bed	*un lit double*
twin beds	*deux lits*
a room with an extra bed	*une chambre avec un lit supplémentaire*
a room with running water and bidet	*une chambre avec cabinet de toilette*
a room with shower and toilet	*une chambre avec douche et WC*
a room with bath and toilet	*une chambre avec salle de bain et WC*
for one/two/three nights	*pour une/deux/troix nuits*
suite	*appartment*
two-level suite	*duplex*
a room on the courtyard	*une chambre sur la cour*
a room over the street	*une chambre sur la rue*
ground floor	*rez-de-chaussée*
first floor	*premier étage*
second floor	*deuxième étage*
sixth floor	*seizième étage*
with a view	*avec vue*
quiet	*calme*
noisy	*bruyant*
breakfast included	*le petit déjeuner compris*
I would like breakfast.	*Je voudrais prendre le petit déjeuner.*
I do not want breakfast.	*Je ne veux pas de petit déjeuner.*
air-conditioning	*climatisé*
blankets	*couvertures*
elevator, lift	*ascenseur*
heat	*chauffage*
to iron	*repasser*
key	*clef*
to do laundry	*faire la lessive*

| pillow | oreiller |
| sheets | draps |

Emergencies

police	police
Stop!	Arrêtez!
help/help me!	Au secours!/Aidez-moi!
Leave me alone.	Laissez-moi tranquille.
I am sick.	Je suis malade.
Call a doctor.	Appelez un médecin.
in case of emergency	en cas d'urgence
hospital	l'hôpital
drugstore	pharmacie
prescription	ordonnance
medicine	médicament
aspirin	aspirine

General Phrases

yes/no	oui/non
okay	d'accord
please	s'il vous plaît
thank you (very much)	merci (beaucoup)
You are welcome.	De rien.
excuse me	excusez-moi, pardon
I am very sorry.	Désolé(e).
Sir, Mr.	Monsieur
Madame, Mrs.	Madame
Miss	Mademoiselle
good morning,	bonjour
good afternoon, hello	
good evening, goodbye	bonsoir, au revoir
How are you?	Comment allez-vous? Vous allez bien?
Fine, thank you, and you?	Très bien, merci, et vous?
What is your name?	Comment vous appelez-vous?
My name is . . .	Je m'appelle . . .
hold the line (telephone)	ne quittez pas
good/well/bad	bon (bonne)/bien/mauvais(e)
small/big	petit(e)/grand(e)
beautiful	beau/belle
expensive/cheap	cher/pas cher
free (without charge)	gratuit
free (unoccupied)	libre
with/without	avec/sans
a little/a lot	un peu/beaucoup
hot/cold	chaud/froid

Getting Around

Do you speak English?	*Parlez-vous anglais?*
I don't speak French.	*Je ne parle pas français.*
I don't understand.	*Je ne comprends pas.*
Speak more slowly, please.	*Parlez plus lentement, s'il vous plait.*
I am American/British.	*Je suis Américain(e)/Anglais(e).*
Where is the nearest métro?	*Où est le métro le plus proche?*
I want to get off at . . .	*Je voudrais descendre à . . .*
Where are the toilets?	*Où sont les toilettes?*
What is it?	*Qu'est-ce que c'est?*
who	*qui*
what	*quoi*
where	*oú*
when	*quand*
why	*pourquoi*
which	*quel*
here/there	*ici/là*
right/left	*à droit/à gauche*
straight ahead	*tour droit*
red/green stoplight	*feu rouge/vert*
far/near	*loin/pas loin*
to cross	*traverser*
How much does it cost?	*C'est combien?/Ça coûte combien?*
Do you take credit cards?	*Est-ce que vous acceptez les cartes de crédit?*
How many?	*Combien?*
I would like . . .	*Je voudrais . . .*
I am going . . .	*Je vais . . .*
it is/it is not	*c'est/ce n'est pas*

Places

airport	*l'aéroport*
bank	*banque*
basement	*sous-sol*
bookstore	*librairie*
bridge	*pont*
bus stop	*l'arrêt de bus*
church	*église*
department store	*grand magasin*
district	*quartier*
garden	*jardin*
laundromat	*laverie*
market	*marché*
museum	*musée*
post office (stamp)	*la poste (timbre)*
street	*rue*

subway	*métro*
ticket office	*vente de billets*
tobacconist	*tabac*
train station/platform/tracks	*gare/chemins de fer/quai*

Signs

caisse	cashier
défense de fumer, nonfumer	no smoking
entrée/sortie	entrance/exit
fermeture annuelle	annual closing
hors service/en panne	out of order
interdit/sens interdit	forbidden/no entry
ouvert/fermé	open/closed
stationnement interdit	no parking
tous les jours	daily
zone piétonne	pedestrian zone

Time

What time is it?	*Quelle heure est-il?*
At what time?	*A quelle heure?*
What time does the train leave?	*Le train part à quelle heure?*
today/yesterday/tomorrow	*aujourd'hui/hier/demain*
this morning	*ce matin*
this afternoon	*cet après-midi*
tonight	*ce soir*

Days

Sunday	*Dimanche*
Monday	*Lundi*
Tuesday	*Mardi*
Wednesday	*Mercredi*
Thursday	*Jeudi*
Friday	*Vendredi*
Saturday	*Samedi*

Months

January	*Janvier*
February	*Fevrier*
March	*Mars*
April	*Avril*
May	*Mai*
June	*Juin*
July	*Juillet*
August	*Août*
September	*Septembre*
October	*Octobre*

| November | *Novembre* |
| December | *Decembre* |

Seasons

spring	*printemps*
summer	*été*
autumn	*automne*
winter	*hiver*

Numbers

0	*zéro*
1	*un, une*
2	*deux*
3	*trois*
4	*quatre*
5	*cinq*
6	*six*
7	*sept*
8	*huit*
9	*neuf*
10	*dix*
11	*onze*
12	*douze*
13	*treize*
14	*quatorze*
15	*quinze*
16	*seize*
17	*dix-sept*
18	*dix-huit*
19	*dix-neuf*
20	*vingt*
21	*vingt-et-un*
22	*vingt-deux*
30	*trente*
40	*quarante*
50	*cinquante*
60	*soixante*
70	*soixante-dix*
80	*quatre-vingts*
90	*quatre-vingt-dix*
100	*cent*
1,000	*mille*
1,000,000	*million*
first	*premier*
second	*deuxième*
third	*troisième*

fourth	*quatrième*
fifth	*cinquième*
sixth	*sixième*
seventh	*septième*
eighth	*huitième*
ninth	*neuvième*
tenth	*dixième*
twentieth	*vingtième*
one-hundredth	*centième*

Colors

black	*noir*
blue	*bleu*
brown	*marron/brun*
green	*vert*
orange	*orange*
pink	*rose*
purple	*violet*
red	*rouge*
white	*blanc*
yellow	*jaune*

Index of Accommodations

Big Splurges

Hotels with Nonsmoking Rooms

Index of Shops

Readers' Comments

While every effort has been taken to provide accurate information in this guide, the publisher and author cannot be held responsible for changes in any of the listings due to rate increases, inflation, the rise and fall of the dollar, the passage of time, management changes, or any other problems—financial or otherwise—that occur between a reader and any person or establishment listed here.

Great Sleeps Paris is updated and revised on a regular basis. For current information on any of the guides in the series, visit either of these Websites: www.greateatsandsleeps.com or www.chroniclebooks.com. If you find a change before I do, make an important discovery you want to pass along to me, or just want to tell me about your trip to Paris, please send me a note stating the name and address of the hotel or shop, the date of your visit, and a description of your findings. As the many readers who have written to me know, your comments are very important to me, and I follow up on every letter received. Because of this, I do not provide an email address, since the volume of mail it would generate would make it impossible to personally reply to each message. I hope you will understand and still take a few minutes to drop me an old-fashioned letter telling me about your hotel and shopping experiences in Paris. Thank you, in advance, for taking the time to write.

Send your letters to Sandra A. Gustafson, *Great Sleeps Paris,* c/o Chronicle Books, 85 Second Street, sixth floor, San Francisco, CA 94105.